# American Religious History

# BLACKWELL READERS IN AMERICAN SOCIAL AND CULTURAL HISTORY

*Series Editor:* Jacqueline Jones, Brandeis University

The *Blackwell Readers in American Social and Cultural History* series introduces students to well-defined topics in American history from a socio-cultural perspective. Using primary and secondary sources, the volumes present the most important works available on a particular topic in a succinct and accessible format designed to fit easily into courses offered in American history or American studies.

# American Religious History

*Edited by*

Amanda Porterfield

BLACKWELL
*Publishers*

Copyright © Blackwell Publishers Ltd 2002; editorial matter and organization copyright © Amanda Porterfield 2002

First published 2002

2 4 6 8 10 9 7 5 3 1

Blackwell Publishers Inc.
350 Main Street
Malden, Massachusetts 02148
USA

Blackwell Publishers Ltd
108 Cowley Road
Oxford OX4 1JF
UK

*Library of Congress Cataloging-in-Publication Data*

American religious history / edited by Amanda Porterfield.
p.cm.–(Blackwell readers in American social and cultural history; 8)
Includes bibliographical references and index.
ISBN 0-631-22321-5 (alk. paper)–ISBN 0-631-22322-3 (pb.: alk.paper)
1. United States–Religion. I. Porterfield, Amanda, 1947– II. Series.

BL2525.A544 2001
200′.973–dc21

2001025262

*British Library Cataloguing in Publication Data*
A CIP catalogue record for this book is available from the British Library.

Typeset in 10/12 pt Plantin
by Kolam Information Services Pvt. Ltd., Pondicherry, India.
Printed in Great Britain by MPG Books Ltd, Bodmin, Cornwall

This book is printed on acid-free paper.

*To my students*

# Contents

# Series Editor's Preface

The purpose of the Blackwell Readers in American Social and Cultural History is to introduce students to cutting-edge historical scholarship that draws upon a variety of disciplines, and to encourage students to "do" history themselves by examining some of the primary texts upon which that scholarship is based.

Each of us lives life with a wholeness that is at odds with the way scholars often dissect the human experience. Anthropologists, psychologists, literary critics, and political scientists (to name just a few) study only discrete parts of our existence. The result is a rather arbitrary collection of disciplinary boundaries enshrined not only in specialized publications but also in university academic departments and in professional organizations.

As a scholarly enterprise, the study of history necessarily crosses these boundaries of knowledge in order to provide a comprehensive view of the past. Over the last few years, social and cultural historians have reached across the disciplines to understand the history of the British North American colonies and the United States in all its fullness. Unfortunately, much of that scholarship, published in specialized monographs and journals, remains inaccessible to undergraduates. Consequently, instructors often face choices that are not very appealing – to ignore the recent scholarship altogether, assign bulky readers that are too detailed for an undergraduate audience, or cobble together packages of recent articles that lack an overall contextual framework. The individual volumes of this series each focus on a significant topic in American history, and bring new, exciting scholarship to students in a compact, accessible format.

The series is designed to complement textbooks and other general readings assigned in undergraduate courses. Each editor has culled particularly innovative and provocative scholarly essays from widely scattered books and journals, and provided an introduction summarizing the major themes of the essays and documents that follow. The essays reproduced here were chosen because of the authors' innovative (and often interdisciplinary) methodology and their ability to reconceptualize historical issues in fresh and insightful ways. Thus students can appreciate the rich complexity of an historical topic and the way that scholars have explored the topic from different perspectives, and in the process transcend the highly artificial disciplinary boundaries that have served to compartmentalize knowledge about the past in the United States.

Also included in each volume are primary texts, at least some of which have been drawn from the essays themselves. By linking primary and secondary material, the editors are able to introduce students to the historian's craft, allowing them to explore this material in depth, and draw additional insights – or interpretations contrary to those of the scholars under discussion – from it.

Jacqueline Jones
*Brandeis University*

# About the Contributors

**Catherine L. Albanese** is Professor of Religious Studies at the University of California at Santa Barbara. Through numerous books and essays including *Nature Religion in America* (1990), Albanese led the way in moving the study of American religion away from the intellectual narrative Perry Miller established toward a broader picture of American religious diversity.

**Randall Balmer** is Ann Whitney Olin Professor of American Religious History at Barnard College of Columbia University and a leading interpreter of American Protestant evangelicalism. In addition to his books on contemporary American Protestantism, including *Mines Eyes Have Seen the Glory* (1993) and *Grant Us Courage* (1996), Balmer has written and hosted three PBS documentaries.

**Gerson D. Cohen** served as the Chancellor of the Jewish Theological Seminary of America from 1972 to 1986 and as Jacob H. Schiff Professor of History until his retirement in 1985. Cohen has been renowned as a spokesman for and interpreter of the Conservative movement in American Judaism.

**Jay P. Dolan** is Professor of History at the University of Notre Dame and former Director of the Cushwa Center for the Study of American Catholicism. His book, *The American Catholic Experience* (1985), was the first to place the revitalization of American Catholicism following the second Vatican Council of the 1960s within the larger context of 500 years of American Catholic history.

**William R. Hutchison** is Professor Emeritus at the Harvard Divinity School and, until his retirement in 1999, Charles Warren Professor of the History of Religion in America at Harvard University. His *Modernist Impulse in American Protestantism* (1976) stands as the definitive study of liberal Protestant thought in the late nineteenth and early twentieth centuries.

**Perry Miller** taught American Literature at Harvard University from 1931 until his death in 1963. In *The New England Mind* (1939), *Jonathan Edwards* (1949), *Roger Williams* (1953), and *Errand into the Wilderness* (1956), Miller emphasized the Puritans' role in shaping American culture and intellectual life.

**Charles S. Prebish** is Professor of Religious Studies at Pennsylvania State University and coeditor of the *Journal of Buddhist Ethics*. His books, *The Luminous Passage* (1999) and *The Faces of Buddhism in America* (coedited with Kenneth K. Tanaka in 1998), are the most comprehensive studies of American Buddhist practice to date.

**Gwendolyn Zoharah Simmons** is Assistant Professor of Religious Studies at the University of Florida in Gainesville. She served on the staff of the American Friends Service Committee for twenty years and is a member of the Sheikh Muhammad Raheem Bawa Muhaiyaddeen Mosque and Fellowship in Philadelphia.

**Ann Taves** is Professor of the History of Christianity and American Religion at the Claremont School of Theology and Professor of Religion at the Claremont Graduate University. In *Fits, Trances, & Visions* (1999), Taves broke new ground in understanding the historical interplay between Protestant religion and the development of American psychology.

# Introduction

## Amanda Porterfield

No place on earth is more ethnically, culturally, or religiously diverse than the United States. With its capitalist economy and great mix of people and traditions, America often seems like a vast marketplace where people with many different outlooks and philosophies coexist, interact, and exchange material and intellectual goods. In the case of religion, an amazing variety of beliefs and practices exists in this country, and flourishes with abundance. America is home to more forms of Christianity, more forms of Buddhism, and possibly more forms of Judaism than anywhere else in the world. It is also home to more new religions and to more new forms of religious hybridization than anywhere else.

In studying American religious history, it is important to attend to this diversity, and to appreciate the range and variety of religious expression that has been and continues to be characteristic of American life. At the same time, it is equally important to see the big picture – to keep the forest in sight while examining some of its many different trees. For all its internal variety and hospitality to new growth, the forest of American religion is also an interdependent, interconnected set of living and once-living things, much like an ecosystem. The overall strength and vitality of its numerous phenomena depend on some basic elements (analogous to certain types of soil and fertile dead matter, predictable amounts of light and moisture, and predominant forms of flora and fauna) common to American religious life as a whole.

This Introduction will identify some of these basic elements and some of the ways they have developed together. Following this, a set of essays

by well-known historians of American religion carries these descriptions
further and explores the historical development of particular faith traditions in more detail. A set of primary documents constitutes the second
and final section of the book. These documents serve as basic reference
points for many of the episodes, themes, and trends discussed in the
Introduction and scholarly essays.

## Foundational Elements of American Religious History

As an overview of American religious history, this Introduction focuses
on religious freedom, individual experience, family life, and social
reform as four interlocking elements that have worked together over
time to define virtually all of the particular religious traditions in America. Each of these foundational elements has worked in relationship with
the others, although not necessarily building on one another in simple or
straightforward ways. New opportunities for religious freedom have
given rise to new forms of individualism within a number of different
faith traditions. And new forms of individualism have inspired new ideas
about family life and social reform. At the same time, however, religious
concerns about excessive individualism have led to conservative efforts
to recover traditional forms of family life and social organization. And
controversies about the meaning of religious freedom, and how extensive
it should be, have divided Americans. Thus Native Americans, Jews,
Catholics, Muslims, Hindus, Buddhists, and Wiccans have all claimed
freedom of religious expression as their right, while conservative Protestants have often wanted to limit the definition of religion to certain
forms of adherence to biblical tradition.

Americans have continually aspired to live in a world in which the four
elements of religious freedom, individual experience, family life, and
social reform coexist in balance with one another. And they have often
agreed that freedom ought to be defined as an enabler of social improvement, not simply as the right to dissent, and that openness to individual
experience should be supported by the stability of family life. But we
have often disagreed about the exact meaning of these fundamental
values and about how to strike the right balance among them. Are
there common ideals to which every individual should aspire? To what
extent are individuals free to interpret religious doctrine according to the
dictates of their own consciences? At what point, if any, should individual expression be sacrificed for the stability of family life? How should
society be reformed? Should women be ordained? Should gay and les-

bian marriages be celebrated? Would society be improved if prayer were allowed in public schools?

In our religiously diverse society, answers and approaches to questions like these are multitudinous. But the underlying commitments to religious freedom, individual experience, family life, and social reform are pervasive. These commitments have shaped American religious history, influencing the development of particular faith traditions, each of which can be understood in terms of their distinctive approaches to these issues. For example, Native Americans have often defined their uneasy relationship to mainstream American society in terms of a religious understanding of family that encompasses ancestral spirits who inhabit Native lands. In recent years, this enlarged sense of family has led many Native Americans to represent themselves as protectors of the environment and its spiritual voices. To take a different example, in their concern to liberate all beings from suffering, Buddhists in the United States have reinterpreted traditional Buddhist teachings to suit American expectations about religious life. In this process, Buddhists have developed effective new ways of attending to the psychological suffering associated with American individualism. Differences between liberal and conservative Christians can be understood as disagreements about family values and their implications for individual experience, social reform, and the meaning of religious freedom, as can differences between liberal and orthodox Jews, or between African American and immigrant Muslims.

This identification of basic elements of American religious life does not mean that a rigid boundary exists between religion in the United States and religion elsewhere, or that American Christians, Jews, Muslims, Hindus, and Buddhists do not also define themselves internationally. The overlap between religious beliefs and practices in the United States and religious beliefs and practices in other parts of the world is considerable. For example, both American Christians and American Muslims emphasize the universal nature of their religious traditions and are often quite eloquent in explaining why their traditions appeal to people in every part of the world. Yet both Christianity and Islam have developed differently in the United States than elsewhere. And American forms of these faith traditions have influenced, and are continuing to influence, the development of those traditions in other parts of the world.

It is important to acknowledge that American religious concerns are, to some extent, universal human concerns. Since time immemorial, human beings have worked to define proper familial relationships, find opportunities for self-expression, and balance those opportunities with the requirements of social stability. Nevertheless, several factors make the American constellation of religious concerns quite distinctive. Investment in religious freedom plays a foundational role in the American system of government and way of life that is unparalleled elsewhere. In the early seventeenth century, Puritans settled in North America for the expressed purpose of practicing their religious beliefs with a kind of freedom they did not enjoy in England. Even if these founders were reluctant to extend the privilege to others, their limited investment in religious freedom played a crucial role in the historical development of American culture and self-understanding.

Strong commitment to the authority of individual experience has also figured prominently in American religious history. The Protestant religious revivals that swept through cities, towns, and frontier areas in the eighteenth and nineteenth centuries often challenged established religious authority in ways that had a democratizing effect both on Protestant churches and on the larger culture. Always centered on the relationship between God and the individual and the need for individual conversion, these revivals lifted up persons who could express religious experience, regardless of wealth or education. In many instances, this emphasis on the importance of the individual experience gave poor people, blacks, and women opportunities for moral authority, social criticism, and influence that they might not otherwise have had.

To be sure, some powerful and fairly conservative religious institutions have also flourished in America, including the hierarchy of the Mormon priesthood, the Southern Baptist Convention, and a sizeable branch of the Roman Catholic Church. But in the nineteenth century, Mormons and Catholics met strong resistance from Protestants who were highly suspicious of the control that institutions of religious authority exerted over individuals. And in all three cases, strong respect for the authority of individual conscience has functioned to limit and moderate institutional control. The Mormon priesthood is known for disciplined uniformity, but also for its focus on individual development, lay leadership, and the potential for every priest to become a god. The Southern Baptist Convention is a conference of churches and church leaders whose purpose is only to guide, not legislate, the religious beliefs and practices of affiliated churches and individual church members, whose authority in matters of conscience is often recognized. In the case of Catholicism, devotion to the poor and readiness to elevate spiritual life above worldly authority are long-standing traits that have often worked to complicate the Church's ties to wealth and political power. Furthermore, Americans have been in the vanguard of worldwide Catholic efforts to recognize the authority of individual conscience, the importance of religious freedom, and the exercise of lay leadership. Compared with Catholics in other parts of the world, Americans are famous (or notorious) for exercising individual choice on matters of Church doctrine, especially birth control, which American Catholics practice at about the same rate as other Americans despite their Church's official ban.

Concerns about the structure of the family and its relationship to both social stability and reform pervade American religious history. While similar to people in other parts of the world in relying on religion to provide guidelines for good family living and proper family relationships, Americans are unusual in their tendency to view the nuclear family as the primary locus of religious life. Belief that religious purity is best attained by living *apart* from family life is strong in many parts of the world, but relatively weak in America. This originally Protestant emphasis on family life as the best context for religious life has shaped the development of American Catholicism, Hinduism, and Buddhism, contributing to the democratization of all three traditions and to increased emphasis within those traditions on the religious significance of ordinary life.

As perhaps their most outstanding characteristic of all, Americans have tended to look to religion as an instrument of world progress and as a means to unprecedented and even revolutionary social change. In other parts of the world and other eras in history, religion has been more of a conserver of cultural tradition and protector of the status quo. The American tendency to conceptualize religion as an engine of progressive social change is so strong that it has challenged, subverted, and sometimes even overturned religion's inherent tendency to cultural conservatism.

## Foundational Elements Rooted in Puritan Culture

In many respects, the constellation of concerns associated with religious freedom, individual experience, family life, and social reform is rooted in New England Puritanism. The Puritans espoused idealized versions of these realities that have continued to shape ideas about what America should be. The Puritans' vision of America figured importantly in the construction of American culture and influenced the development of many other religious traditions in this country.

Puritans have been often (and deservedly) criticized for their hypocrisy in limiting religious freedom to people of their own religious persuasion. In banishing Anne Hutchinson and Roger Williams from the Massachusetts Bay Colony in the 1630s for religious dissent and alleged threats to social order, the Puritans gained a lasting reputation for persecuting others for much the same reason they had been persecuted in England. But this charge could only be leveled because the Puritans were inspired to come to America by a strong but limited desire for religious freedom. If they had been shameless tyrants, they never would have been accused of hypocrisy. The parameters of what religious freedom means have widened over time, and every step in this process has stirred controversy and conflict. Viewed in this historical context, Puritans are rightly remembered as founders of American ideas about religious freedom, and as instigators of ongoing debate about its true meaning and proper extent.

As a result of their investment in religious freedom, the Puritans were strongly but cautiously invested in the authority of individual conscience. Here again, the Puritans disagreed among themselves about the extent to which this authority should be constrained by scripture, ministers, and government. Perhaps the most famous example of this disagreement is Anne Hutchinson's trial in 1637. Later generations have tended to think that the Governor of the Massachusetts Bay Colony, John Winthrop, compromised his own integrity when he denounced Hutchinson for challenging the religious opinions held by several prominent authorities and thereby, in Winthrop's mind, threatening the social order. Although she suffered dearly for it in her own lifetime, Hutchinson has often been praised by later Americans for standing up to Winthrop in court, and defending herself by appeal to the authority of her own conscience.

In another famous case of dissent within the first generation of New England Puritans, Roger Williams accused the Puritan leaders of New England of persecuting others for conscience's sake. These leaders defended themselves by saying that they had come to America in order to have freedom to establish true Christianity, and that they were right not to allow false forms to choke them out. Later generations have tended to agree that Williams had the better argument. Later generations have also commended Williams for his friendships and fair dealings with Native Americans, and for his condemnation of the tendency in many of his fellow Puritans to assume their moral superiority over Native Americans and God-given right to Indian land.

This tendency of the Puritan elite to cast itself as a kind of tribal establishment with a moral right to exert authority over others has echoed down the centuries, not only in how the Puritans have been remembered, but also in the behavior of some of their descendants. In 1963, Digby Baltzell criticized "the Protestant establishment" in American society for behaving as if they were a kind of privileged caste, running the country as if power belonged to them by right, looking down on Catholics, establishing limited quotas for Jews at Ivy League schools, and excluding Jews from membership in country clubs. In Baltzell's opinion, this sort of behavior amounted to a betrayal of the principles of freedom, individuality, and honest work on which the country was founded. Like Roger Williams more than three centuries earlier, Baltzell criticized his fellow Protestants for turning away from their own religious principles.

However conservative in their interpretation, and however resistant to extending its benefits to others, the New England Puritans and their religious descendants prized individual conscience as the prime zone of God's relationship to believers. They opposed any interference that seemed to obscure the individual's relationship to God, or divert attention from it. The Puritan ideal of "the well-ordered household" at once balanced and reinforced this concern for religious individualism. A well-ordered family guided individual development, schooled individual expression, and stabilized society. At the same time, it lent religious sanctity to the relationship of marriage, to the obligations and affections associated with parenting, and to the ordinary challenges and habits of domestic life. As the model of how human society ought to be, the Puritan family was intended to be the microcosm and primary building block of a reformed, Christian society. Relying on the family as a school for individual conscience free from the corruptions of impure influence and interference, Puritans wanted to help God implement his plans for redeeming the world.

Strenuous efforts to create a just and good society in America, and thus to help realize God's design for human history, helped Puritans cope with their anxieties about their own religious worth and integrity. While many among the Puritan elite wanted to limit freedom and preserve their own authority over others, this idealism about American society also inspired people whom the Puritans and many of their successors would have liked to dominate and instruct. The force of Puritan idealism about the promise of world history often helped to defeat the conservatism of Puritan leaders and their descendants.

To return to the metaphor of American religious life as an ecosystem that has developed over time, one might say that people, ideas, and institutions rooted in the New England Puritan tradition dominated American culture at a crucial time in its development. These people, ideas, and institutions functioned as powerful forces to which other religious traditions had to adapt, or learn to resist, in order to survive. As this complex system developed, new forms of growth flourished to such an extent that many of the people, ideas, and institutions identified with early or pristine forms of Puritanism died out. At the same time, many of the ideas associated with Puritanism were rejuvenated in the process of pollinating, hosting, and breeding with other religious people, ideas, and institutions. But not a single Puritan survived, at least not of the same exact type that had established itself so firmly in American soil in the seventeenth century.

While Puritans died out, their influence persisted, much as dead trees help create the soil from which new trees grow. Evangelicals sought to recover the Puritans' sense of religious purpose for America through revivals and missions. Transcendentalists carried forward the investment in the authority of individual conscience that first brought Puritans to America, as did many seekers of metaphysical truth and proponents of social justice. Both Catholics and Jews in America were profoundly influenced by Puritan idealism about America and they, in turn, contributed to the advancement of religious freedom in this country and to explanations about its essential place in American democracy. Like Catholics and Jews, Native Americans often defined themselves against the Protestant establishment that attempted to dominate them. At the same time, they, too, pressed to extend the meaning of religious freedom and its implications. Hindus and Buddhists absorbed democratic tendencies in American culture along with the American emphasis on the moral and religious significance of the nuclear family as a primary context for religious life. At the same time, Hindus and Buddhists have inspired many Americans with the wisdom of their ancient traditions, and with their relevance as antidotes to some of the problems engendered by American individualism.

## Religious Freedom

The First Amendment to the United States Constitution bars the federal government from favoring any one religious group or discriminating against others – "Congress shall make no law respecting an establishment of religion, or prohibiting the free exercise thereof." In defining the federal government's relation to religion by these two negative clauses, the men who drafted the Constitution opened the way for religious experimentation and the proliferation of new religious groups. They did not question the right of state governments to establish religious institutions or seriously entertain the idea that the United States would ever be anything other than a Christian nation. But religious diversity increased after the ratification of the Constitution in 1787, and continues to increase, as a result of their willingness to live without a clear or firm link between church and state.

In addition to providing legal space for the diversification of religion, the First Amendment contributed to increasing religious pluralism. Religious pluralism is related to religious diversity in much the same way that music appreciation is related to music. While religious diversity is a factual reality that people might or might not like, religious pluralism implies respect and even enthusiasm for religious difference, as well as knowledge about different religious groups and their interrelationships. Such respect and understanding involves a process of shedding negative stereotypes about religions other than one's own. As a cultural trend, this process gradually gained momentum over the course of American history and may be never-ending. In other words, religious pluralism in the United States is more of a work in progress than a fully accomplished reality, and not without its obstructers and detractors. But if the expansion of religious pluralism has frequently met with resistance, the respect for individual conscience implicit in the First Amendment has, over the years, supported this increasingly widespread appreciation of religious difference. Although not all have seen it this way, many Americans have interpreted the second clause of the First Amendment to imply that religious freedom is a prerequisite for sincere religious life. This endorsement of religious freedom presumes that genuine religious conviction cannot be coerced, and thus accords a kind of privileged status to individual decision-making. It also diminishes support for the idea that there is one true religion to which all people should conform. If your conscience is a kind of final authority when it comes to your religious beliefs, how can someone else tell you what to believe?

In an indirect but nevertheless powerful way, the First Amendment's restraint on government involvement in religion has fostered the vitality as well as the pluralism of American religious life. The fact that the federal government is prohibited from identifying itself with a particular group has not meant that American people have felt reluctant to identify with religion. Indeed, as some religious leaders discovered to their surprise, the enthusiasm with which Americans have attached themselves to particular religious has often been stimulated by the free and uncoerced nature of those attachments. The idea that freedom is good for religion has underlain much support for the separation of church and state. From the beginning, many of those who have championed the negatively phrased prohibition against government interference in religion have been strong supporters of religion.

Of course, Americans have not always been as free as they are today to practice the religions they choose. With the exception of the short-lived but proudly secular government of Rhode Island established by Roger Williams, the New England colonies prohibited, or tried to prohibit, forms of religious worship that did not conform to Puritan belief. Quakers were persecuted in seventeenth-century Massachusetts and, after the American Revolution, even the elite Church of England had to suffer second-class status until 1833, when the Congregational Church was finally disestablished. Mormons were persecuted for their beliefs in New York and Illinois in the nineteenth century and Utah was not admitted to the United States until Mormons agreed to outlaw their religious practice of polygamy. In the late nineteenth century, the federal government acted to suppress certain rituals practiced by Native Americans. It was not until the American Indian Religious Freedom Act of 1978 that Native Americans won a firm and explicit guarantee of legal protection for their exercise of religious freedom.

From the last decades of the nineteenth century until the 1960s, a *de facto* establishment of Protestant politicians, ministers, lawyers, educators, and business leaders exerted a disproportionate amount of legal, professional, and cultural influence in the United States. Many of these cultural elites were broad-minded and concerned to make American society more just and enlightened. But at the same time, their ideas about other religions were often inaccurate, superficial, and condescending. Because of their privileged place in society and tendency to be condescending, these Protestants were often resented, not only by Catholics and Jews who felt discriminated against, but also by conservative Protestants who thought their ideas about religion were too liberal. As a result of the social upheaval connected with the Civil Rights movement, the Vietnam war, and countercultural rebellions of the sixties and seventies, the cultural influence of liberal Protestants came under attack and began to decline, mainline Protestant churches lost members, new religious movements and new forms of religious dialogue emerged, and the whole religious landscape became at once more complex and more actively interconnected. Commitment to religious freedom, and belief in the authority of individual conscience underlying it, encouraged the fertility of this complex religious ecology. While building on both the broad-mindedness and the individualism of the liberal Protestant tradition, commitment to religious freedom in the late twentieth century worked to erode the privileged status of Protestant elites and to challenge their presumption to act as arbiters of American culture.

The concept of religious freedom emerged in the context of Protestant culture. But it succeeded as a cultural ideal partly as the result of its meaningfulness to Americans whose religions were not Protestant. Because of their history as minority religious groups who would probably have suffered more discrimination if the United States had an established church, and Congress had not been restrained from prohibiting the free exercise of religion, Catholics and Jews have often been among the most eloquent in extolling the virtues of religious freedom. At the same time, their religions have been deeply affected, and even changed, as a result of this embrace of religious freedom and its consequences.

In the nineteenth century, some of America's most influential Catholic leaders favored the principles of religious freedom and separation of church and state, even though the authorities of their Church in Rome disfavored and even denounced those principles. Like Orestes Brownson, a New England Transcendentalist and friend of Ralph Waldo Emerson, several of these leaders were converts from Protestantism. And like Brownson, they not only believed that the Catholic Church would flourish in the United States, but also that it would play a major role in the fulfillment of America's historical destiny as a Christian nation, which Puritans had first foreseen. This American interpretation of Catholicism emphasized the transforming power of the Holy Spirit in the lives of individuals as well as the beauty of the sacraments and authority of the Church. Proponents of this view prized Catholicism for recognizing the corporate nature of humanity and thus providing a balancing force for the individualism of American culture. From their perspective, religious freedom contributed to the strength of the Catholic Church, much as the Catholic Church contributed to the strength of American culture.

In the late nineteenth century, religious authorities in Rome condemned this American interpretation of Catholicism and increased their emphasis on the importance of centralized authority and obedience to the Church's priestly hierarchy and devotional practices. But a later version of this American approach finally gained approval in Rome during the 1960s, when the Second Vatican Council ratified a Declaration on religious freedom. Drafted by the American Jesuit John Courtney Murray with support from a strong contingent of American bishops, this Declaration was the most controversial and, many would argue, most important document of the Council. To many at the Council, endorsing religious freedom meant abandoning the Church's longstanding resistance against the separation of church and state. It also implied that if the Church changed its position on this important issue, other Church teachings might be open to reform as well. As Murray explained, "the real sticking point" in the Council debates about religious freedom was the implied admission that Church doctrine could change over time. But support for the Declaration won out because endorsement of religious liberty reconfirmed the long-standing Catholic principle of human dignity. It also opened the way for Catholics to become more actively engaged with the modern world, which the Council agreed was a priority for the Church. In their vision of the Church leading the way in the fulfillment of God's plan for history, progressive American Catholic leaders since Orestes Brownson had been pushing for just that kind of engagement.

Jews have often been in the forefront in arguing for separation of church and state, not only because this arrangement protected their religious freedom as members of a minority faith, but also because of a strong emphasis within Jewish thought on the importance of individual decision. Rooted in biblical stories that center on the relationship

between God and the individual representative of Jewish community, this
investment in decision-making often required willingness to withstand
social and political pressure. Partly as a result of this ethical emphasis,
and partly as a result of their long history of political oppression, Jews
have also prized political freedom and its opportunities to escape discrimination and to perform religious observances without hindrance.[1]

In the United States, this traditional Jewish love of freedom developed
in new ways. In addition to often being in the forefront as champions of
religious freedom and defenders of the separation of church and state,
American Jews have also taken the interpretation and observance of
Jewish law in directions their ancestors never could have imagined.
Building on the Reform movement that originated in late eighteenth-
century Germany, Reform Jews in the United States left the rigorous
observances of traditional Jewish practice behind to focus on the ethical
force of Judaism and enable Jews to step outside their tribal boundaries
and contribute fully to modern life. An exponent of such progressive
attitudes, Rabbi Isaac Mayer Wise celebrated America as a promised
land for Jews as well as Christians. In Cincinnati, he dispensed with the
practice of confining women to a closed-off section of the synagogue and
instituted family seating in pews. Other Reform Jews made their way into
academic, medical, and business circles, often discriminated against by
Protestants who exerted control in those circles, but still finding greater
opportunity to contribute to public life than in Europe.

At Jewish Theological Seminary in Manhattan, Conservative Judaism
emerged as a new religious movement that bridged the gap between
traditional and Reform Judaism. Focusing on the importance of Jewish
culture, the Conservative movement blended respect for observance of
Jewish tradition with a spirit of flexibility that accommodated middle-
class lifestyles and responded to new opportunities for religious, intellectual, and political expression. The Conservative movement expedited
Jewish assimilation to American culture while at the same time promoting Jewish community. As both a thoroughly American and thoroughly
Jewish phenomenon, the Conservative movement exemplifies the important role that freedom of religious expression has played in the
development of American Judaism.

While American Jews have often been in the forefront of efforts to
defend and promote religious freedom, many American Protestants have
looked to Jewish scripture for inspiration for their own idealism. These
Protestants often knew very little about the living religion of Judaism,
but drew deeply from ancient Jewish thought in their love of freedom,
emphasis on individual experience, respect for family life, and hopes for
a promised land. The New England Puritans hoped that they were
God's chosen people, as they believed the Jews had once been, and

that America would be the New Israel. Growing out of the revivalism that began in the eighteenth century, African American Baptists, Methodists, and later Pentecostals strongly identified with biblical stories of God's relationship with people of Israel. God's deliverance of the Hebrews from slavery in Egypt was a message of hope for many African Americans in the nineteenth century and later emerged as the dominant metaphor of the Civil Rights movement. Taken up by Protestants concerned with freedom from oppressive authority, Hebrew scripture inspired much religious hope and idealism in America both liberal Christians and Jews who found their own traditions recast in the context of American culture.

In this and many other ways, nonProtestant traditions have contributed significantly to the meaning of religious freedom in the United States and to its historical development as a cherished American ideal. Not only Jews, whose own traditions supported it, but Catholics, whose Church officially opposed it until the 1960s, have been eloquent defenders of religious freedom in the United States. Open spaces, new frontiers, and Protestant idealism encouraged people from a variety of different faiths to affirm the principle of religious liberty and contribute to its expansion.

## Individual Experience

Closely linked to the cherishing of religious freedom, the individualism commonly associated with American culture is full of religious implication. Here again, a wide variety of religious and cultural traditions have contributed to diverse forms and expressions of a widely shared American value. As a complex phenomenon rooted in many different traditions, American individualism includes the bravery of Native American heroes, the mysticism of Catholic monastics, the good deeds of Jewish humanitarians, and the self-mastery of practitioners of Hindu and Buddhist meditation, to take just a few examples. At the same time, emphasis on the centrality of individual experience in religious life is deeply rooted in American Protestant culture, as are respect for the moral authority of individual conscience and commitment to the need for religious freedom. In the course of American history, Protestant interpretations of these values have figured importantly in the construction of the larger culture in which other religious have developed. In this process, other religions have added their beliefs and practices to the mix of individual experience available in America, expanding and enriching the meaning of individuality and making it more complicated.

The experience of being in touch with a higher, stronger reality is an essential and universal aspect of religion. Religious experience gives people a sense of power, and makes religion a powerful force in society. At the most basic level, religion engages human feeling, and human feeling is a form of internal, subjective experience. At the same time, religious feeling often brings a sense of being united with others, and with the divine.

What makes Protestant religions unusual is their concentrated focus on the role of the individual will in the production of religious experience. This Protestant focus on the will developed as part of a long history of Christian introspection. This Christian tradition arose out of Jewish scripture and its focus on the covenant relationship between God and Israel, often depicted in terms of a personal relationship between God and man. As Christianity developed in Europe, concern for a personal relationship with God developed in a variety of ways, many of which emphasized the need for both pure-heartedness and good deeds. When Protestantism emerged in sixteenth-century Europe and England, its proponents lifted up the ancient themes of introspection, personal covenant, and moral obligation in the context of a new, incipiently modern interest in individual conscience as a basis of both religious truth and social order. In America, this Protestant investment in individual conscience launched many new communities, cities, and towns. It also contributed to the idea that external government should be as small as possible. While necessary as a means of establishing law and restraining harmful behavior, government should be limited, not only to restrain its inherent tendency to corruption, but also to ensure God-fearing individuals the widest possible scope for their activity and influence.

In both America and England, revivals emerged as a popular arena for religious experience. Preachers encouraged experiences of repentance and conversion, along with new forms of individual expression and performance. All of this popular religious enthusiasm and creativity centered on the individual will; the whole purpose of a revival was to inspire individuals to renounce their willful rebellion against God and to conform their lives to the will of God.

The emergence of revivalism as a major form of American religious expression coincided with the development of a market economy, and innovations in one area fed those of the other. Persuasive evangelists believed that they knew what people needed, and offered promises and hopes of salvation in compelling ways. These skillful preachers inspired commercial advertisers even as they, in turn, were inspired by increasingly sophisticated forms of salesmanship in the American marketplace, and by the growing emphasis on personal choice characteristic of consumer culture. In the religious marketplace of American revivalism, beliefs, practices, and experiences were developed, tested, and exchanged, all focused on the sinfulness, transformation, and purification of the individual will.

One of the most significant cultural developments to emerge out of American revivalism was the exchange between Anglo Protestant and African traditions. Torn away from the protection of African deities, and from the traditional cultures devoted to these deities and their worship, Africans in the New World were attracted to the egalitarian message of the New Testament gospel as well as to the stories of hardship, slavery, and divine justice and liberation in the Old Testament.[2] With its message of salvation, promise of hope to people who suffered, and emphasis on individual experience and freedom from oppressive authority, Protestant Christianity attracted many slaves. At the same time, these converts brought African religious practices and expectations with them into Christianity in ways that affected the development of revivalism and American religious life more generally. African expectations of spirit possession merged with Protestant ideas about the Holy Spirit and its transforming power. African forms of music and dance enriched the emotional intensity and dramatic performances of Protestant worship. The emphasis on individual salvation at the core of Protestant Christianity acquired new force, and new levels of meaning, in the hands of people whose human dignity and individuality were being systematically assaulted. Pentecostalism and other forms of charismatic Christianity emerged out of this synthesis of Protestant revivalism and African religious practice, as did the great secular forms of music for which American culture is so well known – "Rock and Roll" and "Rhythm and Blues." Like their predecessors in religious revivalism, these distinctive forms of American cultural expression focus on individual experiences of pain and sorrow, longing and hope, and on the crucial role of the will in mediating them.

Concentration on the state of individual will, and on the right relationship between the individual and God, gave American Protestant religious thought a strongly psychological quality. In the mid-eighteenth century, the New England pastor Jonathan Edwards produced a number of writings analyzing the psychology of conversion and the transformation of will at its core. Concentrated effort to produce the right relationship between the individual and God involved a particular kind of self-reconstruction characterized by a new openness to God, which Edwards and others described as love toward a greater reality, and assent to a more powerful force, than love toward self. As the Methodist convert Jarena Lee recalled in her memoirs of 1836, excerpted more fully in the primary documents below, "I began to call upon the Lord to

show me all that was in my heart, which was not according to his will."
Sensing "that my heart was not clean in his sight; that there yet remained
the roots of bitterness," she struggled in prayer for months until, finally,
she felt sanctified with a "rush" of "ecstasy (that) caused me to feel as if I
were in an ocean of light and bliss."[3]

As Americans became increasingly skillful in analyzing and managing
this process of self-reconstruction, its therapeutic benefits became increasingly evident. One of the most important writers to explore the
connection between religious experience and psychological health was
the early twentieth-century philosopher William James. Drawing attention to the psychological benefit of believing in a personal relationship
with a higher power, James outlined the stages involved in the conversion
process, and explained the importance of the will in determining human
feeling and behavior. His empathy for religious experience inspired many
readers, including the Catholic convert Dorothy Day, whose devotion to
St. Teresa of Avila originated with her reading of James's account of
Teresa's conversion. At the same time, James's pragmatic approach to
the benefits of conversion shows how a culture strongly influenced by
Protestant evangelicalism provided fertile ground for the growth of
psychotherapy and the flourishing of self-help movements.

American fascination with religious experience has other branches as
well. Among the most notable of these, New England Transcendentalism provided an alternative to the kind of spirituality promoted through
revivalism. In the mid-nineteenth century, Ralph Waldo Emerson shifted
the context of religious experience from the Bible to nature, arguing that
nature was the living expression of God's work and that to know God,
one had to go to nature. Emerson and his followers were no less interested than Protestant revivalists in attaining the right personal relationship between the self and God. And they were equally convinced that to
be open to divine inspiration, one had to avoid selfish attempts at
manipulation. But Emerson and his followers rejected the idea that the
Bible was the only true text of divine revelation. They urged all Americans to establish "an original relation with the universe" that involved
discovering God within the self. One of Emerson's contemporaries,
Emily Dickinson, expressed this approach to religious experience in
one of her poems, "On a Columnar Self – How ample to rely."

New England Transcendentalists were the first Americans to explore
the relationship between Protestant religious experience and Hindu and
Buddhist psychology. Transcendentalists and their successors were in-
trigued by Eastern ideas about the universal flow of consciousness, the
interdependence of all things, and the possibility of attaining a fully
enlightened view of reality. But it was not until the twentieth century

that Americans really began to catch onto the therapeutic and empowering aspects of the Buddhist belief that selfhood was finally an illusion. In the 1950s, Beat poets like Allen Ginsberg saw themselves both as heirs of Transcendentalists and as bringers of Buddhist insight to America. They denounced American bondage to the greedy, grasping, and finally illusory phenomena of selfhood and held out the possibility of compassionate liberation from its desires.

As American interest in Buddhism grew in the late twentieth century, the lifting of strict quotas on Asian immigrants brought more Asian Buddhists and Buddhist teachers to the United States. The growing presence of Buddhist people and ideas opened the way for new developments within Buddhism as well as within American culture. Buddhist practices became more democratic and informal than they were in Asia, and Buddhist ideas became more flexible, especially as they were adapted to American forms of psychotherapy. Buddhist ideas about the causal relation between desire and suffering prodded many Americans to think freshly about the centrality of the will in the individual's search for happiness.

American Jews were drawn to Buddhism in relatively large numbers, and their influence on the development of American Buddhism has been significant. The rationalism of Buddhist psychology, the concern for suffering that Jews and Buddhists share, and Jewish thirst for religious experience all contributed to this attraction. At the same time, Jewish commitments to religious freedom and common decency had a democratizing effect on Buddhism, producing new forms of Buddhist meditation, social action, and psychotherapy.

Catholics drawn to Buddhism brought with them long and highly developed spiritual traditions centered on devotion to the mystical presence of Christ in the sacraments and in the world. At the same time, Buddhist ideas about the illusory nature of selfhood challenged essentialist notions of the soul common in Catholic philosophy in ways that Catholic practitioenrs of Buddhist meditation found liberating. In much the same way, Americans influenced by New England Transcendentalism and other forms of alternative spirituality found the Buddhist concept of the mind-stream, or Big Mind, familiar while being challenged and pushed further by the Buddhist critique of selfhood. In their encounters with Buddhism, American Protestantism, Judaism, Catholicism, and New Age religions grew in new directions. But underlying these new forms of religious syncretism, belief in each individual's need for a right relationship to God (or to the universe, or to life itself) persisted, as did a sometimes troubled but genuine openness to each individual's effort to find that right relationship.

## Family Life

Given their investment in individual experience, it is not surprising that many Americans have stressed the need for community. Throughout American religious history, community has often been championed as a contributor to individual development as well as a counterbalance for excessive individualism. As one of the most common ways in which this recognition of the need for community has been expressed, Americans have often pointed to the family as the primary social unit in which individual development takes place, and the primary social unit upon which religious congregations are based.

As we have seen, the Puritans viewed the nuclear family as the building block of Christian society. Their emphasis on its religious and moral significance as the bedrock of society and the principal social unit responsible for individual development has persisted in American culture as one of the most important legacies of Puritan influence. While many European nations moved far ahead of the United States in creating government-sponsored schools and programs for children, the influence of Puritan ideas about the family contributed to the tendency of many American parents to resist transferring responsibility for children to the state. When children did bad things, many Americans blamed the family rather than larger social causes such as poverty or inadequate schools. Americans tended to regard the nuclear family, however "broken" or even dysfunctional, as a cherished, even sacred, institution.

Marriage was the centerpiece and wellspring of family life, Puritans and their descendants believed, with the relationship between husband and wife mirroring the covenant of grace between God and each saint. In other cultures, gender ties among father, sons, and uncles, or among women and their female kin, figured more prominently in defining family life and the religious institutions associated with it. Indeed, the structure and religious meaning of family life has often shifted for immigrants and their descendants in the process of assimilating to American culture. For example, the German American Protestants who founded St. Paul's Church in nineteenth-century Chicago celebrated the male relationships at the core of family life with elaborate meals for men featuring heavy German foods. By the mid-twentieth century, when the congregants of St. Paul's had become more fully assimilated to American culture, church suppers and other social events at St. Paul's had changed considerably to focus on celebrating and strengthening the nuclear family. Similar trends have been observed among Italian American Catholics, whose appreciation of the religious dimensions of family life shifted from an emphasis on fatherhood and brotherhood as the building block of community to a greater, and more typically American, emphasis on marriage as the family's defining core. As mentioned above, the institution of family seating in most synagogues is one of the major developments in American Judaism. The most obvious difference between Orthodox synagogues, where traditional practices are strictly followed, and more progressive ones developed in the United States is that Orthodox women sit separately behind a partition, while in Reform and Conservative synagogues, husbands and wives sit together.[4]

Implicit in this American emphasis on the nuclear family are complex and far-reaching implications for women's lives. The Puritan idea of marriage included a dimension of partnership between husband and wife; while the husband's authority was assumed to be superior to that of the wife, the bond of marital affection brought husband and wife together as one. This union, along with the wife's capacity to exemplify devotion, gave more than a few women the opportunity to attain indirect authority in their marriages and communities.[5] As Anne Bradstreet's poetry reveals, Puritan theology enabled some women to mesh their religious and marital lives in ways that contributed to respect for women and allowed for at least an element of female equality. But the legacy of this Puritan cherishing of marriage had a restrictive aspect as well. As Randall Balmer observes in his essay on twentieth-century Fundamentalists, these conservative heirs of Puritanism also value the strength and purity of women's love, along with commitment to marriage as the centerpiece of family life. But against what they regard as liberal distortions of Christian thought, Fundamentalists insist that women's place is in the home and that wives should be subordinate to their husbands.

Of course, Puritan theology is not the only source of restrictive ideas about women's roles. Indeed, the tendency to support male authority and to define women's responsibilities in terms of biological fertility and childrearing is so common among the religions of the world that some observers regard it as one of religion's chief and most universal functions. The Puritan-based approach differs from other religious ways of defining women's subordination only in its concentrated focus on the nuclear family and on the central role of marriage in defining family strength. But while it has functioned conservatively, the Puritan tradition has also contributed to American ideas about women's freedom, equality, and individuality, and even to the development of feminism. The Puritan (and larger Protestant) emphasis on marriage and family as the proper context for religious life had the effect of bringing women's religious aspirations and contributions onto more of the same level as men's. To some extent, Protestant rejection of celibacy as a higher form of religious life worked to undermine the idea that the religion transcended sex, flesh, womanhood, and ordinary human life in general. A number of important American women were inspired to great achievement because of tendencies within Puritanism to equalize women in relationship to men, and to equalize women's relationships to God on a par with those of men's. In the seventeenth and eighteenth centuries, these liberal tendencies coexisted with more conservative, gender-restrictive ones, but in the nineteenth century, they became less compatible. Liberal heirs of Puritanism's emphasis on individual development and the authority of individual conscience choice, including Elizabeth Cady Stanton, Lucretia Mott, and Angelina Grimke, were in the forefront of the abolition and women's suffrage movements. In literature, Emily Dickinson brought the Puritan emphasis on individual integrity into modern poetry. She also carried forward the Puritan idea that spiritual life had a courtly, sexual dimension.

In a variety of different American religious traditions, liberals and conservatives have often split over feminism. While liberals endorsed particular forms of feminist theology as authentic and progressive expressions of religious truth, conservatives accused feminists of attempting to destroy the family and, consequently, the moral fabric of society. In other instances, however, feminism and conservative orthodoxy proved more compatible. Tamar Frankiel's exposure to feminism helped to stimulate her appreciation of women's roles in Orthodox Judaism. Gwendolyn Zoharah Simmons sees Islamic feminism as a challenge to corrupt interpretations of Islam in many parts of the world and as a means of recovering the respect for women expressed in the Qur'an and through the life and teachings of the Prophet Muhammad.

## Social Reform

Perhaps the most distinctive aspect of American religious history is the expectation that religion will bring about the moral improvement of both individuals and society. In contrast to the widely prevalent idea in other cultures that religion transcends earthly life, and even offers escape from it, Americans have often looked to religion to make life better. This expectation of religion's human benefit is rooted, at least in part, in the Puritan idea that grace enables moral virtue. Modifying Luther's emphasis on the impossibility of fulfilling God's law, Puritans and other English Protestants believed that grace enabled saints to act in accordance with divine will. This belief gave Puritans, and the larger culture they influenced, a strongly moralistic aspect. It also contributed to the energetic aspect of American culture, and to the expectation that religious people should roll up their sleeves and get busy making the world a better place.

Americans have often expressed their eagerness to participate in God's plans through belief in America as a place where God's Kingdom had already begun to dawn. Americans have often thought about divine providence in terms of God's hand guiding history, not simply intervening in particular situations here and there, but directing the whole course of history in a progressive way. At the same time, we have also expressed uneasiness about this moral vision of history, and about our tendency to identify our own plans with divine will. As Perry Miller pointed out in his famous essay, "Errand into the Wilderness," the Puritans themselves had second thoughts about their hope of carrying out God's mission to make America a light to all nations. Why were their plans not working out more smoothly? Was God really behind their endeavor?

Later in the nineteenth and twentieth centuries, this uneasiness about the idea of America's role as a leader in the progressive enfolding of God's Kingdom on earth turned to outright resistance. In the midst of a groundswell of opposition to belief in historical progress, and of opposition to liberal enthusiasm for modern thought and science, Fundamentalism emerged to challenge liberal optimism about historical progress. Focusing especially on prophesies in the books of Daniel and Revelation, Fundamentalists correlated the signs of cosmic disaster in these prophesies with the moral corruption into which they believed America was sinking. These anti-liberal decoders of biblical prophesy saw America as the realization of all the bad things signified by references to the corrupt Roman Empire in the books of Daniel and Revelation.

However alarming these predictions (and however many Hollywood films were inspired by them), for many Americans, religious life still moved in the direction of commitment to moral progress and social reform. Not only major Protestant denominations adhered to this commitment but Jews, Buddhists, Wiccans, and many American Muslims as well. Most impressive of all was the enormous outpouring of progressive social concern on the part of American Catholics. Partly as a result of the religious energy unleashed by the Second Vatican Council's mandate to open the doors of the Catholic Church to the modern world, and partly as a result of their involvement in the mainstreams of American culture, American Catholics led the way in carrying forward the progressive social vision once associated with mainline Protestantism. Exemplifying both the syncretism and the vitality of American religious life, American Catholics blended the traditional Catholic devotion to the poor with a new commitment to alleviating the social conditions of distress that owed much to the moral activism of Protestant culture. In traditional,

European-style Catholicism, mystical identification with Christ through devotion to the poor had been a means of personal purification, not of social change. But as exemplars of progressive social activism in late twentieth-and early twenty-first-century America, Catholics often led the way in carrying forward the Puritans' religious errand of creating a New Israel. For example, as one of the pioneers of this new American Catholicism, Rosemary Radford Ruether combined spiritual devotion to the poor with activist, feminist, and ecological desires for liberation and world reform.

Similar observations might be made about the historical development of other religious traditions in America. Jews, Muslims, Native Americans, and Wiccans have all been influenced by the Protestant aspect of American culture even as they have contributed to and altered that culture. This process of exchange and syncretism has been abetted by the Protestant emphasis on religious freedom and individual experience. It has also been abetted by American culture's growing freedom from Protestant control. As a general rule, the less control Protestant people and institutions have exerted over others, the more easily Protestant-rooted ideas about religious freedom, individual experience, family life, and moral reform have been absorbed, appropriated, and recast.

## Notes

1 The high value Jews have long placed on political freedom is reflected in the celebration of Passover, which commemorates God's liberation of Jews from slavery in Egypt. As a high point of the Jewish calendar of religious observance, Passover is an occasion to relive that legendary event, to thank God for freedom enjoyed in the present, and to pray for it in the future. Passover is the most popular holiday of the Jewish calendar; according to recent reports, 90 percent of all American Jews celebrate it.

2 The writings of the Christian Old Testament are essentially the same as those in the Hebrew Bible. Christians have often described the New Testament, with its message of Jesus Christ as the redeemer of humankind, as the fulfillment of Hebrew scripture. Christian belief that the New Testament supersedes the Hebrew Bible has also carried the anti-Semitic idea that Jews should give up their stubborn loyalty to an outmoded religious tradition.

3 About questions concerning the will's freedom, and the will's equation with intensity of feeling, Edwards and Lee represent different schools of thought, with Edwards being more skeptical about both. More important, however, they share an underlying agreement about the centrality of the will in religious life, and about the necessity of the will's transformation away from sin toward loving assent to God.

4   For more information on these examples, see Daniel Sack, "Food and Eating in American Religious Cultures," in *Perspectives on American Religion and Culture*, ed. Peter W. Williams (Malden, MA: Blackwell Publishers, 1999), 203–15; Robert Orsi, *The Madonna of 115th Street: Faith and Community in Italian Harlem, 1880–1950* (New Haven: Yale University Press, 1985); and Karla Goldman, "Reform, Gender, and the Boundaries of American Judaism," *Perspectives*, 292–9.

5   Similarly, children were expected to obey their parents, but at the same time, affection drew parents and children together and parental expectations lent children an important element of equality. As church members, parents bestowed indirect authority on their children by presenting them for baptism, hoping that these children would carry on the parents' religious commitments as heads of their own families, and future leaders of the community.

# Part I

# Historical Essays

# 1

# Errand into the Wilderness

*Perry Miller*

## Introduction

In the 1950s, Perry Miller rediscovered the depth of Puritan religious thought. While Puritans were generally understood to have played a formative role in the history of American culture, they were often depicted as sour and heavy-handed moralists who wanted everyone to live according to their rules. At a time when many intellectuals hoped that America might finally break away from puritanical finger-wagging, Miller empathized with the Puritans' predicament in the New World and suggested that modern Americans might better understand their own situation by reflecting on the Puritans' struggle for religious identity. Miller expressed special sympathy for the second and third generations of New England Puritans, whose sense of moral failure was bound up with their idealization of the founding generation.

Miller's work has often been attacked. It has been criticized, among other things, for concentrating on the existential dilemmas of the Puritan elite and thereby overlooking the vitality and pluralism of popular religion. Indeed, Miller's work stimulated many historians of American religion to learn more about the complex world of popular belief and practice in early New England. But however much Miller's work led historians to pursue other stories, his appreciation of the efforts that Puritan leaders made to live up to their forebears still remains instructive. In addition to presenting them as complex

Excerpted from Perry Miller, "Errand into the Wilderness," in Perry Miller, *Errand into the Wilderness* (New York: Harper & Row, 1956), 2–15. Copyright © 1956, 1984 by the President and Fellows of Harvard College.

human beings rather than two-dimensional stereotypes, Miller called attention to the myth of a golden age of American religious purity and to the long
shadow it cast on the religious lives of later Americans.

It was a happy inspiration that led the staff of the John Carter Brown
Library to choose as the title of its New England exhibition of 1952 a
phrase from Samuel Danforth's election sermon, delivered on May 11,
1670: *A Brief Recognition of New England's Errand into the Wilderness*. It
was of course an inspiration, if not of genius at least of talent, for
Danforth to invent his title in the first place. But all the election sermons
of this period – that is to say, the major expressions of the second
generation, which, delivered on these forensic occasions, were in the
fullest sense community expression – have interesting titles; a mere
listing tells the story of what was happening to the minds and emotions
of the New England people: John Higginson's *The Cause of God and His
People In New-England* in 1663, William Stoughton's *New England's True
Interest, Not to Lie* in 1668, Thomas Shepard's *Eye-Salve* in 1672, Urian
Oakes's *New England Pleaded With* in 1673, and, climactically and most
explicitly, Increase Mather's *A Discourse Concerning the Danger of Apostasy* in 1677.

All of these show by their title pages alone – and, as those who have
looked into them know, infinitely more by their contents – a deep
disquietude. They are troubled utterances, worried, fearful. Something
has gone wrong. As in 1662 Wigglesworth already was saying in verse,
God has a controversy with New England; He has cause to be angry and
to punish it because of its innumerable defections. They say, unani-
mously, that New England was sent on an errand, and that it has failed.

To our ears these lamentations of the second generation sound strange
indeed. We think of the founders as heroic men – of the towering stature
of Bradford, Winthrop, and Thomas Hooker – who braved the ocean
and the wilderness, who conquered both, and left to their children a
goodly heritage. Why then this whimpering?

Some historians suggest that the second and third generations suffered
a failure of nerve; they weren't the men their fathers had been, and they
knew it. Where the founders could range over the vast body of theology
and ecclesiastical polity and produce profound works like the treatises of
John Cotton or the subtle psychological analyses of Hooker, or even such
a gusty though wrongheaded book as Nathaniel Ward's *Simple Cobler*, let
alone such lofty and rightheaded pleas as Roger Williams' *Bloudy Tenent*,
all these children could do was tell each other that they were on probation and that their chances of making good did not seem very promising.

Since Puritan intellectuals were thoroughly grounded in grammar and
rhetoric, we may be certain that Danforth was fully aware of the ambi-

guity concealed in his word "errand." It already had taken on the double meaning which it still carries with us. Originally, as the word first took form in English, it meant exclusively a short journey on which an inferior is sent to convey a message or to perform a service for his superior. In that sense we today speak of an "errand boy"; or the husband says that while in town on his lunch hour, he must run an errand for his wife. But by the end of the Middle Ages, errand developed another connotation: it came to mean the actual business on which the actor goes, the purpose itself, the conscious intention in his mind. In this signification, the runner of the errand is working for himself, is his own boss; the wife, while the husband is away at the office, runs her own errands. Now in the 1660s the problem was this: which had New England originally been – an errand boy or a doer of errands? In which sense had it failed? Had it been despatched for a further purpose, or was it an end in itself? Or had it fallen short not only in one or the other, but in both of the meanings? If so, it was indeed a tragedy, in the primitive sense of a fall from a mighty designation.

If the children were in grave doubt about which had been the original errand – if, in fact, those of the founders who lived into the later period and who might have set their progeny to rights found themselves wondering and confused – there is little chance of our answering clearly. Of course, there is no problem about Plymouth Colony. That is the charm about Plymouth: its clarity. The Pilgrims, as we have learned to call them, were reluctant voyagers; they had never wanted to leave England, but had been obliged to depart because the authorities made life impossible for Separatists. They could, naturally, have stayed at home had they given up being Separatists, but that idea simply did not occur to them. Yet they did not go to Holland as though on an errand; neither can we extract the notion of a mission out of the reasons which, as Bradford tells us, persuaded them to leave Leyden for "Virginia." The war with Spain was about to be resumed, and the economic threat was ominous; their migration was not so much an errand as a shrewd forecast, a plan to get out while the getting was good, lest, should they stay, they would be "intrapped or surrounded by their enemies, so as they should neither be able to fight nor flie." True, once the decision was taken, they congratulated themselves that they might become a means for propagating the gospel in remote parts of the world, and thus of serving as steppingstones to others in the performance of this great work; nevertheless, the substance of their decision was that they "thought it better to dislodge betimes to some place of better advantage and less danger, if any such could be found." The great hymn that Bradford, looking back in his old age, chanted about the landfall is one of the greatest passages, if not the very greatest, in all New England's literature;

yet it does not resound with the sense of a mission accomplished –
instead, it vibrates with the sorrow and exultation of suffering, the
sheer endurance, the pain and the anguish, with the somberness of
death faced unflinchingly:

> May not and ought not the children of these fathers rightly say: Our fathers
> were Englishmen which came over this great ocean, and were ready to
> perish in this wilderness; but they cried unto the Lord, and he heard their
> voyce, and looked on their adversitie....

We are bound, I think, to see in Bradford's account the prototype of the
vast majority of subsequent immigrants – of those Oscar Handlin calls
"The Uprooted": they came for better advantage and for less danger,
and to give their posterity the opportunity of success.

The Great Migration of 1630 is an entirely other story. True, among
the reasons John Winthrop drew up in 1629 to persuade himself and his
colleagues that they should commit themselves to the enterprise, the
economic motive frankly figures. Wise men thought that England was
overpopulated and that the poor would have a better chance in the new
land. But Massachusetts Bay was not just an organization of immigrants
seeking advantage and opportunity. It had a positive sense of mission –
either it was sent on an errand or it had its own intention, but in either
case the deed was deliberate. It was an act of will, perhaps of willfulness.
These Puritans were not driven out of England (thousands of their
fellows stayed and fought the Cavaliers) – they went of their own accord.

So, concering them, we ask the question, why? If we are not altogether
clear about precisely how we should phrase the answer, this is not
because they themselves were reticent. They spoke as fully as they
knew how, and none more magnificently or cogently than John Winthrop in the midst of the passage itself, when he delivered a lay sermon
aboard the flagship *Arbella* and called it "A Modell of Christian Charity." It distinguishes the motives of this great enterprise from those of
Bradford's forlorn retreat, and especially from those of the masses who
later have come in quest of advancement. Hence, for the student of New
England and of America, it is a fact demanding incessant brooding that
John Winthrop selected as the "doctrine" of his discourse, and so as the
basic proposition to which, it then seemed to him, the errand was
committed, the thesis that God had disposed mankind in a hierarchy
of social classes, so that "in all times some must be rich, some poor,
some highe and eminent in power and dignitie; others mean and in
subjeccion." It is as though, preternaturally sensing what the promise
of America might come to signify for the rank and file, Winthrop took
the precaution to drive out of their heads any notion that in the wilder-

ness the poor and the mean were ever so to improve themselves as to mount above the rich or the eminent in dignity. Were there any who had signed up under the mistaken impression that such was the purpose of their errand, Winthrop told them that, although other peoples, lesser breeds, might come for wealth or pelf, this migration was specifically dedicated to an avowed end that had nothing to do with incomes. We have entered into an explicit covenant with God, "we haue professed to enterprise these Accions vpon these and these ends"; we have drawn up indentures with the Almighty, wherefore if we succeed and do not let ourselves get diverted into making money, He will reward us. Whereas if we fail, if we "fall to embrace this present world and prosecute our carnall intencions, seekeing greate things for our selves and our posterity, the Lord will surely breake out in wrathe against us be revenged of such a periured people and make us knowe the price of the breache of such a Covenant."

Well, what terms were agreed upon in this covenant? Winthrop could say precisely – "It is by a mutuall consent through a specially overruleing providence, and a more than ordinary approbation of the Churches of Christ to seeke out a place of Cohabitation and Consorteshipp under a due forme of Government both civill and ecclesiasticall." If it could be said thus concretely, why should there be any ambiguity? There was no doubt whatsoever about what Winthrop meant by a due form of ecclesiastical government: he meant the pure Biblical polity set forth in full detail by the New Testament, that method which later generations, in the days of increasing confusion, would settle down to calling Congregational, but which for Winthrop was no denominational peculiarity but the very essence of organized Christianity. What a due form of civil government meant, therefore, became crystal clear: a political regime, possessing power, which would consider its main function to be the erecting, protecting, and preserving of this form of polity. This due form would have, at the very beginning of its list of responsibilities, the duty of suppressing heresy, of subduing or somehow getting rid of dissenters – of being, in short, deliberately, vigorously, and consistently intolerant.

Regarded in this light, the Massachusetts Bay Company came on an errand in the second and later sense of the word: it was, so to speak, on its own business. What it set out to do was the sufficient reason for its setting out. About this Winthrop seems to be perfectly certain, as he declares specifically what the due forms will be attempting: the end is to improve our lives to do more service to the Lord, to increase the body of Christ, and to preserve our posterity from the corruptions of this evil world, so that they in turn shall work out their salvation under the purity and power of Biblical ordinances. Because the errand was so definable in advance, certain conclusions about the method of conducting it were equally evident: one, obviously, was that those sworn to the covenant should not be allowed to turn aside in a lust for mere physical rewards; but another was, in Winthrop's simple but splendid words, "we must be knit together in this worke as one man, wee must entertaine each other in brotherly affection." We must actually delight in each other, "always having before our eyes our Commission and community in the worke, our community as members of the same body." This was to say, were the great purpose kept steadily in mind, if all gazed only at it and strove only for it, then social solidarity (within a scheme of fixed and unalterable class distinctions) would be an automatic consequence. A society despatched upon an errand that is its own reward would want no other rewards: it could go forth to possess a land without ever becoming possessed by it; social gradations would remain eternally what God had originally appointed; there would be no internal contention among groups or interests, and though there would be hard work for everybody, prosperity would be bestowed not as a consequence of labor but as a sign of approval upon the mission itself. For once in the history of humanity (with all its sins), there would be a society so dedicated to a holy cause that success would prove innocent and triumph not raise up sinful pride or arrogant dissension.

Or, at least, this would come about if the people did not deal falsely with God, if they would live up to the articles of their bond. If we do not perform these terms, Winthrop warned, we may expect immediate manifestations of divine wrath; we shall perish out of the land we are crossing the sea to possess. And here in the 1660s and 1670s, all the jeremiads (of which Danforth's is one of the most poignant) are castigations of the people for having defaulted on precisely these articles. They recite the long list of afflictions an angry God had rained upon them, surely enough to prove how abysmally they had deserted the covenant: crop failures, epidemics, grasshoppers, caterpillars, torrid summers, arctic winters, Indian wars, hurricanes, shipwrecks, accidents, and (most grievous of all) unsatisfactory children. The solemn work of the election day, said Stoughton in 1668, is "Foundation-work" – not, that is, to lay a new one, "but to continue, and strengthen, and beautifie, and build upon that which has been laid." It had been laid in the covenant before even a foot was set ashore, and thereon New England should rest. Hence the terms of survival, let alone of prosperity, remained what had first been propounded:

If we should so frustrate and deceive the Lords Expectations, that his Covenant-interest in us, and the Workings of his Salvation be made to cease, then All were lost indeed; Ruine upon Ruine, Destruction upon Destruction would come, until one stone were not left upon another.

Since so much of the literature after 1660 – in fact, just about all of it – dwells on this theme of declension and apostasy, would not the story of New England seem to be simply that of the failure of a mission? Winthrop's dread was realized: posterity had not found their salvation amid pure ordinances but had, despite the ordinances, yielded to the seductions of the good land. Hence distresses were being piled upon them, the slaughter of King Philip's War and now the attack of a profligate king upon the sacred charter. By about 1680, it did in truth seem that shortly no stone would be left upon another, that history would record of New England that the founders had been great men, but that their children and grandchildren progressively deteriorated.

This would certainly seem to be the impression conveyed by the assembled clergy and lay elders who, in 1679, met at Boston in a formal synod, under the leadership of Increase Mather, and there prepared a report on why the land suffered. The result of their deliberation, published under the title *The Necessity of Reformation*, was the first in what has proved to be a distressingly long succession of investigations into the civic health of Americans, and it is probably the most pessimistic. The land was afflicted, it said, because corruption had proceeded apace; assuredly, if the people did not quickly reform, the last blow would fall and nothing but desolation be left. Into what a moral quagmire this dedicated community had sunk, the synod did not leave to imagination; it published a long and detailed inventory of sins, crimes, misdemeanors, and nasty habits, which makes, to say the least, interesting reading.

We hear much talk nowadays about corruption, most of it couched in generalized terms. If we ask our current Jeremiahs to descend to particulars, they tell us that the republic is going on the rocks, or to the dogs, because the wives of politicians aspire to wear mink coats and their husbands take a moderate 5 percent cut on certain deals to pay for the garments. The Puritans were devotees of logic, and the verb "methodize" ruled their thinking. When the synod went to work, it had before it a succession of sermons, such as that of Danforth and the other election-day or fast-day orators, as well as such works as Increase Mather's *A Brief History of the Warr With the Indians*, wherein the decimating conflict with Philip was presented as a revenge upon the people for their transgressions. When the synod felt obliged to enumerate the enormities of the land so that the people could recognize just how far short of their errand they had fallen, it did not, in the modern manner, assume that regeneration would be accomplished at the next election by turning the rascals out, but it digested this body of literature; it reduced the contents to method. The result is a staggering compendium of iniquity, organized into twelve headings.

First, there was a great and visible decay of godliness. Second, there were several manifestations of pride – contention in the churches, insubordination of inferiors towards superiors, particularly of those inferiors who had, unaccountably, acquired more wealth than their betters, and, astonishingly, a shocking extravagance in attire, especially on the part of these of the meaner sort, who persisted in dressing beyond their means. Third, there were heretics, especially Quakers and Anabaptists. Fourth, a notable increase in swearing and a spreading disposition to sleep at sermons (these two phenomena seemed basically connected). Fifth, the Sabbath was wantonly violated. Sixth, family government had decayed, and fathers no longer kept their sons and daughters from prowling at night. Seventh, instead of people being knit together as one man in mutual love, they were full of contention, so that lawsuits were on the increase and lawyers were thriving. Under the eighth head, the synod described the sins of sex and alcohol, thus producing some of the juiciest prose of the period: militia days had become orgies, taverns were crowded; women threw temptation in the way of befuddled men by wearing false locks and displaying naked necks and arms "or, which is more abominable, naked Breasts"; there were "mixed Dancings," along with light behavior and "Company-keeping" with vain persons, wherefore the bastardy rate was rising. In 1672, there was actually an attempt to supply Boston with a brothel (it was suppressed, but the synod was bearish about the future). Ninth, New Englanders were betraying a marked disposition to tell lies, especially when selling anything. In the tenth place, the business morality of even the most righteous left everything to be desired: the wealthy speculated in land and raised prices excessively; "Day-Labourers and Mechanicks are unreasonable in their demands." In the eleventh place, the people showed no disposition to reform, and in the twelfth, they seemed utterly destitute of civic spirit.

"The things here insisted on," said the synod, "have been oftentimes mentioned and inculcated by those whom the Lord hath set as Watchmen to the house of Israel." Indeed they had been, and thereafter they continued to be even more inculcated. At the end of the century, the synod's report was serving as a kind of handbook for preachers: they would take some verse of Isaiah or Jeremiah, set up the doctrine that God avenges the iniquities of a chosen people, and then run down the twelve heads, merely bringing the list up to date by inserting the new and still more depraved practices an ingenious people kept on devising. I suppose that in the whole literature of the world, including the satirists of imperial Rome, there is hardly such another uninhibited and unrelenting documentation of a people's descent into corruption.

I have elsewhere endeavored to argue[1] that, while the social or economic historian may read this literature for its contents – and so construct from the expanding catalogue of denunciations a record of social progress – the cultural anthropologist will look slightly askance at these jeremiads; he will exercise a methodological caution about taking them at face value. If you read them all through, the total effect, curiously enough, is not at all depressing: you come to the paradoxical realization that they do not bespeak a despairing frame of mind. There is something of a ritualistic incantation about them; whatever they may signify in the realm of theology, in that of psychology they are purgations of soul; they do not discourage but actually encourage the community to persist in its heinous conduct. The exhortation to a reformation which never materializes serves as a token payment upon the obligation, and so liberates the debtors. Changes there had to be: adaptations to environment, expansion of the frontier, mansions constructed, commercial adventures undertaken. These activities were not specifically nominated in the bond Winthrop had framed. They were thrust upon the society by American experience; because they were not only works of necessity but of excitement, they proved irresistible – whether making money, haunting taverns, or committing fornication. Land speculation meant not only wealth but dispersion of the people, and what was to stop the march of settlement? The covenant doctrine preached on the *Arbella* had been formulated in England, where land was not to be had for the taking; its adherents had been utterly oblivious of what the fact of a frontier would do for an imported order, let alone for a European mentality. Hence I suggest that under the guise of this mounting wail of sinfulness, this incessant and never successful cry for repentance, the Puritans launched themselves upon the process of Americanization.

However, there are still more pertinent or more analytical things to be said of this body of expression. If you compare it with the great productions of the founders, you will be struck by the fact that the second and third generations had become oriented toward the social, and only the social, problem; herein they were deeply and profoundly different from their fathers. The finest creations of the founders – the disquisitions of Hooker, Shepard, and Cotton – were written in Europe, or else, if actually penned in the colonies, proceeded from a thoroughly European mentality, upon which the American scene made no impression whatsoever. The most striking example of this imperviousness is the poetry of Anne Bradstreet: she came to Massachusetts at the age of eighteen, already two years married to Simon Bradstreet; there, she says, "I found a new world and new manners, at which my heart rose" in rebellion, but soon convincing herself that it was the way of God, she submitted and joined the church. She bore Simon eight children, and loved him sincerely, as her most charming poem, addressed to him, reveals:

> If ever two were one, then surely we;
> If ever man were loved by wife, then thee.

After the house burned, she wrote a lament about how her pleasant things in ashes lay and how no more the merriment of guests would sound in the hall; but there is nothing in the poem to suggest that the house stood in North Andover or that the things so tragically consumed were doubly precious because they had been transported across the ocean and were utterly irreplaceable in the wilderness. In between rearing children and keeping house she wrote her poetry; her brother-in-law carried the manu script to London, and there published it in 1650 under the ambitious title, *The Tenth Muse Lately Sprung Up in America*. But the title is the only thing about the volume which shows any sense of America, and that little merely in order to prove that the plantations had something in the way of European wit and learning, that they had not receded into barbarism. Anne's flowers are English flowers, the birds, English birds, and the landscape is Lincolnshire. So also with the productions of immigrant scholarship: such a learned and acute work as Hooker's *Survey of the Summe of Church Discipline*, which is specifically about the regime set up in America, is written entirely within the logical patterns, and out of the religious experience, of Europe; it makes no concession to new and peculiar circumstances.

The titles alone of productions in the next generation show how concentrated have become emotion and attention upon the interest of New England, and none is more revealing than Samuel Danforth's conception of an errand into the wilderness. Instead of being able to compose abstract treatises like those of Hooker upon the soul's preparation, humiliation, or exultation, or such a collection of wisdom and theology as John Cotton's *The Way of Life* or Shepard's *The Sound Believer*, these later saints must, over and over again, dwell upon the specific sins of New England, and the more they denounce, the more they must narrow their focus to the provincial problem. If they write upon anything else, it must be about the halfway covenant and its manifold consequences – a development enacted wholly in this country – or else upon their wars with the Indians. Their range is sadly constricted, but every effort, no matter how brief, is addressed to the persistent question: what is the meaning of this society in the wilderness? If it does not mean what Winthrop said it must mean, what under Heaven is it? Who, they are forever asking themselves, who are we? – and sometimes they are on the verge of saying, who the Devil are we, anyway?

This brings us back to the fundamental ambiguity concealed in the word "errand," that *double entente* of which I am certain Danforth was aware when he published the words that give point to the exhibition. While it was true that in 1630, the covenant philosophy of a special and peculiar bond lifted the migration out of the ordinary realm of nature, provided it with a definite mission which might in the secondary sense be called its errand, there was always present in Puritan thinking the suspicion that God's saints are at best inferiors, despatched by their Superior upon particular assignments. Anyone who has run errands for other people, particularly for people of great importance with many things on their minds, such as army commanders, knows how real is the peril that, by the time he returns with the report of a message delivered or a bridge blown up, the Superior may be interested in something else; the situation at headquarters may be entirely changed, and the gallant errand boy, or the husband who desperately remembered to buy the ribbon, may be told that he is too late. This tragic pattern appears again and again in modern warfare: an agent is dropped by parachute and, after immense hardships, comes back to find that, in the shifting tactical or strategic situations, his contribution is no longer of value. If he gets home in time and his service proves useful, he receives a medal; otherwise, no matter what prodigies he has performed, he may not even be thanked. He has been sent, as the devastating phrase has it, upon a fool's errand, than which there can be a no more shattering blow to self-esteem.

The Great Migration of 1630 felt insured against such treatment from on high by the covenant; nevertheless, the God of the covenant always remained an unpredictable Jehovah, a *Deus Absconditus*. When God promises to abide by stated terms, His word, of course, is to be trusted; but then, what is man that he dare accuse Omnipotence of tergiversation? But if any such apprehension was in Winthrop's mind as he spoke on the *Arbella*, or in the minds of other apologists for the enterprise, they kept it far back and allowed it no utterance. They could stifle the thought, not only because Winthrop and his colleagues believed fully in the covenant, but because they could see in the pattern of history that their errand was not a mere scouting expedition: it was an essential maneuver in the drama of Christendom. The Bay Company was not a battered remnant of suffering Separatists thrown up on a rocky shore; it was an organized task force of Christians, executing a flank attack on the corruptions of Christendom. These Puritans did not flee to America; they went in order to work out that complete reformation which was not yet accomplished in England and Europe, but which would quickly be accomplished if only the saints back there had a working model to guide them. It is impossible to say that any who sailed from Southampton really expected to lay his bones in the new world; were it to come about – as all in their heart of hearts anticipated – that the forces of righteousness should prevail against Laud and Wentworth, that England after all should turn toward reformation, where else would the distracted country look for leadership except to those who in New England had perfected the ideal polity and who would know how to administer it? This was the large unspoken assumption in the errand of 1630: if the conscious intention were realized, not only would a federated Jehovah bless the new land, but He would bring back these temporary colonials to govern England.

In this respect, therefore, we may say that the migration was running an errand in the earlier and more primitive sense of the word – performing a job not so much for Jehovah as for history, which was the wisdom of Jehovah expressed through time. Winthrop was aware of this aspect of the mission – fully conscious of it. "For wee must Consider that wee shall be as a Citty upon a Hill, the eies of all people are upon us." More was at stake than just one little colony. If we deal falsely with God, not only will He descend upon us in wrath, but even more terribly, He will make us "a story and a by-word through the world, wee shall open the mouthes of enemies to speake evill of the wayes of god and all professours for Gods sake." No less than John Milton was New England to justify God's ways to man, though not, like him, in the agony and confusion of defeat but in the confidence of approaching triumph. This errand was being run for the sake of Reformed Christianity; and while the first aim was indeed to realize in America the due form of government, both civil and ecclesiastical, the aim behind that aim was to vindicate the most rigorous ideal of the Reformation, so that ultimately all Europe would imitate New England. If we succeed, Winthrop told his audience, men will say of later plantations, "the lord make it like that of New England." There was an elementary prudence to be observed: Winthrop said that the prayer would arise from subsequent plantations, yet what was England itself but one of God's plantations? In America, he promised, we shall see, or may see, more of God's wisdom, power, and truth "then formerly were have beene acquainted with." The situation was such that, for the moment, the model had no chance to be exhibited in England; Puritans could talk about it, theorize upon it, but they could not display it, could not prove that it would actually work. But if they had it set up in America – in a bare land, devoid of already established (and corrupt) institutions, empty of bishops and courtiers, where they could start *de novo*, and the eyes of the world were upon it – and if then it performed just as the saints had predicted of it, the Calvinist internationale would know exactly how to go about completing the already begun but temporarily stalled revolution in Europe.[2]

When we look upon the enterprise from this point of view, the psychology of the second and third generations becomes more comprehensible. We realize that the migration was not sent upon its errand in order to found the United States of America, nor even the New England conscience. Actually, it would not perform its errand even when the colonists did erect a due form of government in church and state: what was further required in order for this mission to be a success was that the eyes of the world be kept fixed upon it in rapt attention. If the rest of the world, or at least of Protestantism, looked elsewhere, or turned to another model, or simply got distracted and forgot about New England, if the new land was left with a polity nobody in the great world of Europe wanted – then every success in fulfilling the terms of the covenant would become a diabolical measure of failure. If the due form of government were not everywhere to be saluted, what would New England have upon its hands? How give it a name, this victory nobody could utilize? How provide an identity for something conceived under misapprehensions? How could a universal which turned out to be nothing but a provincial particular be called anything but a blunder or an abortion?

If an actor, playing the leading role in the greatest dramatic spectacle of the century, were to attire himself and put on his make-up, rehearse his lines, take a deep breath, and stride onto the stage, only to find the theater dark and empty, no spotlight working, and himself entirely alone, he would feel as did New England around 1650 or 1660. For in the 1640s, during the Civil Wars, the colonies, so to speak, lost their audience. First of all, there proved to be, deep in the Puritan movement, an irreconcilable split between the Presbyterian and Independent wings, wherefore no one system could be imposed upon England, and so the New England model was unserviceable. Secondly – most horrible to relate – the Independents, who in polity were carrying New England's banner and were supposed, in the schedule of history, to lead England into imitation of the colonial order, betrayed the sacred cause by yielding to the heresy of toleration. They actually welcomed Roger Williams, whom the leaders of the model had kicked out of Massachusetts so that his nonsense about liberty of conscience would not spoil the administrations of charity.

In other words, New England did not lie, did not falter; it made good everything Winthrop demanded – wonderfully good – and then found that its lesson was rejected by those choice spirits for whom the exertion had been made. By casting out Williams, Anne Hutchinson, and the Antinomians, along with an assortment of Gortonists and Anabaptists, into that cesspool then becoming known as Rhode Island, Winthrop, Dudley, and the clerical leaders showed Oliver Cromwell how he should go about governing England. Instead, he developed the utterly absurd theory that so long as a man made a good soldier in the New Model Army, it did not matter whether he was a Calvinist, an Antinomian, an

Arminian, an Anabaptist or even – horror of horrors – a Socinian! Year after year, as the circus tours this country, crowds howl with laughter, no matter how many times they have seen the stunt, at the bustle that walks by itself: the clown comes out dressed in a large skirt with a bustle behind; he turns sharply to the left, and the bustle continues blindly and obstinately straight ahead, on the original course. It is funny in a circus, but not in history. There is nothing but tragedy in the realization that one was in the main path of events, and now is sidetracked and disregarded. One is always able, of course, to stand firm on his first resolution, and to condemn the clown of history for taking the wrong turning: yet this is a desolating sort of stoicism, because it always carries with it the recognition that history will never come back to the predicted path, and that with one's own demise, righteousness must die out of the world.

The most humiliating element in the experience was the way the English brethren turned upon the colonials for precisely their greatest achievement. It must have seemed, for those who came with Winthrop in 1630 and who remembered the clarity and brilliance with which he set forth the conditions of their errand, that the world was turned upside down and inside out when, in June 1645, thirteen leading Independent divines – such men as Goodwin, Owen, Nye, Burroughs, formerly friends and allies of Hooker and Davenport, men who might easily have come to New England and helped extirpate heretics – wrote the General Court that the colony's law banishing Anabaptists was an embarrassment to the Independent cause in England. Opponents were declaring, said these worthies, "that persons of our way, principall and spirit cannot beare with Dissentors from them, but Doe correct, fine, imprison and banish them wherever they have power soe to Doe." There were indeed people in England who admired the severities of Massachusetts, but we assure you, said the Independents, these "are utterly your enemyes and Doe seeke your extirpation from the face of the earth: those who now in power are your friends are quite otherwise minded, and doe professe they are much offended with your proceedings." Thus early commenced that chronic weakness in the foreign policy of Americans, an inability to recognize who in truth constitute their best friends abroad.

We have lately accustomed ourselves to the fact that there does exist a mentality which will take advantage of the liberties allowed by society in order to conspire for the ultimate suppression of those same privileges. The government of Charles I and Archbishop Laud had not, where that danger was concerned, been liberal, but it had been conspicuously inefficient; hence, it did not liquidate the Puritans (although it made halfhearted efforts), nor did it herd them into prison camps. Instead, it generously, even lavishly, gave a group of them a charter to Massachusetts Bay, and obligingly left out the standard clause requiring that the document remain in London, that the grantees keep their office within reach of Whitehall. Winthrop's revolutionaries availed themselves of this liberty to get the charter overseas, and thus to set up a regime dedicated to the worship of God in the manner they desired – which meant allowing nobody else to worship any other way, especially adherents of Laud and King Charles. All this was perfectly logical and consistent. But what happened to the thought processes of their fellows in England made no sense whatsoever. Out of the New Model Army came the fantastic notion that a party struggling for power should proclaim that, once it captured the state, it would recognize the right of dissenters to disagree and to have their own worship, to hold their own opinions. Oliver Cromwell was so far gone in this idiocy as to become a dictator, in order to impose toleration by force! Amid this shambles, the errand of New England collapsed. There was nobody left at headquarters to whom reports could be sent.

Many a man has done a brave deed, been hailed as a public hero, had honors and ticker tape heaped upon him – and then had to live, day after day, in the ordinary routine, eating breakfast and brushing his teeth, in what seems protracted anticlimax. A couple may win their way to each other across insuperable obstacles, elope in a blaze of passion and glory – and then have to learn that life is a matter of buying the groceries and getting the laundry done. This sense of the meaning having gone out of life, that all adventures are over, that no great days and no heroism lie ahead, is particularly galling when it falls upon a son whose father once was the public hero or the great lover. He has to put up with the daily routine without ever having known at first hand the thrill of danger or the ecstasy of passion. True, he has his own hardships – clearing rocky pastures, hauling in the cod during a storm, fighting Indians in a swamp – but what are these compared with the magnificence of leading an exodus of saints to found a city on a hill, for the eyes of all the world to behold? He might wage a stout fight against the Indians, and one out of ten of his fellows might perish in the struggle, but the world was no longer interested. He would be reduced to writing accounts of himself and scheming to get a publisher in London, in a desperate effort to tell a heedless world, "Look, I exist!"

His greatest difficulty would be not the stones, storms, and Indians, but the problem of his identity. In something of this sort, I should like to suggest, consists the anxiety and torment that inform productions of the late seventeenth and early eighteenth centuries – and should I say, some thereafter? It appears most clearly in *Magnalia Christi Americana*, the work of that soul most tortured by the problem, Cotton Mather: "I write the Wonders of the Christian Religion, flying from the Depravations of

Europe, to the American Strand." Thus he proudly begins, and at once trips over the acknowledgement that the founders had not simply fled from depraved Europe but had intended to redeem it. And so the book is full of lamentations over the declension of the children, who appear, page after page, in contrast to their mighty progenitors, about as profligate a lot as ever squandered a great inheritance.

And yet, the *Magnalia* is not an abject book; neither are the election sermons abject, nor is the inventory of sins offered by the synod of 1679. There is bewilderment, confusion, chagrin, but there is no surrender. A task has been assigned upon which the populace are in fact intensely engaged. But they are not sure any more for just whom they are working; they know they are moving, but they do not know where they are going. They seem still to be on an errand, but if they are no longer inferiors sent by the superior forces of the Reformation, to whom they should report, then their errand must be wholly of the second sort, something with a purpose and an intention sufficient unto itself. If so, what is it? If it be not the due form of government, civil and ecclesiastical, that they brought into being, how otherwise can it be described?

The literature of self-condemnation must be read for meanings far below the surface, for meanings of which, we may be so rash as to surmise, the authors were not fully conscious, but by which they were troubled and goaded. They looked in vain to history for an explanation of themselves; more and more it appeared that the meaning was not to be found in theology, even with the help of the covenantal dialectic. Thereupon, these citizens found that they had no other place to search but within themselves – even though, at first sight, that repository appeared to be nothing but a sink of iniquity. Their errand having failed in the first sense of the term, they were left with the second, and required to fill it with meaning by themselves and out of themselves. Having failed to rivet the eyes of the world upon their city on the hill, they were left alone with America.

# Notes

1   See *The New England Mind: From Colony to Province* (1952), Chapter II.
2   See the perceptive analysis of Alan Heimert (*The New England Quarterly*, XXVI, September 1953) of the ingredients that ultimately went into the Puritans' metaphor of the "wilderness," all the more striking a concoction because they attached no significance *a priori* to their wilderness destination. To begin with, it was simply a void.

# Exchanging Selves, Exchanging Souls: Contact, Combination, and American Religious History

*Catherine L. Albanese*

## Introduction

Under and around the long shadow cast by the Puritan struggle for American religious identity, many different religious traditions have flourished, each with its own stories and ceremonies, and each with its own distinctive history of development and change. As Catherine Albanese explains, each religious tradition in America developed in the midst of other traditions declaring themselves, competing for survival and growth, and passing judgment on one another. In contrast to other cultures with less religious competition and fewer religions, American culture has been a vast marketplace for religious goods where people have continually tried out new beliefs and practices and refashioned old ones. If this situation has led to criticism of America for being too trendy and hospitable to religious con artists, it is also responsible for much of the creativity and vitality of American religious life.

The notion of American culture as a marketplace for spiritual as well as material goods points to the important relationship between American religious history and the development of a market economy. As a number of scholars have argued, religion in North America has changed along with the shift from relatively self-sufficient, predominantly local economies to an inter-

Excerpted from Catherine L. Albanese, "Exchanging Selves, Exchanging Souls: Contact, Combination, and American Religious History," in *Retelling U.S. Religious History*, ed. Thomas A. Tweed (Berkeley: University of California Press, 1997), 200–26.

dependent national economy with increasing international connections. Without reducing religion to a simple reflection of this shift toward a global economy, we can appreciate the way in which increased contact among people of different religions, decreased fear of religious strangeness, and growing acceptance of the idea that there are universal religious concerns underlying traditional differences are an important piece of the larger history of American culture as an ever-expanding and increasingly interrelated marketplace.

In the mid-1840s, still in his twenties, Bohemian-born rabbi Isaac Mayer Wise – later to be acknowledged leader of the Jewish Reform movement in America – was riding the railroad in New York state. As he tried to read from a small copy of the Pentateuch with two Aramaic translations and a commentary, his Yankee seatmate grew more and more curious. He wanted to know about Wise's book and about its languages and translations, and Wise explained as best he could. The two got to talking, and the Yankee learned that Wise only recently had arrived in the United States. "Ah, now I know who you are; you are a Jewish bishop," the man declared. Wise recounted what happened next: "I explained to him that the Jews had no hierarchy, but he drew a New Haven newspaper out of his pocket and showed me black on white that a Jewish bishop, Wess or Wiss, who had lately arrived from Jerusalem, had dedicated the synagogue in New Haven." Wise, neither bishop nor Jerusalemite nor dedicator of the New Haven synagogue (he had only preached there), protested in vain. The foreign rabbi had acquired an American identity, and – when later he arrived in Syracuse – he found that the newspaper there already knew it: "N. traveled yesterday from Albany to this city in company with the Jewish Bishop Wess or Wiss (the pronunciation of the name is uncertain), who has lately arrived from Jerusalem."[1]

Another time a country missionary and his wife wanted to meet Wise because, as the man said, "he had never seen a Jew." That task accomplished, the missionary apparently could not contain himself; he let loose a barrage of religious witness in order "to speak in the name of the Lord." But, at least according to his own account, Wise turned out to be better at religious confutation than the missionary. Placing the Hebrew Bible and the Greek New Testament in front of his adversary, he announced, "Here is the Bible. Pray, show me what you may have to object to my Judaism." What followed was Wise's victory: "He confessed that he could read neither the one nor the other, and I attempted to show him how he had learned to know the Bible from the unreliable source of a translation, and that, therefore, he must not discuss Biblical questions with me."[2]

On still a third occasion, in 1850, while Wise was functioning as rabbi at the Bethel congregation in Albany, New York, he became involved in a bitter struggle for control with Louis Spanier, the synagogue's elected president, or parnass. As Wise upheld and Spanier fought violently against the cause of Reform Judaism, Wise found his official preaching garb missing from the synagogue one Sabbath and on another received a message from the parnass not to preach. Blow followed blow in a continuing dispute until it broke through the walls of the synagogue to involve the legal system of the state of New York and the attorney general's office. In the climactic episode of their battle, at one synagogue service that challenged Spanier's authority, the parnass physically obstructed Wise and then struck him with a fist so that Wise's cap fell from his head. Wise, who was arrested, remembered that people "acted like furies" and the synagogue became a "flaming conflagration." The sheriff and his posse who arrived to restore order were "forced out," and then everybody else "surged out of the house" into the street.[3]

Taken together, the three snapshots of Wise – Jewish bishop, missionary's foil, and leader of a faction in a New York synagogue's civil war – invite entry into a world of religious interchange that is often undernoticed and underexplored. Each of the incidents in which Wise functioned as principal actor cast him in a role that was inflected differently, with a distinguishable religious horizon framing the drama in separable ways. Hovering as backdrop for the first was the rumored world of Roman Catholicism, where bishops presided and hierarchies organized religious life. Coming closer in the second episode was the brash and confident world of nineteenth-century Protestant evangelicalism, with militant revival forces ready to do battle for the Lord. And in the third, another sort of battle erupted within the intimacy of a small Jewish congregation. In the Germany and eastern Europe of the past, the rabbi would have reigned supreme, but now the strident echoes of a new land (democracy and religious freedom) and new religious ways (Protestant congregational polity) had brought the authority of the rabbi down.

Whatever else they are about, each of the three episodes from the life of Isaac Mayer Wise are about religious contacts and exchanges in which pluralism and its results must be understood as controlling principles. The exchanges are not exactly symmetrical, and each manifests in a way that seems slightly askew – but the untidiness of the three, their disorderliness, if you will, signals acts in an extended play that tells a new story of religion in America. This tale is one of meeting and change. It is one in which the encounter with the other becomes the invited or (mostly) uninvited gift that transforms the contacting parties – or the gift rebuffed, which still comes back to haunt. And it is one in which transformation comes, sometimes, even through the agencies of third and fourth parties who drift like ghosts on the edge of the cultural horizon.

We may perhaps take a cue from French anthropologist Marcel Mauss. In his provocative *Essai sur le don* (*The Gift*), first published in 1925, Mauss compared a series of cultures past and present to argue that the ritual exchange of gifts functioned as a way to define the social order. Societies avoided war by trading, and in many instances they refined their trading by supplanting written contracts with alliances and gifts. Here they felt the heavy pressure of what became cultures of obligation – pressure to give, to receive, and to repay. According to a Maori proverb, the rule was, Mauss said, "Give as much as you receive and all is for the best."[4]

So gifts, markets, alliances, and constraints were of a piece, part of a continuous social process that maintained the requirements for societal order. Gifts came with strings and prods attached. They extended velvet gloves but masked iron hands beneath. To give a gift meant to coerce with a moral agency that overlay the actual exchange. To receive a gift meant a transaction that might or might not have been equal, and it could also mean possession of what, in effect, had been stolen. Mauss himself was clear about the presence of nonmaterial factors within the created order, pointing to the "various determinants, aesthetic, moral, religious and economic, and the material and demographic factors, whose sum is the basis of society and constitutes the common life."[5]

From a specifically religious perspective, religious exchanges between strangers become cases of what R. Laurence Moore might call "selling God." American religious leaders, he thought, had "learned to operate effectively in the marketplace of American culture"; they had "made that marketplace respond to their concerns," and this was "no mean feat."[6] As for leaders, so for followers and for loners. And when native and would-be Americans met and communicated about their religious ways, they discovered that, as Mauss observed of the Maori, "to give something is to give a part of oneself."[7] So the material gift was also a market exchange and sometime dominative tool in a vast bazaar of the spirit. What was being sold was self and soul. What was being bought was new and combinatory American religions and religion.

This is to argue that, whatever their ascribed religious identity, Americans were professing religions that bore the signs of contact with those who were other and different. American religions were *changed* religions, and they were *new* religions, even if they evoked the stuff of tradition and the trappings of former cultures and times. In this context, discourses about syncretism and "new" – meaning "alternative" – religions are suspect, and what they obscure most of all is the social and spiritual landscape of religious change. Historiographies of consensus begin to unravel, and contested sites for New World potlatches take their place. Gifts are made and remade; they weigh heavily or lightly; they mask oppression and also subvert it. They signal new narratives of contact and combination.

## Indian Episodes

A natural place to begin the story of how all of this worked is with American Indians, earliest residents and partners to processes of exchange. Along the North and Middle Atlantic Coast, Indian contact with Europeans came, initially, through traders and, by the dawn of serious English settlement, their microbes. In the 1610s the plague and in the 1630s the smallpox decimated Indian communities and nations, leaving small, isolated, and seriously demoralized populations. Shamanic powers failed, and the growing encroachment of foreigners outside Indian communities loomed over against the internal havoc wreaked by disease. Cultural collapse seemed imminent, and Indians, at the mercy of disease and foreigners, were strenuously seeking a cure.[8]

No surprise, therefore, that Indians proved vulnerable to Christian teaching and that in New England Puritan missionaries had their modicum of success.[9] But what needs to be added to the picture of "praying Indians" succumbing to the baptismal waters is that if Indians were constrained by circumstance to convert to Christianity, they also did so on their own terms and for their own needs.

Take, for example, the work of the much celebrated John Eliot who, aided by the Society for the Propagation of the Gospel in New England, established a total of fourteen towns of Indian converts, beginning with Natick, Massachusetts, in 1650. In "praying towns" like Natick, the gospel came blatantly with English civilization attached. This conversion scenario is easily read as surrender to a superior culture according to its stipulations, and on many levels that judgment seems correct. Ethnohistorian James Axtell has pointed out, however, that praying towns could function as Indian strategies for survival. Faced with cultural groupings and communities that had dwindled critically and stood in danger of extinction, Indians could band with other native groups in similar circumstance. But the price was higher than many wanted to pay – biological survival in exchange for the death of cultural praxis and ceremony, kinship relations and ways of life. Enter, then, the gatherings that became the praying towns, in which, saved both from their English enemies and from fusions with other tribes, Indian communities could maintain a semblance of their former lives. "By accepting the Christian minister or priest as the functional equivalent of a native shaman and by giving traditional meanings to Christian rites, dogmas, and deities," wrote Axtell, "the Indians ensured the survival of native culture by taking on the protective coloration of the invaders' religion." Indeed, the Indians became, in Axtell's market metaphor, satisfied "cultural customers."[10]

One can question the sanguine reading here and elsewhere – perhaps nowhere more than in eighteenth-century California with its San Diego Indian revolt of 1775 and the Franciscan Junipero Serra's string of missions reinforced by the presence of Spanish military nearby. There the friars got rich on vineyards tended by forced Indian labor, and, as Sherburne Cook writes, "all pretense of voluntary conversion was discarded."[11] Still, at Mission Santa Barbara and other places in the Serra missions, one could see Indian motifs and designs adorning native chapels, and the sacramental spirituality of the Roman church blended with the ceremonial richness of Indian cultural life.[12]

Moreover, contact worked both ways. Beneath the guise of the victorious European extinguishing native cultures and proceeding more or less intact, another tale asks to be told. It is a story about the permeability of any culture and about the conscious and unconscious ways that Indian cultures with their spiritual powers pried open spaces in the seemingly impermeable walls of European civilization. Here the Anglo-American case in point is especially instructive, for the English – considerably more than the Spanish or the French – practiced an ideal of cultural separation. Antimiscegenation held a strong place in English colonial conquest ideology, even if racial conceptions preoccupied the English in their relationship to Indians considerably less than in their relationship to blacks.[13]

Hence, for all the Anglo-American fear of combination, hints of it in specifically religious terms surfaced in seemingly improbable places, forming, sub rosa, part of the fundament in the architecture of an emerging American religious culture. Amanda Porterfield has raised questions about putative shamanic elements in Puritan religion in the context of Algonquian praxis, looking, for example, at the visionary experiences of Puritan saints and the ways that praying, preaching, reading, and writing could function as a shamanic language of power. Porterfield is careful not to argue cause and effect. But staring, even from the safe distance of literature, into the flames of an Algonquian shaman's fire can lead at least to queries about the Indian horizon of awakenings and revivals among the Puritans and other European colonists. Dissociated states, as Ann Taves has shown, are not the comfortable discourse of Western Christian theology.[14]

Meanwhile, there was English trader Thomas Morton of Ma-re Mount. In the 1620s, the existence of his settlement in what is now Quincy, Massachusetts, was a thorn in the side of the Separatist Puritan settlement at Plymouth colony. Morton violated Puritan order by his trading practices with Indians (it was said that he even sold them guns) and by the rumored sexual congress with Indian women practiced at his "plantation." As Ann Taves notes in [her work], Morton and his men erected a maypole. It was not an unconnected symbol – a materialized memory, surely, of the English countryside but also an evocation of pagan rituals of fertility. Thomas Morton's story ended in arrest and deportation by Miles Standish and his men, and it was only from England's rainy shore that Morton could have another word. Significantly, in his *New England Canaan*, published in 1637 to defend the life ways of Ma-re Mount, he argued that union between Indians and the English would bring renewal through the fusion of the vital physical powers of Indians and the civilized intellectual ones of Christians.[15]

Apparently others – even among the Puritans – shared at least some of Morton's sentiment. The New England establishment was regularly embarrassed by whites who, captured in Indian raids or wars, refused to come home when a ransom had been negotiated for them. They chose to remain part of Indian societies, adopted by native peoples to take the place of their own kin lost to war or disease. Former Puritans and now-white Indians, they liked the freedoms they found among Indians; they flourished in their midst.[16]

Contact with Indians found overt representation again, though less straightforwardly, in the Revolutionary War era, when the Sons of Liberty and the Sons of Tammany exploited Indian society to take "Saint Tammany" as cultural icon of their cause. According to popular account, Tammany was Tamanend, a Delaware Indian chief thought to have bid welcome to the newly immigrated William Penn and to have exchanged the land that later came to be known as Pennsylvania for a series of practical gifts. The lore about Tammany grew as – like an early set of tall tales about a Davy Crockett or Daniel Boone – it recounted his amazing deeds and exploits on behalf of whites and all of humankind.[17]

The object of ceremonial attention by 1771 on Tammany Day (Mayday), when colonists dressed as Indians and danced their maypole dances to honor him, Tammany inspired an ample share of ritual songs and poems of celebration. He became the patron of Pennsylvania troops in the Revolutionary War, and by 1778 even George Washington and his army honored Tammany Day by dressing as Indians, singing and dancing around maypoles, and dramatizing his presence. When, after the war, Tammany societies flourished for a time, they copied what they knew of Indian cultures by dividing their membership into thirteen "tribes" with a "sachem" over each and a "grand sachem" over all. Meeting places were called wigwams, and a lunar calendar as a conscious adaptation of Indian time keeping was employed. Tammany societies appropriated the trappings of Indian religions and cultures, as they were understood, mimicking them to express cultural independence from Europe in political and economic contexts. Even when Tammany societies faded in the nineteenth century, one still continued in New York, headquartered in the 1850s at Tammany Hall as the well-remembered Democratic machine organization of the city and the time.

Something of the Tammany societies' impulse and inspiration continued, too, in men's societies that were Indian-identified, such as Lewis Henry Morgan's secret and brief Order of the Iroquois in 1845 and the more sustained Improved Order of Red Men from 1834. By 1850, according to Mark Carnes, the latter group's Grand Lodge went on record declaring that the construction of "effective rituals" constituted its principal business, but the order languished through a series of ritual revisions lasting to the Civil War period. Then, in 1868, it began to offer an Adoption degree that proved the remaking of its fortunes. In the middle of the 1870s, the order was welcoming 10,000 new members annually. "By 1900," Carnes wrote, "approximately 350,000 Red Men were finding their way into wigwams of the order each week. Its annual receipts exceeded a million dollars."[18]

The initiation ceremony that apparently turned so many toward the Red Men featured an extended contemplation of death with a "sachem" as officiant, invoking the Great Spirit on behalf of the new initiate. There were a kindling of actual fire, a donning of moccasins, and a dramatic enactment of an encounter with Indian "hunters" who prepared to burn the initiate at the stake, even as a still more elaborate scenario was enacted in a ritual of adoption.[19] Middle class, urban, and frequented by erstwhile business associates, the lodges of the Red Men were inhabited by mainstream white Protestant men.

If the Indian had become culture broker and, with innuendos of racism, principle of association for them, the figure of the red man functioned similarly for Anglo-Protestants who found their way, less conventionally, into nonmainstream religious groups. From the late 1830s, well before the Red Men had their heyday, members of Shaker communities, who were undergoing a time of revival, claimed to be regularly visited by Indian spirits. In his account of nineteenth-century religious communities, John Humphrey Noyes, himself founder of the Oneida Perfectionists, gave a rare, practical glimpse of a visitation, quoting at length from a source in the Shaker society at Watervliet, New York, during the winter of 1842–3. "Eight or nine sisters became possessed of the spirits of Indian squaws," the sojourner wrote, "and about six of the brethren became Indians." There were "whooping and yelling and strange antics," he told, and – visible only to spirit eyes – the eating of "succotash" with fingers, in wooden dishes on the floor.[20]

Later, American spiritualists joined the ranks of those who said they spent religious time with Indians. After the Civil War, especially, stylized rituals of spirit communication developed, and in the twentieth century Indians were reported to be functioning in key roles. "Indian chiefs" were expected presences at séance gatherings, serving as "gate keepers" to protect mediums by keeping out unwelcome spirits. Moreover, regulars at séances eventually received the names of their own specially designated Indian chiefs as guardians.[21] By century's end, it remained for the children of the New Age to burn sage and sweet grass and to make sweat lodge ceremonies virtually identifying ritual badges for their movement. Indian people could protest in vain about the cooptation of their religious practices by New Age Indian "wannabes," as white Americans signaled their search for closeness to the land and for spiritual transformation. There were ironies and conspiracies of innocence here, gifts that were commandeered and exchanges that were lopsided and unequal. Still, the legacies of contact were real, and they told a story different from those of monochromatic consensus or simple dominance and submission.

## Catholic Encounters

Roman Catholics became involved in ambiguous gift exchanges with native peoples on American shores as early as 1492, when the Italian Christopher Columbus with three crews of Spaniards touched anchor in the Bahamas. What Jay P. Dolan calls the "marriage between conquest and conversion" became a standard arrangement in the fifteenth and sixteenth centuries as Spanish ritual crosses were planted in the Americas to signal the coming of gospel and gun.[22] Here the transition from warring to gift giving was fragilely wrought in a Catholic pale of trade and settlement that stretched through the territories of New France and New Spain, as Catholic missionaries and native peoples struggled through acts of contact.

As political power settled out and Anglo-Protestants ruled, Catholic encounters with strangers took new turns in the former Atlantic seaboard colonies and their western extensions. Earliest Catholic presence among Anglo-Protestants in America had come with Leonard Calvert of the Baltimore clan, who arrived as first governor of the Maryland colony in 1634. With him, the *Ark* and the *Dove* brought two Jesuit priests and a lay brother, and they were joined soon afterward by a third priest and second brother. At first the Jesuits evangelized among the Indians with familiar goals of converting them to "civility" as well as to Roman Catholic Christianity. By 1645, however, when Protestants from Virginia invaded Maryland and deposed the Calverts, Jesuit mission ventures among the Indians ended. The continuing religious contacts of Roman Catholics were to be with Anglo-Protestants.[23]

From the first, the Calvert plan had been to make that religious contact minimal, with written instructions that "all Acts of Romane Catholique Religion ... be done as privately as may be" and that Roman Catholic settlers be told "to be silent upon all occasions of discourse concerning matters of Religion." The plan worked poorly though, and Protestant hostilities toward Calvert and Catholic presence did not fail to surface, as the later history of the colony showed.[24] With the exception of Pennsylvania, conditions were likewise unfavorable for Catholics in the other colonies. A brief era of toleration ended in Rhode Island in 1664, and the period of toleration in New York before the Revolution also was brief. Thus, it was the religious settlement forced by political circumstance in the new United States that initiated widespread legal toleration of Roman Catholicism – and this only gradually, as state governments fell into line behind the federal model. Moreover, Catholics had continuing reasons to be wary of Protestant power, whatever the formal declarations of the law.

To complicate matters for Roman Catholics further, the contact situations they met were internal as well as external. As Catholics from widely disparate ethnic groups found themselves members of the same American church, they were forced to recognize their kinship even as they often wanted to stress their difference. English, French Canadian, German, and Irish Catholics were hardly easy comrades, and by the end of the nineteenth century when they were joined by southern and eastern Europeans the stresses were even more noticeable. A small and continuing African American presence in the church and a rapidly growing Latino population added further to ethnic diversity and to strain.

Robert Orsi's account of the twentieth-century *festa* devoted to Our Lady of Mount Carmel by Italian Americans in Harlem, New York, is an instructive case.[25] As Italian Harlem gave way to the Spanish brand, the July *festa* with its flamboyant public procession transporting a statue of the Madonna through the streets meant, more and more, Orsi argued, an expedition into "foreign" territory controlled, especially, by Puerto Ricans. Dark-skinned and ambiguously understood as "black," the Puerto Ricans evoked Italian American memories and fears of their own ambiguity in Anglo-America, where initially their swarthy complexions had been cause for racial comment. In their turn, Puerto Ricans reciprocated by conspicuously ignoring the *festa*.

In contrast, when another dark-skinned people, the Haitians, began to enter Harlem in appreciable numbers, Italian Americans gave them a decidedly different reception. The Haitians found in the Madonna and the Carmel church ritual support for their own mixed practice of Catholicism and *vodou*. The Madonna granted miracles to the Haitians, it was said, and the appearance of the Haitians themselves was understood, as Orsi recounted, "as something of a mystery and miracle, an uncanny event."[26] That the Haitians spoke French and could command the Latin language of the liturgy on occasion were credits in their cause. And, finally, in an act of denial, Italian Americans did not consider the Haitians black. As if in a laboratory report on ethnic – and racial – contact and conflict, Italian Americans displayed the subtleties of the meeting of Catholic with Catholic across lines of language and culture. They deflected attention away from the Anglo-Protestant world that has occupied so much of American religious historiography to point to processes of exchange where gifting and its refusal went on behind and beyond a specifically Protestant gaze. Yet in their concern regarding ethnic and racial identity – their preoccupation with "blackness" – they hinted at memories of their contact with Protestant America and the exchanges that it brought.

Contact with Protestant America led not merely to inner conflict, though. There also could be exercises of active emulation: from a Catholic immigrant's stance, Protestants, who were people of power and definers of the socially real, could be good to imitate. For evidence, consider the lay-trustee conflicts of the late eighteenth and antebellum nineteenth centuries and the Americanist controversy after the Civil War. In the case of the former, congregational church governance – the kind of polity in which an individual congregation called its pastor and in effect hired and fired him – became the envy of the Catholic laity and the ambiguous gift of Anglo-Protestantism to them. Moreover, envy and gift mingled with ethnic tensions and antagonisms within the American church. In the case of the Americanist controversy, ethnic quarrels blended with ideologies of American freedom and activist democracy to yield a "phantom heresy."

As early as the 1780s, in the wake of the American Revolution and its republican ideology, New York and Philadelphia Catholics were moving toward a lay-trustee system of church governance. Here those members of a parish who rented pews elected trustees annually to represent them by presiding over practical affairs within a congregation. Along the frontier in the New West as well, Catholic laity banded together, elected representatives, and purchased land for church buildings. But control of practical affairs escalated into a desire for control of policy and personnel, and soon decision-making regarding clergy was claimed by lay trustees. At St. Peter's Church in New York City, for example, the congregation divided over the pastoral virtues of two Irish-born Capuchin priests, Charles Whelan and Andrew Nugent.[27]

Even more seriously, in Philadelphia the German national parish at Holy Trinity Church, founded at the initiative of German lay immigrants and reluctantly approved by Archbishop John Carroll, elected the German Capuchin John Charles Helbron as their pastor over Carroll's objections. And when Irish lay trustees assumed control of church finances in Norfolk, Virginia, in 1808, they went on to challenge the authority of the archbishop of Baltimore over the appointment of French pastors. Not only did they appeal to the pope (Pius VII) and to the Roman Congregation for the Propagation of the Faith, but they turned as well to Virginia state officials, to the United States Congress, and to President Thomas Jefferson.[28]

## Protestant Relations, African American Ports of Call, Jewish Alliances, and Asian Junctures

The First Great Awakening already had counted black converts among those who embraced Christianity, and by 1760 the presence of African American Christians had surely become noticeable. But in the nineteenth century Methodists and Baptists succeeded among slaves and free blacks as earlier Anglicans never had. In considerable part, whites gave the Christian gift with conscious manipulation – as a way to control their slaves and ensure submissive slave societies. But African Americans were not blind to the elements of resistance and rebellion contained in the Christian message and especially in its apocalyptic strands, as the experiences of Denmark Vesey (1822) and Nat Turner (1831) attest. In a developed *habitus* that was far more prevalent, though, African Americans in the American South themselves created a combinatory Christian faith that is often hailed as an "invisible institution." Here the contact meant a mingling of what Charles H. Long has called West African structures of consciousness (the slaves generally came from West Africa) with the historical experience of involuntary presence in America and the overt language of Christian belief and practice.[29]

In this process a common West African belief in a noninterfering high God, who was not ritually involved, could support a theodicy in which slavery could be accepted as a fact of life without imputing God. And West African ritual habits involving active possession states, when intermediary Gods mounted and "rode" – like horses – individual devotees, could lend themselves to revival praxis in strongly toned conversion experiences. Baptist worship as embraced by African Americans in the American Southwest could echo traditional African ritual frames and rhythms that transported from melancholy to ecstasy. Spiritual churches in New Orleans, with their female leadership, could welcome the Holy Spirit and also the spirit guides of American spiritualism and Haitian *vodou*.[30]

In this context to speak of an "African spiritual holocaust," as Jon Butler has, may obscure as much as, or more than, it reveals.[31] Intact religious systems may not have survived the contact, but their underlying structures surely did. These intellectual, emotional, and physical ways of being in the world governed the way blacks faced their New World encounters, what they took, what they gave, and how and what they combined. Some joinings of distinctively African and Christian elements were obvious, as in *vodou*, in Cuban Santería, and in other Afro-Caribbean religions that made their way, with twentieth-century Caribbean immigrants, into East Coast cities such as New York and Miami.[32]

Yet many of the combinations present earlier in the United States bypassed Christian themes or radically transformed them in religious survivals that bore little, if any, relationship to organized religion. Traditions of root work and conjure, use of the Bible itself as a conjure book, folk fables passed on as in the Brer Rabbit tales, old shamanic memories of magical human flight revived to assuage the pain of slavery – much of the time none (or, as with the Bible, only some) of this could be cast within a Christian mold.[33] Still, all such practice and discourse involved religious combination, as elements from the past were adapted and reinvented under new circumstances.

That the contact between blacks and whites worked both ways is nowhere more evident than in the origins and transformations of the spiritual in what became a black master art and genuinely American musical culture, a process that has been traced effectively by Lawrence W. Levine.[34] However, if white Americans were principal partners for the African contact, they were surely not the only ones. Cultural amalgamation between Africans and Indians, for example, could be found in Cape Cod and some New England towns, in New York City, Long Island, and the Hudson River Valley, in small tri-ethnic (black, Indian, white) enclaves in Delaware, Maryland, Virginia, and North Carolina, and, especially, in South Carolina and Georgia.

Although interaction between blacks and Indians was discouraged by whites in the South, for fear of combined insurrections, numbers of slaves found sanctuary in Indian communities. Gary Nash has suggested that "so common was Afro-Indian contact in the Southern colonies that the term *mustee* was added to the Southern vocabulary in order to categorize the offspring of African and Indian parents."[35]

And the tracks of the exchange were left, at least, in a discourse that the two peoples shared. Joel Chandler Harris's *Uncle Remus* stories with their Brer Rabbit exploits, for example, paralleled similar tales that were told in Cherokee and Creek societies. Trickster tales and animal stories from African-American and southeastern Indian cultures, generally, shared thematic content and a common fund of popular wisdom and spirituality.[36]

Trickster tales on an American landscape bespeak the role of culture heroes in creating the practical cosmos of a richly pluralist society, and in America, there were culture heroes too numerous to count. If the African diaspora with its culture heroes resulted in a multifaceted complex of New World religious exchanges, so, too, did the American diaspora of the Jews. We already have met Isaac Mayer Wise traveling the trains in upper New York state and fielding inquiries and blows from assorted strangers and former friends. Wise's exchanges took on the high drama of his public persona in his autobiographical reminiscences, but other Jewish gifts and exchanges were as important. Wise's contemporary, Isaac Leeser, for example, upheld traditional orthodoxy against Wise's Reform leadership. For Leeser and others, though, religious contraction and consolidation were relative commodities. At Philadelphia's Sephardic Mikveh Israel Congregation, well before Wise's arrival in America, the twenty-three-year-old Lesser – not officially a rabbi but reader for the congregation – began to preach regularly from 1829. "At that period, the duties of the minister were confined to the conducting of the public worship in the synagogue and elsewhere," he later recalled, "and it was not accepted that he should be at the same time a preacher and exhorter."[37] Preaching was not the only adaptation from the evangelical Protestant mode that could be attributed to Leeser; he also advocated use of the English language and supported Rebecca Gratz in the initiation of a Sunday school in Philadelphia in 1838. A year later, he published a catechism to help replace texts like the scripture lessons from the Christian Sunday School Union, used in Gratz's school – as Rosa Mordecai remembered – by "pasting pieces of paper over answers unsuitable for Jewish children."[38]

Leeser went on to inaugurate a traditionalist journal, the *Occident and American Jewish Advocate* in 1843. But by 1844, he was editorializing in favor of the distinctly nontraditional idea of a *"federative* union." Later he adapted and elaborated an earlier plan for union formed with Louis Salomon, leader of Philadelphia's Ashkenazic Congregation Rodeph Shalom. Then, with the support of a third Philadelphia synagogue, Beth Israel, the plan, which called for a national Jewish congress, was published and endorsed in the pages of the *Occident*.[39] Jews at the time were not ready for "traditionalist" Leeser's unionist plans on an American federal model. Still, the long-term trajectory of American Judaism would be one of religious expansionism.

Joseph L. Blau has stressed the compatibilities between traditional Judaism and Anglo-Protestant America, pointing, for example, to the similarities between a Jewish biblical ethic that viewed scripture under the character of law and a Calvinist one with its own lawyerly grasp of the Old Testament.[40] Judaism, Blau argued, embodied a series of major characteristics of American religion: its protestantism, its pluralism, its moralism, and, especially, its voluntaryism. In Blau's terms, "protestantism" (lower case) meant the religious impulse toward creedal freedom, the allowance of multiple conclusions. A foundational characteristic of historic Protestantism (upper case), it was also, said Blau, a significant part of a Jewish tradition that did not put its premium on religious creed to begin with. In contrast, pluralism directed attention away from conclusions and toward beginnings, operating on the premise that all originating points in religion possessed equal validity. Even with their ideology of chosenness, Jews had historically known significant experience with cultural pluralism, and they had thrived in the pluralistic matrix of America.

Again, the moralism that Blau named was for him an expression of an American pragmatism that put its stock in "immediate practical consequences," a habitual stance that was reflected in a Jewish social concern for goodness. And voluntaryism – for Blau the right of people living in a free society to choose freedom *from* religion – became in his reading of immigrant Jewry an American Protestant gift that was received with enthusiasm. Evoking a model of Judaisms in America, he concluded that it was voluntaryism most of all that shaped Jews into "an American Jewry made in the reflection of American cultural and religious patterns."[41]

So there were Jewish atheists and socialists in America, and there were Jews who enthusiastically endorsed Freemasonry. There were Black Jews and Jewish Humanists and a Jewish founder and membership for the Ethical Culture Society. In the twentieth century, Jews marched beside blacks and liberal Protestants in the civil rights movement of the sixties and helped to found the National Association for the Advancement of Colored People. Meanwhile, beginning with the Puritan collective vision of their society as the New Israel, Jewish threads had been woven into the general fabric of American religion. It was true that on the cultural seesaw of the nation's history, Judaism was at times figured as the enemy – in clear patterns of anti-Semitism and refusal of the gift. At other times, though, Judaism to the contrary figured the warmth and security of family and home, as in advertising slogans such as the invitational, "You don't have to be Jewish to love Levy's Jewish Rye bread."[42]

Significant numbers of unhyphenated Americans, apparently, liked consuming Jewish gifts. They also were ardent consumers of Asian ones, and their consumption was hardly limited to Chinese and Japanese culinary productions. For what many Americans consumed from the Orient – before, for the most part, they encountered Asian peoples themselves – was Eastern culture and religion. In the years following the Revolution, American ships sailed for Asian ports, returning with Chinese and Indian goods to grace households and shops in New England and Middle Atlantic coastal cities. Along with the material culture of Asia came some of its sacred texts, and there was a smattering of interest among elites.[43] It remained for the nineteenth century, however, to see a more serious interest in Asian peoples and their religions develop on the part of non-Asian Americans. It may have been a straw in the wind that, in 1801, a handbook claiming to describe the religions that had arisen since the dawn of the Christian era included, in its third edition, a thirty-page section on the religions of Asia. Hannah Adams's *A View of Religions* reflected the sources and knowledge of its time as well as the shock, for her, of the Asian encounter. The "incredible tortures" of a Hindu yogi revolted the author. She confessed that "a minute description of the voluntary sufferings of the Indian devotee" brought "increasing horror" to the mind and froze "the astonished reader to a statue, almost as immoveable as the suffering penitent."[44]

Still, Adams had worked hard to present all that was known, spending time reading at booksellers' quarters because she could not afford the price of the books that she needed. She also had worked hard to be fair. Her interest presaged that of the New England Transcendentalists nearly four decades later and, after that, a steady procession of Anglo-American inquirers. Thus, when Edward Elbridge Salisbury lectured on the history of Buddhism at the American Oriental Society's first annual meeting in 1844, he stood at the launch of a Victorian American romance with things Buddhist. Here, as Thomas A. Tweed has shown, Buddhism was read by Anglo-American converts and sympathizers as supportive of the best in American individualism, optimism, and activism.[45] As in a Judaism that found the part of itself that fit the exchange rate in American society, the new Buddhism of these Americans was transmuted into the coin of the realm.

After these beginnings, the postbellum Gilded Age brought the presence of Asia and its religions still closer to Anglo-America. By 1878, Helena Blavatsky and Henry Steel Olcott, cofounders of a still-infant Theosophical Society, set sail for India and, especially for Olcott, began a serious commitment to Buddhism. What had started as a spiritualist reform society with a preoccupation with the occult now stretched to include the study of Asian religions, even if the study was premised on an underlying orientalism that read Buddhism in unconscious Western and Theosophical terms.[46] Then, by 1893, as numbers of Chicagoans perused the pages of the Chicago *Daily Inter Ocean* with its reports on the World's Parliament of Religions, a sizable population of non-Asian Americans was becoming superficially acquainted with Asian religions for the first time.

The parliament had been held in conjunction with the Columbian Exposition marking the four-hundred-year anniversary of European contact with the Americas and bringing twenty-seven million visitors from seventy-two nations.[47] Racism and colonialism pervaded the exposition, reflected in its hegemonic construction of the White City – a specially designed assemblage of buildings – and its relegation of non-American "others" to grounds outside it as so many exhibits at which fair-goers might ogle. The parliament itself, with 150,000 spectators over seventeen days, was held away from the White City in downtown Chicago.[48] But the parliament shared the condescension and colonialism of the fair toward the world's peoples.[49] So the translation of Asian – religions or peoples – read "exotic," and accounts of Swami Vivekananda's orange and crimson robes and accompanying turban made impressions as strong or stronger than the subtleties of what he taught. A contemporary poem by Minnie Andrews Snell, appearing in a Chicago journal, the *Open Court*, offered a useful summary of popular surmise. In "Aunt Hannah on the Parliament of Religions," Snell's Aunt Hannah confessed how she "listened to th' Buddhist, in his robes of shinin' white," then "heered th' han'some Hindu monk, drest up in orange dress, / Who sed that all humanity was part of God – no less."[50]

Still, despite the superficialities and cultural imperialism, important exchanges occurred, and Asian parliament representatives in their speeches often inverted the assumptions of conference organizers.[51] They also used the occasion as a springboard for later missionary work in America. In fact, the parliament was, as Kenten Druyvesteyn argued, a watershed for Eastern religions in the United States.[52] Meanwhile, on the West Coast, the ethnic presence of Asia was visible and, with it, traditional Asian religions. Chinese immigrants had come as early as the 1840s, bringing Buddhism, Taoism, and Confucianism intermingled as they were in their own culture. Japanese missionaries accommodated their own people in Hawaii from 1889 and in California a decade later, carrying Pure Land Buddhism with its devotion to Amida Buddha and hope of attainment, after death, of the Pure Land, or Western Kingdom. Here the contact was easy to trace institutionally in titles, designations, and the most visible signs of American accommodation. The Jodo Shinshu (Pure Land) movement in America became, from 1899 to 1944, the North American Buddhist Mission; after that, it was the

Buddhist Churches of America. Regular services were inaugurated, unlike the pattern of devotion in the Buddhist temples of Japan, and Buddhist "bishops" came to oversee American worship, even as Sunday schools flourished along with the Sunday services.

Hence, as all of this already testifies, the American contact produced two characteristic forms of Asian religions overall. *Export* religions were embraced by non-Asian Americans; *ethnic* religions were observed by Asian immigrants and/or their children. Often the two forms were widely divergent, with export versions stressing philosophy, meditation traditions, and esoterica, and ethnic forms concerned with ritual and cultural praxis. Moreover, the gifts of the contact often spawned combinations that perhaps surprised even the participants. When, for example, the International Society for Krishna Consciousness (ISKCON) found itself dwindling after its American countercultural heyday in the late sixties and seventies, it was Asian Indian immigrants who rescued the Hare Krishna movement after most of the non-Asian converts had gone.[53]

Other South Asians, who built lavish temples to grace the American landscape, often found themselves more observant of their traditions in this nation than they had been in India. They used religion as a carrier of culture, and they worked to preserve language, tradition, art, music, and folkways over the sign of the Gods. Concerned for their children in huge and crime-ridden American cities and worried about an American moral culture they often found decadent, they turned to the new temples they erected as tools for cultural contraction, for the maintenance of islands of integrity in an America they found too culturally and religiously promiscuous. Yet, as Joanne Punzo Waghorne's study of the Sri Siva-Vishnu Temple in suburban Washington, DC, has shown, South Asians could not go home again religiously. The suburban temple in Lanham, Maryland, was neither an intact replica of South Asia nor a totally American creation. Rather the temple's design – with its split-level construction that forced a non-Indian separation of sacred rituals from more ordinary cultural activities – openly articulated theological change.[54] Built into the material reality of the temple, the new distinctions were a product of the contact; they signaled a change in the habits of mind and life that constituted religious culture for these South Asian Indians.

# Notes

1   Isaac M. Wise, *Reminiscences*, trans. David Philipson, 2nd ed. (New York: Central Synagogue of New York, 1945), in Jacob Rader Marcus, ed., *Memoirs of American Jews, 1775–1865* (Philadelphia: Jewish Publication Society of America, 1955), 2:104–5.

2   Ibid., 108.

3   Ibid., 120–5, 125–6.

4   Marcel Mauss, *The Gift: Forms and Functions of Exchange in Archaic Societies*, trans. Ian Cunnison (New York: W. W. Norton, 1967), 69. The recent thinking of my colleague Charles H. Long has sparked my own interest in the work of Mauss and its applicability to scenarios of religious contact.

5   Ibid., 81.

6   R. Laurence Moore, *Selling God: American Religion in the Marketplace of Culture* (New York: Oxford University Press, 1994), 275. Moore's book, though, is written in a decidedly different key from this essay, since his concern is the commercialization and commodification of organized religion, while I focus here on the issue of the processes of contact and exchange in a pluralist society.

7   Mauss, *The Gift*, 10.

8   The classic exposition of the size of Native American populations before and after the European conquest is Henry F. Dobyns, "Estimating Aboriginal American Population: An Appraisal of Techniques with a New Hemispheric Estimate," *Current Anthropology* 7 (1966): 395–416. Useful accounts of the cultural meetings that ensued may be found in James Axtell, *The European and the Indian* (New York: Oxford University Press, 1981); idem, *The Invasion Within: The Contest of Cultures in Colonial North America* (New York: Oxford University Press, 1985); idem, *After Columbus: Essays in the Ethnohistory of Colonial North America* (New York: Oxford University Press, 1988); idem, *Beyond 1492: Encounters in Colonial North America* (New York: Oxford University Press, 1992); Francis Jennings, *The Invasion of America: Indians, Colonialism, and the Cant of Conquest* (Chapel Hill: University of North Carolina Press, 1975); Gary B. Nash, *Red, White, and Black: The Peoples of Early America* (Englewood Cliffs, NJ: Prentice-Hall, 1974); and Neal Salisbury, *Manitou and Providence: Indians, Europeans, and the Making of New England, 1500–1643* (New York: Oxford University Press, 1982).

9   For a review of recent thinking on the success or failure of seventeenth-century Indian missions and an independent assessment, see James Axtell, "Were Indian Conversions *Bona Fide*?," in *After Columbus*, 100–21.

10  James Axtell, "Some Thoughts on the Ethnohistory of Missions," in ibid., 54–5. See also idem, "Native Reactions to Invasion," in *Before 1492*, especially 116–18.

11  Sherburne F. Cook, *The Conflict between the California Indian and White Civilization* (Berkeley: University of California Press, 1976), 76. For a useful discussion of Roman Catholic–Indian mission contact, see Jay P. Dolan, *The American Catholic Experience: A History from Colonial Times to the Present* (Garden City, NY: Doubleday, 1985), 15–68.

12  Sandra S. Sizer (Tamar Frankiel) explores some of the ways that the California Indians related to Franciscan Catholic religious practices in terms of their own ceremonial life in "Native Americans, Franciscans, and Puritans: Problems of Translation," an unpublished paper to which I am indebted.

13  For an argument that racial preoccupations were not important in early English colonial views of American Indians, see Karen Ordahl Kupperman, *Settling with the Indians: The Meeting of English and Indian Cultures in America, 1580–1640* (Totowa, NJ: Rowman and Littlefield, 1980).

14  Amanda Porterfield, "Algonquian Shamans and Puritan Saints," *Horizons* 12, 2 (1985): 303–10; Ann Taves, "Knowing through the Body: Dissociative Religious Experience in the African-and British-American Methodist Traditions," *Journal of Religion* 73, 2 (April 1993): 220–2.

15  For a short and useful account of Ma-re Mount, see Salisbury, *Manitou and Providence*, 152–65.

16  See James Axtell, "The White Indians of Colonial America," in *European and Indian*, 168–206.

17  My treatment of Tammany and Tammany lore here and in what follows is indebted to Sarah McFarland Taylor of the University of California, Santa Barbara, whose unpublished paper "Customs, Costumes, and Ritual: Constructions of White 'Native' Identity and Origin in American History" explores the Tammany literature in greater depth than I can offer here. For more on Tammany, see Oliver E. Allen, *The Tiger: The Rise and Fall of Tammany Hall* (New York: Addison-Wesley, 1993); Edwin Kilroe, *Saint Tammany and the Origin of the Society of Tammany or Columbian Order in the City of New York* (New York: Columbia University Press, 1913); Carl Lemke, ed., *Offical History of the Improved Order of Red Men: Compiled under the Authority from the Great Council of the United States by Past Great Incohonees, George Linsay of Maryland, Charles Conley of Pennsylvania, and Charles Litchman of Massachusetts* (Waco, Tex.: Davis, 1965); Gustavus Myers, *The History of Tammany Hall* (New York: Burt Franklin, 1917); and M. R. Werner, *Tammany Hall* (Garden City, NY: Doubleday, Doran, 1928).

18  Mark C. Carnes, *Secret Ritual and Manhood in Victorian America* (New Haven: Yale University Press, 1989), 99, 97–9.

19  Ibid., 99–101.

20  John Humphrey Noyes, *Strange Cults and Utopias of Nineteenth-Century America* [*History of American Socialisms*] (1870; reprint, New York: Dover, 1966), 605.

21  See the discussion in J. Stillson Judah, *The History and Philosophy of the Metaphysical Movements in America* (Philadelphia: Westminster Press, 1967), 70.

22  Dolan, *American Catholic Experience*, 16.

23  For an account of the Jesuit contact with Indians in the Maryland colony, see James Axtell, "White Legend: The Jesuit Missions in Maryland," in *After Columbus*, 73–85.

24  Instructions of Cecil Calvert to his brother Leonard, as quoted in Dolan, *American Catholic Experience*, 74; see also 69–85.

25  Robert Orsi, "The Religious Boundaries of an Inbetween People: Street Feste and the Problem of the Dark-Skinned Other in Italian Harlem, 1920–1990," *American Quarterly* 44, 3 (September 1992): 313–47.

26  Ibid., 333.

27  For an estimate of the Protestantizing nature of what was happening, see the letter of John Carroll to the Trustees of St. Peter's Church, New York City, 25 January 1786, in John Tracy Ellis, ed., *Documents of American Catholic History, vol. 1, 1493–1865* (Wilmington, Del.: Michael Glazier, 1987), 152.

28  See Trustees of the Roman Catholic Congregation of Norfolk and Portsmouth, 14 January 1819, in ibid., 221–3, and the introduction by Ellis on 220.

29  For a short and helpful introduction to themes of religion and rebellion in African American religious history, see Gayraud S. Wilmore, *Black Religion and Black Radicalism: An Interpretation of the Religious History of Afro-American People*, 2nd ed. (Maryknoll, NY: Orbis Books, 1983), especially 53–73. For the best study of the "invisible institution" among the slaves, see Albert J. Raboteau, *Slave Religion: The "Invisible Institution" in the Antebellum South* (New York: Oxford University Press, 1978). Charles H. Long has argued the case for West African structures of consciousness in numerous teaching situations throughout his career. For a related written discussion of some of his ideas that I cite here, see Charles H. Long, "Perspectives for a Study of Afro-American Religion in the United States," in *Significations: Signs, Symbols, and Images in the Interpretation of Religion* (Philadelphia: Fortress Press, 1986), 173–84.

30  See, for example, Walter F. Pitts, Jr., *Old Ship of Zion: The Afro-Baptist Ritual in the African Diaspora* (New York: Oxford University Press, 1993), and Claude F. Jacobs and Andrew J. Kaslow, *The Spiritual Churches of New Orleans: Origins, Beliefs, and Rituals of an African-American Religion* (Knoxville: University of Tennessee Press, 1991).

31  Jon Butler, *Awash in a Sea of Faith: Christianizing the American People* (Cambridge, Mass.: Harvard University Press, 1990), 129–63. In a work that predated Butler's by some six years, Gary B. Nash observed that "Africans in the English plantations [in America] adapted elements of African culture to the demands of a new life and a new environment. . . . This continuous infusion of African culture kept alive many of the elements that would later be transmuted almost beyond recognition. Through fashioning their own distinct culture, within the limits established by the rigors of the slave system, blacks were able to retain semiseparate religious forms, their own music and dance, their own family life, and their own beliefs and values" (Nash, *Red, White, and Black*, 211–12).

32  For elaboration, see Joseph M. Murphy, *Working the Spirit: Ceremonies of the African Diaspora* (Boston: Beacon Press, 1994), and idem, *Santería: An African Religion in America* (Boston: Beacon Press, 1988).

33  See, for example, Theophus H. Smith, *Conjuring Culture: Biblical Formations of Black America* (New York: Oxford University Press, 1994); Alan Dundes, ed., *Mother Wit from the Laughing Barrel: Readings in the Interpretation of Afro-American Folklore* (1973; reprint, Jackson: University Press of Mississippi, 1990), especially 357–427, 523–48; Langston Hughes and Arna Bontemps, eds., *Book of Negro Folklore* (New York: Dodd, Mead, 1958),

especially 1–329; and Zora Neale Hurston, *Mules and Men* (1935; reprint, Bloomington: Indian University Press, 1978).

34  See Lawrence W. Levine, *Black Culture and Black Consciousness: Afro-American Folk Thought from Slavery to Freedom* (New York: Oxford University Press, 1977), especially 19–30, 136–297. See also Don Yoder, *Pennsylvania Spirituals* (Lancaster, Pa.: Pennsylvania Folklife Society, 1961), 20–32. I am indebted to Leonard Norman Primiano for bringing the Yoder source to my attention.

35  Nash, *Red, White, and Black*, 296.

36  For a useful discussion that argues for a black provenance for these tales, see Alan Dundes, "African Tales among the North American Indians," in *Mother Wit*, 114–25. And for Cherokee examples of the phenomenon, see James Mooney, *Myths of the Cherokee*, Smithsonian Institution, Bureau of American Ethnology Nineteenth Annual Report, 1897–98, pt. 1 (Washington, DC: Government Printing Office, 1900); this work has been reprinted in James Mooney, *Myths of the Cherokee and Sacred Formulas of the Cherokees* (Nashville, Tenn.: Charles and Randy Elder, Booksellers, in collaboration with Cherokee Heritage Books, 1982).

37  Quoted in Winthrop S. Hudson and John Corrigan, *Religion in America*, 5th ed. (New York: Macmillan, 1992), 176.

38  Rosa Mordecai, "Recollections of the First Hebrew Sunday School," *Hebrew Watchword and Instructor* 6 (1897), in Marcus, *Memoirs of American Jews*, 1:283.

39  See the account in Joseph L. Blau, *Judaism in America: From Curiosity to Third Faith* (Chicago: University of Chicago Press, 1976), 31–2.

40  Ibid., 112–13.

41  Ibid., 1–20, 20.

42  Quoted in ibid., 135. For a brief but germane discussion of anti-Semitism, see Catherine L. Albanese, *America: Religions and Religion*, 2nd ed. (Belmont, Calif.: Wadsworth, 1992), 509–12.

43  For a useful discussion of eighteenth-century American contacts with Asia, see Carl T. Jackson, *The Oriental Religions and American Thought: Nineteenth-Century Explorations* (Westport, Conn.: Greenwood Press, 1981).

44  Hannah Adams, *A View of Religions in Two Parts . . . The Whole Collected from the Best Authors, Ancient and Modern*, 3rd ed. (Boston: Manning and Loring, 1801), 409 n., quoted in Jackson, *Oriental Religions and American Thought*, 17.

45  For an elaboration of these themes, see Thomas A. Tweed, *The American Encounter with Buddhism, 1844–1912: Victorian Culture and the Limits of Dissent* (Bloomington: Indiana University Press, 1992).

46  For the early Theosophical Society as a Spiritualist reform movement, see Stephen Prothero, "From Spiritualism to Theosophy: 'Uplifting' a Democratic Tradition," *Religion and American Culture: A Journal of Interpretation* 3, 2 (summer 1993): 197–216; see also Bruce F. Campbell, *Ancient Wisdom Revived: A History of the Theosophical Movement* (Berkeley: University of California Press, 1980). For orientalism, cast in linguistic terms as creolization, see Stephen Prothero, *The White Buddhist: Henry Steel Olcott and the*

*Nineteenth-Century American Encounter with Asian Religions* (Bloomington: Indiana University Press, 1996), especially 7–9, 176–82.

47    The best one-volume introduction to the World's Parliament of Religions is Eric J. Ziolkowski, ed., *A Museum of Faiths: Histories and Legacies of the 1893 World's Parliament of Religions* (Atlanta: Scholars Press, 1993).

48    John Henry Barrows, ed., *The World's Parliament of Religions: An Illustrated and Popular Story of the World's First Parliament of Religions, Held in Chicago in Connection with the Columbian Exposition of 1893* (Chicago: Parliament Publishing, 1893), 2:1558, quoted in Ziolkowski, *Museum of Faiths*, 8.

49    See the account of the parliament and its foundation in the "Columbian myth," in Richard Hughes Seager, *The World's Parliament of Religions: The East/West Encounter, Chicago, 1893* (Bloomington: Indiana University Press, 1995).

50    Minnie Andrews Snell, "Aunt Hannah on the Parliament of Religions," *Open Court* (October 12, 1893), stanzas 4–5, quoted in Ziolkowski, *Museum of Faiths*, 17.

51    For an instructive account of this process, see Seager, *World's Parliament of Religions*, 94–120.

52    Kenten Druyvesteyn, "The World's Parliament of Religions," Ph.D. dissertation, University of Chicago, 1976.

53    On ISKCON, see Raymond Brady Williams, *Religions of Immigrants from India and Pakistan: New Threads in the American Tapestry* (Cambridge: Cambridge University Press, 1988), 130–7.

54    Joanne Punzo Waghorne, "The Hindu Gods in a Split-Level World: The Sri Siva-Vishnu Temple in Suburban Washington, D.C.," in Robert Orsi, ed., *Gods of the City* (Bloomington: Indiana University Press, forthcoming).

# 3

# Shouting Methodists

## Ann Taves

## Introduction

While Anglo Americans shaped American religious history in important ways, African Americans have hardly been less influential. As slaves brought to this country in chains to be sold as property, torn from their cultures of origin and forced to adapt to harsh new realities, African Americans experienced the moral failure and hypocrisy of American culture first hand. They also contributed in many ways to the freshness and vitality of American religious life. Largely as a result of the resonance between their life in America and biblical stories of suffering and oppression, many blacks converted to Protestant Christianity during the religious revivals of the eighteenth and nineteenth centuries. In their embrace of Christianity, American blacks not only introduced elements of traditional African belief and practice into Methodist and Baptist churches but also sharpened and intensified the equation between Christian salvation and the overcoming of suffering, oppression, and death.

African American interpretations of the Bible worked as a democratizing force on both Christianity and Judaism in America. The Exodus story of God's freeing his people from bondage and the dream of living in a promised land acquired progressive social meaning as a result of black interpretation. No less important, the performance of Protestant evangelicalism, and the impact of evangelicalism on the performing arts in America more generally, expanded greatly as a result of the emotional intensity and artistic brilliance of black

Excerpted from Ann Taves, *Fits, Trances, & Visions: Experiencing Religion and Explaining Experience from Wesley to James* (Princeton: Princeton University Press, 1999), 76–108.

Christians who communicated the power of the Spirit in exciting new ways. As Ann Taves explains in her discussion of Protestant revivalism, blacks contributed significantly to the performance of evangelical religion, and thereby to its popularity, growth, and development.

Among the camp-meeting songs that have come down to us from the early nineteenth century is one titled simply "The Methodist." From it we learn not only that Wesley's followers in America were "despised... because they shout and preach so plain," but also that they proudly referred to themselves as "shouting Methodists."[1] Because the tradition of "shouting" was developed and passed on by means of embodied performance, the sources do not tell us what it meant to "shout" in any systematic fashion. We get glimpses of what it meant and how it changed over time from the letters and journals of participants in early American Methodist revivals and from camp-meeting songs preserved in later collections of black and white spirtuals. Perhaps the single most helpful source, and one to which I return frequently throughout this chapter, was written by John Fanning Watson, a lay Methodist from Philadelphia alarmed by the ritualistic elaboration of shouting in the context of public worship.

Watson's book, titled *Methodist Error; or, Friendly Christian advice to those Methodists who indulge in extravagant emotions and bodily exercises,* was published anonymously in 1814.[2] In it, Watson emphasized that he was not opposed to extravagant emotions and bodily exercises at the time of conversion or in private devotion, but on the part of converted Christians in the context of public worship.[3] Reflecting the standards disseminated among Methodists through Wesley's editions of Edwards's writings, Watson argued that such exercises were appropriate in "closet" devotions because it was there, rather than in public or social worship, that persons "enter more peculiarly into the very presence of Deity" and because there persons might be "as vehement" as they liked "without offense to others" (*ME*-1819, 27).

Watson framed the practices he found objectionable as "enthusiasm," providing numerous extracts on the subject from the writings of John Wesley, John Fletcher, Adam Clarke, Jonathan Edwards, and John Locke in his introduction and appendices. In the main body of the work, he specified the practices he deplored and the scriptural passages used by Methodists to legitimate them. He anticipated that his "expos-ures" would lead "some well-meaning Methodists" to conclude that he had betrayed their cause through indiscretion. But he justified his forth-rightness on the grounds that such exercises were prejudicing their fellow Philadelphians against them (*ME*-1814, 13) and he addressed Methodists with the evident hope that "respectable" Philadelphians would be reading, so to speak, over his shoulders. Drawing these on-lookers in, he admitted to them what "we [Methodists] have all long known," that is, "that there has been considerable division of sentiment among us, respecting the *character* of our religious exercises." While the majority of Methodists were, he claimed, "sober and steady" and de-sired decent and orderly worship, "the minor part, have been, on the contrary, very zealous for... outward signs of the most heedless emo-tion" (*ME*-1814, 7). It was this "minor part" of Methodism that had given it a reputation that was, in his view, undeserved.

Watson marginalized these more "zealous" Methodists by positioning them as a minority and marking them both in terms of race and class. Those, he wrote, who "learn a *habit* of vehemence [are]... mostly per-sons of credulous, *uninformed* minds; who, before their change to grace had been of rude education, and careless of those prescribed forms of good manners and refinement, of which polite education is never divested – and which, indeed, religion ought to cherish. They fancy that all the restraints of conduct, viz. 'sobriety, gravity and blameless-ness,' is a formality and resistance of the Spirit; – and so to avoid it, they seem rather to go to the other extreme, and actually run before it" (*ME*-1814, 10). He noted, too, that the new songs, "often miserable as poetry, and senseless as matter,... [are] most frequently composed and first sung by the illiterate *blacks* of our society" (*ME*-1814, 15). After de-scribing the noisiness of a service at Bethel, the "mother" church of African Methodism, he stated that "they have now parted from us [the MEC], and we are not sorry" (*ME*-1814, 13).

In his preface to the "improved edition" of 1819, he reported that Methodism had gone up in the eyes of outsiders as a result of his book, "because they now perceive that the excesses *of a few*, were never the acts *of the whole*." He made it clear that he had written with the interests of "the great 'substantial middle class'" in mind, those who, in his words, "were too often offended in their instinctive sympathies, tastes and feelings, to come enough among us, to be profited by the soundness of our general doctrine." Because Methodists taught that "Christ died *for all*[,]... to be content with any partial success, or to regard the poor, or illiterate, as their only hope, or only accountable charge, would be neither Scriptural, nor politic; and certainly contrary to obvious fact" (*ME*-1819, v). Not only were the "excesses of the few" firmly identified with the poor and illiterate, but in a new footnote he also took pains to locate the origins of these "errors" elsewhere. "It began," he said, "in Virginia, and as I have heard, among the blacks" (*ME*-1819, 27 [note]).

While Watson was forthcoming in his examples and free with his opinions in a way that clearly made the Methodist clergy uncomfort-able,[4] he provided historians with an invaluable resource. His descriptions of worship at the Bethel Church in Philadelphia and of singing and dancing at camp meetings in the area by blacks and whites provide some of the earliest Protestant accounts of the call-and-response style in worship, the spirituals, and the ring shout. In his discussions of exegesis, we have clues as to the biblical typologies that informed the emergent camp-meeting tradition and the later interracial Holiness and Pentecostal movements. In short, Watson provided us with evidence to suggest that a new style of public worship had already emerged among Methodists by the first decades of the nineteenth century and that this form of worship had it roots in Virginia. As Methodist itinerant George Roberts stressed, what reformers found most offensive about this new style of worship was not "the involuntary loud hosannas of...pious souls, [but]...forming jumping, dancing, shouting, &c. into a *system*, and pushing our social exercises into those extremes."[5]

In this chapter, I focus on the emergence of "shouting Methodists," what Watson referred to as "Methodist enthusiasm and errors," and more specifically the process whereby "jumping, dancing, [and] shouting" were formed into "a system" in the context of public worship. In the previous chapter, I emphasized the role of narratives in the construction of British Methodist experience in class meetings, bands, love-feasts, and watch nights. This chapter emphasizes the way in which "shouting Methodists" utilized biblical narratives and bodily knowledges handed down from Europe and Africa to elaborate on the narratives of their British counterparts and constitute a distinctively American Methodist experience of the power and presence of God in new public spaces. These new public spaces – the quarterly conferences of the late eighteenth century and the camp meetings of the early nineteenth century – emerged as primary contexts in which Methodists might expect to see the power of God manifest through bodily experience.

I argue that shouting Methodists elaborated on the experience of their British counterparts in two ways: by pushing the Methodist performance tradition in a more interactive direction and by interpreting their bodily experiences in light of biblical typologies. The chapter is divided into two parts. The first part surfaces the idioms of the shouting Methodists as they emerged in the interracial revivals in Virginia in the 1770s and 1780s, in the Mid-Atlantic in the 1790s, and in the camp meetings of the early 1800s. I locate what I take to be the shouters' central interpretive act – the association of weeping, crying out, falling to the ground, and shouting for joy with the presence of the power of God – in relation to grassroots pressures to make preaching and worship more interactive. The shouters' attempts to push the Methodist tradition in a more interactive direction were contested by others. Analysis of these controversies suggests that the shouters presupposed a bodily knowledge, derived from the African performance tradition, which insisted that the presence and power of God was most fully realized in the dynamic interaction of the group.

In the second half of the chapter I analyze the idioms of the shouting Methodists as they surfaced through songs, autobiographies, journals, and diaries, focusing on the way shouters used the biblical narrative to sacralize their bodily experiences and the space of the camp. They did so, I argue, through the typological exegesis of scripture, that is, by casting themselves as the "new Israelites" and the camp as "Zion." While the use of typology was not new, scholars have largely missed the way that typological exegesis was employed at the grassroots level, especially in contexts where it was enacted rather than preserved in written commentaries on scripture.[6] The emergence of "shouting Methodists" and the development of the camp-meeting tradition more generally illustrate the role that typological interpretation played in the construction of religious experience at a grassroots level. More comprehensively, analysis of the shouting Methodists allows us to see the way in which early American Methodist narratives of experience drew upon bodily knowledges and biblical narratives, which they both acquired and assumed in practice. These narratives of experience in turn constituted the bodies of believers and the spaces in which they experienced religion in the distinctive form that later generations referred to as "old-time Methodism."

## The Shout as Interactive Performance

Scholars generally trace the origins of the shout tradition back to the revivals of the late eighteenth century, note its connection with the camp meetings of the early nineteenth century, and acknowledge its continued existence within the Sanctified, Holiness, and Pentecostal churches of the early twentieth century.[7] Although most scholars agree that the shout tradition has both European and African roots, recent scholarship, relying on primary sources from the late nineteenth and early twentieth centuries, has emphasized the African and Baptist side of that heritage.[8] Relatively little attention has been paid to the emergence of the shout tradition in the context of the late eighteenth-century revivals.[9] These revivals took place in the region surrounding the Chesapeake Bay in the 1760s, 1770s, and 1780s. While the revivals of the 1760s took place among Baptists and Presbyterians, Baptists and the newly arrived Methodists dominated the revivals of the 1770s and 1780s.[10]

As Russell Richey has pointed out, the historic roots of American Methodism lie in the areas surrounding the Chesapeake Bay: the

Delmarva Peninsula, the Western shore from Baltimore to Washington, DC, and eastern Virginia and northeastern North Carolina.[11] Methodism's rapid rise to become the nation's largest Protestant denomination began with the revivals of the mid-1770s and late 1780s. In the 1770s, growth was most rapid in Virginia and neighboring North Carolina, in part due to the involvement of Devereux Jarratt, an Anglican priest and Methodist sympathizer, whose parish lay within the boundaries of the famous Brunswick circuit near Petersburg, Virginia. Between 1774 and 1777, the Brunswick circuit went from 218 members to 1,360, with its newly formed daughter circuits (Amelia, Sussex, and North Carolina) claiming an additional 2,277 members. Membership again jumped dramatically in a number of circuits in the mid-to-late 1780s. In this period, too, growth was most dramatic on the Brunswick and adjacent circuits.[12]

*Components of the tradition*

While Methodists played a considerably larger role in the creation of the shout tradition than has been recognized and provided some of the best documentation for the early period, I do not mean to suggest that they did so alone. Surviving sources suggest that both Separate Baptists and Methodists played a significant role. Nor was shouting mostly a "white" or European American phenomenon. Black membership in the Methodist Episcopal Church was disproportionately concentrated in the Chesapeake Bay region. Although one-fifth of the total de nomination was of African descent in 1790, a third or more of Methodists were of African descent in many of the circuits around the Chesapeake. In Virginia, nearly half the population was of African descent as of the late 1780s.[13] By the 1790s, somewhere between a quarter and a third of the Separate Baptists and Methodists in Virginia were black. The revivals of the 1770s and 1780s in Virginia, thus, were thoroughly interracial affairs and the shout tradition was, to paraphrase Mechel Sobel, a tradition "they [Europeans and Africans] made together."

My aim in discussing the shout tradition as a Methodist or, more broadly, a Protestant phenomenon is not to obscure its Africanness, but to document the sacralization of certain kinds of experience within *Christianity* in an interracial and more importantly a *multicultural* context.[14] In order to give a clearer sense of this multicultural mix, I will briefly discuss some of the key ingredients: first, those derived from broad differences in African and European performance styles and, second, specific contributions of the Separate Congregationalists (turned Separate Baptists) and the English Methodists.[15]

## EUROPEAN AND AFRICAN PERFORMANCE STYLES

Two very different performance styles – the African and European – met in the context of the Virginia revivals. The most notable differences involved the relationship between music and worship and the interaction between leader and people. Where European worship, especially in the Protestant traditions, placed the emphasis on the word, whether spoken or sung, African worship placed the emphasis on rhythmic interaction, whether spoken or enacted in bodily movements. Where the former encouraged a relatively static relationship between leader and people structured around the formal preaching and singing of the word, the latter emphasized a dynamic interaction between leader and people structured by means of music. The effect of this confluence of styles was apparent in singing, preaching, the use of the body, and the level and meaning of interaction in worship.

Whereas the words of the eighteenth-century hymns were largely derived from Isaac Watts and Charles Wesley, the wandering choruses and spiritual songs were most likely a product of the (interracial) late eighteenth-century revivals and the early nineteenth-century camp meetings. The specifically African, as opposed to European or interracial, character of the sung tradition lies in the condensation of meaning,[16] repetition of musical phrases, and marked changes in performance style. Such changes included an emphasis on the improvisation of words and melodies, call-and-response, multiple rhythms operating simultaneously (polyrhythm), and the use of hand-clapping for percussion, all of which are among the most basic and widespread features of African music.[17]

The impact of the African musical tradition reached well beyond singing, in the conventional Western sense of the term, to preaching and dance. In the African context, speech and music were frequently integrated, running on a continuum from speech, recitative, and chant to song. Songs might move into speech and vice versa during the course of a performance, and the entire performance could be shot through with the rhythms of call-and-response or verse and chorus.[18] That the African musical tradition influenced the black preaching styles of the nineteenth and twentieth centuries is widely recognized. LeRoi Jones, for example, describes "the long, long, fantastically rhythmical sermons of the early Negro Baptist and Methodist preachers." Shaped by the traditional African call-and-response song, "the minister would begin slowly and softly, then built his sermon to an unbelievable frenzy with the staccato punctuation of his congregation's answers."[19] We will see that there was considerable congregational pressure on eighteenth-century Methodist preachers to develop a more interactive preaching style. This congregational pressure most likely had its roots in the call-and-response styles to which Africans were accustomed.

Movement and music were also integrated in the African context. Movement was typically an integral part of the music-making process, such that dancers and musicians were often one and the same.[20] African dancing was typically circular. Some early observers commented on a "predilection for 'principally confining [movement] to the head and upper parts of the body' and for 'scarcely moving their feet' or using a shuffle like step." Musicians were often placed in the center of the ring.[21] The ring shout, a circular dance, frequently described in post-Civil War accounts of slave religion, has been widely interpreted as an African dance of this sort.[22] Some of the earliest American accounts of such circular dances appear in conjunction with Methodist camp meetings.

Overall, and perhaps most crucially, the nature of African music was interactive. As John Miller Chernoff points out, African music, because of its emphasis on polyrhythm and call-and-response, is always the product of a group interaction. A focus on African rhythms encourages us to shift our mode of viewing away from the actions of individuals – the preacher, the convert, the shouter – to the *interaction* among people in a group. Oddly enough, such an approach brings us back full circle to Chauncy and Edwards's observations about the *interaction* between preacher and congregation. This time, however, such interaction, and indeed the constructedness of the rhythmic interaction, is not a means of *explaining away* the action of the Spirit, but precisely the means whereby the dynamic rhythmic interconnection of individuals-within-a-group emerges and the Spirit is known.[23]

## SEPARATE BAPTIST

While Methodism in its British phase constituted a largely separate cultural as well as religious world, this was not the case for indigenous American denominations, such as the Separate Baptists. As descendants of the radical wing of the Great Awakening, the Separatist tradition, as Albert Raboteau and David Wills have shown, was multi-ethnic (European, Indian, and African) in its make-up and probably to some extent multicultural in its practices from the start.[24] Thus, while it is clear that the Separate Baptists carried the distinctive forms of worship and religious experience of the radical wing of the New England awakening into the South, the radicalness of such practices in a transatlantic perspective may be due, at least in part, to Indian and African involvement beginning in New England.

Unfortunately for the historian, the Separate Baptist commitment to direct religious experience was linked to an unwillingness to put things down on paper. This unwillingness extended even to confessional statements. Where Regular (that is, firmly Calvinist) Baptists, in keeping with the Baptist Association of Philadelphia, adopted the London Confession of Faith (1689), the Separates, to the consternation of the Regulars, adhered simply to the Bible, fearing, in the words of one early historian, that "a confession of faith . . . would lead to formality and deadness."[25] Given this fear, as well as their general lack of literacy, it is not surprising that few descriptions of their experiences come to us by way of their own first-person accounts.[26] Most of the early accounts are histories written by Baptist clergy, most notably, Morgan Edwards, John Leland, Robert Semple, and David Benedict, after the Separate Baptists had merged with the Regular Baptists.[27]

According to Morgan Edwards, Separate Baptist "ministers resemble[d] . . . [the radical Congregationalists of New England] in tones of voice and actions of body; and the people in crying-out under the ministry, falling-down as in fits, and awaking in extacies; and both ministers and people resemble those in regarding impulses, visions, and revelations."[28] Leland indicates that "the Regulars were orthodox Calvanists [sic], and the work under them was solemn and rational; but the Separates were the most zealous, and the work among them was very noisy."[29] Robert Semple describes "most of the *Separates*" as having "strong faith in the immediate teachings of the spirit," but does not give specific instances of this.[30] David Benedict indicates the Separates held in their early years to "nine Christian rites, viz. *baptism, the Lord's supper, love-feasts, laying-on-of-hands, washing feet, anointing the sick, right hand of fellowship, kiss of charity, and devoting children*," based on their reading of scripture. Again, presumably in an attempt to follow scriptural precedent, the Separates not only appointed men as elders and deacons, but also women as "eldresses" and "deaconesses."[31]

The Separate Baptists' penchant for developing a ritual life directly derived from their reading of scripture without the benefit of mediating theological, devotional, or confessional traditions, was undoubtedly a stimulus to what scholars have called an "iconic" or "pictorial" reading of scripture, in which biblical "scenes" are reenacted in the present. This approach to scripture will characterize the shout tradition more broadly, and is specifically attacked by John Watson in *Methodist Error*. Moreover, one of these practices, the giving of the "right hand in fellowship," still survives in black Baptist churches. In some post-Civil War accounts of ring shouts in slave communities, the giving of the right hand of fellowship marked the transition from the "praise meeting," devoted to singing, praying, and preaching, and the "ring shout."[32]

John Williams, an unusually bookish convert to the Separate Baptist ministry, provided our only first-hand account of Separatist ritual practice. In his journal, he gives a detailed description of a "great meeting" held in Virginia on June 25, 1771, in which the ministers proceeded through cycles of preaching, exhorting, and the taking of experience, punctuated by the "ordinance" of footwashing, and culminating in baptism.[33] The Baptists' ritual focus on baptism by immersion, often in rivers, was as many have noted a key point of contact for European and African Baptists. The River Jordan, a very prominent image in the spirituals associated with the shout tradition, does not come to the fore in Methodist sources and probably reflects the emphasis on baptism on the Baptist side of the shout tradition. Both Methodists and Baptists, however, testified to their experience. In post-Civil War accounts of black Christian practice under slavery, there are numerous references to shouting at "experience meetings."[34]

Separate Baptist preachers also were known for a distinctive preaching style that, like the sermons of Whitefield and Davenport, was extemporaneous and musically inflected. Morgan Edwards described the voice of Shubal Stearns, a Whitefield convert from New England and the "father" of the Separate Baptist movement in the South,[35] as "musical and strong." Stearns managed his voice "in such a manner as...to make soft impression on the heart, and fetch tears from the eyes in a mechanical way; and anon, to shake the very nerves and throw the animal system into tumults and perturbations." Moreover, according to Edwards, all the Separate ministers copied him "in tones of voice and actions of body; and some few exceed[ed] him."[36] "Old-time" black Baptist preachers preserved much of the flavor of Separate Baptist preaching. According to William Montgomery, the greatest asset of successful Baptist preachers was their language skills, including their ability to create vivid word pictures and "their feel for the rhythms that evoked bodily responses."[37]

There is also evidence, as we have seen, that the repetitive spiritual songs that John Watson deplored had roots in the New England awakening as well. While the hymns of Isaac Watts were the general standard for Virginia's Baptists, Leland noted that they did not confine themselves to them. "Any spiritual composition," he reported, "answers to their purpose." Leland also commented that with respect to the "great meetings" of the 1780s, "in some places, singing was more blessed among the people than the preaching was...At meeting, as soon as preaching is over, it is common to sing a number of spiritual songs; sometimes several songs are sounding at the same time, in different parts of the congregation."[38]

## The Shout as Biblical Interpretation

When critics such as John Fanning Watson referred to shouting as "noise" and linked it to "extravagant emotions" or "a habit of vehemence," they obscured what shouting meant to shouters. Shouting did not simply involve performance, it also involved narrative, sometimes in the context of performance and sometimes after the fact. Such narratives were not simply individual accounts, but located the individual in relation to the group. They did so by constituting personal experience in the idioms of the biblical narrative, that is, by placing the individual within the collective narrative of the people of God. Many of the biblical idioms that shouters used to characterize their experience surfaced in accounts of the late eighteenth-century revivals; the interpretive process was most fully realized, however, in the context of the nineteenth-century camp meeting.

The continuous line of development from the late eighteenth-century Methodist quarterly conferences to the early nineteenth-century Methodist-dominated camp meetings has been obscured by a traditional emphasis on the camp meeting's roots in Presbyterian sacramental meetings, its emergence in the context of the Kentucky revival, and its links with the frontier and/or the South.[39] Since my concern here is with religious experience, claims to primacy are less important than the traditions of practice and experience that converged in the camp meeting. Although references to "camp meetings" *per se* are rare before 1800, large outdoor gatherings of various sorts were common in a number of Protestant traditions during the eighteenth century. The three most important were the Presbyterian sacramental meetings, the Methodist quarterly conferences, and the Separate Baptist "big" or "great" meetings.[40] The Red River meeting in Kentucky, sometimes designated as the first camp meeting, represented the confluence of Presbyterian and Methodist traditions and illustrates the interplay between bodily knowledge and interpretation in the construction of religious experience.

Accounts indicate that the Red River meeting was jointly organized by four Presbyterians, James McGready, John Rankin, William Hodge, and William McGee, all with experience of sacramental meetings; and John McGee, a Methodist elder with experience at quarterly conferences in the Carolinas, Tennessee, and Kentucky. John McGee reported that on the third day of the meeting, while he was preaching, the "glory of God" broke out among the people. In the familiar idiom of the shout tradition McGee reported that "some fell to the floor, screaming and praying for mercy, while others shouted aloud the praises of God." McGee, who almost fell himself, "went through the house shouting and exhorting with all possible ecstasy and energy, and the floor was soon covered with the slain."[41] The Presbyterian ministers, not knowing what to make of this, turned to the Methodist for guidance. John Rankin later wrote that "on seeing and feeling his [John McGee's] confidence, that it was the work of God, and a mighty effusion of his spirit, and having heard that he was acquainted with such scenes in another country, we acquiesced and stood in astonishment, admiring the wonderful works of God."[42] McGee here passed on a tradition of interpretation extant among Methodists "in another country" (i.e., back east) to the Presbyterians in Kentucky. Without McGee's confident interpretation of this performance as "the work of God," it would have been incomprehensible to the Presbyterian ministers.

For several years after this meeting, Presbyterians, Methodists, and to a lesser extent Baptists, held "General Meetings" or "General Camp Meetings" in the West and deep South in which Presbyterians invited Methodists and Baptists to their sacramental occasions and Methodists invited Presbyterians and Baptists to their quarterly conferences.[43] Russell Richey emphasizes Francis Asbury's role in promoting camp meetings among Methodists. In an episcopal directive issued in December 1802, Asbury bestowed his blessing on the (general) camp meetings in the Carolinas and Georgia (in which "hundreds have fallen and have felt the power of God") and called for a (denominational) camp meeting to be held in conjunction with a conference outside Baltimore.[44] By 1802, a rising tide of opposition to camp meetings among the more conservative Baptist and Presbyterian ministers in the South and West led many of the more revivalistically oriented Presbyterians to join the Cumberland Presbyterian Church, the "Christian" movement, or in a few cases, the Shakers.[45] By 1804, the cooperative arrangements had largely broken down and the Methodists had embraced the camp meeting as their own.[46]

Letters from Methodist itinerants reflected both the Methodist embrace of and the Calvinist retreat from camp meetings. Through 1802 the preachers' letters referred to quarterly conferences and general (i.e., multidenominational) camp meetings in the West and the South. After 1803, the letters regularly referred to Methodist, but rarely multidenominational, camp meetings, not only in the deep South and West, but in Virginia and Maryland as well.[47] The first Methodist camp meeting in the New York City area was held in 1804 and on the Delmarva Peninsula in 1805.[48] Camp meetings under Methodist auspices, as Richey makes clear, were not simply associated with the frontier, but took place in the established heartlands of Methodism from New York to Georgia. There were undoubtedly many reasons why the Methodists took on the camp meeting as their own. One reason was that the Methodists extended the narrative embedded in the shout tradition from the body of the believer to the space of the camp and in doing so constructed the camp meeting as a public space with sacred significance. Just as shouting for shouters was not just noise, the camp was not just a collection of tents, but the new Zion where the people of God recognized the presence of God by shouting with joy.

Methodists of various sorts described their experiences at early nineteenth-century camp meetings. A number of them record how the meeting ground itself was laid out. Itinerant Samuel Coate described a three-day Methodist camp meeting held "in a grove or forest" near Baltimore in 1803. "A stand [was] erected in the midst of a piece of ground containing three or four acres; and round this, the tents, waggons, carts, coaches, stages, and the like were arranged in a circular form; and fires were kindled at the front of the tents to accommodate those who lodged in them." Jesse Lee described the layout of the typical Methodist camp meeting as an "oblong square," and indicated that some had two preaching stages, one at either end of the area bounded by the tents. Zilpha Elaw, who attended Methodist camp meetings in New Jersey a decade or so later, described the typical camp meeting, like Coate, as circular. "A large circular inclosure of brushwood is formed; immediately inside of which the tents are pitched, and the space in the centre is appropriated to the worship of God, the minister's stand being on one side, and generally on a somewhat rising ground." In contrast to later camp-meeting observations, none of these early Methodists note any area being set apart for mourners.[49]

Like quarterly conferences, camp meetings were interracial events. How relations between the races were configured spatially seems to have varied. In his history of the camp meeting, Kenneth Brown indicates that in the deep South, "black Christians had to conduct their own services, with their own preachers, in their own quarters; in effect, they had to hold their own separate camp meeting." Segregation was apparently also the norm on the Delmarva Peninsula from an early date. Robert Todd, referring to the "old-time" camp meetings, states that "a portion of the circle to the rear of the preacher's stand [was] ... invariably set apart for their [the 'colored people's'] occupancy and use," with a plank partition separating the white and colored sides of the encampment. Segregation may not have been the custom everywhere, however. Although Jesse Lee mentioned separate seating for men and women in his general description of the layout of Methodist camp grounds, he made no reference to race. Nor did Zilpha Elaw, in her descriptions of meetings in New Jersey in the 1810s and early 1820s, give the impression that she as a free black woman was encamped or seated in a distinctive space. The only seating she mentioned (and she was seated) was located "in the space before the platform."[50]

Coate, Elaw, and Lee offered similar descriptions of the "religious exercises" that structured the camp meeting. The two itinerants, Coate and Lee, used much the same language to describe these exercises, although Lee went into considerably more detail. In Jesse Lee's words:

> soon after the dawn of day, a person walks all round the ground in front of the tents, blowing a trumpet as he passes; which is to give the people notice to rise; about ten minutes after the trumpet is blown again with only one long blast upon which, the people in all their tents begin to sing, and then pray, either in their tents, or at the door of them, as is most convenient. At the rising of the sun a sermon is preached, after which we eat breakfast. We have preaching again at 10 o'clock, and dine about one. We preach again at 3 o'clock, eat supper about the setting of the sun, and have preaching again at candle light. We generally begin these meetings on Fridays, and continue them until the Monday following about the middle of the day.[51]

While Zilpha Elaw described the same basic format, the language she used to do so differed sharply from that of Jesse Lee and Samuel Coate. Where in Lee's account a person awakened the people by blowing a trumpet, in Elaw's "watchmen proceed round the inclosure, blowing with trumpets to awaken every inhabitant of this City of the Lord." Where Lee indicated that "we have preaching again at 10 o'clock," Elaw wrote,

> At ten o'clock, the trumpets sound again to summon the people to public worship; the seats are all speedily filled and as perfect a silence reigns throughout the place as in a Church or Chapel; presently the high praises of God sound melodiously from this consecrated spot, and nothing seems wanting but local elevation to render the place a heaven indeed. It is like God's ancient and holy hill of Zion on her brightest festival days, when the priests conducted the processions of the people to the glorious temple of Jehovah.[52]

Richey argued that, in the Methodist context, the camp meeting "recalled the memory of intense community and the dramatic revivalistic response at Methodist conferences – quarterly and annual," while at the same time permitting a separation of the business of the denomination from the business of revival.[53] It did this, I agree, but it also did more. In separating business and revival, Methodism took the final step in a process of creating a *public* time and place where (to paraphrase Watson) "the very presence of the Deity" was manifested in and through the bodily exercises and extravagant emotions of the faithful. In the words of Zilpha Elaw we get a glimpse of the biblical idioms involved in the sacralization of the camp. For shouters, the sacralization of the body, the sacralization of the camp, and the passage from sin to salvation were intimately linked through a series of biblical typologies.

*The sacralization of the body*

Like quarterly conferences, early descriptions of camp meetings drew on the language of the shout tradition. As in the earlier accounts, sinners falling and saints shouting were linked with the felt power or presence of God, most typically in association with prayer or singing. James Jenkins wrote regarding a camp meeting on the Bladen circuit near Wilmington, North Carolina, in 1804: "We began the exercises after breakfast, and continued nearly till night, with very little stir; but under the last prayer *the power of God came down* among the people. The saints began to shout aloud and praise God. And sinners began to cry for mercy. In a little time, there were many agonizing on the ground." Thomas Sargent used similar language to describe a camp meeting near Baltimore the same year: "Our strong lunged men exerted themselves until the whole forest echoed, and all the trees of the woods clapped their hands. *God came near,* sinners fell in abundance, christians rejoiced and shouted, and a glorious sacrifice of praise ascended to God.[54]

# Notes

1   *The Chorus,* compiled by A. S. Jenks and D. S. Gilkey (Philadelphia, 1860), #241, quoted in Winthrop S. Hudson, "Shouting Methodists," *Encounter* 29 (1968): 73.

2   The manuscript version of *Methodist Error* is at the Huntington Library, San Marino, California. A number of letters and reviews of the work bound in the volume establish the author as John Fanning Watson. Watson was for a time a bookseller (in Philadelphia from 1806 to 1814), a bank cashier (in Germantown from 1814 to 1848), a writer, and a local historian. He is best known as the author of the *Annals of Philadelphia and Pennsylvania, in the olden time; being a collection of memoirs, anecdotes, and incidents of the city and its inhabitants* (Philadelphia, 1830). Although he described himself as a "Wesleyan layman," Deborah Waters states that "while a bookseller, Watson pleased his mother by embracing religion, initially following his mother's Methodism, but remaining within the Episcopal Church" ("Philadephia's Boswell: John Fanning Watson," *The Pennsylvania Magazine of History and Biography* 98 [1974]: 7–9).

3 [James Fanning Watson], *Methodist Error* (1814), 10; [Watson], *Methodist Error* (Trenton: D. & E. Fenton, 1819), 15. Hereafter *Methodist Error* will be cited in the text as either *ME*-1814 or *ME*-1819.

4 The Methodist ministers of Philadelphia, according to Watson, concurred with him "so far as *his main object* is concerned," but claimed that they could "manage *their objections* to these things, *with more discretion and moderation*" than Watson could (*ME*-1819, 193–4).

5 George Roberts, *The substance of a sermon (but now more enlarged) preached to, and at the request of the Conference of the Methodist Episcopal Church, held in Baltimore, March, 1807* (Baltimore: Henry Foxall, 1807), 29–30 (emphasis added).

6 The earliest Christians read the Septuagint (the Greek translation of Hebrew scriptures) as "prefiguring" Christian developments. In the New Testament itself, Paul depicted Adam as the "figure" or "type" of Christ and thus Christ as the "antitype" of Adam. Although the Protestant reformers rejected much of the more elaborate allegorical exegesis of the early and medieval church, even the most conservative Protestant exegetes recognized the legitimacy of the typologies instituted in the New Testament. The Puritan use of typology has been extensively discussed, but scholars have paid relatively little attention to the use of typology by nineteenth-century religious groups other than Mormons. On typology, see Sacvan Bercovitch, ed., *Typology and Early American Literature* (Amherst: University of Massachusetts Press, 1972), 3–46; George P. Landow, *Victorian Shadows, Victorian Types: Biblical Typology in Victorian Literature, Art, and Thought* (Boston: Routledge & Kegan Paul, 1980), 1–64; Conrad Cherry, *Nature and Religious Imagination from Edwards to Bushnell* (Philadelphia: Fortress Press, 1980), 14–25. On typology in the early national period, see Mark A. Noll, "The Image of the United States as a Biblical Nation, 1776–1865," in Nathan O. Hatch and Mark A. Noll, eds., *The Bible in America* (New York: Oxford University Press, 1982), 39–58. On the Mormon use of typology, see Philip L. Barlow, *Mormons and the Bible* (New York: Oxford University Press, 1991), 35–8, 66–9, 75–7, 83–4.

7 Most scholars acknowledge these touchstones in the history of the shout tradition, but it has been of particular interest to scholars of African American religion. The ring shout has received considerable attention from scholars concerned with slave religion and the survival of African traditions in the American context. In this regard, see Albert J. Raboteau, *Slave Religion: The "Invisible Institution" in the Antebellum South* (New York: Oxford University Press, 1978); Melville Herskovits, *The Myth of the Negro Past* (Boston: Beacon, 1958); Sterling Stuckey, *Slave Culture: Nationalist Theory and the Foundations of Black America* (New York: Oxford, 1987), 3–97; and Robert Simpson, "The Shout and Shouting in Slave Religion in the United States," *The Southern Quarterly* 23, 3 (1985): 34–47. The origin of the music associated with the shout tradition has been the subject of extensive debate among musicologists over the years. For a review of the scholarship through 1959, see D. K. Wilgus, *Anglo-American Folksong Scholarship Since 1898* (New Brunswick, NJ: Rutgers University Press, 1959), 345–64.

8  Mechael Sobel, *Trabelin' On: The Slave Journey to an Afro-Baptist Faith* (Westport, CT: Greenwood Press, 1979), and Walter F. Pitts, Jr., *Old Ship of Zion: The Afro-Baptist Ritual in the African Diaspora* (New York: Oxford University Press, 1993). Hudson emphasized the Euro-American and Methodist side of the tradition in "Shouting Methodists," 73–84. See Ann Taves, "Knowing Through the Body: Dissociative Religious Experience in the African-American and British-American Methodist Traditions," *Journal of Religion* 73, 2 (April 1993): 200–2, for my initial attempt to present the Methodist side of the shout tradition in a way that did justice to both its European and African roots.

9  A number of dissertations and books have appeared since this was largely completed, including Lester Ruth, "'A Little Heaven Below': Quarterly Meetings as Seasons of Grace in Early American Methodism" (Ph.D. dissertation, University of Notre Dame, 1996); William C. Johnson, "'To Dance in the Ring of All Creation': Camp Meeting Revivalism and the Color Line, 1799–1825" (Ph.D. dissertation, University of California at Riverside, 1997); Christine L. Heyrman, *Southern Cross: The Beginnings of the Bible Belt* (New York: Alfred A. Knopf, 1997); John H. Wigger, *Taking Heaven by Storm: Methodism and the Popularization of American Christianity* (New York: Oxford University Press, 1998). Deborah Vansau McCauley's *Appalachian Mountain Religion* (1995) is the most important study that has come to my attention since this was written. Working backwards from contemporary sources, McCauley attempts to construct a historical framework for the distinctive religiosity of the Appalachian region. She locates its roots in "pietism, Scots-Irish sacramental revivalism, Baptist revival culture during the Great Awakening in the mid-South, and plain-folk camp-meeting religion" (36). The analysis presented here is derived independently from (mostly) early Methodist sources. The emphasis on Methodist sources from the revivals in the mid-South in the 1770s and 1780s and in the mid-Atlantic in the 1790s and beyond illuminates Methodist and African American contributions to a tradition of camp-meeting religion that was not limited to either the frontier or the southern "high country." McCauley's work, taken together with the analysis presented here, begins to suggest the broader contours of an experiential tradition, which (with some distinctive variations) has been claimed as the distinctive center of both the religion of mountain whites and enslaved blacks.

10  I have found only a few disparate references to shouting or a shout prior to the Virginia revivals – one in the context of a sacrament Sunday at Edinburgh College (*Diary of Samuel Sewell*, 2 vols. [New York: Farrar Straus & Giroux, 1973], 1: 352, quoted in Ward, *Protestant Evangelical Awakening*, 17) and another in an account of black conversions on the Bryan Plantation in South Carolina in 1741 written by Salzburger immigrants. The latter refers to "those who love Christ... shouting and jubilating" (the relevant passage from the *Detailed Reports* of the Salzburger immigrants is quoted in Albert J. Raboteau and David W. Wills, "Slave Conversions on the Bryan

Plantations [Nov–Dec 1741]," *Afro-American Religion* [Working Draft (Dec. 1994)] vol. 2, chap. 5, doc. 27).

11 Russell Richey, *Early American Methodism* (Bloomington: Indiana University Press, 1991), 50.

12 *Minutes of the Annual Conferences of the Methodist Episcopal Church for the Years 1773–1828*, vol. 1 (New York: Mason and Lane, 1840). In 1790 the circuits ringing the Chesapeake included Severn and Calvert on the western shore of Maryland; Cecil, Kent, Talbot, and Dorchester on the Delmarva Peninsula; and Portsmouth in Virginia. From the time racially differentiated statistics began to be kept in 1786 until 1790, more than half the members of the Calvert circuit were black (ibid.).

13 According to Leland, the ratio of blacks to whites in Virginia in 1788 was approximately six to seven (John Leland, "The Virginia Chronicle" [1790] in *The Writings of John Leland* [New York: G. W. Wood, 1845], 93).

14 I am adopting here what Mary Louise Pratt refers to as a "contact perspective." Such a perspective, in her words, "emphasizes how subjects are constituted in and by their relations to each other. It treats the relations among colonizers and colonized, . . . not in terms of separateness or apartheid, but in terms of copresence, interaction, interlocking understandings and practices, often within radically asymmetrical relations of power" (*Imperial Eyes: Travel Writing and Transculturation* [London and New York: Routledge, 1992], 7).

15 There is a large general literature on the revivals in Virginia, including Rhys Isaac, *The Transformation of Virginia, 1740–1790* (Chapel Hill: University of North Carolina Press, 1982); Wesley M. Geweher, *The Great Awakening in Virginia, 1740–1790* (Durham: Duke University Press, 1930); Mechal Sobel, *The World They Made Together: Black and White Values in Eighteenth-Century Virginia* (Princeton: Princeton University Press, 1987).

16 On the condensation of meaning, see John W. Work, *American Negro Songs* (New York: Howell, Soskin & Co., 1940), 9–10.

17 Eileen Southern, *The Music of Black Americans: A History*, 2nd ed. (New York: Norton, 1983), 15–20; John Storm Roberts, *Black Music of Two Worlds* (Trivoli, NY: Original Music, 1972), 168–74; LeRoi Jones, *Blues People: Negro Music in White America* (New York: William Morrow, 1963), 41–7; Brett Sutton, *Primitive Baptist Hymns of the Blue Ridge* (Chapel Hill: University of North Carolina Press, 1982), compare contemporary black and white congregational singing of the hymn tradition.

18 Southern, *Music of Black Americans*, 18–20.

19 LeRoi Jones, *Blues People*, 45–6. There is a large literature on the chanted sermon in both black and white contexts. See, for example, Gerald L. Davis, *I Got the Word in Me and I Can Sing It, You Know: A Study of the Performed African-American Sermon* (Philadelphia: University of Pennsylvania Press, 1985); William H. Pipes, *Say Amen Brother!* (New York: The William-Frederick Press, 1951); Bruce A. Rosenberg, *Can These Bones Live? The Art of the American Folk Preacher*, rev. ed. (Urbana and Chicago: University of Illinois Press, 1988); on chanted sermons among white

Baptists, see especially Jeff Titon, *Powerhouse for God: Sacred Speech, Chant, and Song in an Appalachian Baptist Church* [recording] (Chapel Hill: University of North Carolina Press, 1982).

20 Olly Wilson, "The Association of Movement and Music as a Black Conceptual Approach to Music-Making," in *More Than Dancing: Essays on Afro-American Music and Musicians*, ed. Irene V. Jackson (Westport, CT: Greenwood Press, 1985), 10–11.

21 Southern, *Music of Black Americans*, 20–1.

22 See, for example, Raboteau, *Slave Religion*, 66–73; Stuckey, *Slave Culture*, 53–64, 83–98.

23 John Miller Chernoff, *African Rhythm and African Sensibility: Aesthetics and Social Action in African Musical Idioms* (Chicago and London: University of Chicago Press, 1979).

24 Raboteau and Wills, "Slave Conversions," in *Afro-American Religion*, vol. 2., chap. 5, doc. 17–24; Goen, *Revivalism and Separatism*, 90–1.

25 William Fristoe, *History of the Ketocton Baptist Association* (Staunton, VA: William Lyford, 1808), 21–2, quoted in Geweher, *Great Awakening in Virginia*, 109; John Leland, "Virginia Chronicle," 105.

26 The most notable exception to this is a journal kept by Separate Baptist John Williams during 1771; see John S. Moore, "John Williams' Journal: Edited with Comments," *Virginia Baptist Register* 17 (1978): 795–813. Letters to Rippon's *Baptist Register*, which began publication in 1790, are also a source of first-hand materials, but since the Separates had largely lost their distinctive character by that time and blended in among the Regulars, these letters do not provide much first-hand documentation of the Separates.

27 For the South and especially Virginia, the most important sources are Morgan Edwards, *Materials Towards a History of the Baptists*, 2 vols., 1770–1792 (Danielsville, GA: Heritage Papers, 1984); Isaac Backus's diary entries relating to his travels through Virginia in 1789; Leland, "Virginia Chronicle" (1790); Fristoe, *Ketocton Baptist Association* (1808); Robert Semple, *History of the Rise and Progress of the Baptists in Virginia* (Richmond: By the Author, 1810); David Benedict, *A General History of the Baptist Denomination*, 2 vols. (Boston: Lincoln & Edmands, 1813).

28 M. Edwards, *History of the Baptists*, 2: 90.

29 Leland, "Virginia Chronicle," 105.

30 Semple, *Baptists in Virginia*, 2.

31 Benedict, *Baptist Denomination*, 2: 107.

32 On contemporary Primitive Baptists, see Sutton, *Primitive Baptist Hymns*, album notes, 16. Prior to the Civil War, according to Simpson ("Shout and Shouting"), such gatherings consisted of a "praise meeting" that included preaching, followed by "a 'shout.' " A "transition ritual of solemn handshaking" marked the transition between the two parts of the meeting (37).

33 Moore, "John Williams' Journal," 803–4.

34 On experience meetings in the context of slavery, see, for example, "The Religious Life of the Negro Slave," *Harper's New Monthly Magazine* 27 (1863): 680–2.

35   Goen, *Revivalism and Separatism*, 296–7.

36   M. Edwards, *History of the Baptists*, 2: 93.

37   William E. Montgomery, *Under Their Own Vine and Fig Tree: The African American Church in the South, 1865–1900* (Baton Rouge: Louisiana State University Press, 1992), 284, 310. See also William E. Hatcher, *John Jasper: The Unmatched Negro Philosopher and Preacher* (New York, 1908; reprint New York: Negro University Press, 1969).

38   Leland, "Virginia Chronicle," 115.

39   Charles A. Johnson, *The Frontier Camp Meeting: Religion's Harvest Time* (Dallas: Southern Methodist University Press, 1955; 2nd edition, 1985); Dickson D. Bruce, Jr., *And They All Sang Hallelujah: Plain-Folk Camp-Meeting Religion, 1800–1845* (Knoxville: University of Tennessee Press, 1974); John B. Boles, *The Great Revival, 1787–1805: The Origins of the Southern Evangelical Mind* (Lexington: University Press of Kentucky, 1972). Most studies have noted, but not adequately explained, the virtual Methodist takeover of this institution within a few years of its emergence. For a critical perspective on this historiographical tradition, see Richey, *Early American Methodism*, 21–32.

40   On the Presbyterian sacramental meetings in Scotland and America, see Schmidt, *Holy Fairs*; on the continuity between Methodist quarterly conferences and camp meetings, see Richey, *Early American Methodism*, 21–32. There is little secondary literature on either German pietist or Baptist "big meetings." For descriptions in primary sources, see *Rippon's Register* [1790]: 105–6, which describes "big meetings" as "the common practice in Georgia, South and North Carolina, and in Virginia, in what we call the back parts of the country."

41   John McGee, "Commencement of the Great Revival," *Methodist Magazine* 4 (1821): 190, quoted in Kenneth O. Brown, *Holy Ground: A Study of the American Camp Meeting* (New York: Garland, 1992), 18.

42   Rankin's account was originally published in J. P. MacLean, "The Kentucky Revival and Its Influence on the Miami Valley," *Ohio Archaeological and Historical Publications* 12 (1908): 280, quoted in Brown, *Holy Ground*, 19. Others also comment on falling as "a new thing among Presbyterians" and one that "excited universal astonishment"; see "Extract of a Letter from the Rev. G. Baxter . . . to the Rev. Dr. Archibald Alexander," *Arminian Magazine* [London] 26 (Feb. 1803): 88.

43   For accounts of such meetings, see *Rippon's Register*, 1009, 1104; Lorenzo Dow, *Extracts from Original Letters to the Methodist Bishops, Mostly from their Preachers and Members in North America . . .* (Liverpool: H. Forshaw, 1806), 10, 20–1, 24–5, 27, 30–1, 38–41, 52. Both Baptists and Methodists commented on the "extraordinary meeting" at Washaws, SC, in May 1802. It was organized by the Presbyterians around a sacramental meeting, with Methodists and Baptists invited to participate (*Rippon's Register*, 1104; Dow, *Extracts*, 20–1). The Methodist *Arminian Magazine* [London] published letters from Presbyterian ministers William Hodge, J. Hall, and Samuel McCorkle describing cooperative revivals in Tennessee and North

Carolina (24 [June 1803]: 268–85; see also reports from Methodists 26 [Sept. 1803]: 418–19).

44  Richey, *Early American Methodism*, 31–2; Zachary Myles to William Myles, Jan. 11, 1803, *Arminian Magazine* 26 (June 1803): 285.

45  Boles, *The Great Revival*, 94–100.

46  Charles A. Johnson, *Frontier Camp Meeting*, 50–51.

47  Dow, *Extracts*; Jesse Lee, *History of the Methodists*, 286–96.

48  Rev. Robert W. Todd, *Methodism of the Penninsula* (Philadelphia: Methodist Episcopal Book Room, 1886), 35; George White, *A Brief Account of the Life, Experience, Travels, and Gospel Labours of George White, An African* (New York, 1810), in *Black Itinerants of the Gospel*, ed. Graham Russell Hodges (Madison: Madison House, 1993), 54.

49  Dow, *Extracts*, 61; Zilpha Elaw, *Memoirs of the Life, Religious Experience, Ministerial Travels, and Labors of Mrs. Zilpha Elaw*, in *Sisters of the Spirit: Three Black Women's Autobiographies of the Nineteenth Century*, ed. William L. Andrews (Bloomington: Indiana University Press, 1986), 65.

50  On the Carolina meetings in the 1790s, see Brown, *Holy Ground*, 8; on the Delmarva Peninsula, see Todd, *Methodism of the Penninsula*, 179, 182; on meetings in Pennsylvania and New Jersey, see Elaw, *Memoirs*, 65. Both Charles A. Johnson (*Frontier Camp Meeting*, 46), probably following Todd, and D. Bruce (*And They All Sang Hallelujah*, 73), citing Gorham's *Camp Meeting Manual* (1854), confidently state that camp meetings were segregated with whites sitting in front of the preaching stand and blacks gathering at the back. The variability and complexity of interactions around separate and shared space is suggested by Richard Bassett, an itinerant stationed on the Dover circuit in Delaware, who referred to separate black and white love-feasts at the annual conference in 1802, but in the next breath described "twelve to fifteen hundred [who] came to the Lord's table, white and coloured people" (Dow, *Extracts*, 19).

51  Jesse Lee, *History of the Methodists*, 366–7; for Coate, see Dow, *Extracts*, 61–2, also the letter of Daniel Hitt in Dow, 57.

52  Elaw, *Memoirs*, 65–6.

53  Richey, *Early American Methodism*, 24.

54  Dow, *Extracts*, 55, 59, emphasis added; see also 24, 28, 29, 31, 33, 37, 38, 43, 71.

# 4

# Protestantism as Establishment

*William R. Hutchison*

## Introduction

During the nineteenth century, American Protestants from several denominations cooperated on a variety of different outreach projects. Especially in foreign missions, where funding was often scarce and competition among different Protestant groups was sometimes embarrassing, American Protestants strove to work together toward common goals. As a growing network of cooperating individuals and institutions expanded in influence, fissures developed that split this network into several groups. Liberals interested in defining the gospel in terms of social justice pulled away from more conservative types who focused on the doctrines of biblical revelation separating Christians from others. In the twentieth century, another group emerged to emphasize spirituality as something different from either social Christianity or fundamentalism. Meanwhile, black Protestants, along with other groups that had been excluded from or marginalized by Protestant missionary cooperation, became increasingly well-organized and visible participants in American public life, as did Catholics and Jews, who had once been targets of missionary conversion.

Even as differences between liberal and conservative Protestants were solidifying, and as other groups were becoming more powerful, liberal Protestants were increasingly prominent and sophisticated players in national and

Excerpted from William R. Hutchison, "Protestantism as Establishment," in *Between the Times: The Travail of the Protestant Establishment in America, 1900–1960*, ed. William R. Hutchison (New York: Cambridge University Press, 1989), 3–18.

international life. Many new developments in government, business, and higher education emerged through their influence, often supported by philanthropic agencies such as the Ford, Rockefeller, and Carnegie foundations. As William Hutchison explains, this liberal Protestant "establishment" defined the international face of America during the first half of the twentieth century and set important agendas for both foreign policy and higher education in America for decades to come.

Historians of American religion have generally taken for granted the existence of a Protestant establishment. Sydney Ahlstrom's *Religious History of the American People* used that terminology repeatedly. Robert T. Handy's arguments concerning an alleged "second disestablishment" of Protestantism after about 1920 (the first having occurred soon after the American Revolution) have been well received. Richard Neuhaus in the 1980s attributed the decline of religious influence in the civic order to, among other things, a "final disestablishment of mainline Protestantism." And E. Digby Baltzell, with a sociological more than religious definition in mind, used the term to identify certain breeding-grounds for anti-Semitism.[1]

Possibly such authors have alluded to something that, even if real, is not at all definable. Richard Rovere, who helped to give the term "establishment" the currency it enjoyed in this country after 1960, acknowledged that experts will always disagree about what a given establishment is and how it works, but he added that experts have also disagreed about the nature and operation of the Kingdom of God without on that account denying its existence. Leonard Silk and Mark Silk, in their volume of 1980, *The American Establishment*, acknowledged that the entity to which they had devoted their days and nights might be "a spirit, a ghost borne on the wind"; yet they remained convinced it was a reality.[2]

## The Denominational Matrix

Plausible working definitions do, in any case, seem attainable with respect to religion. This is especially true if one begins, as we do in this volume, with the modest proposition that in the earlier years of this century an establishment, identifiable both as a group of denominations and as a network of leaders in general connected with them, existed *within* American Protestantism. This intra-Protestant entity, if fuzzy at the edges and changeable over time, was not much more so than, say, the Republican Party or the American Federation of Labor (which as a federation provides a pretty good analogy). It was, at any rate, stable and definable enough to present one with an initial object of research, a starting point or base for inquiries into the dynamics of American religious and cultural history.

Let me be more specific. When historians, in their analyses of nineteenth-century religion, have used terms like establishment or mainline in a more-than-regional sense, they almost always have meant Congregationalists, Episcopalians, Presbyterians, and the white divisions of the Baptist and Methodist families. For the decades since 1900, the Disciples of Christ and the United Lutherans usually have been added, while the vast southern segment of the Baptists (unlike Southern Methodists or Presbyterians) has been seen as increasingly and intentionally removing itself from such a category.

These seven denominations represented well over half the constituency of the Federal and National Councils of Churches, supplied an overwhelming amount of their leadership, and to an amazing degree dominated the various enterprises ancillary to the main conciliar organizations. When "American Protestantism" dispatched delegates to the twelve-hundred-member World Missionary Conference at Edinburgh in 1910, all these groups except the Lutherans sent from 20 to 123 representatives. (American Methodists alone accounted for over 10 percent of the delegates at a gathering touted as broadly representative of world Christianity.)[3]

When the International Sunday School Council in 1922 formed an American subcommittee, these denominations provided at least 90 of the 109 members, and all of the fourteen officers. When American denominations in 1924 joined in establishing a National Council for the YMCA, it was these bodies (along with the Dutch and German Reformed churches and the Society of Friends) that made up the council. When John D. Rockefeller, Jr., and others in 1930 set in motion a "laymen's inquiry" into foreign missions, the same churches (minus the Lutherans) provided the ecclesiastical sponsorship. All of these churches (excluding the Disciples but including three different groups of Presbyterians) ranked among the top ten suppliers of Protestant missionary personnel; and all including the Disciples ranked in a top ten with respect to missionary budgets.[4]

The ability of the largest Protestant bodies to flood mission fields and international gatherings with their personnel, and to supply a huge proportion of the leadership, in some ways gave a distorted image of their position in American religious life. To speak only of numbers, their dominance among Protestants at home amounted to something like 60 percent, not 90 percent. But the resulting misperceptions, for example among European co-workers and observers, could in themselves work to strengthen the establishment's real authority, both at home and abroad. Exaggerated estimates, in other words, were to some extent self-fulfilling.

One can illustrate that phenomenon by reference to the period just after the First World War, when many people had come to think of "American Protestantism" as the principal creative and executive force in European reconstruction. In those years the Federal Council of Churches, which in its first decade (1908–18) had experienced only mixed success in unifying the American churches and directing their social outreach, gained enormously in international visibility, prestige, and prophetic standing. Europeans who admired "American religion" idealized the Federal Council both as a reliable representation of that larger entity, and as the leading model for structures of worldwide Christian unity and reconciliation. But even those who habitually distrusted American activism – and they were many – applauded the Council's insistent lobbying against the isolationist or recriminatory actions of Allied governments. Such American bodies and their leaders were viewed askance for undue paternalism and efficiency-mindedness, yet still admired extravagantly as religious America's rebuke to the United States Senate. These perceptions in turn helped produce the larger-than-life status that American "liberal" Protestantism was to enjoy in international settings for at least the next three decades.[5]

If the unity and effectiveness of the establishment could be exaggerated, especially from distant perspectives, so of course could that of any given denominational family within it. As an earlier allusion to three Presbyterian bodies indicated, several of these families – the Baptists, Lutherans, and Methodists as well as the Presbyterians – were exceedingly diverse. The number of ecclesiastical organizations "denominated" by the same name varied, as of 1920, from ten among the Presbyterians to twenty-two among the Baptists; and, except for an increase in Baptist groups, those numbers remained much the same in 1960. But any close look at relative numbers and resources within each denominational family will reinforce the conclusion that control was concentrated in a very few large bodies.[6]

One finds represented on the boards of the establishment organizations both those "family members" (United Presbyterian, Methodist Protestant) that eventually would merge with a more powerful sibling, and other Protestant bodies that were destined to maintain a separate identity (black Baptists, the Reformed churches, Quakers, Moravians). Yet the small scale of such representation, for example in the case of black churches with huge constituencies, again underscores the establishment's dominance. Blacks, along with Mennonites, Free Methodists, and Seventh-Day Adventists, were represented at the Edinburgh meeting of 1910. But delegation size had been determined by the size of mission budgets, and these churches had been allotted only one to three delegates each.[7]

Not all the pieces in the mosaic of American institutional religion contribute in that way to the clarity of a central pattern. The establishment, though massive and seemingly very much in control, was not a monolith. Some American denominations that took no part in establishment enterprises – usually because they chose not to – could nonetheless boast competitive membership statistics, or a large degree of regional authority, or both. (The leading examples of "both" were the Southern Baptist Convention, the Missouri Synod Lutherans, and the Mormons.)[8] In any given area of activity, moreover, one or more "outsider" groups were likely to rank among a top ten or top twelve.

In foreign missions, the mainline churches shared prominence with outsider groups that specialized in such activity – especially with the Christian and Missionary Alliance and the Seventh-Day Adventists. In domestic social activism (judging from a longitudinal study, made in the 1950s, of the denominations' welfare enterprises), all except the Disciples ranked at the top; but the mainline churches were joined there by such specialists in city mission work as the Salvation Army and the Volunteers of America. When it came to concern for higher education (as reflected in official sponsorship of colleges and universities), this set of churches, minus the Episcopalians, again dominated the statistics, with the seven leading groups, at any given time, supporting over half of the Protestant institutions; but in this area they shared leadership with the Roman Catholics.[9]

## The Establishment as a Personal Network

If these "Seven Sisters" continue, after careful nuancing of the description, to look like an established church operating without parliamentary sanction, that is partly because the American establishment was a personal network as well as a congeries of institutions. The historian James A. Field in the 1970s called attention to the familial, social, and old-school-tie relationships, in many areas of the world, not only among missionaries, but between the missionaries on one hand and entrepreneurs, educators, philanthropists, and diplomats on the other. Such interrelationships had been visible in an earlier period when the medical missionary Peter Parker, whose wife was a Webster, held a series of diplomatic posts including, in the 1850s, that of American minister to China. By the twentieth century, partly because of what Field (a former naval officer) called "lack of intertheater transfer," mission-family dyn-asties had grown up in several areas of the world: Gulicks in Hawaii and Japan, Scudders in India, Underwoods in Korea, and many others.[10]

Field suggested that the situation in the Mediterranean world, where the "web of interconnected influence" had been established earlier than elsewhere, was an especially graphic single-theater epitome of more far-reaching networks extending across familial, occupational, and also national boundaries. And the overseas-based networks resembled, or actually extended, others that seem to have operated only on the national scene. The prospect therefore is that, just as historians of American foreign relations have had to take account of the interconnected influ-ence of the Dodge, Stokes, Phelps, and Bliss families (with special attention to Woodrow Wilson's lifelong friend and adviser Cleveland Dodge),[11] so the aims and operations of the Protestant leadership at home probably will not be adequately understood until we have worked through the relationships, official and personal, of those who managed or supported the Protestant enterprise.

That word "work" should be emphasized. Historical name dropping, however intriguing and usefully suggestive, will tell us little about how the personal network operated – for example, about who influenced whom. We know already, however, that friendships like those linking the Fosdicks (Harry Emerson and his brother Raymond) with the Rock-efellers, or the ecumenical executive John R. Mott with Woodrow Wilson, or Reinhold Niebuhr with leaders of the academic and foreign-policy establishment, figure in the stories both of mainline Protestantism and of its attempted cultural outreach and control. Mott's most exhaust-ive biographer, C. Howard Hopkins, scattered through his book refer-ences to Mott's interviews and other contacts with nine presidents of the United States. On one red-letter day in 1923, this particular lion of the religious establishment "began with William Howard Taft at 9:30, lunched with President Coolidge, and visited with his old friend Wood-row Wilson at 3:30."[12]

Similarly, biographers of the theologian Reinhold Niebuhr have docu-mented his extensive and intimate involvement in secular branches of the establishment. Richard Fox, recounting Niebuhr's participation in a State Department consultation of 1949, surmises that

> both he and the assembled foreign-service officers and department spe-
> cialists learned something of value from one another. No doubt too he and
> the State Department officials lent one another a certain amount of pres-
> tige: he basked in the aura of high affairs of state, they lingered briefly in
> the presence of a celebrity intellectual. They helped augment his standing
> as a significant Establishment figure, he helped elevate their own image as

intellectually vigorous officials, not narrow-minded technicians. If Niebuhr did not influence government policy, he did participate in a system of influence in which some individuals and agencies established themselves as authoritative voices.

Two weeks later, according to Fox, Niebuhr learned that he was being seriously considered for a post "at the very summit of the Establishment," the presidency of Yale University. His sponsors included Jonathan Bingham, the lawyer and later New York congressman, Chester Bowles, who was then governor of Connecticut, and the historian Arthur Schlesinger, Jr.[13]

Such information – the kind that relates to well-known personages and is likely to be mentioned in printed sources – would be merely the tip of a vast iceberg. The personal network in question also operated through less official contacts, both among the preeminent lay and clerical figures and among the rank and file. To cite one example: If we are to understand more fully the tensions in mainline Protestantism before and during the fundamentalist – modernist controversy (ca. 1910–30), we should learn not only how the various participants carried out their official duties, or what they said at conferences, but also how they spent their leisure time, and with whom.

The Presbyterian and ecumenical leader Robert E. Speer (a man often thought to have *had* no leisure time) spent part of most summers from 1901 to 1925 at Camp Diamond in northern New Hampshire, fishing and otherwise consorting with a number of persons whose names are well known to historians of missions or of Presbyterianism – with Robert Wilder, Charles Erdman, Henry Frost, the Hudson and Howard Taylors, and a great many others. As those same historians would know, Speer's fellow fishermen, and the organizations to which they were linked (the Student Volunteer Movement, Princeton Seminary, the China Inland Mission), played important and at some points sharply opposed roles in Speer's public career. The story of Speer's involvement in such a community could throw light on his willingness to be a contributor, along with Erdman and Frost, to the series of pamphlets that helped launch the fundamentalist movement. The circumstances, or just the fact, of his quitting Camp Diamond in 1925 (along with the Erdmans and the Wilders; the Frosts and Taylors stayed on) would at the least add dimension to what we know of the epochal falling-out, in the mid-twenties, between the fundamentalists on one hand, Speer and the Princeton Seminary moderates on the other.[14]

If such communities (the better known would include, for example, Silver Bay and Chautauqua in New York State, and Estes Park in Colorado) have their stories to tell of the religious establishment's less guarded moments, the more numerous "Pequod Islands," where members of *different* elites met and mingled, could tell us about its relations to the business, educational, and other secular worlds. The novelist John P. Marquand may well have based his evocation of Pequod Island, the beloved summer home of George Apley and his friends, on such real locations as Mount Desert Island, off the Maine coast. On Mount Desert, year after year, Browns and Peabodys of the religious establishment vacationed with Eliots, Rockefellers, and Peppers – that is, with educational, business, and political leadership. Although it was common in the languid, cheery recollections of these bucolic seasons to stress one's democratic or even egalitarian credentials (most memoirs include tributes to the sturdy locals and their ancestral wisdom), George Apley's poignant rumination is also apt: "Sometimes here on Pequod Island and back again on Beacon Street, I have the most curious delusion that our world may be a little narrow." A good many summer colonies were playgrounds, and to some extent workplaces, for a tight and well-defined social organization in which the leaders of mainline Protestantism were fixtures.[15]

Professor William Adams Brown, of Union Seminary in New York, devoted a section of his autobiography to "Forty Years of Mount Desert." Brown, a leading liberal theologian who during the First World War had been Speer's deputy in directing the War-Time Commission of the Churches, was prominent in both the intra-Protestant and the more general power structure. As a distant cousin to the Adamses of presidential lineage and a descendant of leading merchant bankers (Brown Brothers), he was a veritable embodiment of the network in its historical dimension; and his beloved summer place represented its contemporary form.

Brown's memoir mentions only the Mount Desert "names" that might be household words among the educated, rich, and famous – again, tips of an iceberg. But these are enough to make the point: university presidents such as Eliot of Harvard and Gilman of Johns Hopkins; Professors Dana (Yale) and Peabody (Harvard); and Seth Low, the Columbia University president who was also a reform politician. There were Fords and Morgans as well as Rockefellers; Lord Bryce, the British ambassador, as well as Senator George Wharton Pepper of Pennsylvania.

Vacation communities, though undoubtedly good points of entry for an understanding of the religious power structure and its outer connections, would represent only one starting point. Investigators have, for example, long since detected the Protestant establishment's massive footprints in the biographical dictionaries. When C. Luther Fry, in 1931, surveyed the stated religious affiliations of *Who's Who* biographees, he found that among 16,600 who listed a preference, fully 7,000 were either Episcopalians or Presbyterians. Congregationalists, despite the smaller size of that denomination, numbered an equally astounding 2,000. Baptists, with Northern Baptists probably overrepresented, Southern and black Baptists undoubtedly underrepresented, came in at about 1,500. Unitarianism evoked Emerson's "congress of kings" by weighing in with 1,000 biographees. Catholics, Lutherans, Disciples, Jews, and Quakers, in that order, could claim from 750 to 180.[16]

Here again, in other words, the bodies we are concerned with ranked in a top ten. Some of them, obviously, ranked embarrassingly high, enough so that Fry wondered, as have others before and since, whether Episcopalianism made for leadership or leaders simply made for the Episcopal churches. For us it makes little difference, just as it makes little difference whether mainline male persons were enormously influential or were greatly overrecognized. (I think both explanations are correct.) Either way, we are dealing with a network of Protestant leadership that, whatever its degree of actual hegemony, lasted well into the era of the more differentiated mainstream (one including Catholics and Jews) that Will Herberg charted in the 1950s,[17] and possibly into the era, three decades later, when it became common to suppose that evangelical and "third force" Protestantism had subverted the influence of the old-line denominations.

Another dimension needing exploration is the one embodied in the structures of leadership and influence in local communities. Only after the completion of many new studies, chosen with attention to reasonable sampling criteria, will it be possible with any specificity to relate these local establishments to the ones that dominated nationally or regionally. Meanwhile, however, sociological descriptions of such communities as W. Lloyd Warner's "Yankee City" can at least be accepted as presenting "variations within a [national] type,"[18] and therefore as providing bases for some starting reflections.

This would seem to be true, at least, for communities in those regions that were well represented within the national religious establishment. The New England community selected by Warner and his associates in the 1930s contained fifteen congregations, of which eleven were Protestant Christian. Three of these churches were Congregational, while Presbyterians, Methodists, Baptists, and Christian Scientists had one apiece. The Episcopalians and the Unitarians each sponsored a church and a chapel.[19] Studies of the network of personal and institutional leadership in such towns, or of the mainline Protestant presence in more diverse communities such as the "Middletown" community studied by Robert and Helen Lynd, would undoubtedly deepen our understanding of the national establishment, how it operated – and also how and why it changed.

In the midwestern "Middletown" of the 1920s, for example, the Lynds found, among both townspeople and ministers, evidence of decline in ministerial prestige. Despite "a widespread attitude of respect and in many cases warm affection and esteem" toward local ministers, "especially among the women," Middletown business leaders appeared to find excuses for excluding the clergy from the all-important Rotary Club. The Lynds gained "an impression of the ministers as eagerly lingering about the fringes of things trying to get a chance to talk to the men of the city who in turn are diffident about talking frankly to them."[20]

Whether such signs and complaints of alienation, even if common beyond Middletown, were in any way new to the 1920s is an extremely tricky question. Laments concerning "ministerial decline," laid end to end, would form a wide and solid line from 1630 to 1930 and, if valid, would document the ending of all ministerial influence in America sometime before the Revolution. It would be rash, moreover, to take exclusion from the Rotary Clubs of the 1920s, or terror in the face of such exclusion, as indicating permanent deterioration in ministerial standing. Clearly, the sociological data concerning denominational strengths and memberships, to say nothing of sociologists' "impressions" about local networks, will need to be treated comparatively, both over time and across the country.

The task, however, like that of inquiring into the nationwide web of individual relationships, becomes less formidable when one considers that at least some of the preliminary work – in one case local history and sociology, in the other case individual biography – has been done and sits waiting to be synthesized.

## Liberalism and the Protestant Establishment

Of all the terms used in recent years for what we are calling the Protestant establishment, the one least likely to be employed in this book as an actual synonym is "liberal Protestantism." Liberalism in all the most usual senses – theological, social, and ecumenical – was undeniably an important element in the common life of these churches, as well as in their doctrinal development and their bureaucratic and other leadership. But the habit of designating the Protestant mainline churches simply as "liberal," which is at least understandable if one has in mind the alignments of the 1970s and 1980s, is problematic for earlier periods.

The churches, church constituencies, and leaders we are talking about, when forced to choose between modernism and fundamentalism, or between the social gospel and more individualistic modes, did tend strongly to make the more "liberal" choice; and the fact that they did so is a vitally important part of their story. In making such choices, however, they were not in all instances – probably not in most instances – opting for what those churches and people would have spoken of as liberalism, to say nothing of modernism.

The Protestant establishment can in fact be understood as a "broad church" that held together, and exercised whatever cultural authority it did enjoy, precisely because it retained the adherence, at all levels, of many besides liberals. While it is probably true that few who called themselves fundamentalists were able to remain comfortably in these churches after about 1930, all the evidence indicates that "liberal" was rarely a preferred term outside the theological seminaries and the more sophisticated periodicals. (During the time of neo-orthodox reaction against conventional liberalism – that is, between 1930 and 1960 – such terminology was a bit suspect in those precincts as well.) Most establishment leaders and people, if forced to use limiting terms, were likely to designate their own positions as evangelical, confessional, progressive, or – calling on that all-time favorite among weasel words – moderate.

One can refuse to take such protestations seriously. We might insist that most of the so-called moderates, and most of those in furious neo-orthodox revolt, were in fact liberals – that "establishment" and "liberalism" are in the end best understood as synonymous terms. The habit of equating them developed, after the 1950s, largely because many evangelicals, along with nearly all fundamentalists, did make exactly that assertion about the old-line churches, and particularly about their intellectual and bureaucratic leadership. It became common to insist that those establishment functionaries, whatever fancy or fudging names they might give themselves, were all basically liberals. It was also charged that much of the rank and file, in failing either to speak out in their denominations or to defect from them, were fellow-traveling liberals as well.

Among a number of evangelicals who built polemics and programs on such allegations, one of the more discriminating was James DeForest Murch. Just after the period considered in this book, Murch sought to rally true Christians against a liberal superchurch that he thought was conspiring, especially through the ecumenical movement, to impose liberal and collectivist thought all across American culture. "It needs to be made clear," he explained in the first pages of *The Protestant Revolt* (1967), "that there is a liberal ecclesiastical establishment which sets the tone for and influences the direction of modern institutional Protestantism."[21]

Murch, far from assuming that all adherents of the old-line churches deserved to be branded as liberals, asserted that "thousands upon thousands" within those churches had discerned the contrast between true Christianity and "the pronouncements and practices of the Councils of Churches and the Liberal Establishment." Multitudes, he thought, were ready for active revolt. Even within the "small body of 'key men'" who managed the selection of "the 'right people' to all important positions in the ecclesiastical machine," many would not call themselves liberal. These leadership groups, he conceded, included "theologians of various persuasions (except 'fundamentalists')." The liberal establishment, in other words, was made up, basically, of just two kinds of people: Although doubtless controlled by actual liberals, it included all too many others who merely tolerated their thinking and connived in their machinations.[22]

Perceptions of an essentially liberal establishment and its dangers, while perhaps most intense at this moment of renewed evangelical consciousness, were by no means new. In 1923, as the fundamentalist controversy heated up, the periodical *Ministers' Monthly* (founded a year earlier to counter the "controlled press" of the major denominations) devoted two articles to "the flood tide of liberalism." This tide, it was said, had engulfed not only the theological seminaries, but also foreign missions, the religious press, and "the ecclesiastical machinery in nearly all of the leading denominations." J. Gresham Machen, chief scholarly mentor of the fundamentalists, sounded some of the same notes in his *Christianity and Liberalism* (also 1923), and the plaint could be heard amid the rhetoric of the Scopes trial two years later. The allegation that liberalism was taking over was in fact as old as the reactions, early in the century, to denominational "social creed" legislation and to the formation of the Federal Council of Churches. It was as venerable as fundamentalism itself.[23]

Card-carrying liberals, especially if social action was foremost in their religious thinking, acquiesced readily enough in this equation between "mainline" and "liberal"; and the tendency to make such an identification was strengthened accordingly. But the degree to which liberal ideas actually had come to pervade the establishment and its strategies remains an important open question.

What are we justified in assuming, meanwhile, about liberalism's importance in the twentieth-century development of these denominations? Estimates by such historians as C. Howard Hopkins and the present author may be reliable so far as they go: Hopkins identified very strong social gospel influence, and official denominational acceptance, in all of our seven bodies and nine others.[24] My own *Modernist Impulse* was inclined to see roughly as much liberal and modernist commitment within mainline Protestantism as conservatives found there (and in the same places: among the intellectual and bureaucratic leadership). The subject is, however, sufficiently complex that one will need to look behind the statistics, public pronouncements, and informed impressions on which such accounts have relied. In the meantime (and perhaps afterward as well), "liberal" must remain a term that, while it clearly helps to define the establishment, in no sense exhausts its definition.

Whatever the case with other establishments, this one was not a "ghost borne on the wind," but was defined concretely in the management of American Protestant life. The nature of its extension outward, its interconnection with other organizations and elites, is bound to remain somewhat more elusive. Even harder to answer definitively are questions of "influence" and of broad cultural authority – how much of the earlier hegemony endured or was successfully refashioned in the new conditions of the twentieth century. The difficulty of drawing the final and comprehensive map is not an excuse for failing to explore a few specific and vital territories.

# Notes

1 Sydney E. Ahlstrom, *A Religious History of the American People* (New Haven: Yale University Press, 1972); Robert T. Handy, *A Christian America: Protestant Hopes and Historical Realities* (New York: Oxford University Press, 1971), chapter 7; Richard John Neuhaus, *The Naked Public Square: Religion and Democracy in America* (Grand Rapids, Mich.: Eerdmans, 1984), ix; E. Digby Baltzell, *The Protestant Establishment: Aristocracy and Caste in America* (New York: Random House, 1964).

2 Richard Rovere, "The American Establishment," *Esquire* 57 (May 1962): 106; Leonard Silk and Mark Silk, *The American Establishment* (New York: Basic Books, 1980), 328.

3 World Missionary Conference, 1910, *History and Records and Addresses* (Edinburgh: Oliphant, Anderson & Ferrier, 1910), 51–63.

4 Herbert H. Smith (ed.), *Organized Sunday School Work in North America, 1918–1922: Official Report of the Sixteenth International Sunday School Convention* (Chicago: International Sunday School Council, 1922), 4–6; S. Wirt Wiley, *History of Y.M.C.A.-Church Relations in the United States* (New York: Association Press, 1944), 115; William E. Hocking et al., *Re-Thinking Missions: A Laymen's Inquiry After One Hundred Years* (New York: Harper, 1932), v–vi, ix–x; James Dennis et al. (eds.), *World Atlas of Christian Missions* (New York: Student Volunteer Movement, 1911), 16–29; Joseph I. Parker (ed.), *Interpretative Statistical Survey of the World Mission of the Christian Church* (New York: International Missionary Council, 1938), 43–5.

5 Adolf Keller, *Dynamis: Formen und Kräfte des amerikanischen Protestantismus* (Tübingen: Mohr, 1922), chapter 5; Karl Bornhausen, *Der Christliche Activismus Nordamerikas in der Gegenwart* (Breslau: Alfred Töpelmann, 1925).

6  *1919 Year Book of the Churches* (New York: Federal Council of Churches, 1919), 196 and 205; *1962 Yearbook*, 249 and 254. See generally the Federal and National Council of Churches' *Yearbooks*, published since 1916. (Cited hereafter as *Yearbook* or *Handbook* with date.)

7  World Missionary Conference, 1910, *History*, 55, 58, 51.

8  *1962 Yearbook*, 8, 249–54; *1951 Yearbook*, 2, 234–9; *1941 Yearbook*, 88, 129–35; *1931 Handbook*, 160, 259–63.

9  Parker, *Survey*, 43–5; *1919 Yearbook*, 211–14; *1934 Handbook*, 208–81; *1935 Yearbook*, 14–17; Horace R. Cayton and Setsuko Matsunaga Nishi, *The Changing Scene: Churches and Social Welfare*, vol. 2 (New York: National Council of Churches, 1955), 180–214; *1916 Yearbook*, 43–157; *1933 Yearbook*, 103–216; *1951 Yearbook*, 210–19.

10  James A. Field, "Near East Notes and Far East Queries," in John King Fairbank (ed.), *The Missionary Enterprise in China and America* (Cambridge, Mass.: Harvard University Press, 1974), 51 and 23–55 *passim*; Edward V. Gulick, *Peter Parker and the Opening of China* (Cambridge, Mass.: Harvard University Press, 1973).

11  Field, "Near East Notes," 53–5.

12  C. Howard Hopkins, *John R. Mott, 1865–1955* (Geneva: World Council of Churches, 1979), 665.

13  Richard Wightman Fox, *Reinhold Niebuhr: A Biography* (New York: Pantheon, 1985), 239.

14  Helen Waite Coleman, *The Camp Diamond Story*, privately printed, n.d. (ca. 1942); William R. Hutchison, *Errand to the World: American Protestant Thought and Foreign Missions* (Chicago: University of Chicago Press, 1987), 164–75.

15  William Adams Brown, *A Teacher and His Times* (New York: Scribner's, 1940), 144–55.

16  *1933 Yearbook*, 311–16. Methodists, more proportionately, numbered 2, 500.

17  Will Herberg, *Protestant-Catholic-Jew: An Essay in Religious Sociology* (New York: Doubleday, 1955).

18  W. Lloyd Warner and Paul S. Lunt, *The Social Life of a Modern Community* (New Haven: Yale University Press, 1941), 5.

19  Ibid., 188–93.

20  Robert S. Lynd and Helen Merrell Lynd, *Middletown: A Study in Contemporary American Culture* (New York: Harcourt, Brace, 1929), 349–50.

21  James DeForest Murch, *The Protestant Revolt: Road to Freedom for the American Churches* (Arlington, Va.: Crestwood Books, 1967), 25.

22  Ibid., 27–8.

23  William R. Hutchison, *The Modernist Impulse in American Protestantism* (Cambridge, Mass.: Harvard University Press, 1976), 260 and chapters 6–8 *passim*.

24  C. Howard Hopkins, *The Rise of the Social Gospel in American Protestantism, 1865–1915* (New Haven: Yale University Press, 1940), 280–98.

# 5

# American Fundamentalism: The Ideal of Femininity

## Randall Balmer

## Introduction

Belief in the sacredness of women's roles as wives and mothers in the context of their submission to male authority is one of the most significant features of religious conservatism in America today. This conservative idealization of women's domestic roles is partly a reaction to feminism, especially to feminism's attack on gender-role stereotypes and corresponding commitment to women's empowerment and self-fulfillment. At the same time, the conservative idealization of women's domestic roles reflects an even deeper desire to recover a well-ordered world of the past in which the confusions, corruptions, and instabilities of the present are resolved. In this respect, the idealization of women's domestic roles among religious conservatives in America today exemplifies a basic conservative tendency, often inherent in religion itself, to believe in a mythical world of the past that sets the standard for human behavior in the present.

In the context of American religious history, images of the Puritan family contribute to this mythology of the past. Not only did Puritans themselves idealize affectionate, hierarchical marriage and well-ordered family life, but later Americans, especially conservative Protestant Americans, idealized the Puritan family as part of their own religious identity. In addition, as Randall

Excerpted from Randall Balmer, "American Fundamentalism: The Ideal of Femininity," in *Fundamentalism and Gender*, ed. John Stratton Hawley (New York: Oxford University Press, 1994), 47–62. Copyright © 1994 by Oxford University Press, Inc. Used by permission of Oxford University Press, Inc.

Balmer explains, the conservative Protestant ideal of femininity reflects elements of nineteenth-century American Victorian culture, especially its celebration of maternal tenderness and the sweet comforts of home. The Victorian ideal of domestic femininity, along with its partner, an ideal of manhood emphasizing the husband's role as protector and provider, play important roles in the mythology of American fundamentalism and, in varying degrees, in the mythologies of other forms of American religious conservatism.

During a 1989 television interview, Bailey Smith, a fundamentalist and an official in the Southern Baptist Convention, offered his views of women. "The highest form of God's creation," he said, "is womankind."[1]

Such pronouncements are so commonplace among American fundamentalists that it is easy to gloss over their significance. Those who purport to be the twentieth-century guardians of Christian orthodoxy – a tradition that, more often than not, has blamed Eve for Adam's downfall – now trumpet the unique purity of women, the "highest form of God's creation."

These encomiums permeate fundamentalist piety. If you page through a fundamentalist songbook, you will find all sorts of examples of women alternately praying and weeping for their children, waiting for wayward, sometimes drunken, sons to come home. "Tell Mother I'll Be There," for instance, is a forlorn, anguished cry from one such son who wants desperately to assure his mother, now "home with Jesus," that her prayers have been answered. These paeans to female piety intensify as Mother's Day approaches each year:

> Mother is the sweetest word
> You and I have ever heard!
> Mother, oh how dear the thought,
> A bit of heaven you have brought![2]

Or consider the rather unpoetic chorus from a song entitled "Praying Mothers" by Tammy Deville:

> Praying mothers, Christian homes,
> Keeping families together where they belong;
> Teaching trust, respect, faith and love,
> Reverence to our God above.
> With love to godly mothers,
> We sing this song.[3]

All of this might be dismissed merely as vulgar sentimentality, the Protestant counterpart to popular Catholic pinings for the Virgin

Mary, but the celebration of female piety by fundamentalists has a particular focus in the home. If the Blessed Virgin ever sorted socks, scrubbed the kitchen floor, or worried about ring around the collar, we seldom hear about it, even from her most devoted followers.

Not so for fundamentalist women, who are overwhelmingly white and middle class. Their identity is tied almost exclusively to motherhood and to what one fundamentalist writer has called "the oft-maligned delights of homemaking."[4] You do not have to look very far in fundamentalist literature to find celebrations of motherhood and female domesticity. "Raising children is a blessing from the Lord, and I can't imagine a home without the mother being there," Nancy Tucker, a "stay-at-home mother," wrote in a fundamentalist magazine.[5] "Being a mother, and filling mother's place, is one of the greatest responsibilities there is in this ... world," an editorial in *The Way of Truth* proclaimed. "Those who feel that a woman is wasting her time, and burying her talents, in being a wife and mother in the home, are simply blinded by the 'gods' of this world." Such domestic duties, the editorial continued, must not be taken lightly:

> What a grave and sacred responsibility this is. To provide food, clothing, and shelter, may be the easiest part for many couples. To be a true *mother* goes far beyond supplying these temporal needs. The love, the nurturing, the careful guiding, the moral example, the moral teaching, the training, is the most important of all.[6]

An article in *Kindred Spirit*, a magazine published by Dallas Theological Seminary, echoes this theme. "In many ways God measures a woman's success by her relationship with her husband and children," the author, a woman, writes. "Many women ache to learn how to be truly successful in marriage and motherhood."[7]

This ideology, of course, is cloaked in biblical literalism. Paul, the apostle, is not usually regarded as a feminist, and fundamentalists generally refuse to see his proscriptions as culturally conditioned. While most fundamentalists have maneuvered around Paul's insistence that women keep their heads covered in church, they cannot see – or have elected *not* to see – his commands to keep silence and to be submissive as similarly culture-bound. Consequently, fundamentalist women are expected to be submissive, to demand no voice of authority in the church or in the home. As the article in *Kindred Spirit* puts it, "Young women need to be taught a biblical view of their roles and relationships with their husbands in order to truly liberate them to be all that God intended them to be and to experience the best that He has for them."[8] Paradoxically, then, fundamentalist women are supposed to feel a kind of liberation in this submission to their husbands. "In seeking to recognize the crucial role of the husband and father as head of the household," the argument goes, "perhaps we have lost sight of the ways that family warmth is generated by the love and security given by a godly wife and mother."[9]

It was not always thus in American history, even in the evangelical tradition.[10] I have already alluded to the discrepancies between historic Christian theology and the contemporary lionization of women by fundamentalists. Through the centuries, Christian theology has often portrayed women as temptresses, the descendants of Eve, the inheritors of a wicked, seductive sensuality that could only be tempered through subordination to men. John Robinson, pastor of the Pilgrims in Plymouth, Massachusetts, for instance, enjoined a "reverend subjection" of the wife to her husband, adding that she must not "shake off the bond of submission, but must bear patiently the burden, which God hath laid upon the daughters of Eve."[11] The Puritans of New England also imbibed traditional suspicions about women; consider their treatment of Anne Hutchinson, their contempt for the Quakers' egalitarian views of women, and the evident misogyny of the Salem witch hysteria. More important, the Puritans regarded the man as both the head of the household and the person responsible for the spiritual nurture and welfare of his children.

Around the turn of the eighteenth century, however, the sermonic rhetoric in New England betrays a shift in sentiment. Women, who joined the churches in far greater numbers than men, began to be extolled as uniquely tender and loving and, hence, as spiritually superior to their husbands, who were increasingly involved in commercial pursuits.[12] Although during the interregnum of the revolutionary era *virtue* was chiefly a political term applied to the fusion of civic humanism with evangelical ardor, by the end of the eighteenth century *virtue* had become synonymous with femininity.[13]

The nineteenth century witnessed a domestic revolution in American life, with the romanticization of the home, changes in gender roles, and, finally, the idealization of female piety. While there is some evidence that the republican ideals of the revolutionary era permeated family life and led, at least for a time, to the relative equality of husbands and wives, the real changes occurred during the Second Great Awakening early in the nineteenth century, when women were freed from institutional restraints in the enthusiasm of the revival.[14] The Second Awakening taught that everyone was equal before God, a notion that combined roughly equal parts of republican ideology and Arminian theology. Charles Grandison Finney's "new measures," moreover, encouraged women's participation in revival meetings, and evangelical women began to assert themselves as leaders of various benevolent and social-reform movements.[15] Some women, such as Phoebe Palmer and Margaret (Maggie) Van Cott, became important evangelists.

Despite the temporary loosening of restraints during times of revival, nineteenth-century women rarely ascended to positions of religious authority. Whenever evangelical women aspired to leadership they were met with stern warnings. Presbyterian minister Ashbel Green, sometime president of the College of New Jersey, reminded his auditors in 1825 that Christ framed women "with that shrinking delicacy of temperament and feeling, which is one of their best distinctions, which renders them amiable." Green acknowledged that this female characteristic, "while it unfits them for command" and "subjects them, in a degree, to the rougher sex, gives them, at the same time, an appropriate and very powerful influence." Green concluded that women could not, however, expect that Christ, "who formed them with this natural and retiring modesty, and under a qualified subjection to men, would ever require, or even permit them, to do anything in violation of his own order."[16]

Did this mean that women had no spiritual role to play whatsoever? On the contrary, women must assume responsibility for the home and, in particular, for the spiritual nurture of the children. "The female breast is the natural soil of Christianity," Benjamin Rush, a fervent evangelical, opined.[17] "It is one of the peculiar and most important duties of Christian women," Ashbel Green wrote, "to instruct and pray with children, and to endeavor to form their tender minds to piety, intelligence and virtue."[18] Here was the proper sphere of female spirituality – as moral guardians of the home, in charge of the religious instruction and nurture of the children. "The family state," Catharine Beecher and Harriet Beecher Stowe wrote in 1869, "is the aptest earthly illustration of the heavenly kingdom, and in it woman is its chief minister."[19] Nineteenth-century evangelical literature fairly brims with examples of maternal piety and persistent prayers that eventually, sometimes even after her death, effect the conversion of a mother's children.[20]

This idea of women as spiritual titans was new in the nineteenth century and peculiar to America. "Although the women of the United States are confined within the narrow circle of domestic life, and their situation is in some respects one of complete dependence," Alexis de Tocqueville, the peripatetic French observer, wrote in 1835, "I have nowhere seen woman occupying a loftier position." After outlining Americans' distinctive and careful division of "the duties of man from those of woman," Tocqueville attributed America's "singular prosperity and growing strength" to "the superiority of their women."[21] Ann Douglas calls this development the "feminization" of American culture, the product of a collusion between nineteenth-century clergy, whose power and status were waning, and housewives eager for some emotional outlet.[22] Males came to be characterized as aggressive and indifferent to godliness, whereas women became the lifeblood of the churches. They were the repositories of virtue, meek and submissive – like Jesus himself.

Thus, female spirituality was upheld as an ideal, a notion taken to its extremes in Shaker theology and even in Christian Science, both of which asserted explicitly the superiority of the feminine and linked the perfection of humanity to womanhood. Women were implicitly more spiritual in nineteenth-century America. They were morally superior to men; they had a greater capacity for religiosity. Women, therefore, became responsible for the inculcation of virtue into their daughters, sons, and husbands. The evangelical women of Utica, New York, for instance, organized themselves in 1824 into a Maternal Association that met biweekly and required that each member pledge to pray for her children daily, to read literature on Christian child-rearing, to set a pious example, and to spend the anniversary of each child's birth in fasting and prayer.[23]

Other forces besides revivalism lay behind this transition from the spiritual patriarchy of the Puritan family to the evangelical household of the nineteenth century. The early republic witnessed the gradual emergence of a market economy and the stirrings of nascent industrialization. Men began to work outside the home and the farm. They eventually organized into guilds as their labor became increasingly specialized. Traditional family and kinship networks thus gave way to associations among fellow workers. Families were no longer self-sufficient; they depended on the fathers' wages. Gender roles became more distinct. "From the numerous avocations to which a professional life exposes gentlemen in America from their families," Benjamin Rush wrote, "a principal share of the instruction of children naturally devolves upon the women."[24] Men increasingly distanced themselves from domestic chores and activities, and women succumbed to the "cult of domesticity" or the "cult of true womanhood," marked by purity, piety, and domesticity.

Thus sentimentalized, women assumed responsibility for domestic life, especially the religious instruction of the children. For many, in fact, the two were inseparable. In his *Treatise on Bread, and Bread-Making*, Sylvester Graham, temperance lecturer and health reformer, explicitly assigned to mothers the responsibility for both the physical and the moral well-being of their children. It is the mother, wrote Graham, "who rightly perceives the relations between the dietetic habits and physical and moral condition of her loved ones, and justly appreciates the importance of good bread to their physical and moral welfare."[25]

Indeed, the sphere of domesticity – including the home, the education and nurture of children, and religious matters generally – was the one area where the nineteenth-century woman reigned supreme, her judgments largely unchallenged. "In matters pertaining to the education of their children, in the selection and support of a clergyman, and in all benevolent enterprises, and in all questions relating to morals or manners, they have a superior influence," Catharine Beecher wrote in *A Treatise on Domestic Economy* in 1841. "In all such concerns, it would be impossible to carry a point, contrary to their judgement and feelings; while an enterprise, sustained by them, will seldom fail of success."[26]

An important theological development – a new focus on religious instruction and socialization – reinforced the importance of female nurture. The tides of revival early in the nineteenth century swept away strict Calvinist doctrines of depravity and original sin, thereby emphasizing the ability of the individual to control his or her spiritual destiny; eventually this downplaying of depravity and the elevation of human volition undermined the traditional emphasis on dramatic conversions. Indeed, Horace Bushnell's *Christian Nurture*, published in 1847, urged that children should be reared from birth as though they were Christian, and insisted that parents should not expect a dramatic conversion experience in their children. Hence, children should be educated and socialized in such a way that they would always consider themselves Christian or, in Puritan terms, among the elect. Who should perform this duty, especially in a society with increasingly differentiated gender roles? With men away at the mill or the factory all day, the task of "Christian nurture" fell to women.

The home thus became the sphere that both defined and delimited female influence. As the Victorian era unfolded, moreover, mechanized production and a commercial economy increasingly eased domestic burdens, especially for the middle-class mother, who often had a hired girl (usually a recent immigrant) to help with household chores. No longer must a woman spend her hours sewing, weaving, making soap, or butchering meat for her home. Instead, her husband's wages and the commercial economy gave her time to fuss over it. A passel of magazines, such as *Godey's Lady's Book*, instructed the Victorian woman on how to decorate her home with ornate woodworking and carvings and a vast array of furnishings – bookcases, clocks, overstuffed chairs – that lay within her budget. The invention of the power loom in 1848 made carpets plentiful and affordable. The parlor organ became a kind of domestic shrine, with its high verticality, its carved, pointed arches, and its nooks, crannies, and shelves for family photographs and mementos. The organ itself, used for family hymn-singing, both symbolized and reinforced religious notions and the ideal of feminine domesticity.

*Mother* played the organ and thereby cemented her role as the religious keystone of the family.[27]

These notions about feminine spirituality have persisted among fundamentalists in the twentieth century. Many of the taboos devised by fundamentalists in their time of beleaguerment in the 1920s and 1930s centered on women. In reaction to the perceived moral laxity of the larger culture, which was careening stubbornly toward judgment, fundamentalists insisted that women forswear worldly adornments, especially jewelry and cosmetics. They devised elaborate parietal rules intended to protect the sexual innocence of their children, especially the girls, who were perceived as vulnerable to the animal cravings of less-spiritual males.

The Victorian myth of feminine spiritual superiority is so entrenched in twentieth-century fundamentalism that many preachers have felt obliged to shake men out of their spiritual complacency.[28] Consider, for instance, the machismo posturings of evangelist Billy Sunday, who insisted that in Jesus we find "the definition of manhood."[29] "God is a masculine God," the fundamentalist firebrand John R. Rice insisted to a male audience in 1947. "God bless women, but He never intended any preacher to be run by a bunch of women."[30] But the intensity of Rice's protestations merely verifies the pervasiveness of the myth. Presbyterian preacher Donald Grey Barnhouse confirmed this in his characterization of a typical Christian household. "The husband is not interested in the things of God, so the family drifts along without any spiritual cohesion," he wrote. "Perhaps they all go to church together on Sunday morning, and the wife goes to all the activities of the week, but the husband seems uninterested." Barnhouse then offered a familiar, albeit paradoxical, prescription for this malaise: feminine submission. "With delight she learns the joy of knowing it is her husband's house, his home; the children are his; she is his wife," he wrote. "When a woman realizes and acknowledges this, the life of the home can be transformed, and the life of her husband also."[31]

This notion reached its apotheosis in the 1970s with the enormous popularity of Marabel Morgan's book *The Total Woman*. The answer to a troubled marriage, Morgan preached, lay in becoming a "Total Woman," a wife who submitted abjectly to her husband and who burrowed herself ever deeper into the putative bliss of domesticity. "A Total Woman caters to her man's special quirks, whether it be salads, sex, or sports," Morgan wrote. "She makes his home a haven, a place to which he can run."[32]

Against the background of this ideal of feminine domesticity, fundamentalists have found the rapidly changing views of women in recent decades utterly disconcerting. Perhaps nothing – not even Darwinism and higher criticism, the issues of the 1920s – has contributed so greatly to their sense of cultural dislocation. American fundamentalists were caught off guard by *The Feminine Mystique*, and the ensuing feminist movement has left them confused and full of resentment because the domestic ideal that fundamentalism has reified since the nineteenth century is now derided as anachronistic by the broader culture. More confusing still is the fact that many fundamentalist women, like American women everywhere, have joined the workforce in the past two decades. On the one hand they are beset by calls from feminists for liberation and self-assertion, and on the other they are peppered from the pulpit by insistent rehearsals of the nineteenth-century ideal of femininity. Those who resist the workplace inevitably feel anger and even shame about being labeled "just a housewife," and they protest loudly about the nobility of tending the home. Often, however, general economic stringency, an unemployed husband, or divorce tips the balance in the general direction of the feminists. But those fundamentalist women are then left with what Leon Festinger calls cognitive dissonance: on the one hand, the necessity of employment; and on the other, the need they feel to perpetuate fundamentalist standards. More often than not, they feel guilt and confusion for "abandoning" their homes and families, thereby violating the fundamentalist feminine ideal.

A question-and-answer exchange in the May 1989 issue of James Dobson's *Focus on the Family* magazine illustrates poignantly this confusion and anger, as well as this pining for a halcyon past. "As a homemaker," the question from an anonymous reader begins, "I resent the fact that my role as wife and mother is no longer respected as it was in my mother's time. What forces have brought about this change in attitudes in the Western world?" Dobson's response is equally illuminating:

> Female sex-role identity has become a major target for change by those who wish to revolutionize the relationship between men and women. The women's movement and the media have been remarkably successful in altering the way females "see" themselves at home and in society. In the process, every element of the traditional concept of femininity has been discredited and scorned, especially those responsibilities associated with homemaking and motherhood.
>
> Thus, in a short period of time, the term *housewife* has become a pathetic symbol of exploitation, oppression, and – pardon the insult – stupidity, at least as viewed from the perspective of radical feminists. We can make no greater mistake as a nation than to continue this pervasive disrespect shown to women who have devoted their lives to the welfare of their families.[33]

Dobson, of course, failed to acknowledge that his "traditional concept of femininity" (and presumably the one shared by his distraught reader) was a nineteenth-century construct.

More significantly, Dobson's response identified the enemy: "radical feminists," the women's movement, and the media. In the face of such a conspiracy, fundamentalists have had to muster their troops, something they have done with remarkable success over the past decade. What is especially striking about the exertion of fundamentalist influence in the American political arena is the extent to which issues of gender – the Equal Rights Amendment, private sexual morality – have shaped their political agenda. Fundamentalists regularly attach the sobriquet "anti-family" to policies and to politicians they regard as inimical; and they have, curiously, attached singular attention to the issue of abortion.

In recent years, fundamentalists have tried, with considerable success, to propel abortion to the center of political debate. A group of activists calling itself Operation Rescue, many of whose members are fundamentalists, has picketed and blocked abortion clinics in New York, Atlanta, Wichita, and other cities around the country. Anti-abortion hecklers regularly disrupted Democratic rallies during the 1988 presidential campaign.

The Supreme Court's *Roe* v. *Wade* decision on January 22, 1973, which effectively struck down existing state laws banning an abortion, was initially greeted with silence or indifference by fundamentalists; but by the end of the decade, as they began to mobilize politically, the abortion issue helped to galvanize them into a potent political force. Jerry Falwell, for instance, credited that decision with awakening him from his apolitical stupor, even though he had declared some years earlier that he "would find it impossible to stop preaching the pure saving gospel of Jesus Christ, and begin doing anything else – including fighting Communism, or participating in civil-rights reforms." Falwell thereby articulated a fairly common fundamentalist attitude in the mid-sixties. "Nowhere are we commissioned to reform the externals," he said. "We are not told to wage war against bootleggers, liquor stores, gamblers, murderers, prostitutes, racketeers, prejudiced persons or institutions, or any other existing evil as such."[34]

*Roe* v. *Wade*, however, together with what Falwell regarded as sundry assaults on the family, triggered an about-face. By the end of the decade Falwell had shed his political naïveté and had organized his "Moral Majority" to counter the evil influences in American culture that threatened to subvert the fundamentalist ideal of femininity. Other fundamentalist leaders have professed similar reactions and indignation to *Roe* v. *Wade*, and I have spoken with many fundamentalists who become visibly angry, almost apoplectic, when discussing abortion.

On the face of it, abortion is an odd issue to use as a rallying point. Fundamentalists pride themselves on taking the Bible literally, but, all of their tortured exegeses notwithstanding, nothing in the scriptures *explicitly* dictates a "pro-life" position. Nor does the fundamentalist fervor over abortion arise from any abstract commitment to the sanctity of all real and potential human life (in that respect, the "pro-life" moniker, which the activists prefer to "anti-abortion," is something of a misnomer). Many fundamentalists who decry abortion will, in the next breath, declare their unequivocal support for capital punishment. And fundamentalists have never been squeamish about the exercise of military force by the United States or its proxies, even when directed against civilians: witness their overwhelming support for the Contras of Central America, the US bombing of Libya, and the wars in Vietnam, Grenada, Panama, and the Persian Gulf.

Why, then, have so many fundamentalists invested such extraordinary passion into this crusade? Why would hundreds of otherwise law-abiding citizens be willing to go to jail to underscore their opposition to abortion? I do not wish to trivialize fundamentalist convictions on this issue. I find some of their arguments compelling and most of them sincere; but it is difficult, at first glance, to understand the centrality of abortion to the fundamentalist political agenda.

I think the answer to this conundrum lies more in the realm of symbols than in ideology, and it relates in particular to the historical circumstances of fundamentalism in the twentieth century. For much of the century, fundamentalists have felt beleaguered and besieged by forces beyond their control. Whereas in the nineteenth century evangelicals had shaped much of the nation's social and political agenda, by the late 1800s rapid urbanization, industrialization, and the massive arrival of immigrants (most of them non-Protestants) made America look a good deal less congenial to evangelicals than it had during the evangelical heyday earlier in the century. Teeming, squalid tenements no longer resembled the precincts of Zion.

By the late nineteenth and early twentieth centuries, moreover, evangelicals felt the sting of evolutionary theory, which, pressed to its logical conclusions, undermined literal understandings of the Bible. The Scopes trial of 1925 finally convinced many fundamentalists that American culture had become inhospitable, even hostile, so they retreated into their own subculture of denominations, publishing houses, mission societies, Bible camps, and Bible institutes.

Although other factors played a role in their reentry into public life in the mid-1970s – a resurgent patriotism after the national ignominies of Vietnam and Watergate and following the presidential candidacy of a Southern Baptist Sunday-school teacher (whom they later abandoned) –

fundamentalists latched onto the abortion issue with a vengeance. Given their own history, however, their identification with the fetus is not surprising. For fundamentalists, the fetus serves as a marvelous symbol, not only because of its Freudian or psychoanalytic connotations of crawling back into the womb to escape the buffetings of the world, but because they see it in their own image. "Abortion is the symbol of our decline," Randall Terry, head of Operation Rescue, told a reporter for the *New York Times*, "the slaughter of the most innocent."[35] Nothing is so pure and untainted as an unborn child; fundamentalists, in turn, view themselves as the guardians of moral purity in an immoral world.

At the same time, nothing is so vulnerable as a fetus, and fundamentalists for decades have seen themselves as vulnerable. "We are providing a voice and a defense for the human and civil rights of millions of unborn babies," Falwell wrote in 1987, explaining the political agenda of Moral Majority.[36] "The most dangerous place to be these days is inside a mother's womb," an anti-abortion activist in Iowa told me just before the precinct caucuses in February 1988. Many fundamentalists, I believe, readily identify with that sentiment. Despite their political successes in the past decade, contemporary fundamentalists, like their predecessors in the 1920s, still see American culture as alien and their own existence as precarious. They must exercise extraordinary vigilance lest the forces of evil and darkness, usually identified as "secular humanism," overtake them. In a fund-raising letter issued after the Supreme Court's *Webster* v. *Reproductive Health Services* decision, which allowed the State of Missouri to impose new restrictions on the availability of abortions, James Dobson reminded his readers that "the pro-life movement is only part of a much larger conflict that rages today. What is really at stake is the future of the Judeo-Christian system of values in this country." Dobson concluded the letter by assuring his readers (and contributors) that "we will fight to the death for the moral values in which we believe."[37]

Abortion, moreover, violates the cherished fundamentalist ideal of feminine domesticity. If women guarded their purity and contented themselves with their divinely ordained roles as mothers and housewives, abortion would never be though necessary at all. For fundamentalists, the very fact that abortion is a political issue in the first place provides an index of how dramatically American culture has deserted their ideal of femininity. The roots of the "disorder," then, can be found in female restiveness, a popular unwillingness to accept the role that God had designed for women. According to Susan Key, a homemaker from Dallas, Texas, who devised a course for women called Eve Reborn, God gave women "a unique capacity for submission and obedience and when this capacity is thwarted by rebellion and deceit, it becomes a capacity to destroy which begins to work within her heart and then sulks out to her intimate relationships, widens to her acquaintances, to society, and then into history."[38]

But if benighted and wayward women contributed to the massive cultural malaise that fundamentalists so decry, women also, because of their exalted spirituality, hold the key to redemption. "I firmly believe the role of a woman today is to nurture our next generation," Maxine Sieleman of Concerned Women for America said during the 1988 presidential primaries, thereby echoing nineteenth-century evangelical notions of virtue. "She has the power within her hands to either make or break a nation. A good woman can make a bad man good, but a bad woman can make a good man bad. . . . Women are the real key for turning this country around. . . . I firmly believe that God has always worked through women."[39] Phyllis Schlafly, who almost singlehandedly defeated the proposed Equal Rights Amendment to the constitution, said it more succinctly in *The Power of the Positive Woman*. The ideal woman, according to Schlafly, was not merely a housewife but a "patriot and defender of our Judeo-Christian civilization." Moreover, "It is the task of the Positive Woman to keep America good."[40] Compare the sentiments of Catharine Beecher in *A Treatise on Domestic Economy*, published in 1841:

> The mother writes the character of the future man; the sister bends the fibres that hereafter are the forest tree; the wife sways the heart, whose energies may turn for good or for evil the destinies of a nation. Let the women of a country be made virtuous and intelligent, and the men will certainly be the same.

Beecher added that "the formation of the moral and intellectual character of the young is committed mainly to the female hand."[41]

The political agenda of contemporary fundamentalists, then, represents a desperate attempt to reclaim the nineteenth-century ideal of femininity both for themselves and for a culture that has abandoned that ideal. For American fundamentalists, women serve as a kind of bellwether for the culture at large. If women allow themselves to be seduced by "radical feminists" into abandoning their "God-given" responsibilities in the home, America is in trouble. If, however, women cling to Victorian notions of submission, nurture, and domesticity, the future of the republic is secure. Far from the temptress of earlier Christian orthodoxy, the contemporary woman, in the rhetoric of American fundamentalism, can be a redeemer. What better demonstration of her superior spirituality?

Such notions, however, face tough opposition in the latter decades of the twentieth century. Despite their recent political success, American fundamentalists remain on the defensive, trying to shore up what the broader culture now considers a quaint, anachronistic view of women. Whatever the merits of their arguments, the fundamentalist political agenda and particularly their struggle against abortion may represent, at some (albeit subconscious) level, a battle for their own survival as well as a struggle for the preservation of a nineteenth-century ideal.

## Notes

1 Bailey Smith, on *Larry King Live*, March 21, 1989.
2 Edward M. Brandt, "Mother," *The Way of Truth* 47 (May 1989): 2.
3 Tammy Deville, "Praying Mothers," *The Way of Truth* 47 (May 1989): 2.
4 Barbara A. Peil, "A Seasoned Approach," *Kindred Spirit* II (Spring 1987): 13.
5 "Motherhood in the '90s," *Focus on Family* 14 (January 1990): 2.
6 "Mother," *The Way of Truth* 47 (May 1989): [ii], 1.
7 Peil, "Seasoned Approach," 12.
8 Ibid., 13.
9 Ibid.
10 I shall use the term *evangelical* to refer to conservative Protestants of the nineteenth century. Because fundamentalists derive their name from the series of pamphlets published between 1910 and 1915, it would be ana-chronistic to refer to their nineteenth-century evangelical forebears as *fundamentalists*, even though the two share many beliefs in common.
11 Cited in Rosemary Radford Ruether and Rosemary Skinner Keller, eds., *Women and Religion in America*, 3 vols. (San Francisco: Harper & Row, 1981–6), 2: 161.
12 Gerald F. Moran, " 'Sisters in Christ': Women and the Church in Seven-teenth-Century New England," in Janet Wilson James, ed., *Women in American Religion* (Philadelphia, 1976), 47–65; Laurel Thatcher Ulrich, "Vertuous Women Found: New England Ministerial Literature, 1668–1735," in *Women in American Religion*, 67–88.
13 Ruth H. Bloch, "The Gendered Meanings of *Virtue* in Revolutionary America," *Signs* 13 (1987): 37–58.
14 See Jan Lewis, "The Republican Wife: Virtue and Seduction in the Early Republic," *William & Mary Quarterly*, 3d ser., 44 (October 1987): 689–721.
15 Susan Juster writes: "The restoration of agency is the key to understanding women's experience of grace. . . . these women were empowered by recover-ing their sense of self through the assertion of independence from others." " 'In a Different Voice': Male and Female Narratives of Religious Conversion in Post-Revolutionary America," *American Quarterly* 41 (March 1989): 53.
16 *Women and Religion in America*, 1:34.
17 *Women and Religion in America*, 2:402.
18 *Women and Religion in America*, 1:36.

19  Catharine E. Beecher and Harriet Beecher Stowe, *The American Woman's Home; or, Principles of Domestic Science; being a Guide to the Formation and Maintenance of Economical Healthful Beautiful and Christian Homes* (New York: J. B. Ford, 1869), 19.

20  For one particularly well-known example, see *The American Woman's Home*, 28–9. See also Sandra S. Sizer, *Gospel Hymns and Social Religion: The Rhetoric of Nineteenth-Century Revivalism* (Philadelphia: Temple University Press, 1978), chapter 4.

21  Alexis de Tocqueville, *Democracy in America*, trans. Henry Reeve, ed. Henry Steele Commager (New York: Oxford University Press, 1947), 401, 403.

22  Ann Douglas, *The Feminization of American Culture* (New York: Alfred A. Knopf, 1977).

23  Mary P. Ryan, "A Women's Awakening: Evangelical Religion and the Families of Utica, New York, 1800–1840," in *Women in American Religion*, 107.

24  *Women and Religion in America*, 2:401.

25  Sylvester Graham, *A Treatise on Bread, and Bread-Making* (Boston: Light & Stearns, 1837), 105–6.

26  Catharine E. Beecher, *A Treatise on Domestic Economy, for the Use of Young Ladies at Home, and at School* (Boston: March, Capen, Lyon, and Webb, 1841), 9.

27  These ideas of Victorian domestic culture are developed nicely by Colleen McDannell, *The Christian Home in Victorian America, 1840–1900* (Bloomington: Indiana University Press, 1986).

28  The "feminization" of American Protestantism in the nineteenth century extended well beyond the evangelical ambit, and so did the various reclamation efforts undertaken early in the twentieth century. See Gail Bederman, " 'The Women Have Had Charge of the Church Work Long Enough': The Men and Religion Forward Movement of 1911–1912 and the Masculinization of Middle-Class Protestantism," *American Quarterly* 61 (1989): 432–65.

29  Quoted in Douglas Frank, *Less than Conquerors: How Evangelicals Entered the Twentieth Century* (Grand Rapids: W. B. Eerdmans, 1986), 192.

30  *Women and Religion in America*, 3:260, 261.

31  Ibid., 261, 262.

32  Marabel Morgan, *The Total Woman* (Old Tappan, NJ: Fleming H. Revell, 1973, 55.

33  "Dr. Dobson Answers Your Questions," *Focus on the Family* (May 1989): 8.

34  Quoted in Frances FitzGerald, "A Disciplined, Charging Army," *New Yorker*, May 18, 1981, p. 63.

35  Tamar Lewin, "With Thin Staff and Thick Debt, Anti-Abortion Group Faces Struggle," *New York Times*, June 11, 1990, p. A11.

36  Jerry Falwell, "An Agenda for the 1980s," in Richard John Neuhaus and Michael Cromartie, eds., *Piety and Politics: Evangelicals and Fundamentalists Confront the World* (Washington, DC: Ethics and Public Policy Center, 1987), 114.

37 Letter, dated August 1989, from James Dobson, *Focus on the Family*, 2, 7.
38 Quoted in Carol Flake, *Redemptorama: Culture, Politics, and the New Evangelicalism* (Garden City, NY: Anchor Press, 1984), 70.
39 Quoted in Randall Balmer, *Mine Eyes Have Seen the Glory: A Journey into the Evangelical Subculture in America* (New York: Oxford University Press, 1989), 120–1.
40 Quoted in Flake, *Redemptorama*, 87.
41 Beecher, *Treatise on Domestic Economy*, 13.

# 6

# Catholicism and American Culture: Strategies for Survival

## Jay P. Dolan

## Introduction

During the sixteenth century, Christians in Europe and Britain divided into two main branches, those who remained loyal to the Church of Rome, with its long history as a unifying force in the Western world, and those who joined Protestant sects and churches that expressed a new, modern spirit of individualism. Like other Protestants, the Puritans who carried the Protestant Reformation forward in England and America often defined themselves in opposition to the Church of Rome, which they claimed had infected the original purity of Christianity with priestly corruption. Meanwhile, Catholics worked to defend themselves against Protestant intolerance on one hand and to define their own understanding of the role of Christianity in the modern world on the other.

In America, Catholics were divided on the issue of the Church's relationship to modern society, and to American society in particular. As Jay Dolan explains, many embraced democracy with enthusiasm and were optimistic about the fit between Catholicism and American society and the role the Catholic Church was destined to play in American religious history. Others took a more traditional view of the Church, emphasizing the dissonance between American democracy and Catholic teaching and piety, and expressing pessimism about the relationship between Christianity and modern soci-

Excerpted from Jay P. Dolan, "Catholicism and American Culture: Strategies for Survival," in *Minority Faiths and the Protestant Mainstream*, ed. Jonathan D. Sarna (Urbana: University of Illinois Press, 1998), 61–80.

ety. For these conservative Catholics, the Church stood in opposition to the progressive, individualistic spirit of modern America, as well as to the atheism associated with Marxist ideology and the rise of communism.

During the second Vatican Council of the 1960s, the Catholic Church reversed its official rejection of modern society, proclaiming that the Church had a pastoral mission to the modern world and that the people of God and their presence in the world defined the Church as much as its priestly hierarchy and historic buildings. In response to this reversal, conservative Catholics developed countercultural constituencies within the Church. Progressive Catholics, once a minority tradition within the Church, became a majority after Vatican II, especially in the United States.

The relationship between religion and American culture has fascinated scholars for years. Protestants, Catholics, and Jews have grappled with the issue since setting foot on the North American continent. For Cecil Calvert, the English Catholic founder of Maryland, it was an issue that surfaced in England even before the first wave of settlers set sail for Maryland in 1633. To encourage Protestants to join his Maryland adventure, he issued strict instructions to his brother Leonard, the governor of the new colony, urging that Catholic adventurers practice their religion in private during the course of the journey across the ocean lest they offend the sensibilities of the numerous Protestants sailing with them.

Once a government was established in Maryland, one of its first acts was to pass a law in 1639 to guarantee that the "Holy Churches within this province shall have all their rights and liberties." Ten years after this legislation, the Maryland assembly passed another, more detailed law known as the Act Concerning Religion, which sought to guarantee the toleration of differing Christian religions. Although it was neither an eloquent statement on behalf of religious freedom nor a radical proposal for the separation of church and state, it did represent a significant effort to adapt the Catholic European tradition regarding the relationship between church and state to a New World environment.

Throughout the colonial era Catholics in Maryland continued to modify their religious traditions to fit the Chesapeake situation. Given the absence of churches, their religion became centered in the home; given the scarcity of clergy, lay people became more involved in maintaining and sustaining the Catholic tradition. Such persistent efforts represented a conscious attempt to design a strategy for the survival of religion in a new cultural context. This was true not just for Catholics but for Protestants and Jews as well.

Although numerous examples of the adaptation of Catholicism to American culture were present during the colonial era, a more significant place to begin an examination of that relationship is the republican era that began in the late eighteenth century (1780–1820). The American Revolution and the birth of a new nation had begun a period that historians are inclined to label the age of democracy. It was a transitional time that transformed religion in America in the same manner that it changed political life. In religion as in politics, the people's choice became determinative. People sought to gain control over their own destinies, spiritual as well as political. Heaven was democratized, and salvation became a possibility for all God's children not just the Calvinist elect. This democratic surge altered the landscape of American religion. It was the driving force behind the growth of Methodism, it gave birth to the Disciples of Christ, and it was a major reason for the popularity of Joseph Smith and the Mormons. It also shaped the organization of synagogues as Jews sought to declare their rights and privileges. The passion for democracy permeated the Catholic community as well, particularly in the government of local parishes.

The American legal system encouraged the development of the trustee form of church government, a style Catholics quickly adopted. The system endorsed four major principles of the democratic experience: the sovereignty of the people, popular elections, religious freedom, and a written constitution. In his study of trusteeism in this period, Patrick Carey has shown how the spirit of democracy surged through the Catholic community and changed how people thought about their church. In desiring to have it adapt to American culture, Catholics wanted their religion to be more in step with the times and reflect the prevailing democratic spirit.[1]

Catholics who advocated this new style of government were pushing for more than just accommodation. They had a different understanding of what the church should be. In their opinion, the monarchical tradition of European Catholicism was not suited to the United States. As one prominent Catholic layman put it, "This people never will submit to the regime in civil or ecclesiastical affairs that prevails in Europe. . . . a different order prevails in this country. . . . The extreme freedom of our civil institutions has produced a corresponding independent spirit respecting church affairs. . . . The opinion and the wishes of the people require to be consulted to a degree unknown in Europe."[2] Mathew Carey, who wrote these words, and others like him wanted the church to be more democratic and less monarchical or authoritarian; they wanted "a National American Church with liberties consonant to the spirit of government under which they live."[3] In advocating more democracy they articulated in an inchoate manner an understanding of church that was modern and democratic rather than feudal and monarchical.

Just as the spirit of democracy influenced the way Catholics thought about their church, the spirit of the Enlightenment changed the way they thought about their God. Joseph Chinnici has written extensively on this subject and in a convincing manner has documented how the Enlightenment influenced Catholic thought.[4] John Carroll, for example, the first bishop of Baltimore, was a child of the Enlightenment; he endorsed religious toleration, the separation of church and state, the personal, interior dimension of religion, and the support of benevolent causes. His was a reasonable piety rooted in natural reason but perfected by divine revelation. Mathew Carey, a prominent Irish Catholic immigrant in Philadelphia, was yet another example of the Enlightenment way of thought. Carey was a strong advocate of the "spirit of toleration" that he said "distinquishes this enlightened age." His religion had a strong personalist quality as well as a heavy dose of moralism. A humanist, he found inspiration in the classical writers and what he termed their "genuine Roman or Grecian spirit."[5] In addition, he found nurture in the ritual and sacraments of Catholicism and respected the authority of the clergy. Like many people of his time who sought "to adapt their belief in God to modern ideas," Carey integrated the doctrine of Catholicism with the demands of reason so central to Enlightenment thinking.[6] He was able to reconcile moralism and spirituality, faith and reason, and nature and the supernatural. In this manner Carey integrated his religion with the culture of the age so that his Catholicism blended with the prevalent Enlightenment culture.

It is evident that throughout the republican era some Catholics attempted to adapt their religion to the American cultural environment, which was permeated by Enlightenment thought and inspired by democratic ideals. But this was not the only strategy of adaptation Catholics adopted. Another understanding of Catholicism was prevalent in the United States, and that view eventually became the dominant model. It was a more traditional model of the church that emphasized the weakness of human nature, the prevalence of sin, and the need for the church and its clergy to help people overcome the worldly environment. It stressed the authority of the hierarchy and the subordinate role of the laity; its model of government was the medieval monarchy and not the modern republic. Historians have labeled this model of Catholicism "Tridentine Catholicism" after the Council of Trent because that sixteenth-century church council promoted the reformation of Catholicism by endorsing such a style of religion. Tridentine Catholicism was prevalent in eighteenth-century Europe, and by the middle of the nineteenth century, after a brief period when Enlightenment-inspired Catholicism had gained popularity, the model was revived and restored to prominence.

A fine exemplar of Tridentine Catholicism was Ambrose Marechal, John Carroll's successor as the archbishop of Baltimore. Born in France,

Marechal joined the Sulpicians, a society of diocesan priests, and was ordained a priest in 1792 in Paris. He fled Paris because of the turmoil of the French revolution, not even taking time to celebrate his first Mass as a priest. He headed for the United States, where he worked primarily as a missionary in Pennsylvania and Maryland and also taught some courses at St. Mary's, a seminary operated by the Sulpicians in Baltimore. When the revolution cooled, he returned to France for a few years and then was sent back to Baltimore to teach again at St. Mary's. In 1817 he was appointed the archbishop of Baltimore.

As the archbishop of Baltimore, Marechal strongly opposed any efforts to promote a republican model of Catholicism. He endorsed the idea of religious liberty but wanted no part of democracy in the church. As far as he was concerned, the spirit of democracy was the reason for many of the church's problems in the new nation. Americans loved "the civil liberty which they enjoy," he wrote. As he put it, "The principle of civil liberty is paramount with them," and even the lowest magistrate is elected by the vote of the people. Such principles governed Protestant churches, and in his opinion Catholics "are exposed to the danger of admitting the same principles of ecclesiastical government." Marechal strongly opposed this tendency and sought to establish the supreme authority of the clergy and weaken the power of the lay trustee system.[7] His model of the church was very French and very monarchical. Moreover, it was the model gaining ascendency in France after the downfall of Napoleon in 1814.

Like Marechal, many other French clergy fled to the United States during the revolution, and most of them included in their cultural bagage a traditional understanding of Catholicism. Their presence was especially influential in Kentucky, where they sought to shape the piety of the people according to the French model. The French-born Stephen Badin and his Belgian-born contemporary Charles Nerinckx were pioneer priests in Kentucky. They brought their own style of Catholicism to the new nation, and any idea of adapting the traditional French style of Catholicism to the United States was totally foreign to them. They were especially noted for promoting a stern code of morality that discouraged dancing and theatergoing. Although Enlightenment Catholicism encouraged a personal and plain style of religion that stressed the positive side of human nature, toleration, and the reasonableness of religion, the moralism of Badin and Nerinckx was rooted in a negative view of human nature and the need to curb its evil tendencies. Their severity in the confessional was well known, and people complained continuously about both men. Nerinckx, for example, told people to rise at 4 a.m. and forbade them to dance; Badin would impose such penances as holding a hot coal while reciting the Our Father and the Hail Mary or digging a shallow grave and lying in it a brief time each day for a week. Although they were eccentric in their understanding of spiritual life, the priests shared a fundamentally pesimistic view of human nature characteristic of European Catholicism. Many Kentucky Catholics did not approve of that style of piety, and their resistance suggests that they were attuned to a more moderate and positive type of spirituality.[8]

Badin conducted many parish missions, the Catholic counterpart to Protestant revivals, along the Kentucky frontier, and they too promoted this understanding of Catholicism in which sin and fear were the foundation on which religion rested. These French missionaries were bringing their own style of Catholicism to the new nation, and any idea of adapting the traditional French style of Catholicism to the United States was totally foreign to them.

Kentucky was also the setting for clashes between the monarchical and republican models of Catholicism. Kentucky Catholics were known as ardent Jeffersonians and supported a republican view of government in both the civic and religious arena. The absence of clergy encouraged lay leadership, and most congregations organized themselves into religious societies and wrote republican constitutions that supported the idea of lay trustees. Badin, however, resisted what he called such "extravagant pretensions of Republicanism" and continually opposed any manifestation of lay independence. The bishop of Bardstown, Benedict Flaget, also had to deal with such independence and acknowledged that the people were indeed "good republicans."[9]

The contrast between the two opposing views of the church was captured clearly in a letter written by the French-born bishop of New Orleans to a Vatican official: "It is scarcely possible to realize how contagious even to the clergy and to men otherwise well disposed, are the principles of freedom and independence imbibed by all the pores in these United States. Hence I have always been convinced that practically all the good to be hoped for must come from the Congregations or religious Orders among which flourish strict discipline."[10] Discipline in a hierarchical church was essential, whereas independence and freedom were counterproductive to the goals of an organization based on authority and the chain of command.

By 1800 it was clear that Catholics in the United States supported two different and competing understandings of Roman Catholicism. One encouraged the idea of the adaptation of religion to the American cultural environment, and the other sought to transplant the European model intact. The dilemma facing US Catholics concerned how to be both Catholic and American. The traditional understanding of Catholicism emphasized such virtues as authority and conformity, which seemingly went against the grain of the American ideals of freedom and independence; the more American, more modern understanding stressed such virtues as democracy and toleration, which appeared incompatible with the traditional Tridentine model. The tension between the two understandings had existed since the earliest days of the Maryland colony, when the Calverts, who supported an accommodationist view, did battle with Jesuit missionaries who wanted to transplant the clerical privileges they enjoyed in Europe to the Maryland frontier. Matters became more intense after the American Revolution, when a popular surge of democracy took hold in an environment greatly influenced by Enlightenment thought.

The end of the republican period coincided with the advent of large-scale immigration, and Roman Catholicism was one of the religions most affected by that development. Immigrant laity and clergy brought to the United States a European model of church that was not in harmony with the spirit of democracy. As a result, the republican style of Catholicism that surfaced during the decades following the Revolution became less popular and plausible. Catholicism became a church of immigrants, and the major challenge for much of the nineteenth century was to provide for their religious needs. The visibly immigrant nature of Catholicism intensified with each decade and raised the question of the relationship between Catholicism and American culture, an issue that would persist throughout the century of immigration from 1820 to 1920. It became especially significant during the 1850s.

The protagonist of this discussion was Orestes Brownson, a recent American convert to Catholicism and a well-known writer. In the summer and fall of 1854 Brownson published a series of controversial articles in *Brownson's Quarterly Review*, arguing that the Irish and all other immigrants "must ultimately lose their own nationality and become assimilated in general character to the Anglo-American race." The Irish resented this and accused Brownson of being anti-Irish and soft on anti-Catholic nativists.[11] He had clearly endorsed the Americanization strategy – that is, the need for Catholics to adapt to American culture – and reiterated that theme two years later at a July commencement address at St. John's College. In the address, most of which appeared in an essay Brownson published in the fall of 1856, he celebrated the American nation, "a people with a great destiny, and a destiny glorious to ourselves and beneficent to the world."[12]

The essay, "Mission of America," was in the spirit of Manifest Destiny, a popular expression and belief that celebrated the providential role and destiny the United States possessed. Brownson rejected the idea that Catholics should "separate themselves from the great current of American nationality, and . . . assume the position in political and social life of an inferior, a distinct, or an alien people, or of a foreign colony planted in the midst of a people with whom they have no sympathies." Rather, he wanted them to "take their position as free and equal American citizens, with American interests and sympathies, American sentiments and affections, and throw themselves fearlessly into the great current of American national life." For Brownson, being American meant possessing "self-reliance, energy, perserverance," what he called "the chief elements of success." Most important, he believed that the future of America rested in the hands of Catholics. "It is only through Catholicity that the country can fulfill its mission. . . . The salvation of the country and its future glory depend on Catholics." He concluded by warning that it was "the duty of all Catholic citizens . . . to be, or to make themselves, thorough-going Americans." Those who would not he considered to be " 'outside barbarians' and not within the pale of the American order."[13]

It would be hard to find a more explicit endorsement of the Americanization strategy, but it was not to go unchallenged. At the end of the St. John's commencement ceremony, the archbishop of New York, John Hughes, addressed the students. As one person noted, he "harangued the graduates with completely opposing views, denying the existence of the advantages the laws of the country are said to offer Catholics, which Brownson had taken pains to emphasize; asserting further that liberty for Catholics existed only on paper, and not in fact, and exhorting them to prepare for days of oppression and persecution in the future."[14] Hughes clearly wanted Brownson to avoid any "allusion to the nationality of our Catholic brethren" and did not want him to "write or say anything calculated to represent the Catholic religion as especially adapted to the genius of the American people as such."[15]

Even though Hughes was clearly not launching an anti-American tirade, he did not agree with Brownson about the advantages that the United States held for Catholics. This was not surprising, given the wave of anti-Catholicism sweeping the country in the 1840s and 1850s. He also wanted to avoid endorsing any nationality over another. But Hughes did go further, and in a letter to Brownson he denied the convert's contention that "if the Catholic religion had been or could now be presented to the American people through mediums and under auspices more congenial with the national feelings and habits, the progress of the Church and the conversion of Protestants would have been far greater."[16]

What Hughes was saying was that Catholicism could not and should not adapt to American culture. Brownson had hinted at this in an imperfect manner, but he never developed it or explained how it would happen. The most he could say was that "grace does not destroy nature, nor change the national type of character. It purifies and elevates nature, and brings out whatever is good, noble, and strong in the national type."

If Catholicism could be "adapted to the wants of the simple, the rude, the barbarian, and the savage," he said, surely it could adapt itself to the "active, energetic, self-reliant American character."[17]

The controversy between Brownson and Hughes was about more than nationality. Brownson clearly wanted Catholics to become more American, and Hughes saw this emphasis as divisive. He wanted to emphasize the Catholic dimension of the American Catholic dilemma. He was more interested in self-defense, intent on transplanting the Catholicism of the Old World to the United States and establishing an immigrant church strong enough to withstand the attacks of a nativist American society. But Brownson wanted Catholicism – "Catholicity" was the word he used – to adapt itself to the American culture. He never explained how that would take place, and within a year he had repudiated the idea, most likely in response to Hughes's strong objection.

The repudiation took place in a review Brownson had written of Isaac Hecker's *Aspirations of Nature*. He explicitly denied any "design to Americanize Catholicity" and sought to distance himself from any group (or "new school," to use Hughes's phrase) that sought to achieve this.[18] It appears evident from Brownson's strong repudiation of his earlier position and Hughes's equally strong condemnation of any attempt to "Americanize Catholicity" that both men were talking about the relationship between religion and American culture.

The "new school" to which Hughes referred was a small group of clergy and laymen in New York City who met regularly during the 1850s to discuss issues of mutual interest. Their chief concern was the relationship between American culture and Catholicism. As Hughes put it, they wanted to "show that the Catholic religion and the American Constitution would really fit each other as a key fits a lock; that without any change in regard to faith or morals, the doctrines of the Catholic church may be, so to speak, Americanized – that is represented in such a manner as to attract the attention and win the admiration of the American people."[19] The one person who would develop that theme more than anyone else was Isaac Hecker. Although not a regular member of the new school, it provided him with "the moral support and intellectual stimulation" he needed to articulate his vision of a Catholic America.[20]

Like Brownson, Hecker was a convert to Roman Catholicism; after his conversion he joined the Redemptorist order and was ordained a priest in 1849. He eventually left the Redemptorists and in 1858 founded a new order, the Paulists, officially known as the Missionary Society of St. Paul the Apostle. Hecker was enthusiastic about Manifest Destiny, as many Protestant evangelicals were. But he gave it a different twist. In his opinion, the providential destiny of America would be realized only when America became Catholic. According to Hecker, the destinies of the United States and American Catholicism were so bound together that Catholics alone would be able to guide the nation toward "its highest destinies." To achieve that goal it would be necessary for Catholics "to put aside European ways and adapt to American conditions."[21] As he put the matter in a letter to his colleagues in the Redemptorist order, "So far as it is compatible with faith and piety, I am for accepting the true American civilization, its usages and customs; leaving aside other reasons it is the only way in which Catholicity can become the religion of our people." And in a letter to a Catholic laywoman he reiterated that point and wrote, "Our faith must take root in our national characteristics."[22] "Every age has its own characteristics," he told her, and therefore the type of spirituality suitable for American Catholics must reflect the age in which they lived. What this consisted of exhibited some of Brownson's ideas, concepts also popular among many American intellectuals. These included such ideas as personal initiative, self-reliance, freedom of action, and a positive attitude toward the world. Hecker's positive regard for the world, or what he called "the age," was rooted in his belief that the divine spirit becomes more manifest as history unfolds; that is, with each passing age God becomes more present in the world through the medium of the church.

Hecker's vision of religion was so dynamic that he envisioned Catholicism transforming American society, but that could not take place until Catholicism became more American. One of his most explicit statements was a comment he made shortly before his death regarding the recent establishment of Catholic University in Washington, DC. "The work of the new University," he wrote, "planted in the political center of this free and intelligent people, will tend to shape the expression of doctrines in such wise as to assimilate them to American intelligence – not to minimize but to assimilate. To develop the mind there is never need to minimize the truth; but there is great need of knowing how to assimilate the truth to different minds."[23] The statement was reminiscent of his belief that the spirituality of the people must be in tune with the age; in other words, religion, both in its doctrinal and spiritual expression, must adapt itself to the age.

Given Hecker's vision, it was clear what his strategy would be for the survival of Catholicism in the United States. Catholicism must become American, and only then will it prosper. As his epitaph phrased it, "In the union of Catholic faith and American civilization a new birth awaits them all, a future for the Church brighter than any past."[24] If it remained a foreign colony, as some of his contemporaries described the church, then it would never realize its destiny in America.

Throughout his life as a Catholic, Hecker strived to adapt his religion to the American environment. In addition to founding a new religious order that would seek to unite Catholicism and American life, he developed a new apologetic in the hope that his reasoning would influence Protestant Americans; he encouraged a new type of spirituality that emphasized sanctity in the world and not apart from it; he founded a press to distribute religious pamphlets and books; he established a periodical that would address the issues of the day; and he lectured throughout the nation hoping to gain converts to Catholicism. His was an energetic style of Catholicism that encouraged the involvement of the laity and sought sanctification in the world, not apart from it.

John Hughes was the antithesis of the American-born Hecker. An Irish-born immigrant who grew up in Ireland, a culture steeped in religious conflict and discrimination, he viewed Protestant America as a religiously hostile environment. He became a strong advocate of Catholic schools and separate institutions for the sick and dying, orphans, and delinquent children, as well as a devotional Catholicism that emphasized the role of the clergy and the need for external rituals. Hecker, by contrast, stressed the interior workings of the spirit in each individual. Although Hughes was clearly not anti-American, his model of Catholicism was the fortress community that opposed the dominant culture, not in a prophetic manner but as an adversary.

Hughes represented the majority opinion of Catholics in the nineteenth century. Throughout the era, clergy and laity worked together to establish parish communities that served the needs of immigrants. In these parishes immigrants could hear the gospel preached in their own languages, and they could sing the familiar hymns of the old country. Many parishes had elementary schools, and some even had high schools. Through these institutions each wave of immigrants passed the faith on to the next generation. The ethos that inspired the schools was the preservation of the faith; there was no question of adapting Catholicism to the American environment. The religion of the Old World was to be transplanted intact to the United States and passed on to succeeding generations. Although people could become American, their religion could not. Nevertheless, the dilemma of how to be both American and Catholic, and the tension that this created, did not go away. Others who followed Hecker sought to adapt the religion of Catholicism to the American culture, a practice that became most evident in the late nineteenth century.

The late nineteenth century was, in the words of Arthur Schlesinger, Sr., "a critical period" in the development of American religion.[25] An emerging urban and industrial nation presented formidable challenges to churches. Equally formidable were the challenges presented by developments in the intellectual realm. Darwin's theory of evolution occupied the attention of theologians for years as they sought to come to terms with the biblical account of creation and Darwin's evolutionary theory about the origins of life. A new theology that was more humanistic and ethical in focus was gaining popularity and would radically change the way people thought about religion. New theories of biblical criticism challenged the accuracy of many biblical stories; indeed, they challenged the very truthfulness of the Bible itself. New universities, more secular and less religious, became the citadels of the new learning, and for the first time in American history unbelief became as respectable as belief. Knowledge and learning had become America's icons. William Onahan, a Chicago Catholic layman, spoke for many when he underscored the necessity of education. "The age has become inspired by a passion for knowledge and is athirst for more and higher learning," he said. "This higher learning is everywhere in request, and the young man who aspires to highest rank and position must be equipped with this higher knowledge. There is room only in the lowest plane for the ignorant and the illiterate."[26]

The new intellectual environment radically transformed the religious landscape. Protestantism became more fragmented with the emergence of theological modernism and fundamentalism, and American Judaism witnessed the consolidation of the Reformed tradition and eventually underwent further division with the founding of the Conservative tradition. Even though Catholicism did not undergo the radical fragmentation experienced by Protestants and Jews, the new social and intellectual environment presented formidable challenges for Catholics in the United States. A key issue was the one Hecker had considered all his Catholic life: the relation between Catholicism and American culture. Now, however, the discussion would move beyond the idea of American culture to include the broader concept of modernity or modern culture.

Unlike earlier discussions of the relationship between Catholicism and American culture, the debate during the 1880s and 1890s was not confined to a handful of individuals. It involved leading members of the hierarchy, numerous clergy, and some lay people, and it occurred in periodicals and along the lecture circuit for a decade and more. It was as public and heated as any previous debate in American Catholic history.

The key figure in the hierarchy was John Ireland, the archbishop of St. Paul, Minnesota. Joining Ireland were John Keane, bishop of Richmond, Virginia, and later rector of Catholic University, and Denis O'Connell, rector of the North American College in Rome. Another prelate with a decidedly Americanist impulse was John L. Spalding of Peoria, Illinois, but he was not as actively involved in the discussion as the others. Cardinal James Gibbons, archbishop of Baltimore, was also a strong supporter of Ireland and the others.

The relationship between Catholicism and America was a theme John Ireland had been developing for many years. In November 1884, speaking before bishops gathered at the Third Plenary Council of Baltimore, he first gave "formal expression" to the issue that "was to dominate his thought and action for many more years to come."[27] His most developed thoughts on the issue were later presented in two other speeches, one entitled "The Mission of Catholics in America" was delivered in 1889 on the occasion of the centennial celebration of the establishment of the American hierarchy, and a second, "The Church and the Age," was given in 1893 on the anniversary of Cardinal Gibbons's episcopal consecration. In both speeches Ireland came across as American as Uncle Sam and as Catholic as the pope. He wanted to launch what he called "the new, the most glorious crusade. Church and age!" He also wanted to unite the two, making them mutually compatible and harmonious because "in both the self-same God" works so that "they pulsate alike."[28] This would first mean that Catholics would have to cast aside their foreign traits and become American. It was a theme he hammered home most energetically in discussions about the Germans. But for Ireland, more than just the question of nationality was involved.

John Ireland also believed that the religion of Catholicism had to adapt itself to American culture. As he put it, "The Church must herself be new, adapting herself in manner of life and in method of action to the conditions of the new order, thus proving herself, while ever ancient, to be ever new, as truth from heaven it is and ever must be."[29] This meant adopting new ways to present the Catholic message to American society. That involved change, and Ireland realized the challenge that posed. "The Church never changes," he said, "and yet she changes." To solve the dilemma, he like Hecker distinguished between the divine and the human, the essentials and the accidents. "The divine never changes," he wrote, "it is of Christ, the same ... forever. But even in the divine we must distinguish between the principle and the application of the principle; the application of the principle, or its adaptation to environment, changes with the circumstances. And thus, at times, there seems to be a change when there is not change." The "Church," he said, "while jealously guarding the essentials," should be ready "to abandon the accidentals, as circumstances of time and place demand."[30]

What Ireland was trying to do in these lectures – and throughout his life – was "to justify his deep-seated conviction that the Church must initiate an over-all rapprochement with a modern culture which at some point in the past had passed her by."[31] More than ethnic identity was at issue. Ireland realized the need for the church to change and adapt to the age. In his mind it had done this in the past, and it must do it once again.

But as Dennis Dease observed, "Ireland inevitably ran up against the problem of change in the Church; he knew that the Church must at times listen to the voice of the world and read the signs of the times. Yet Ireland's basic concept of the Church, like that of Brownson and Hecker, was ahistorical: he regarded the Church as transcending history and as unchanging in essence."[32] For this reason he could never fully develop his life-long belief that Catholicism must adapt to the age and the culture in which it is situated. He did not have the theological tools or methods to develop the idea in more than a general way.

Reinforcing John Ireland's crusade to unite church and age was the emergence of a Catholic middle class that also sought to adapt the Catholic way of life to American culture. Its members gave the "American Victorian values of male and female roles, home life, self-culture and education, temperance, sabbatarianism, and good citizenship . . . a Catholic form."[33] This was confirmation of the timeliness and value of Ireland's crusade.

Ireland's agenda, and that of his Americanist allies, was quite clear. They favored a more tolerant attitude toward Protestants, a more favorable attitude toward public schools, and even the possibility of some type of arrangement whereby Catholic children could be encouraged to attend public schools. Ireland also endorsed the American idea of the separation of church and state and was enthusiastic about the virtues of democracy, believing that the rest of the world should imitate the United States. He was inspired by his enthusiastic belief in progress and the idea that the present age was superior to what had gone before it.

For Ireland, the United States represented the apogee of progress. This belief in the progressive or evolutionary development of civilization was central to the Americanist point of view and provided the energy and enthusiasm necessary to sustain the crusade to unite church and age. Critics clearly recognized that fact and saw this principle as essentially hostile to the Catholic faith. In an astute, historically important article, Thomas Preston, a key aide to Archbishop Michael Corrigan of New York, the most formidable opponent of the Americanists, underscored the point emphatically: "The doctrine, that we have greater light in our age, that we better understand the truths of our revelation than the ages before us; that we have theologically taken upon ourselves the wings of human progress, is not simply an empty boast, it is a serious error." Preston warned that "there is no more dangerous disposition, if it should ever become popular, than the belief that there is an American Catholicity which is in advance of past times, which differs materially from the faith once delivered to the Church and always preserved by her, which boasts of a freedom from restrictions which bind the ages of the past."[34] It is clear from Preston's critique of the agenda of what he called an

"American Catholicity" that much more was at issue in this debate than ethnic identity.

For Preston, the solution to the American Catholic dilemma was to preserve the faith intact and oppose any attempt to adapt it to the American environment. But other Catholic intellectuals were trying to do just that. This was most evident among theologians who wrote in the late nineteenth century. As Scott Appleby has argued, there was a link between the progressivism of Americanists such as Hecker and Ireland and the modernist theologians who followed them. Americanists wanted Catholicism to "adapt itself to the values of the modern American republic"; modernist theologians wanted Catholicism to adapt itself to the best that modern philosophy and science had to offer. The theologians took the desire for adaptation beyond the pragmatic, political platform of the Americanists and fashioned an ideology of theological adaptation that represented the "theological and philosophical expression of Americanism."[35] Like the Americanists, they argued that if Catholicism was to survive in the United States and in the modern world it would have to reconcile with the age. For the theologians this meant more than political, social, or cultural adaptation. It meant reconciling the ancient beliefs of Catholicism with the new learning.

The issue that most challenged the foundations of Christianity during these decades was Darwin's theory about evolution and his concept of natural selection. Among Catholics, the debate over evolution was not as prolonged and divisive as it was among Protestants. Nonetheless, it was a popular theme in the 1890s. The key person in this discussion was John Zahm. A Holy Cross priest on the faculty of the University of Notre Dame, Zahm was an accomplished scientist and educator. After he entered the evolution discussion during the 1880s he lectured widely and wrote numerous essays promoting the compatibility of science and religion. By the 1890s he had clearly endorsed the theory of evolution and was widely praised for his efforts. In 1896 he published his major work on the topic, *Evolution and Dogma*. The book was the culmination of his thinking and confirmed his reputation "as a leading Catholic apologist and educator."[36]

Zahm's endorsement of theistic evolution eventually attracted the attention of Catholic theologians in Rome and elsewhere, who viewed evolution in particular and modernity in general as hostile to religion. By 1898 opposition against Zahm had escalated to such an intense degree that church authorities in Rome condemned his book and prohibited further publication. The condemnation persuaded Zahm to abandon his efforts to reconcile theology and modern science although it was clear to him that the survival of Catholicism depended on adaptation to the modern world, specifically to modern science and the concept of evolution. In that sense he was clearly an apologist for modernity.

There were others, however, who pushed the concept further and self-consciously sought to reconcile Catholic beliefs with modern thought. The most important center for this school of thought was St. Joseph's Seminary in New York, established in 1896 and directed by priests of the Society of St. Sulpice. Following the lead of seminaries in Boston and Baltimore, which the Sulpicians also administered, St. Joseph's Seminary sought to modernize the traditional program of formation and adapt it to the American culture. This meant a modification of a stern French Sulpician tradition of seminary formation, a mentality that "often regarded as a sin against the spirit to complain of cold rooms, bad food, poor hospital treatment, long kneeling at prayers, and other violations of the rules of health and common sense."[37] Other adaptations included the encouragement of physical exercise; lectures by distinguished visiting scholars, both Protestant and Catholic; and reading rooms where students could find some of the best secular magazines and newspapers along with the usual collection of Catholic periodicals. Seminarians also attended classes at New York University and Columbia University. But the Sulpicians wanted to do more than promote physical fitness and good reading habits. The faculty at St. Joseph's sought to teach the modern approach to such ancient disciplines as history, philosophy, and theology. That meant rejection of the traditional neo-scholastic methodology and its ahistorical, classicist perspective and an endorsement of an historical, critical approach in theology. In this way they hoped to achieve a "synthesis of modern science and revealed truth."[38]

The area undergoing the most change was the study of the Bible. Propelled by the new history and its concern for data and new techniques in textual criticism, dramatic changes were occurring. A major issue concerned the authorship of the Pentateuch; another was the meaning of inspiration and inerrancy. At St. Joseph's and other Sulpician seminaries the latest advances in Bible studies became part of the curriculum, and the writings of European scholars who supported a more modern approach to the study of the Bible were made available to students.

Another important development at St. Joseph's Seminary was the founding of a journal, *New York Review*, in 1905 that sought to educate the American clergy in the new theology emerging in Europe. Its goal was to reconcile an ancient faith with modern thought. As one of its editors put it, the purpose of the journal was "not to abandon the old in favor of the new, but rather to interpret with becoming care and reverence the old truths in the light of the new science." What this meant, according to Appleby, was "to provide for the American Catholic church the epistemological, theological, apologetic, and ecclesiological foundations for the new worldview" that was emerging.[39]

For the theologians at St. Joseph's Seminary, the Catholic strategy for survival was clear. It had to reconcile the ancient truths of Catholicism with modern thought. Americanists such as Ireland wanted Catholicism to become more American, a general feeling that was widespread within the Catholic culture. It could mean a multitude of things – endorsing democracy, supporting the temperance crusade, or promoting patriotism, for example. The theologians pushed the Americanist agenda one step further and advocated the modernization of Catholic thought, bringing it into harmony with the advances of modern learning. Both positions generated a good deal of debate, and by the 1890s two opposing schools of thought existed among Catholics. Americanists and modernists were in the minority, however. The majority opinion did not endorse the historical, developmental methodology of the modernists and rejected their efforts to synthesize traditional beliefs of Catholics and modern thought. Those who opposed any such synthesis controlled the seats of power in Rome and were able to persuade the papacy to condemn any efforts at Americanization or modernization.

The first such condemnation came in 1899, when Pope Leo XIII condemned what he called "Americanism" and labeled as "reprehensible" the idea that "the Church ought to adapt herself somewhat to our advanced civilization, and relaxing her ancient rigor, show some indulgence to modern popular theories and methods." The pope also warned against the concept that the church in America could be "different from that which is in the rest of the world."[40] The condemnation effectively ended John Ireland's crusade to unite church and age. But it did not end the debate about the church adapting itself to the modern age; that continued for several years in an intellectually robust manner as Catholic intellectuals sought to reconcile Catholicism and modern thought. Then, in 1907, Pope Pius X condemned what he labeled modernism and published a syllabus of errors, effectively ending the search for a synthesis between modern thought and traditional Catholic belief. The ahistorical, classicist methodology of neo-scholasticism continued to be the dominant theological system within Roman Catholicism.

The consequences of that development were significant. Theologically, it meant that American Catholics could no longer, publicly at least, seek to reconcile modern thought with traditional Catholic doctrine. The theological strategy was to resist modernism as much as possible and punish those intellectuals who thought differently. Pastorally, it meant a strategy of religious separatism whereby the parish became an island community set apart from the rest of the nation's religiously pluralistic society. For many people the parish became a total community where all religious, social, and recreational needs were met through a host of societies and organizations. This was especially true in parishes organized for recently arrived immigrants from Eastern and Southern Europe. But it was also the case in Irish and German parishes in this pre-World War I era. As one woman described her parish, "Our lives were centered around Sacred Heart church and one another."[41] The centerpiece of the strategy was the parish school, which served as a "culture factory" for Catholics and passed on and preserved intact the tradition of Catholicism. Any effort to fashion a Catholicism that was in tune with American culture was no longer encouraged. This would hold fast through the 1920s, when 100 Percent Americanism engulfed the church as well as the nation.

Ever since Catholics set foot on the shores of North America they have sought to adapt their religion to the new environment. This desire has always ignited a debate about what is the best strategy for survival in the new land. On one side, integrationists wanted Catholicism to adapt to American culture. At virtually every important juncture in the brief history of Catholicism in the United States they have raised the issue and sought to persuade others that Catholicism must adapt. On the other side, separatists wanted to maintain the integrity of Catholicism by maintaining its traditions and resisting adaptation.

In the 1890s and early 1900s the debate took on greater significance because the issue included not just the relationship of Catholicism to American culture, or what can be called the question of group identity. It also included the relationship of Catholicism to the broader theme of modern culture, especially modern thought. Separatists won out each time and were able to fashion a religious culture that was enormously successful in meeting the needs of a predominantly immigrant people. Yet the question of adaptation would not go away. During the decades between the two world wars, especially the 1930s, Catholics once again raised the issue of adaptation. The relationship between Catholicism and American culture became the center of a vigorous debate in the late 1940s and 1950s. This debate has continued to the present day. Once again it has gone beyond the issue of the Americanization of Catholicism to include the larger theme of the stance of Catholicism toward modern thought and culture. How to be both Catholic and American still remains a dilemma for American Catholics.

# Notes

1 Patrick W. Carey, *People, Priests, and Prelates: Ecclesiastical Democracy and the Tensions of Trusteeism* (Notre Dame: University of Notre Dame Press, 1987).

2 Mathew Carey, *Address to the Rt. Rev. Bishop Conwell and the Members of St. Mary's Congregation* (Philadelphia, 1821), 3–4; Mathew Carey, *Address to the Rt. Rev. The Bishop of Pennsylvania and the Members of St. Mary's Congregation, Philadelphia* (Philadelphia: n.p., 1820), 3.

3 Quoted in Patrick W. Carey, "Republicanism within American Catholicism, 1785–1860," *Journal of the Early Republic* 3 (Winter 1983): 416.

4 Joseph P. Chinnici, *Living Stones: The History and Structure of Catholic Spiritual Life in the United States* (New York: Macmillan, 1989).

5 Quoted in Edward C. Carter II, "The Political Activities of Mathew Carey, Nationalist 1760–1814," Ph.D. diss., Bryn Mawr College, 1962, 25; Diary of Mathew Carey, Dec. 1, 1824, Rare Book Room, University of Pennsylvania.

6 See James Turner, *Without God, Without Creed: The Origins of Unbelief in America* (Baltimore: Johns Hopkins University Press, 1985), 35ff.

7 "Archbishop Marechal's Report to Propaganda, October 16, 1818," in *Documents of American Catholic History*, ed. John Tracy Ellis (Chicago: Henry Regnery, 1967), 1:214.

8 Clyde F. Crews, *An American Holy Land: A History of the Archdiocese of Louisville* (Wilmington: Michael Glazier, 1987), 64.

9 Crews, *An American Holy Land*, 102; Jay P. Dolan, *The American Catholic Experience: A History from Colonial Times to the Present* (New York: Doubleday, 1985), 119–20.

10 Dolan, *The American Catholic Experience*, 121.

11 Ibid., 296.

12 Orestes A. Brownson, "Mission of America," in *The Works of Orestes A. Brownson*, ed. Henry F. Brownson (Detroit: T. Nourse, 1884), 11:567.

13 Brownson, "Mission of America," 556–7, 576, 584.

14 Quoted in Thomas R. Ryan, *Orestes A. Brownson: A Definitive Biography* (Huntington, Ind.: Our Sunday Visitor, 1976), 534.

15 Quoted in Henry F. Brownson, *Orestes A. Brownson's Later Life: From 1856–1876* (Detroit: H. F. Brownson, 1900), 71.

16 Brownson, *Orestes A. Brownson's Later Life*, 71–2. Hughes wrote an important essay on this topic in November 1856: "Reflections and Suggestions in Regard to What Is Called the Catholic Press in the United States," in *Complete Works of the Most Rev. John Hughes, D. D., Archbishop of New York*, ed. Lawrence Kehoe (New York: Lawrence Kehoe, 1865), 2:686–701.

17 Brownson, "Mission of America," 559.

18 David J. O'Brien, *Isaac Hecker: An American Catholic* (New York: Paulist Press, 1992), 121–3; William LeRoy Portier, "Providential Nation: An Historical-Theological Study of Isaac Hecker's Americanism," Ph.D. diss., University of St. Michael's College, Canada, 1980, 309.

19   Hughes, "Reflections and Suggestions," 688.

20   Portier, "Providential Nation," 319.

21   Quoted in Dolan, *The American Catholic Experience*, 308, and O'Brien, *Isaac Hecker*, 154.

22   Quoted in O'Brien, *Isaac Hecker*, 154, and Portier, "Providential Nation," 324.

23   Quoted in O'Brien, *Isaac Hecker*, 316.

24   Portier, "Providential Nation," 320.

25   Arthur M. Schlesinger, Sr., "A Critical Period in American Religion, 1875–1900," *Massachusetts Historical Society Proceedings* 65 (1930–2): 523–46.

26   William Onahan, "The Jesuits in Chicago," address given at the silver jubilee of St. Ignatius College, June 24, 1895, Chicago, Ill.

27   Marvin R. O'Connell, *John Ireland and the American Catholic Church* (St. Paul: Minnesota Historical Society, 1988), 193.

28   Quoted in Dolan, *The American Catholic Experience*, 309.

29   Ibid.

30   Quoted in R. Scott Appleby, *Church and Age Unite: The Modernist Impulse in American Catholicism* (Notre Dame: University of Notre Dame Press, 1992), 85, and Dennis J. Dease, "The Theological Influence of Orestes Brownson and Isaac Hecker on John Ireland's Ecclesiology," Ph.D. diss., Catholic University of America, 1978, 220.

31   Dease, "The Theological Influence," 221.

32   Ibid., 244.

33   Paul G. Robichaud, "The Resident Church: Middle Class Catholics and the Shaping of American Catholic Identity, 1889 to 1899," Ph.D. diss., University of California Los Angeles, 1989, 297.

34   Thomas S. Preston, "American Catholicity," *American Catholic Quarterly Review* 15 (April 1891): 399, 408.

35   Appleby, *Church and Age Unite*, 7–8.

36   Ibid., 36.

37   Quoted in Joseph M. White, *The Diocesan Seminary in the United States: A History from the 1780s to the Present* (Notre Dame: University of Notre Dame Press, 1989), 230.

38   Appleby, *Church and Age Unite*, 109.

39   Ibid., 109, 163.

40   Pope Leo XIII, *Testem Benevolentiae*, in *Documents of American Catholic History*, ed. Ellis, 2:539, 546.

41   Quoted in Dolan, *The American Catholic Experience*, 206.

# 7

# Conservative Judaism

## Gerson D. Cohen

## Introduction

Jews can be distinguished from other religious groups partly by their adherence to a ritual calendar of holy days that link the seasons of the year with major events in Jewish history and special times of introspection. The most commonly observed holidays are Passover in early spring, which celebrates the Hebrew Exodus from bondage in ancient Egypt, and the early fall holidays of Yom Kippur and Rosh Hashanah, the Day of Atonement and the Jewish New Year. Respect for both the religious meaning of Jewish history and for the sacred nature of the created world underlies this ritual calendar and helps to construct Jewish identity.

But while they share the same ritual calendar, American Jews have differed among themselves about what it means to be Jewish. The high degree of religious freedom available in the United States has contributed to divisions among Jews about the meaning of Judaism and the nature of Jewish life. As a middle way between the liberalism of Reform Judaism and the traditionalism of Orthodox Judaism, Conservative Judaism celebrated diversity of opinion about Jewish theology while retaining commitment to the observance of halakhah (the rules and applications of Jewish law). As Gerson Cohen explains, the Conservative movement emerged among Jews in New York City in the late nineteenth century as an affirmation of the dynamic, historical nature

---

Excerpted from Gerson D. Cohen, "Conservative Judaism," in *Contemporary Jewish Religious Thought: Original Essays on Critical Concepts, Movements, and Beliefs*, ed. Arthur A. Cohen and Paul Mendes-Flohr (New York: Free Press, 1987), 91–9.

of God's covenant relationship with the Jewish people. Pointing to the many different ways in which Jews have conceptualized their relationship with God, Conservative Jews have stressed the religious significance of intellectual freedom and creativity, not only for Jews, but for all humankind.

Conservative Judaism, the largest of the three major Jewish religious classifications in the United States and Canada, is most accurately described as a number of organizational affiliations of rabbis and congregations as well as laity who identify themselves and who are identified by others as Conservative. While the name embraces a variety of theological orientations and norms of religious usage, Conservative Judaism bears certain identifying marks and professes certain standards that set it apart from all other contemporary Jewish religious groups.

Despite the impressive increase in recent years of Conservative Jewish institutions and congregations in Israel and in many countries – particularly in Latin America and Europe – Conservative Judaism is primarily an American movement whose religious orientation has been determined by the institution that continues to be its chief academic and ideological center, the Jewish Theological Seminary of America. Established in New York in 1886 by Rabbi Sabato Morais of Philadelphia as a traditionalist but modern rabbinical school, the Seminary was reorganized in 1902 under the academic and religious leadership of Solomon Schechter. He mobilized a young but impressive faculty, all of whom were endowed with formidable training in rabbinics – indeed, in all of classical Hebrew literature – and all of whom possessed doctorates in Hebrew and classical studies earned in secular universities. Simultaneously, the lay leadership of the Seminary placed at its disposal a small but highly impressive library that, in time, has grown into the largest collection of rare Judaica and Hebrew manuscripts ever assembled under one roof in all of Jewish history.

Early in the history of the reorganized Seminary the name *Conservative* was adopted by its faculty and lay leadership in order to reinforce recognition of its total commitment to traditional rabbinic Judaism and to the reformulation of that tradition in modern terms and forms. The best summary of the mission that the Seminary saw itself fulfilling was given by Solomon Schechter in his *Seminary Addresses and Other Papers*, which, despite occasional polemic and apologetics, remains the most lucid affirmation of the traditionalist but modern Judaism that the founding fathers of the Seminary upheld. Nevertheless, while the name *Conservative* was meant to set the Seminary and its scholarship apart from the contemporary Orthodox world, with its antimodernist postures in learning and custom, the two currents the new Seminary was most concerned to stem were Reform Judaism and nineteenth-century Protestant Christian scholarship in the Bible and rabbinics. The Reform movement had renounced three of the basic pillars of Judaism: halakhah, the hope for national deliverance, and the *de facto* centrality of Hebrew in the synagogue service. Although it insisted on maintaining the commitment to a discrete Jewish people and faith, it focused its emphasis on "prophetic ethics" and dismissed the ritual usage that constituted the framework of rabbinic Judaism.

As for nineteenth-century Protestant biblical and rabbinic critical scholarship, Schechter and his colleagues opposed it vehemently because of the "higher anti-Semitism" that pervaded so much of it. In nineteenth-century Protestant thought, Hebrew monotheism was seen to have developed relatively late in the biblical period and soon thereafter to have become incurably corrupted by the relegation of prophetic monotheism to a place far below that of priestly ritual. By the days of the Second Temple, according to this perception, Judaism had become so intensely nationalistic and so Temple-centered that its pristine message could be restored only by the ideological and behavioral revolts of Jesus, Paul, and their disciples. It was sensitivity to this animus that underlay the decision of the new rabbinical Seminary to omit higher biblical criticism, especially of the Pentateuch, and, indeed, to omit even the study of much apocryphal and apocalyptic literature from its curriculum, and to encourage, albeit discreetly, such eminent non-Jewish scholars as George Foot Moore to correct the generally distorted Christian reading of Jewish materials then commonplace.

The urgent desire to develop a form of traditional Judaism that was responsive to a post-Enlightenment world and at the same time to rescue Jewish history from the scrap heap of Western culture had led, in Germany and Central Europe in the nineteenth century, to the development of a movement called *Wissenschaft des Judentums* (Science of Judaism). Outside of Eastern Europe no religious group in modern Jewish history was so directly oriented toward the study of its basic texts and religious practices as the advocates of *Wissenschaft des Judentums*. The scholars of this movement were obsessed with the necessity of convincing themselves and the rest of the world that at no stage in its development had Judaism ever been just a faith, but that at every stage it had been – and still was – a culture, one that was properly understood and defined only when examined in light of the contemporary Jewish and secular historical moment.

These men dedicated themselves to the elucidation of texts and forms that had been ignored by Jews and Christians alike during the days of the Enlightenment: the casuistry of the Babylonian Talmud, the medieval poets, and medieval Jewish philosophy, to name but three fields of the many to which they devoted themselves. From their research they came to believe – as Conservative Judaism continues to believe – that just as Jews have carried their Torah with them wherever they have gone, so they have also carried with them the mandate to make their tradition – law, liturgy, midrash, and theology – relevant and meaningful to every generation.

In the twentieth century Solomon Schechter and his colleagues dedicated themselves to the continuation of this work. It is not fortuitous that Conservative Judaism has made its schools of learning – the Seminary itself, the University of Judaism in Los Angeles, and Neve Schechter in Jerusalem – its spiritual centers. The centrality of these institutions to the Conservative movement and the academic foundation they give it are reflected in the veneration that the movement has accorded its scholars, not only those who were its founding fathers – Israel Davidson, Israel Friedlaender, Louis Ginzberg, Alexander Marx, Solomon Schechter – but also the next generation of scholars, such as Louis Finkelstein, H. L. Ginsberg, Robert Gordis, Abraham Joshua Heschel, Saul Lieberman, Shalom Spiegel, and Moses Zucker. Each of these men has radically extended and deepened our contemporary understanding of the Jewish religious and cultural heritage.

Indeed, if there is anything Conservative Judaism has accomplished in the last hundred years, it has been the total transformation of the concept of Jewish history and culture; its scholarship has been the basis of the development of a cultural self-understanding that is profoundly new. The students and scholars in the Conservative movement do not confine their study of Torah to Bible and Talmud; for them the study of Torah embraces the religious literature of every age. Ideally, every Jew should become aware of the great variety of Jewish religious expression that has been produced over the centuries, because its existence is witness to a religious experience that has been far more multifaceted and multicolored than anything understood heretofore. At the Seminary a knowledge of midrash, philosophy, liturgy, medieval poetry, modern theology, and modern Hebrew literature is considered to be indispensable both to the rabbi and to the learned Jewish layman.

Nevertheless, the unquestioning affirmation of historic Jewish doctrines and the unquestioning acceptance of traditional Jewish practices that were characteristic of Conservative Judaism in its first two decades began to show some internal weakening by 1910. Although the small group of scholars who stood at the academic and religious helm of the seminary at that time were giants in the field of twentieth-century Jewish scholarship, a younger member of the faculty, Mordecai M. Kaplan, began to take issue with his colleagues' policy of encouraging theological, philological, and textual debate while resisting any consideration of change with respect to traditional concepts and practices. Kaplan was impatient with a system that coupled dispassionate scholarship with theological immobility and that was receptive to novelty in exegesis but impervious to the need of the ordinary American Jew for guidance in responding to the challenges of modernity and citizenship. Although at first Kaplan confined his dissident views to the Seminary and his pulpit, it was clear that a vigorous attack on Conservative Judaism was germinating within the highest ranks of the movement itself. Nor, despite an initial attempt to dissuade Kaplan from continuing to speak out, did Schechter ever consider more punitive steps against a member of the Seminary faculty.

Kaplan's monumental work *Judaism as a Civilization* (1934) contained, among other themes, nothing less than a complete repudiation of traditional Conservative Judaism as it had been expressed up to that point. The critical examination of classical Jewish texts had demonstrated to Kaplan, as it had to so many others, that the history of the Jewish tradition was a history of constant development and renewal. But to him it was also immediately evident that Judaism was once more in urgent need of rejuvenation. He felt a vacuum in the Jewish life he saw around him – especially in Conservative Jewish life – that led him to question the continued relevance of the traditional authority, faith, and practice that Schechter and his faculty had defended so vigorously. Even though Kaplan's plea for halakhic reconstruction and his continued devotion to the concept of the centrality of the Jewish people, to the renewal of Hebrew as a spoken language and as a literature, indeed his continued observance of Jewish rituals, and to the reestablishment of a strong Jewish presence in Palestine set him clearly apart from Reform Judaism, he was, nonetheless, fierce in his polemic against traditional Conservative Judaism. He was dismayed, for instance, by the refusal of the faculty to confront the fact not only that most American Jews were failing to observe the practices considered by the traditionalists to be essential, but that they were not even committed to these practices in theory.

To be sure, even Schechter and his disciples had not been insensitive to the problems articulated by Kaplan. He himself had been inspired by Zacharias Frankel's view that Judaism was the product of a positive historical development and had suggested that what had governed the process of development within the tradition was the consensus of *Kelal Yisrael*, a phrase he translated as "catholic Israel." What *Kelal Yisrael* said and did represented the manifestation at that particular moment of divine inspiration, that is, of the development of Torah in theory and practice at that point. Of course, the concept of catholic Israel did not include those who had renounced the obligations and demands of their faith. To be counted in the consensus one had to be knowledgeable in the traditional literature and to have set oneself to live by the results of the exegesis and reasoning that formed the tradition.

For Schechter, however, the process of religious development had been slow and quietly effective; whatever changes had been introduced into the tradition had not challenged the basic foundations of faith. Not that Judaism had escaped controversy. The impact of Saadiah Gaon and Moses Maimonides on their generations belies the perception by both Jews and non-Jews of a monolithic Jewish community. Still, in the final analysis the work of these men had challenged existing institutions, not the unquestioned validity of rabbinic authority. Kaplan, on the other hand, insisted – and others came to agree with him – that since scholarship had illuminated the actual dynamics of change, that is, since it had revealed to us the laws and mechanisms within Judaism and the halakhah that had permitted the continuous evolution of Jewish culture, it could now be used more actively – even aggressively – to modify law, practice, and even canons of belief.

Although Conservative Judaism has largely rejected Kaplan's theology (Kaplan's followers have established a new Reconstructionist movement and theological seminary), his vocabulary and fundamental idiom permeated the religious approach of virtually every member of the Rabbinical Assembly (the official organization of Conservative rabbis) and generated a new temper among the Conservative laity. In 1948 the Committee on Jewish Law and Standards of the Rabbinical Assembly was recognized and began, albeit slowly, to break with many of the traditional attitudes toward faith and ritual held by the majority of the Jewish Theological Seminary faculty. Thanks to the influence of Kaplan's perception of religion, the standards of Jewish behavior could no longer be determined exclusively by the hitherto acknowledged supreme halakhic authorities of Conservative Judaism. In truth, the ideas of Mordecai Kaplan caused such a basic reorientation within Conservative Judaism that its posture today is at variance with that which obtained in the years following its birth.

While retaining the basic principles of traditional faith and practice, the rabbinate and laity of Conservative Judaism are today increasingly reflective, if unconsciously, of the insights derived from the critical study of Jewish sources, and consciously open to the possibilities of new exegesis. The primary desire of Conservative Judaism's leaders and scholars is to translate law and usage into renewed expressions of an ancient tradition – to employ all the knowledge they have gained of the development of the Jewish tradition, as well as their contemporary moral perceptions, in order to come to halakhic decisions that will be acceptable to the learned believer in the modern world. They are committed to promulgating fresh formulations of the components of a totally authentic, yet modern, Jewish life – formulations that will rearticulate the fundamental principles of normative Judaism as interpreted in the light of the latest advances in technology, sociopolitical organization, and modern moral values. These extra-legal considerations are vital because if the yardsticks for religious validity or for change are restricted to the traditional halakhic ones, the Jews of the modern world are then caught in a web of precedents established in different settings and in different ages with vastly different conceptions of morality and conscience. There are two questions Conservative Judaism asks in gauging the authenticity of any halakhic decision: (1) Is it grounded in the history and wording of the law itself? and (2) Will it result in the enhancement of Torah as a whole? If the Committee on Jewish Law and Standards of the Rabbinical Assembly permits the modification of a talmudic norm regarding the Sabbath, it is because it is believed that the modification will result in increased observance.

The most widely known departures of Conservative Judaism from established practice have been in the decisions of the committee to permit riding to the nearest synagogue on the Sabbath, to count women as legitimate members of a minyan, and most recently – and most resoundingly – the decision of a majority of the Seminary faculty to admit women to the rabbinical school as candidates for ordination. After reading the report of a commission appointed by the chancellor that had traveled throughout the country to sound out the opinions of large numbers of Conservative Jews to establish a consensus of the movement on this matter, and after reading numerous halakhic opinions submitted by faculty members, the faculty put the question to a vote. Those who voted in favor of the motion did so, first, because they believed that it was halakhically sound, that there was nothing in rabbinic Judaism to inhibit women from functioning as rabbis; and, second, because they believed that since it was halakhically sound, it was religiously imperative, in the context of the Conservative Jewish community, to move on the issue at that time. They believed that to continue to deny admission to the rabbinical school to women who are committed to halakhah and dedicated to God, the service of Torah, and Israel would fail to be responsive to the felt desire of the greater part of the community and of Conservative Judaism altogether. Instead they, and through them the Conservative movement, have opened the gates of Jewish leadership to new sources of vitality, dedication, and talent.

It should be obvious – although frequently it seems not to be – that this faculty decision obligated no one and no congregation. It merely meant that – as the Conservative movement interpreted the halakhah with respect to this issue – there is a choice. It recognized – as has the tradition since the rabbinic age – that there may be more than one acceptable opinion about the application of a particular law to a particular set of circumstances. In the past thirty-seven years the Committee on Jewish Law and Standards has consistently circulated both majority and minority opinions, leaving the final decision to the individual rabbi and congregation. Indeed, the vitality of Conservative Judaism will depend, for the foreseeable future, not only on the authenticity and wisdom of its interpretations of halakhah, but also on the recognition of all concerned of the validity even of legitimate interpretations with which they may disagree.

Flexibility can engender fear. Many require a religious movement to be unequivocal in its ideology and to advocate, at least in theory, a unitary form of ritual practice. But the leadership of the Conservative movement functions on the principle that competent authorities can reach a variety of authentic answers to the complex issues of faith and life. In fact, it is when seen from this perspective that the Conservative movement can be said to be quasi-congregationalist in its organization, each congregational unit (rabbi and synagogue membership) deciding for itself which of the positions deemed acceptable by the Committee on Jewish Law and Standards it wishes to adopt.

Nevertheless, although Conservative Judaism endorses a pluralistic approach in matters of doctrine and observance, it insists, at the same time, upon the acceptance of certain basic categories of faith and worship. All Conservative congregations affirm the binding obligation of halakhah, the Sabbath, the festivals, *kashrut*, circumcision, daily prayer, marriage, divorce, and conversion according to Jewish law, and the centrality of Hebrew in the synagogue service. And all affirm the spiritual centrality of the land of Israel and the people of Israel. It is important to emphasize here, however, that whereas the word *Israel* in this formulation means Israel in its transtemporal and transgeographic sense, the fact is that the State of Israel and its Jewish population bear a spiritual importance that transcends their local existence. Moreover, it is also important to emphasize in regard to the concept of the people of Israel that just as the Conservative movement tolerates diversity within its own camp, it tolerates diversity outside itself as well. In other words, Conservative Judaism has always insisted on the solidarity of the Jewish people as a whole, in all its myriad forms and orientations. From the Conservative perspective the secular Jew is as much a Jew as the observant Jew, and the destiny and welfare of the non-Conservative as much the concern of the movement as the destiny and welfare of those within its fold.

Conservative Judaism is not monolithic. As it takes root in different parts of the world, it will express itself in each case in a dialect that is appropriate to each particular situation. Nevertheless, wherever Conservative Judaism will be found, it will be found to be dedicated to fostering a life of Torah – in the synagogue, in the home, in the school, and in the community. The Jewish people has acquired the ability to reinterpret its Torah, linguistically and conceptually, in every generation. This is what Conservative Judaism is trying to do for the contemporary generation of Conservative Jews both within the United States and outside it. For unless each generation of Jews, no matter where they may find themselves, can master this process of reinterpretation, the Jewish tradition will lose its hold in that place. Conservative Judaism is not a halfway point between Orthodoxy and secularism. On the contrary, for the past century, combining the critical study of Jewish texts and Jewish history with an unalterable commitment to the Jewish tradition, Conservative Judaism has offered a fresh and authentic approach to the modern world.

# 8

# "Introduction," The Faces of Buddhism in America

## Charles S. Prebish

## Introduction

As Charles Prebish explains, the history of Buddhism in the United States dates back to the 1840s, when Chinese immigrants brought Buddhist traditions to cities and settlements along the West Coast. At about the same time, New England Transcendentalists discovered Buddhist and Hindu writings and fused Buddhist ideas about the universal flow of Mind with their own Romantic ideas about nature and poetic inspiration. In the late nineteenth and early twentieth centuries, Buddhist ideas and practices persisted among both ethnic and intellectual minorities, but often in marginalized and apparently exotic pockets apart from the mainstreams of American culture.

In the 1960s, immigration quotas changed dramatically, allowing more people from Asia than ever before to enter the United States. At the same time, the shaking of American values associated with the war in Vietnam drew many Americans who had been raised as Christians or Jews to the wisdom of Asian religions. New forms and interpretations of Buddhism developed in rapid succession as many of these Americans incorporated Buddhist insights into their lives, and as the United States became home to more forms of traditional Buddhism than anyplace else in the world.

Nothing better illustrates the creative, and typically American, process of religious growth and diversification than the development of Buddhism in late

Excerpted from Charles S. Prebish, "Introduction," in *The Faces of Buddhism in America*, ed. Charles S. Prebish and Kenneth K. Tanaka (Berkeley: University of California Press, 1998), 1–10.

twentieth-century America. Since the 1960s, the growing presence of cradle Buddhists with backgrounds in Asian cultures and the cross-fertilization of ideas, not only among Buddhists themselves, but also between Buddhists and Christians and Jews, contributed to a general rise in American interest in Buddhism and to the establishment of many new centers of Buddhist study and practice.

Between the months of June and November 1994, features on American Buddhism appeared in such popular print media as the *Wall Street Journal*, *USA Today*, *Newsweek*, *New York Magazine*, and *Christianity Today*. The *Newsweek* article, titled "800,000 Hands Clapping," focused on a varied group of American Buddhists that included John Daido Loori, the abbot of Zen Mountain Monastery in upstate New York, well-known actor Richard Gere, Mitchell Kapor of Lotus Development Corporation, Phil Jackson, coach of the world champion Chicago Bulls professional basketball team, and even rock group The Beastie Boys, who recorded "The Bodhisattva Vow," a rap tribute to the Buddhist path. *New York Magazine* went even further, categorizing American Buddhists as "Beat Buddhists" (such as Gary Snyder, Allen Ginsberg, Philip Whalen, and Lawrence Ferlinghetti), "Celluloid Buddhists" (including Willem Dafoe, Oliver Stone, and Ellen Burstyn, along with Gere), "Art Buddhists" (Milton Glaser, Robert Moscowitz, Roy Lichtenstein, and Robert Rauschenberg, among others), "Power Buddhists" (Jerry Brown), and "Benefit Buddhists" (like Porter McCray and Bokara Legendre).

Also in 1994, American Buddhism was presented as a major feature on the *ABC Nightly News with Peter Jennings* (with scholar-Buddhists Robert Thurman and me serving as scholarly consultants) as well as on *Talk of the Nation* on National Public Radio (with Helen Tworkov and Kenneth Tanaka fielding questions from a national audience). Peter Jennings's researchers estimated the American Buddhist population to be between four and six million individuals, composed of both Asian American and Euro-American ethnic groups, making American Buddhism a religious movement significantly larger than many Protestant denominations.

The flurry of national media attention devoted to American Buddhism has continued almost nonstop since. And it's expanding. The *Utne Reader* ran a short feature titled "Buddhism American Style" in the issue for January–February 1995, and the *New York Times* ran an article on October 15, 1995, on apartments that were being turned into would-be *zendōs* for informal mediation sessions. Moreover, American youngsters are even being identified as incarnations of famous Buddhist teachers. On January 25, 1996, *USA Today* ran the story of Sonam

Wangdu, a young boy born in Seattle to an American mother and Tibetan father who was identified as the incarnation of Lama Deshung Rinpoche III, a Tibetan teacher who died in Seattle in 1987.

Rodger Kamenetz, author of *The Jew in the Lotus*, a best-selling book on the Jewish–Buddhist dialogue, wrote a popular article titled "Robert Thurman Doesn't *Look* Buddhist" (*New York Times Magazine*, May 5, 1996), highlighting Thurman's role as one of the most visible members of a new breed of scholar-Buddhists, or well-credentialed academic investigators of the Buddhist religion who also happen to be Buddhist practitioners. Thurman is especially visible as one of the Dalai Lama's chief American translators, as well as being the father of noted actress Uma Thurman. Even the newspaper layout of news on American Buddhism foreshadows its growing normative status in mainline American religion. On June 26, 1996, the *New York Times* juxtaposed an article on the construction of Odiyan, a Tibetan Buddhist temple in northern California, alongside an article on the suspected Unabomber's not-guilty plea. And the cover story of *Time* magazine's October 13, 1997, edition was titled, "America's Fascination with Buddhism."

Although there is little consensus on an explanation for the growing popularity of American Buddhism in the latter half of the twentieth century, Peter Berger's perceptive comment of more than thirty years ago still seems applicable today: "Secularization brings about a demonopolization of religious traditions and thus, *ipso facto*, leads to a pluralistic situation." Berger goes on to say that "the key characteristic of all pluralistic situations, whatever the details of their historical background, is that the monopolies can no longer take for granted the allegiance of their client populations.... The pluralistic situation is, above all, a *market situation*."[1] That Buddhism was able to exploit this "market situation" is now widely acknowledged. Robert Bellah, for example, has noted: "In many ways Asian spirituality provided a more thorough contrast to the rejected utilitarian individualism than did biblical religion. To external achievement it posed inner experience; to the exploitation of nature, harmony with nature; to impersonal organization, an intense relation to a guru."[2] In this complex social situation, in addition to its Asian American constituents, the Buddhist movement in America has been especially attractive to individuals from Jewish backgrounds, as Rodger Kamenetz has pointed out;[3] to many African Americans, following the highly visible Buddhist involvement of Tina Turner and bell hooks;[4] to those steeped in the new language of the wellness movement, conversant with the works of Jon Kabat-Zinn,[5] Mark Epstein,[6] and others; and to a small but continually growing portion of the highly literate, socially and politically active Euro-American urban elite.

Not all of the attention highlighting American Buddhism has occurred in the popular press and print media. Following a profusion of scholarly publications, Syracuse University sponsored a major conference in spring 1977 with the exuberant and perhaps presumptuous title, "The Flowering of Buddhism in America." The trend has continued, expanding to include panels at professional meetings, doctoral dissertations, and even university courses.

More recently, the Institute of Buddhist Studies in Berkeley, California, with funding from the Bukkyo Dendo Kyokai (founded by Reverend Dr. Yehan Numata in Japan), sponsored a twelve-week lecture series organized by Kenneth Tanaka and entitled "Buddhisms in America: An Expanding Frontier" during the fall of 1994. In January 1997, the most ambitious conference of its kind on the topic, titled "Buddhism in America: A Landmark Conference of the Future of Buddhist Meditative Practice in the West," was held in Boston, and in May 1997, Harvard University's Harvard Buddhist Studies Forum sponsored a highly comprehensive conference on the academic investigation of American Buddhism called "Scholarly Contributions to the Study of Buddhism in America."

## Historical Concerns

Although it is now rather common to refer to Oriental influences in the writings of such prominent American literary figures as Henry David Thoreau, Ralph Waldo Emerson, and Walt Whitman, and to point to the impact of the Theosophists on the Oriental movement in America, the more specific beginnings of Buddhism in America can be traced to the Chinese immigrants who began to appear on the West Coast in the 1840s.[7] Prior to the discovery of gold at Sutter's Mill, the number of Chinese immigrants was small, but with the news of the golden wealth in the land, the figure increased exponentially. Rick Fields, author of *How the Swans Came to the Lake: A Narrative History of Buddhism in America*, has suggested that by 1852, twenty thousand Chinese were present in California, and within a decade, nearly one-tenth of the California population was Chinese.[8] In the Chinese temples that dotted the California coastline and began to appear in the Chinatown section of San Francisco, the religious practice was an eclectic blend of Buddhism, Taoism, and Confucianism, and although there were many Buddhist priests in residence, a distinctly Chinese Buddhism on the North American continent did not develop until much later.

The Japanese presence in America developed more slowly than the Chinese, but had much greater impact. By 1890, when the Chinese presence was already quite apparent, the Japanese population was barely two thousand. The World Parliament of Religions, however, held in conjunction with the Chicago World's Fair in 1893, radically changed the entire landscape for Japanese Buddhism in America. Among the participants at the parliament was Shaku Sōen, a Rōshi who was to return to America a decade later and promote the school of Rinzai Zen (one of the two major branches of Japanese Zen Buddhism). Sōen Rōshi returned to America in 1905, lecturing in several cities and establishing a basic ground for the entry of Zen. Upon his return to Japan in 1906, three of his students were selected to promote the Rinzai lineage in America.

The first of Sōen Rōshi's students, Nyōgen Senzaki, came to California in the first decade of the twentieth century, but delayed his teaching mission until 1922. Sōen Rōshi's second disciple, Shaku Sōkatsu, lived in America from 1906 to 1908, and again from 1909 to 1910, but eventually returned to Japan without having made much impact. By far Sōen Rōshi's most noted disciple, and the man who made the most impact on the early growth of Buddhism in America, was Daisetz Teitaro Suzuki. Suzuki worked for Open Court Publishing Company in LaSalle, Illinois, from 1897 to 1909, but returned to Japan to pursue a career in Buddhist Studies. He visited America again from 1936 until the beginning of World War II, and eventually returned for a final time from 1950 to 1958, lecturing frequently in American universities and cities.

Nonetheless, the Rinzai lineage was not the only one to develop in America. The Sōtō tradition (the other major branch of Japanese Zen) began to appear in America in the 1950s. By the mid-1950s, Soyu Matsuoka Rōshi had established the Chicago Buddhist Temple, and Shunryu Suzuki Rōshi arrived in San Francisco in 1959, founding the San Francisco Zen Center shortly thereafter. The Dharma successors to Suzuki Rōshi have continued the Sōtō lineage, while other teachers in this lineage (including one of the few female rōshis, Jiyu Kennett) have also appeared.

In addition to the traditional forms of Rinzai and Sōtō Zen, still another form of Zen has appeared in America, one that attempts to harmonize the major doctrines and practices of each school into a unified whole. This movement owes its American origins to Sogaku Harada, although he never visited the United States himself. Proponents of this approach included Taizan Maezumi Rōshi (arriving in 1956), Hakuun Yasutani Rōshi (who visited the United States first in 1962, and who visited regularly until his death in 1973), and Philip Kapleau, an American by birth who first learned about Japanese religion and culture while serving as a court reporter in 1946 during the War Crimes Trials held in Tokyo. Maezumi Rōshi and Kapleau Rōshi have been enormously successful. Maezumi Rōshi established the Zen Center of Los Angeles, where he resided until his death in 1995. He left a dozen Dharma heirs, many of whom have developed their own vital, creative communities. Kapleau Rōshi too was quite successful, having built a stable Zen community in Rochester, New York, that was notable for its attempt to develop an American style for Zen practice; it recently celebrated its thirtieth anniversary. Other significant teachers are Robert Aitken Rōshi, who founded the Diamond Sangha in Hawaii in 1959, Eidō Shimano Rōshi, who first came to the United States as a translator for Yasutani Rōshi, and Joshu Sasaki Rōshi, who founded the Cimarron Zen Center in Los Angeles in 1966 and the Mount Baldy Zen Center five years later.

Zen was surely not the only Japanese Buddhist tradition to make an appearance in America before the turn of the twentieth century. In 1898 two Japanese missionaries, Shuye Sonoda and Kakuryo Nishijima, were sent to San Francisco to establish the Buddhist Mission of North America, an organization associated with a Pure Land school of Japanese Buddhism. Although their formation was seriously hampered by the Japanese Immigration Exclusion Act of 1924, thirty-three main temples were active by 1931. With the outbreak of World War II, more than one hundred thousand Japanese Americans (more than half of whom were Buddhist and two-thirds American born) were relocated to internment camps. In 1944, the name Buddhist Mission of North America was changed to Buddhist Churches of America. With headquarters in San Francisco, this Buddhist organization remains one of the most stable Buddhist communities in North America.

In the 1960s, another form of Japanese Buddhism appeared on the American landscape. It was known as Nichiren Shōshū of America, and by 1974 it boasted 258 chapters and over 200,000 members (although these figures were highly suspect). This group grew out of the Sōka Gakkai movement in Japan, a nonmeditative form of Buddhism that based its teachings on the thirteenth-century figure Nichiren (1222–82) and his emphasis on the doctrines and practices focusing on or deriving from the famous *Lotus Sūtra*. Brought to this country by Masayasa Sadanaga (who changed his name to George Williams), the organization set up headquarters in Santa Monica, California, where it began an active program of proselytizing. Although the group has recently splintered, it remains a formidable Buddhist presence in America, having become extremely attractive among Euro-American and African American Buddhists.

The Chinese are once again making their presence visible in American Buddhism. Although not nearly so visible as the Japanese Buddhist groups, several Chinese Buddhist organizations have appeared in the last half-century. Perhaps the most notable of these is a largely monastic group originally known as the Sino-American Buddhist Association which, until his recent death, was under the direction of a venerable monk named Hsüan-Hua. Established in 1959, this organization has developed a huge monastery in Talmage, California, known as the "City of Ten Thousand Buddhas," which serves as the headquarters of what is now identified as the Dharma Realm Buddhist Association. Of even larger size (and quite possibly importance) is the Hsi Lai Temple outside Los Angeles, founded in 1978, and now offering a wide variety of Buddhist teachings and services. Other Chinese Buddhist groups can be found in virtually every major metropolitan area. There are approximately 125 Chinese Buddhist organizations in the United States, more than half of which are in California and one-fifth of which are in New York. The religious practice of the Chinese Buddhist groups in America is largely an eclectic combination of various Buddhist schools, combining Ch'an, Vinaya, T'ien-t'ai, Tantra, and Pure Land practices. Most of these practices are Mahāyāna-based, and a similar kind of approach is followed by the Vietnamese Buddhist groups that have begun to appear in urban areas, mostly as a result of a large influx of Vietnamese immigrants following the termination of the United States' involvement in Vietnam. To some degree, this eclectic approach can also be seen in the various Korean Buddhist groups that began appearing in the United States in the latter half of the twentieth century.

The Buddhist culture to enter America most recently is the Tibetan. Although a few Buddhist groups appeared in the West prior to 1960, the majority came after the Tibetan holocaust, during which the Communist Chinese made every effort to extinguish religion in Tibet. Following an immediate exile in India, Bhutan, Nepal, and Sikkim, the diaspora has widened, with many Tibetans seeking to reestablish their sacred lineages on American soil. Communities from each of the four major Tibetan sects can now be found in America, with those founded by Tarthang Tulku and Chögyam Trungpa Rinpoche being especially popular and visible. The Tibetan groups are the most colorful of all the Buddhist groups now prospering in America, possessing a rich tradition of Buddhist art and a powerful psychological approach to mental health. They continue to grow rapidly, being very attractive to Euro-American Buddhists. It is no wonder, then, that they quote the thousand-year-old saying attributed to the sage Padmasambhava to explain their rapid growth: "When the iron bird flies, and horses run on wheels, the Tibetan people will be scattered like ants across the World, and the Dharma will come to the land of the Red Man."

The final sectarian tradition to be considered is that of the Theravāda, which permeated South Asia following the missionary tradition of the

Indian King Aśoka in the third century BCE, and which continues today. Until quite recently, most Thervāda groups in the United States were similar to the Buddhist Vihāra Society in Washington, DC, an organization founded in 1965 under the direction of the Venerable Bope Vinita from Sri Lanka, and appealing to the large diplomatic community in the nation's capital. Now, however, as many Buddhists from Laos, Cambodia, Thailand, and Burma have migrated to the United States to escape the economic and political uncertainty of their native homes, there is a vigorous new infusion of Theravāda Buddhism into America. Temples are appearing in major cities, as these immigrant groups have tended to settle in ethnic communities not unlike the Chinese and Japanese communities of the early decades of the twentieth century.

## Developmental Issues

Outlining the historical details of the Buddhist movement in America tells but a small part of the story, for the growth of American Buddhism is far more than its history. Rather, it presents a struggle to acculturate and accommodate on the part of a religious tradition that initially appeared to be wholly foreign to the American mindset. It is important to realize that two different groups were primarily responsible for Buddhism's earliest growth in America. On the one hand, Buddhism is the native religion of a significant number of Asian immigrants. On the other hand, it became the religion, or at least the subject of serious personal interest, for an ever-increasing group of (mostly) Euro-Americans who embraced Buddhism primarily out of intellectual attraction and interest in spiritual practice. This latter circumstance has created its own Buddhist subculture that is literate, urban, upwardly mobile, perhaps even elite in its life orientation. That bifurcation makes even the issue of Buddhist identity and membership a murky problem, further exacerbated with confusion about various Buddhist positions on ethical issues, sexuality, gender roles, and the like. This developmental pattern and the issues associated with it need to be explored alongside a careful consideration of each of the Buddhist traditions now present on American soil.

Thomas Tweed's important and influential book *The American Encounter with Buddhism 1844–1912: Victorian Culture and the Limits of Dissent* suggests a variety of reasons for late-Victorian America's fascination with Buddhism.[9] Clearly, there was a growing dissatisfaction with the answers provided by the traditional religions of the time, and apologists, such as Paul Carus, were quick to suggest that imported Asian religions might well offer more satisfactory answers to the religious needs of Americans. Additionally, several Asian teachers, such as Anagarika

Dharmapala and D. T. Suzuki, had sufficient personal charisma to advance that cause. Few Asian Buddhist teachers took up residence in America, however, and the two primary Buddhist organizations – the American Maha Bodhi Society and the Dharma Sangha of Buddha – were institutionally weak. Tweed notes well that while Buddhist sympathizers resonated favorably with the mid-Victorian period's emphasis on optimism and activism as important cultural values, on the whole, Buddhism's presumed characterization as pessimistic and passive made a much more compelling argument for its detractors. Tweed's insightful postscript[10] suggests that, because they were also faced with the serious lack of accurate textual translations, most Victorians, however disillusioned they may have been, looked elsewhere for potential resolutions to their spiritual crises.

That American Buddhism in the late twentieth century seems to be far more extensive than it had at the end of the previous century, and far more visible in American culture, suggests that many of Tweed's postulates for the failure of Victorian Buddhism in America have been remedied. And indeed they have – especially so in the last half of the century.

By 1970, virtually the full extent of Asian Buddhist sects was represented in America, and there was a plethora of Asian Buddhist teachers in permanent residence in the growing number of American Buddhist centers. The growth of these centers has been so staggering in the second half of the twentieth century that in 1988 Don Morreale was able to catalogue nearly 350 pages of listings for these groups in *Buddhist America: Centers, Retreats, Practices*. A new edition has now appeared, aided by a register service posted on the World Wide Web. Dozens of rōshis, along with their Dharma heirs, many Tibetan *tulkus*, Chinese monks and nuns, and an increasing number of Theravāda monks from various South and Southeast Asian cultures are now visibly active on American soil. The presence of a growing number of Asian Buddhist teachers in America has been complemented and augmented by regular visits from global Buddhist leaders such as the Dalai Lama and Thich Nhat Hanh.

Further, these Asian Buddhist teachers, and the gradually increasing number of American Buddhist masters, are beginning to establish an institutional foundation that is stable, solid, and even ecumenical. In 1987 the "World Buddhism in North America" conference was held at the University of Michigan,[11] during which a statement of consensus was promulgated (1) "to create the conditions necessary for tolerance and understanding among Buddhists and non-Buddhists alike," (2) "to initiate a dialogue among Buddhists in North America in order to further mutual understanding, growth in understanding, and cooperation," (3) "to increase our sense of community by recognizing and understanding our differences as well as our common beliefs and practices," and (4) "to cultivate thoughts and actions of friendliness towards others, whether they accept our beliefs or not, and in so doing approach the world as the proper field of Dharma, not as a sphere of conduct irreconcilable with the practice of Dharma." Geographically organized organizations, like the Sangha Council of Southern California, and associations of the students of famous Buddhist masters, such as the White Plum Sangha, linking the Dharma heirs of Taizan Maezumi Rōshi, are now becoming commonplace in the American Buddhist movement.

The availability of accurate primary and secondary literature has expanded almost exponentially in the latter half of the twentieth century. Several university presses, such as the State University of New York Press, University of Hawaii Press, University of California Press, and Princeton University Press, have been leaders in publishing scholarly books devoted to the study of Buddhism, and a variety of trade publishers has emerged as well, such as Snow Lion and Wisdom Publications, that emphasize Buddhism specifically. Reliable translations of the entire Pāli canon are now readily available throughout the world, and a project to publish translations of the entire Chinese Buddhist canon is currently under way, sponsored by the Bukkyo Dendo Kyokai. This translation endeavor represents a significant step forward in the American Buddhist movement because it requires extensive language training in Sanskrit, Pāli, Chinese, Japanese, and Tibetan. This training is usually, although not exclusively, obtained in American universities. As of 1994, nearly two dozen North American universities could boast at least two full-time faculty devoted to the academic discipline of Buddhist Studies, and nearly 150 academic scholars of Buddhism are located on the North American continent, many of whom can best be identified as "scholar-practitioners." Moreover, the American Buddhist movement is aided by the presence of a growing number of individuals who have traveled to Asia for extensive training and then returned to the United States to share their approach with Americans. One of the most successful enterprises of this kind is the Insight Meditation Society in Barre, Massachusetts, initially guided by Joseph Goldstein, Jack Kornfield, Sharon Salzberg, and Christina Feldman, each of whom received extensive *vipassanā* training in Asia.

Certainly, the issue of social and religious anomie is no less critical in the latter years of the twentieth century than it was in the previous century. A quick perusal of Theodore Roszak's *Making of a Counter Culture*, Harvey Cox's *Secular City*, or Peter Berger's *Sacred Canopy* shows how the pervasive influence of secularism and pluralism created the same kind of religious crisis as witnessed prior to the World Parliament of Religions, held in Chicago in 1893.[12] Roszak even argued that the counterculture of the 1960s was, "essentially, an exploration of the politics of consciousness."[13] The counterculture of the twentieth century differed from that of the preceding century, however, in that it was no longer either passive or pessimistic, and this was clearly obvious in the American Buddhist movement.

Quite apart from issues relating to the specificity with which American Buddhist life is manifested (lay versus monastic ideals; urban versus rural lifestyle), a distinct and unique application of Buddhist ethics, creatively called "socially engaged Buddhism," is emerging that demonstrates in dramatic fashion both the *active* and the *optimistic* approach of today's American Buddhism. The overarching approach of socially engaged Buddhism is clearly portrayed in Ken Jones's useful book *The Social Face of Buddhism*, and summarized extremely well in Kenneth Kraft's introduction to his edited volume *Inner Peace, World Peace*.[14] Organizations like the Buddhist Peace Fellowship, founded in 1978, aggressively demonstrate how to strike a careful balance between meditational training and political activism. Their task in bringing this activism and optimism to the American Buddhist public is aided by a strong new Buddhist journalism in America that has fostered exciting publications such as *Tricycle: The Buddhist Quarterly*, the *Shambhala Sun*, and *Turning Wheel: Journal of the Buddhist Peace Fellowship*, as well as many publications of individual Buddhist centers. In addition, the useful and productive development of the Internet has allowed American Buddhism to expand its sphere of influence to a *sangha* not necessarily limited to a given geographic space. The electronic *Journal of Buddhist Ethics*, for example, in its "Global Resources for Buddhist Studies" component, has created links to literally hundreds of American Buddhist *sanghas* across the totality of North America.

Thus the faces of Buddhism in America are many. They are diverse, and enthusiastic, and active, and forward looking in their optimism.

# Notes

1  Peter Berger, *Sacred Canopy: Elements of a Sociological Theory of Religion* (Garden City, NY: Doubleday, 1966), 134, 137.
2  Robert N. Bellah, "The New Consciousness and the Crisis in Modernity," in Charles Y. Glock and Robert N. Bellah, eds., *The New Religious Consciousness* (Berkeley: University of California Press, 1976), 341.
3  See the discussion of so-called JUBUs in Rodger Kamenetz, *The Jew in the Lotus* (San Francisco: HarperSanFrancisco, 1994), 7–15.
4  See bell hooks's interesting short article on racism, "Waking Up to Racism," *Tricycle: The Buddhist Review* 4, 1 (Fall 1994): 42–5.
5  See, for example, Jon Kabat-Zinn, *Wherever You Go, There You Are: Mindfulness Meditation in Everyday Life* (New York: Hyperion, 1995).

6  See, for example, Mark Epstein, *Thoughts Without a Thinker: Psychotherapy from a Buddhist Point of View* (New York: Basic Books, 1995).

7  For an introduction to the historical development of Buddhism in America, see Charles S. Prebish, *American Buddhism* (North Scituate, Mass.: Duxbury Press, 1979): chapter 1 discusses the entry of the Japanese, Chinese, Tibetan, and South Asian Buddhist traditions; the following three chapters discuss problems of growth and acculturation.

8  Rick Fields, *How the Swans Came to the Lake: A Narrative History of Buddhism in America*, 3rd ed. (Boston: Shambhala, 1992), 70–1.

9  See especially chapter 6, "Optimism and Activism," in Thomas A. Tweed, *The American Encounter with Buddhism 1844–1912: Victorian Culture and the Limits of Dissent* (Bloomington: Indiana University Press, 1992), 133–56.

10  Ibid., 157–62.

11  For an account of the conference, see Eleanor Rosch, "World Buddhism in North America Today," *Vajradhatu Sun* 9, 1 (October–November 1987): especially 28.

12  See Berger, *Sacred Canopy*; Harvey Cox, *The Secular City* (New York: Macmillan, 1966); and Theodore Roszak, *The Making of a Counter Culture* (Garden City, NY: Anchor Books, 1969).

13  Roszak, *The Making of a Counter Culture*, 156.

14  See Ken Jones, *The Social Face of Buddhism: An Approach to Political and Social Activism* (London: Wisdom Publications, 1989); and Kenneth Kraft, ed., *Inner Peace, World Peace: Essays on Buddhism and Nonviolence* (Albany: State University of New York Press, 1992).

# 9

# Striving for Muslim Women's Human Rights – Before and Beyond Beijing: An African American Perspective

## Gwendolyn Zoharah Simmons

## Introduction

Like the history of Buddhism, the history of Islam in America involves a mixture of distinctly American religious tendencies with religious customs brought to the United States by immigrants from a number of different cultures. But unlike Buddhism, Islam incorporates universal forms of prayer and fasting that devout Muslims around the world perform in synchronicity. Muslims are also united by intense reverence for the Qur'an, the sacred book believed to contain the perfect and final revelation uttered by God to his prophet Muhammad. From Muslim perspectives, this final revelation completes and supersedes the revelations given to the prophets of Judaism and Christianity.

For a significant minority of African Americans, the universality of Islam, its historic ties to Africa, and its inclusion of many dark-skinned peoples have made Islam an ideal alternative to the patterns of racial segregation and white privilege perceived to characterize American Christianity. But this commitment to racial equality invoked by Muslims of African American descent has

Excerpted from Gwendolyn Zoharah Simmons, "Striving for Muslim Women's Human Rights – Before and Beyond Beijing: An African American Perspective," in *Windows of Faith: Muslim Women Scholar-Activists in North America*, ed. Gisela Webb (Syracuse: Syracuse University Press, 2000), 197–208.

coincided with ideas about sexual inequality introduced by immigrants and visitors from strict Islamic countries. As Gwendolyn Simmons explains, this mixture of ideas has become more complicated with the adoption of restrictive attitudes toward women by increasing numbers of African American Muslims, a trend that reflects fundamentalist currents within American culture as well as patterns of gender inequality characteristic of Islamic cultures in other parts of the world.

At the same time, progressive Islamic women around the world have been working to improve women's health and education and to challenge cultural ideas about female inferiority that, in their view, corrupt the true message of Islam. This worldwide network of culturally progressive Islamic women draws support from agencies based in the United States and reflects the global aspect of religion today as well as the ongoing international scope of American outreach once associated with "the Protestant establishment" described in William R. Hutchison's essay.

It has become more of a practice now for academicians writing about social, political, or anthropological issues to state up front the grounds on which they stand and the perspective they bring to their research and writing. I shall follow that practice. I am a practicing Muslim and an Islamic scholar, presently pursuing both a doctorate in Islamic studies and a certificate in women's studies at Temple University in Philadelphia, Pennsylvania. In part of 1996 and 1997 I spent fifteen months in Jordan and, to a lesser extent, in Palestine researching the women's movements there. My research activities were made possible through a United States Information Agency Near and Middle East Research Training Act (USIA NMERTA) Fellowship granted through the American Center For Oriental Research (ACOR) and a Fulbright dissertation research fellowship. A fair amount of the progressive women's movement activities that I observed in both countries were directly related to their earlier work in preparation for Beijing and their follow-up activities to secure implementation of the Platform For Action (PFA) ratified at the Fourth World Conference on Women (FWCW) held in September of 1995 in Beijing, China. I led an American Friends Service Committee (AFSC) delegation of nine women to Beijing. There I was actively involved with various Muslim women's workshops, especially those related to securing human rights.

For me as an American woman convert to Islam, engaging in the research and writing of this chapter is more than an academic exercise. This is an issue of real concern to me as I navigate my way through the spiritual, cultural, and legal aspects of my religion. I am also a feminist and an activist. I began my activist work in the US Civil Rights movement in the 1960s. I was both a leader and a foot soldier in that historic struggle for justice and equality. I grew up in the Jim Crow South (Memphis, Tennessee) where I experienced the United States's own brand of racial apartheid. In my early life I was relegated to the back of the bus, to the "colored" toilets, water fountains, theater balconies, and hamburger joints (if at all). I was accustomed to not having hotel accommodations when traveling or entrance to the public library or the zoo (except on designated days; in Memphis, Thursdays were "colored" people's day). There were many other indignities I experienced but never accepted, such as whites routinely calling me *"nigger"* or *"gal"* and the ever-present fear that I might be the victim of a racially motivated hate crime with little hope for justice. As a black women, there was the added fear of being the victim of white male sexual assault with the knowledge that if it occurred, justice was not likely to prevail.

What I now know in retrospect is that the worst part of being an African American person in that era was the almost complete erasure of my people's heritage and contributions as actors on the grand stage of history. Racist white America had worked thoroughly to delete Africa and its children from the history books, movies, and television programs. For the most part, I thought, then, that my *"real"* history began with slavery, for which it was suggested I should be thankful because the slavers had *"rescued"* my ancestors from a *"barbarous and uncivilized land and life"* in the jungles of Africa. Because my knowledge of Africa was largely gleaned from Tarzan movies that I saw in sequel every Saturday at the black theater in my neighborhood, there was a subtle and hidden shame for being so visibly a descendent of the *"dark continent."* (I am a dark brown woman with African features.) I internalized the racist history and ideology and secretly longed to be other than myself. Seeing my reflection in the mirror often caused me pain.

My journey to full personhood was accelerated with my recruitment by the Student Nonviolent Co-ordinating Committee (SNCC) workers to join the demonstrations to desegregate the restaurants, hotels, public libraries, train and bus stations, and other public places from which African Americans were barred. Repeatedly confronting the racist establishment owners and workers besides the Atlanta police forces (defenders of injustice) gave me a newfound pride and courage. From these beginning assertions of full personhood, I increased my involvement and commitment to securing justice for me and my people. Jailings, beatings, vicious racist attacks, and the courage of my compatriots, some of whom were only in junior high, heightened my resolve to continue in the struggle. When I made the decision to go to Mississippi in the summer of 1964 as a participant in the Mississippi Freedom Summer Project, I went against my family's wishes and my own fear of the worst state in the Union for blacks. All of my life as a child in Memphis, Tennessee, I had heard of the horrors of Mississippi. My family knew blacks who had literally escaped from plantations where they had been held in virtual slavery (as indentured servants) as late as the fifties and sixties. Because I had become part of the student leadership of SNCC, I had participated in the SNCC decision to do the project. *"To crack the state"* was the goal of the summer project, Bob Moses, state director of the Mississippi project, would often say.

I knew the death toll of blacks in the state. The *Jet Magazine* picture of the swollen body of thirteen-year-old Emmit Till, when it was pulled from a river in Mississippi (he was killed, tied to weights, and thrown in a river for allegedly whistling at a white girl) when I was ten or twelve years old, is indelibly imprinted in my memory. I knew about Medgar Evers (the brilliant civil rights leader who was shot down on his front porch in Jackson, Mississippi, for his efforts to secure black rights), too, and several others whose deaths were reported in the Memphis black press. Yet, I *had* to participate fully in the movement to make blacks *"free"* in spite of my fear. What had been a three-month commitment to Mississippi turned into almost two years. I, by default, became the project director of the Laurel, Mississippi, project (the original director was arrested and run out of town). I could not leave at summer's end because our work was only beginning, and the local folks needed a few of us "outsiders" to stay to help keep the fledgling movement growing. Although I gave my all in that project, I went away with much more than I gave. Any internalized myths and stereotypes about blacks' happiness with the status quo or our inability to organize potent movements for change were eradicated. Dispelled also were all embedded stereotypes about women's weakness, lack of skills, and inability to lead. Of course I was already aware of the strength of women as religious and political leaders from my exposure to women of power and courage throughout my life, beginning with my own grandmother, Rhoda Douglas. It was during this period in Mississippi that I began identifying myself as a feminist. The African American women of Laurel and the whole state of Mississippi were the backbone of the Freedom movement. Their involvement outnumbered the men's. And in most instances, their commitment and endurance were greater. They were both leaders and foot soldiers. The Fanny Lou Hammers, Victoria Grays, Eunita Blackwells, Annie Devines, Euberta Spinks, Susie Ruffins, Carrie Claytons, and many others too numerous to list are etched in my heart and memory forever. I was favored by God to get to know and to work closely with these strong women in helping to build the Mississippi movement. These women helped mold and shape my character.

As a result of my years in the Civil Rights movement and the Black Power movement that it helped to ignite, I learned that most, if not all, of what I had imbibed of white racism as a child were lies perpetuated by a system hellbent on keeping my mind enslaved, even if it had grudgingly and partially *"freed"* my people's bodies. The lies and stereotypes about women as the "weaker sex" were also exposed for what they are, men's efforts to maintain power over women through systematic brainwashing. Religion, tradition, and culture, I learned, have been used historically to convince women of their inferiority and their second-class status just as they had been used to convince African Americans of the same.

Over the decades spent in the various movements of my time (civil rights, peace, and women's), I have engaged in a deprogramming process, an unlearning of all the internalized oppressions ingested since my childhood. Little by little, I have been able to stand tall and take my place as a full-fledged human being at life's table. This has meant divesting myself of racist and sexist images of divinely decreed inferiority. I had thrown off much of the internalized racism and sexism before becoming a Muslim in the mid-1970s. Clearly, I had no desire to reoppress myself as a woman in the name of religion. I found unacceptable the notion that woman is a secondary creation made for man's use.

Therefore, my relationship with my chosen religion, Islam, has been wrought with ambivalence and tension. My biggest problem has been with the traditional depiction of women and our role in both the religion and in society. You may ask how I came to be a Muslim given the above brief biographical account and given the stereotypical depiction in the West of Islam as the most misogynist of the three Abrahamic Traditions.

My conversion to Sunni Islam was through the example and guidance of a Sufi teacher from Sri Lanka, Sheikh Muhammad Raheem Bawa Muhaiyadeen. I was drawn to the religion by its mystical and spiritual aspects as taught by him. The beautiful prayer rituals, the month of fasting, the pilgrimage to Mecca (which I was recently graced by God to make), the particularly Sufistic practices, such as *dhikr* and the *maulid*s, and the Sufi stories of mystical quests leading to union with God drew me to the religion. Bawa, as he is affectionately called by all of his disciples, taught an Islam of love, compassion, wisdom, and human unity. His own life mirrored what he taught. He was a wise, compassionate, and loving human being. In his daily discourses which he gave for more than fifteen years of his life here in the United States, Bawa pleaded with his racially and gender mixed audiences to love one another, eschew violence, racial intolerance, separations, egotism, anger, and injustice. He urged his followers, who were from a variety of religious traditions, to come into their true birthright and live as *"real human beings"* (*insan al-kamil*) and to exemplify in their every thought, word, and deed, the *"three thousand gracious qualities of Allah"* *and His ninety-nine attributes*, which include patience, tolerance, and compassion. In the foreword to Bawa's book, *Islam and World Peace: Explanations of a Sufi*, Annemarie Schimmel, retired professor of Indo-Muslim culture at Harvard University, wrote, "Real Islam is a deep and unquestioning trust in God, the realization of the truth that there is no deity save God" and of the threefold aspect of religious life: that of *islam*, complete surrender to God; *iman*, unquestioning faith in Him and His wisdom; and *ihsan*, to do right and to act beautifully, because one knows that God is always watching man's actions and thoughts (Muhaiyaddeen 1987, iii).

Bawa taught that true Islam is "equality, peacefulness, and unity"; that it is exemplified in the human being's life by "inner patience, contentment, trust in God, and praise of God." This person will become God's representative on earth. That person in his or her own life will demonstrate God's qualities, God's action, and God's conduct. Bawa made it perfectly clear that this was a spiritual state accessible to human beings of both genders, equally.

This was the Islam that I embraced unequivocally and joyously. For those who sat with Bawa and understood his message, there is no question about equality between males and females (spiritually or intellectually). From the very beginning Bawa picked women for leadership roles in the community, a practice that continues to this day. Women and men work freely together in an atmosphere of sisterly and brotherly love. Although modesty and chastity are observed, this is done without rigid enforcement of gender segregation. Nor is there a need for hierarchical gender arrangements. Women perform tasks that are often said to be "male" jobs and, likewise, men perform tasks mistakenly thought to be "for women only." For example, women head many of the Fellowship's departments; one of the organization's three presidents is a woman; the executive secretary who runs Fellowship operations is a woman; several women sit on the organization's board and on the Mosque Committee. Women often head the committees that oversee the *Ids* and other religious and commemorative festivals that are observed. Women also often lead the weekly public meetings, presenting their interpretations and understandings of Bawa's teachings. Women serve as presidents of some of the Fellowship branches (chapters) located around the United States. In his discourses Bawa often used feminine images in his descriptions of God's care for his creation and in his descriptions of his relationship to members as their sheikh. He often referred to himself as *"having given birth to all of us, his disciples,"* and he would say that he was *"nursing us from his breast of wisdom."* He constantly reiterated the "feminine" qualities of Allah, His *compassion* and His *mercy* for his creations as being two of the most important of Allah's attributes.

Bawa, believed by many to be a *Qutb* (a reviver of the faith and a divinely inspired wise man) was not interested in returning his disciples to a culturally Arab seventh-century Islam. His was a twentieth-century Islam that adhered to the foundations and to the eternal and universal principles of the religion while it embraced the knowledge and understanding of this era. A saying that the Chinese Women's movement popularized some years ago – "Women hold up half of the sky" – is amply exemplified in the Fellowship Community.

As a Muslim woman, when I remain within my own religious community, for the most part, there is no problem with overt sexism or exclusion. But once I venture out into the larger US Islamic community or into the Islamic practices that I found in parts of the Middle East, I find a very different situation, a difficult one for me to accept. Here in the States, many *imams* and other religious leaders, including some in the African American Muslim community, seem to embrace the most conservative views when it comes to Islamic interpretations of the role of Muslim women. Practices are embraced here that are either severely questioned or even under attack in the Muslim Middle East and other parts of the Islamic world by progressive Muslim men and women. Examples of these expanding practices in the States include the following: growing numbers of polygamous marriages, young women being encouraged to marry early, produce many children, and even give up their schooling to do so, the discouraging of women's participation in the public prayers in the mosque, the urging of women's withdrawal from public life, the insistence that their only role is that of mother and homemaker, increased face veiling, unquestioned obedience to male family members, and rigid gender segregation. I have also found that some of the more misogynist passages from the *hadith* and sexist interpretations of Qur'anic texts are often quoted as the justification for the views and practices being embraced. I find these trends troubling and unacceptable for me personally.

In addition, there is widespread resistance to a public exchange of ideas within the Muslim community, especially when initiated by women, who are expected to simply "accept" male perspectives and interpretations. These conservative interpretations defy what I, and many other progressive Muslims, see as the essentially egalitarian message of the Holy Qur'an and of the early Islamic community. These conservative views deeply offend my notion of what is just. Furthermore, given the historic role that African American women have played in women's struggle for justice, it is unbelievable that African American male Muslim leaders seek to marginalize women in the Islamic community, attempting to relegate them solely to domestic and silent roles. In my opinion, such practices will only accelerate the growing decline in impoverished African American communities at a time when it needs its best religious minds (male and female) engaged in the project to rebuild inner-city communities and to rescue large numbers of children from crime, drugs, and despair. *"No Nation can rise higher than the status of its women"* is an old proverb that is as true today as it ever was. I fear that this attempted relegation of women to domestic roles is a manifestation of male egotism and an expression of the long-held belief by black men that black women have too much power. Unfortunately, this is an old issue in the African American community, long predating the black large-scale entry into Islam. I experienced it often in the Civil Rights and in the Black Power movements. It was rife in what was called the Black Nationalist movement of the seventies and eighties. Many black men have longed to participate as full members in the *patriarchy*. This *"right"* was taken from them as the result of slavery and its aftermath. In its own horrible way, slavery put enslaved African males and females on the same level as far as work and responsibility were concerned. After slavery, economics demanded that black women continue to work to help maintain their families. This gave black women a semblance of independence, which has long been resented by some black men. I fear that Islam is being used as a cover to continue this age-old struggle to bring black women under black men's control.

Many leaders in the Muslim world have discovered that it is very difficult to build modern national states while oppressing one-half of the population. It would be good if African American male Muslim leaders could learn from these leaders' experiences about the negative consequences to the whole society of oppressing more than half of their population.

## Muslim Women Struggle for Human Rights: The Context

Most non-Muslims credit Islam as being the root cause of the oppression of women in the Muslim world. In a special Middle East report, "Women's Rights in the Arab World", authors Ramla Khalidi and Judith Tucker write:

> For many Westerners, the issue of Arab Women's rights and the broader problematic of gender and power in the region can be neatly summed up in one word, "Islam." The image of Islam as the fount of unmitigated oppression of women, as the foundation of a gender system that categorically denies women equal rights and subjects them to men, recurs in the movies, magazines and books in our popular culture as well as in much academic discourse.
>
> *(Khalidi and Tucker n.d., 2)*

But, of course, it is not that simple. A growing number of Muslim women scholars and activists have begun to challenge the notion that Islam is synonymous with the oppression of women. These women, many of whom consider themselves feminists, are questioning the male and often misogynist interpretations of the sacred tenets of Islam. They are focusing a women's, or feminist, lens on Islam's canon, and they are deriving different interpretations from those that have prevailed for centuries. As the two authors quoted above write: "[Seeing] a single essence or 'spirit' of Islam, a single blueprint for gender roles . . . proves difficult. Islam is not one thing, but is rather a set of beliefs and values that has evolved over time in rhythm with changing historical conditions and local customs and practices with which it came into contact" (Khalidi and Tucker n.d., 2).

It is these women scholars and activists who are bringing this insight and information to the forefront. They argue convincingly that Islam is not a monolithic structure etched immutably in stone for eternity. They are seeking to separate Islam, the religion, from culture, tradition, and social mores. They are calling for, and are themselves reinterpreting, the sacred texts. They are reviewing the history of the religion, at times bringing to the foreground the interpretations of earlier sects or groups in Islam who were labeled heterodox and their views dismissed. Just as happens among Christian and Jewish feminists, some Muslim women express anger toward religious institutions that undergird the oppression of them and their sisters. But, for the most part, these women want to work within their religious tradition and seek to reinterpret, reconceptualize, contextualize, and historicize Islam and their societies' rituals and practices. All of the women activists with whom I have spoken or whose materials I have read realize that they have a difficult task before them. Thirteen centuries of belief and cultural traditions are difficult to change.

As many, if not most, of the Muslim feminists see the need to change their societies within an Islamic context, they question Western feminist paradigms. There is also the problem of the heritage of colonialism. In the nineteenth and early twentieth centuries, colonial powers repeatedly used the issue of gender to advance their own agendas in the region. They argued that the oppression of women justified colonial intervention and that the imperial project would elevate women to the standard of equality putatively present in northern Europe. As Khalidi and Tucker point out, "the linking of gender issues to Western intervention and the invocation of Western standards to which all must aspire left a bitter legacy of mistrust. This legacy continues to cloud relations between women in the West and women in the Arab [Muslim] world" (Khalidi and Tucker n.d., 2).

Women here in the West use certain benchmark aspects in a society to measure the position of women within it. These include legal equity, reproductive freedom, and the opportunity to express and fulfill the individual self through work, through art, or through sexuality. But are these the only criteria by which one should assess the status of women in a particular society? Are these the universals of "feminism"? If one looks at what the women in the Muslim or Islamic world say are their main concerns, one gets a somewhat different list of priorities. They want legal equity, political participation, education, health care, and the right to employment (Khalidi and Tucker n.d., 2). Although there are similarities and overlap, what is quite obviously missing is the emphasis on the opportunity to express and fulfill the *individual self* through work, through art, or through sexuality.

On a group trip to the Middle East in October 1994, we met with a Muslim woman feminist psychologist on the faculty at the University of Jordan in Amman, Dr. Arwa al-Amry. She spoke with us about the state of women in Jordan. Although she noted that there had been great strides in education, health care, and equal pay for equal work, there had been little advancement in the area of gender relationships, particularly on the domestic front. Dr. al-Amry said that the model of gender relations in the Western world was not attractive to women in her part of the world. She spoke of the commodification and appropriation of women's sexuality and their bodies for commercial purposes in the West. She described the way that they see it: "Males in the Islamic world control women by veiling them and keeping them secluded; in the West, males control females by stripping them naked and exposing their nudity for sexual gratification and commercialization." For Dr. al-Amry and her feminist colleagues at their Women's Center, both positions are objectionable.

Two main factors must be understood in assessing gender issues in the Muslim world. One is the Islamic view of gender, which is, of course, based upon the sacred texts of Islam. First is the Qur'an, considered the divine revelations from God to the Prophet Muhammad, which is, for the most part, uncontested. The Qur'an does prescribe gender differences in terms of responsibilities and rights. The *surah* (chapter) most often quoted to support male control and domination is *Surah* 4:34. A traditional interpretation of it states: "Men are the protectors and providers (*qawwamma ala*) of women." Muslim women scholars, such as Amina Wadud and Azizah al-Hibri, are questioning this translation and the interpretation of this particular verse. Muslim women scholars say that many of the Qur'anic verses upon which women's subjugation is built are difficult to translate and are subject to varying interpretations (Wadud 1992; al-Hibri 1985). The Qur'anic verse most often used to impose dress codes on women, "women cover your adornments" (*Surah* 24:31), can be understood as mandating veiling for the good Muslim woman or simply as requiring reasonably modest dress.

The question of equality in the Qur'an is mixed. The sacred book clearly equates the genders in the spiritual or religious realms. Men and women have equal religious responsibility and will receive the same reward or punishment for their behavior. Yet there are statements that seem to indicate differences between men and women that disadvantage women and privilege men over them: for example, that women's legal testimony is worth one-half a man's or that women's inheritance is one-half that of their male relatives. Some Muslim feminists say that although these stipulations had their reasons and, perhaps, justification in the middle of the seventh century, there is no need or justification for a continuation of these practices in the last decade of the twentieth century. Herein lies the controversy. Of course, this argument brings these women interpreters into conflict with a huge number of people in the Muslim world who believe that the Qur'an, as the immutable and unchangeable word of Allah, is the *literal truth* for all times. This prevalent view holds that the interpretation of the holy book is not subject to context or history but is to be accepted literally as a whole. This is a major issue that Muslim feminists who hold a different view will have to struggle with for some time to come. Many of the women activists with whom I worked and spoke saw this issue of "literal" interpretation versus a contextual and historical interpretation of the sacred Islamic texts as a large and difficult matter with which to contend. Many of them even dread having to face it and are actually avoiding it for as long as possible. This was true in both Jordan and Palestine. The issue of textual interpretation is a potentially volatile one, and these women, for the most part, are handling it gingerly if at all. Yet most will acknowledge that it will be next to impossible to avoid it in the effort to change the public's perceptions of women's roles in society.

## Works cited

al-Hibri, Azizah. 1985. "Women In Islam." *Hypatia* (Special issue no. 2). New York: Pergamon Press.
Khalidi, Ramla, and Tucker, Judith. N.d. "Women's Rights in the Arab World." Special report of the Middle East Research and Information Project (MERIP), 2–8.
Muhaiyaddeen, M. R. Bawa. 1987. *Islam and World Peace: Explanations of a Sufi.* Philadelphia: Fellowship Press.
Wadud, Amina (authorship listed as Wadud-Muhsin). 1992. *Qur'an and Woman.* Kuala Lumpur: Penerbit Fajar Bakti. SDN.BHD.

# Part II

# Primary Documents

# 10

# A Model of Christian Charity
# (1630)

*John Winthrop*

## Introduction

In this excerpt from his address onboard the flagship *Arbella* en route to New England, John Winthrop expressed a vision of Christian community that he hoped Puritans would soon actualize in America. Echoing the New Testament's radical call for perfect love, Winthrop urged his fellow travelers to be "knit together...as one man" in intense but peaceful devotion to God and compassion for one another. Echoing stories about God's relationship to Israel in the Hebrew Bible, Winthrop warned that God expected more from the New England Puritans than from other people. If God promised to love and cherish them above others, he also asked more from them, and would be angrier if they disobeyed. In Winthrop's view, then, the Puritan adventure in America was an extension of biblical history. It also held a promise of America's becoming a Christian nation whose goodness and justice would culminate biblical history.

As governor of Massachusetts Bay Colony, Winthrop played a central role in constructing social order in New England. His devotion to the Puritan vision of Christian community helped pull people together in common cause. At the same time, however, this vision served as a constant reminder of the Puritans' many failures, God's judgment upon them, and the punishments they

Excerpted from John Winthrop, "A Model of Christian Charity" (1630), *Old South Leaflets*, no. 207, reprinted in *The Puritans in America: A Narrative Anthology*, ed. Alan Heimert and Andrew Delbanco (Cambridge, Mass.: Harvard University Press, 1985), 89–92.

deserved for their dissension, greed, and hypocrisy. Nothing rooted within Puritanism has lasted longer than this tendency to condemn America for its betrayal of religious ideals.

Whatsoever we did or ought to have done when we lived in England, the same must we do, and more also, where we go. That which the most in their churches maintain as a truth in profession only, we must bring into familiar and constant practice, as in this duty of love. We must love brotherly without dissimulation; we must love one another with a pure heart fervently. We must bear one another's burthens. We must not look only on our own things, but also on the things of our brethren, neither must we think that the Lord will bear with such failings at our hands as he doth from those among whom we have lived; and that for three reasons:

First, in regard of the more near bond of marriage between him and us, wherein he hath taken us to be his after a most strict and peculiar manner, which will make him the more jealous of our love and obedience. So he tells the people of Israel, "You only have I known of all the families of the earth, therefore will I punish you for your transgressions." Secondly, because the Lord will be sanctified in them that come near him. We know that there were many that corrupted the service of the Lord, some setting up altars before his own, others offering both strange fire and strange sacrifices also; yet there came no fire from heaven or other sudden judgment upon them, as did upon Nadab and Abihu,[1] who yet we may think did not sin presumptuously. Thirdly, when God gives a special commission he looks to have it strictly observed in every article. When he gave Saul a commission to destroy Amalek, he indented[2] with him upon certain articles, and because he failed in one of the least, and that upon a fair pretense, it lost him the kingdom which should have been his reward if he had observed his commission.[3]

Thus stands the cause between God and us. We are entered into covenant with him for this work. We have taken out a commission, the Lord hath given us leave to draw our own articles. We have professed to enterprise these actions, upon these and those ends, we have hereupon besought him of favor and blessing. Now if the Lord shall please to hear us, and bring us in peace to the place we desire, then hath he ratified this covenant and sealed our commission, [and] will expect a strict performance of the articles contained in it. But if we shall neglect the observation of these articles which are the ends we have propounded and, dissembling with our God, shall fall to embrace this present world and prosecute our carnal intentions, seeking great things for ourselves and our posterity, the Lord will surely break out in wrath against us, be revenged of such a perjured people, and make us know the price of the breach of such a covenant.

Now the only way to avoid this shipwrack, and to provide for our posterity, is to follow the counsel of Micah, to do justly, to love mercy, to walk humbly with our God. For this end, we must be knit together in this work as one man. We must entertain each other in brotherly affection, we must be willing to abridge ourselves of our superfluities, for the supply of others' necessities. We must uphold a familiar commerce together in all meekness, gentleness, patience, and liberality. We must delight in each other, make others' conditions our own, rejoice together, mourn together, labor and suffer together, always having before our eyes our commission and community in the work, our community as members of the same body. So shall we keep the unity of the spirit in the bond of peace. The Lord will be our God, and delight to dwell among us as his own people, and will command a blessing upon us in all our ways, so that we shall see much more of his wisdom, power, goodness, and truth, than formerly we have been acquainted with. We shall find that the God of Israel is among us, when ten of us shall be able to resist a thousand of our enemies; when he shall make us a praise and glory that men shall say of succeeding plantations, "the Lord make it like that of New England." For we must consider that we shall be as a city upon a hill.[4] The eyes of all people are upon us, so that if we shall deal falsely with our God in this work we have undertaken, and so cause him to withdraw his present help from us, we shall be made a story and a byword through the world. We shall open the mouths of enemies to speak evil of the ways of God, and all professors for God's sake. We shall shame the faces of many of God's worthy servants, and cause their prayers to be turned into curses upon us till we be consumed out of the good land whither we are agoing.

And to shut up this discourse with that exhortation of Moses, that faithful servant of the Lord, in his last farewell to Israel, Deuteronomy 30: Beloved, there is now set before us life and good, death and evil, in that we are commanded this day to love the Lord our God, and to love one another, to walk in his ways and to keep his commandments and his ordinance and his laws, and the articles of our covenant with him, that we may live and be multiplied, and that the Lord our God may bless us in the land whither we go to possess it. But if our hearts shall turn away, so that we will not obey, but shall be seduced, and worship other gods, our pleasures and profits, and serve them; it is propounded unto us this day, we shall surely perish out of the good land whither we pass over this vast sea to possess it.

Therefore let us choose life,
that we and our seed
may live by obeying his
voice and cleaving to him,
for he is our life and
our prosperity.

## Notes

1　Aaron's sons, whom God destroys by fire in anger at their disobeying his injunction against burnt offerings.
2　Made a formal agreement.
3　Saul spared the livestock of the Amalekites, thereby incurring the wrath of God, who had ordered their total destruction (1 Samuel 15).
4　Matthew 5:14–15.

# 11
# Examination of Mrs. Anne Hutchinson (1637)

## Introduction

One of the first and most serious questions faced by New England Puritans was the extent to which community leaders should exert authority over individuals in matters of conscience. Believing that God acted primarily through individuals, Puritans justified the move to New England as a means of escaping the corrupt authority they believed that both church and state in England imposed on individual conscience. In their idealism about Christian community, many who immigrated believed that the consciences of individual Christians would conform to the will of good leaders who would guide New England churches and govern its towns. These advocates of Christian unity were unprepared for Anne Hutchinson's appeal to her own conscience as something above her obligation to the ministers and magistrates of New England.

Hutchinson and her husband had immigrated to Boston to be with their teacher, John Cotton, one of the most charismatic preachers of his day. More than other ministers, Cotton stressed the need for immediate experience of the Holy Spirit. Hutchinson became a popular advocate for the kind of personal assurance that Cotton celebrated, especially among the women she attended in childbirth, many of whom met together for regular religious instruction in her kitchen. But she went beyond Cotton in condemning other

Excerpted from "Examination of Mrs. Anne Hutchinson," in *The Antinomian Controversy, 1636–1638: A Documentary History*, ed. David D. Hall (Middletown, Conn.: Wesleyan University Press, 1968), 336–7.

ministers for their failure to emphasize the need for direct experience of the Spirit. More conservative Puritans saw a grave threat to social order in Hutchinson's preaching, growing popularity, and boldness in behaving in ways they thought improper in a woman. Brought before the General Court, Cotton failed to defend her and she was condemned to banishment. After some years in Rhode Island with her family and followers, she died in an Indian attack in New York in 1643.

*Mrs. H.* If you please to give me leave I shall give you the ground of what I know to be true. Being much troubled to see the falseness of the constitution of the church of England, I had like to have turned separatist; whereupon I kept a day of solemn humiliation and pondering of the thing; this scripture was brought unto me – he that denies Jesus Christ to be come in the flesh is antichrist[1] – This I considered of and in considering found that the papists did not deny him to be come in the flesh, nor we did not deny him – who then was antichrist? Was the Turk antichrist only? The Lord knows that I could not open scripture; he must by his prophetical office open it unto me. So after that being unsatisfied in the thing, the Lord was pleased to bring this scripture out of the Hebrews.[2] He that denies the testament denies the testator, and in this did open unto me and give me to see that those which did not teach the new covenant had the spirit of antichrist, and upon this he did discover the ministry unto me and ever since. I bless the Lord, he hath let me see which was the clear ministry and which the wrong. Since that time I confess I have been more choice and he hath let me to distinguish between the voice of my beloved and the voice of Moses, the voice of John Baptist and the voice of antichrist, for all those voices are spoken of in scripture. Now if you do condemn me for speaking what in my conscience I know to be truth I must commit myself unto the Lord.

*Mr. Nowell.* How do you know that that was the spirit?

*Mrs. H.* How did Abraham know that it was God that bid him offer his son, being a breach of the sixth commandment?

*Dep. Gov.* By an immediate voice.

*Mrs. H.* So to me by an immediate revelation.

*Dep. Gov.* How! an immediate revelation.

*Mrs. H.* By the voice of his own spirit to my soul. I will give you another scripture, Jer. 46. 27, 28 – out of which the Lord shewed me what he would do for me and the rest of his servants. – But after he was pleased to reveal himself to me I did presently like Abraham run to Hagar. And after that he did let me see the atheism of my own heart, for which I begged of the Lord that it might not remain in my heart, and being thus, he did shew me this (a twelvemonth after) which I told you of before. Ever since that time I have been confident of what he hath revealed unto me.

## Notes

1   1 John 2: 18.
2   Hebrews 9: 16.

# 12

# A Key into the Language of America (1643)

*Roger Williams*

## Introduction

Although many New England leaders respected his devotion to Christ, Roger Williams was banished from Massachusetts Bay because of the perceived threat that his ideas posed to social order. In his tendency to carry moderate Puritan ideas to their logical and radical conclusion, he argued, among other things, that civil authorities had no right to judge or coerce people in matters of conscience and that Christian principle mandated religious freedom. As founder and governor of Rhode Island, he established the world's first secular state, which served as a haven for Quakers, Catholics, and other religious outsiders in Puritan New England.

After his banishment from Massachusetts Bay, Williams lived with Narragansett Indians who befriended him. Unlike other English settlers who simply claimed land for England and themselves, Williams purchased land for an English colony from Narragansett Indians living south of Massachusetts Bay. He also studied their language and customs and produced one of the first sustained depictions of Indian life, still valued by historians of Indian cultures today. Of course, Williams viewed the Narragansett people in terms of his own theological ideas and never showed much respect for their religious beliefs, or any deep understanding. But he did appreciate the honesty, gener-

Excerpted from Roger Williams, *A Key into the Language of America: Or, An help to the Language of the Natives in that part of America, called New-England*, ed. John J. Teunissen and Evelyn J. Hinz (Detroit: Wayne State University Press, 1973), 85–6, 133, 135.

osity, and openness of his Indian friends and believed Indians to be superior in these respects to many English people he knew.

From *Adam* and *Noah* that they spring, it is granted on all hands. But for their later *Descent*, and whence they came into those parts, it seems as hard to finde, as to finde the *Wellhead* of some fresh *Streame*, which running many miles out of the *Countrey* to the salt *Ocean*, hath met with many mixing *Streames* by the way. They say themselves, that they have *sprung* and *growne* up in that very place, like the very *trees* of the *Wildernesse*.

They say that their *Great God Cawtántowwit* created those parts, as I observed in the Chapter of their *Religion*. They have no *Clothes, Bookes,* nor *Letters*, and conceive their *Fathers* never had; and therefore they are easily perswaded that the *God* that made *English* men is a greater *God*, because Hee hath so richly endowed the *English* above *themselves*: But when they heare that about sixteen hundred yeeres agoe, *England* and the *Inhabitants* thereof were like unto *themselves*, and since have received from *God, Clothes, Bookes, &c.* they are greatly affected with a secret hope concerning *themselves*. [. . .]

Other opinions I could number up: under favour I shall present (not mine opinion, but) my *Observations* to the judgement of the Wise.

[1.] First, others (and my selfe) have conceived some of their words to hold affinitie with the *Hebrew*.

Secondly, they constantly *annoint* their *heads* as the *Jewes* did.

Thirdly, they give *Dowries* for their wives, as the *Jewes* did.

Fourthly (and which I have not so observed amongst other *Nations* as amongst the *Jewes*, and *these*:) they constantly seperate their Women (during the time of their monthly sicknesse) in a little house alone by themselves foure or five dayes, and hold it an *Irreligious thing* for either *Father* or *Husband* or any *Male* to come neere them.

They have often asked me if it bee so with *women* of other *Nations*, and whether they are so separated: and for their practice they plead *Nature* and *Tradition*.

2. Yet againe I have found a greater *Affinity* of their Language with the *Greek* Tongue. As the *Greekes* and other *Nations*, and our selves call the seven *Starres* (or Charles Waine) the *Beare*, so doe they *Mosk* or *Paukunnawaw* the Beare.

3. They have many strange Relations of one *Wétucks*, a man that wrought great *Miracles* amongst them, and *walking upon the waters, &c.* with some kind of broken Resemblance to the *Sonne of God*.

[4.] Lastly, it is famous that the *Sowwest (Sowaniu)* is the great Subject of their discourse. From thence their *Traditions*. There they say (at the *South-west*) is the Court of their *great God Cautántouwit*: At *the South-*

*west* are their *Forefathers* soules: *to the South-west* they goe themselves when they dye; From the *South-west* came their *Corne,* and Beanes out of their Great *God Cautántowwits* field: And indeed the further *Northward* and *Westward* from us their Corne will not grow, but to the *Southward* better and better. [. . .]
More particularly:

> [1.] *Boast not proud* English, *of thy birth & blood,*
> *Thy brother* Indian *is by birth as Good.*
> *Of one blood God made Him, and Thee & All,*
> *As wise, as faire, as strong, as personall.*

> [2.] *By nature wrath's his portion, thine no more*
> *Till Grace* his *soule and* thine *in Christ restore,*
> *Make sure thy second birth, else thou shalt see,*
> *Heaven ope to* Indians *wild, but shut to thee.*

[. . .] *Obs.* As one answered me when I had discoursed about many points of God, of the creation, of the soule, of the danger of it, and the saving of it, he assented; but when I spake of the rising againe of the body, he cryed out, I shall never believe this.

# 13

# Poems (1640–1665)

## Anne Bradstreet

## Introduction

As daughter and wife of men in the government of Massachusetts Bay, Anne Dudley Bradstreet did not share the radical religious zeal of either Anne Hutchinson or Roger Williams. As a highly educated English woman and America's first published poet, she expressed a broad-minded outlook on the world that reflected the most liberal aspects of Puritan culture. In *The Tenth Muse Lately Sprung Up in America*, published in London in 1650, Bradstreet wrote long, elegant poems that showed her knowledge of classical literature and Christian humanism as well as her impatience with negative views of female intelligence.

Bradstreet also wrote poems about her personal feelings and domestic life that were not published until long after her death but are regarded today as her finest work. Viewed in terms of American religious history, these poems are outstanding expressions of the investment in marital love and family life characteristic of Puritan culture and American life more generally. Bradstreet's domestic and personal poetry shows how the Puritan analogy between the covenant of marriage and the covenant of grace encouraged familial imagery for God and desire for an intimate relationship with him. Her poetry also shows how this analogy helped to make earthly marriage and family life the primary context for religious feeling and introspection.

---

Anne Bradstreet, "To my Dear and loving Husband," "*His Epitaph*" (in "To the Memory of my dear and ever honoured Father Thomas Dudley Esq"), "An Epitaph On my dear and ever honoured Mother Mrs. Dorothy Dudley," "Upon the burning of our house, July 10th, 1666" and "In memory of my dear grand-child Elizabeth Bradstreet," in *Poems of Anne Bradstreet*, ed. Robert Hutchinson (New York: Dover, 1969), 41, 53–7.

## To my Dear and loving Husband

If ever two were one, then surely we.
If ever man were lov'd by wife, then thee;
If ever wife was happy in a man,
Compare with me ye women if you can.
I prize thy love more than whole Mines of gold,
Or all the riches that the East doth hold.
My love is such that Rivers cannot quench,
Nor ought but love from thee, give recompence.
Thy love is such I can no way repay,
The heavens reward thee manifold I pray.                    10
Then while we live, in love lets so persever,
That when we live no more, we may live ever.

## To the Memory of my dear and ever honoured Father Thomas Dudley Esq, *His Epitaph*

*Within this Tomb a Patriot lyes*
*That was both pious, just and wise,*
*To Truth a shield, to right a Wall,*
*To Sectaryes a whip and Maul,*
*A Magazine of History,*
*A Prizer of good Company*
*In manners pleasant and severe*
*The Good him lov'd, the bad did fear,*
*And when his time with years was spent*
*If some rejoyc'd, more did lament.*                    10

## An Epitaph On my dear and ever honoured Mother Mrs. Dorothy Dudley, who deceased Decemb. 27. 1643. and of her age, 61

Here lyes,
*A Worthy Matron of unspotted life,*
*A loving Mother and obedient wife,*

*A friendly Neighbor, pitiful to poor,*
*Whom oft she fed, and clothed with her store;*
*To Servants wisely aweful, but yet kind,*
*And as they did, so they reward did find:*
*A true Instructer of her Family,*
*The which she ordered with dexterity.*
*The publick meetings ever did frequent,*
*And in her Closet constant hours she spent;*                    10
*Religious in all her words and wayes,*
*Preparing still for death, till end of dayes:*
*Of all her Children, Children, liv'd to see,*
*Then dying, left a blessed memory.*

# Upon the burning of our house, July 10th, 1666

In silent night when rest I took,
For sorrow neer I did not look,
I waken'd was with thundring nois
And Piteous shreiks of dreadfull voice.
That fearfull sound of fire and fire,
Let no man know is my Desire.

I, starting up, the light did spye,
And to my God my heart did cry
To strengthen me in my Distresse
And not to leave me succourlesse.                    10
Then coming out beheld a space,
The flame consume my dwelling place.

And, when I could no longer look,
I blest his Name that gave and took,
That layd my goods now in the dust:
Yea so it was, and so 'twas just.
It was his own: it was not mine;
Far be it that I should repine.

He might of All justly bereft,
But yet sufficient for us left.                    20
When by the Ruines oft I past,
My sorrowing eyes aside did cast,
And here and there the places spye
Where oft I sate, and long did lye.

Here stood that Trunk, and there that chest;
There lay that store I counted best:
My pleasant things in ashes lye,
And them behold no more shall I.
Under thy roof no guest shall sitt,
Nor at thy Table eat a bitt.                                    30

No pleasant tale shall 'ere be told,
Nor things recounted done of old.
No Candle 'ere shall shine in Thee,
Nor bridegroom's voice ere heard shall bee.
In silence ever shalt thou lye;
Adeiu, Adeiu; All's vanity.

Then streight I gin my heart to chide,
And did thy wealth on earth abide?
Didst fix thy hope on mouldring dust,
The arm of flesh didst make thy trust?                         40
Raise up thy thoughts above the skye
That dunghill mists away may flie.

Thou hast an house on high erect
Fram'd by that mighty Architect,
With glory richly furnished,
Stands permanent tho' this bee fled.
It's purchaséd, and paid for too
By him who hath enough to doe.

A Prise so vast as is unknown,
Yet, by his Gift, is made thine own.                           50
Ther's wealth enough, I need no more;
Farewell my Pelf, farewell my Store.
The world no longer let me Love,
My hope and Treasure lyes Above.

## In memory of my dear grand-child Elizabeth Bradstreet, who deceased August, 1665. being a year and a half old

Farewel dear babe, my hearts too much content,
Farewel sweet babe, the pleasure of mine eye,
Farewel fair flower that for a space was lent,
Then ta'en away unto Eternity.
Blest babe why should I once bewail thy fate,

Or sigh thy dayes so soon were terminate;
Sith thou art setled in an Everlasting state.


        2
By nature Trees do rot when they are grown.
And Plumbs and Apples throughly ripe do fall,
And Corn and grass are in their season mown,                10
And time brings down what is both strong and tall.
But plants new set to be eradicate,
And buds new blown, to have so short a date,
Is by his hand alone that guides nature and fate.

# 14

# The Nature of True Virtue (1765)

## Jonathan Edwards

## Introduction

Often regarded as America's greatest theologian, Jonathan Edwards defended the intellectual fiber and emotional realism of Puritan theology against religious writers who wanted to define God in gentler and more humane terms. His best-known sermon, "Sinners in the Hands of an Angry God" (1734), used terrifying images of hell to awaken people to their internal rottenness, and to the need to cast off their complacency. As a result of his promotion of a religious awakening in his own parish of Northampton in 1734, Edwards became famous as a defender of religious revivals. He was an influential supporter of the Great Awakening of 1740–34, which swept through many of the English colonies in America and helped to create a sense of shared American identity that contributed to American independence from Britain. But while he supported the Awakening as a work of the Holy Spirit, he also criticized misguided forms of enthusiasm that he thought were mixed in.

Edwards believed that religious virtue was essentially a matter of will, and that natural tendencies to self-love had to be uprooted so that the will could be reoriented toward God. Certain qualities of will characterized genuine love to God, he believed, including benevolence, sincerity, humility, and meekness of spirit. *The Nature of True Virtue* (published seven years after Edwards's death) defines this reorientation of the will in philosophical terms as responsiveness to the beauty of being in general. Remarkable for its

Excerpted from Jonathan Edwards, *The Nature of True Virtue* (1765; written 1755), ed. William K. Erankena (Ann Arbor: University of Michigan Press, 1960), 1–10.

avoidance of explicitly Christian terminology, this dissertation stands as an important link between Puritan theology and the religious thought of Ralph Waldo Emerson and other New England Transcendentalists of the nineteenth century.

## Showing Wherein the Essence of True Virtue Consists

Whatever controversies and variety of opinions there are about the nature of virtue, yet all excepting some sceptics, who deny any real difference between virtue and vice, mean by it something beautiful, or rather some kind of beauty or excellency. It is not all beauty that is called virtue; for instance, not the beauty of a building, of a flower, or of the rainbow; but some beauty belonging to beings that have perception and will. It is not all beauty of mankind that is called virtue; for instance, not the external beauty of the countenance or shape, gracefulness of motion, or harmony of voice: but it is a beauty that has its original seat in the mind. But yet perhaps not every thing that may be called a beauty of mind, is properly called virtue. There is a beauty of understanding and speculation; there is something in the ideas and conceptions of great philosophers and statesmen, that may be called beautiful: which is a different thing from what is most commonly meant by virtue.

But virtue is the beauty of those qualities and acts of the mind that are of a moral nature, i.e. such as are attended with desert or worthiness of praise or blame. Things of this sort it is generally agreed, so far as I know, do not belong merely to speculation: but to the disposition and will, or (to use a general word I suppose commonly well understood) to the heart. Therefore I suppose I shall not depart from the common opinion when I say, that virtue is the beauty of the qualities and exercises of the heart, or those actions which proceed from them. So that when it is enquired, what is the nature of true virtue? This is the same as to enquire what that is, which renders any habit, disposition, or exercise of the heart truly beautiful?

I use the phrase true virtue, and speak of things truly beautiful, because I suppose it will generally be allowed, that there is a distinction to be made between some things which are truly virtuous, and others which only seem to be so, through a partial and imperfect view of things: that some actions and dispositions appear beautiful, if considered partially and superficially, or with regard to some things belonging to them, and in some of their circumstances and tendencies, which would appear otherwise in a more extensive and comprehensive view, wherein they are seen clearly in their whole nature, and the extent of their connections in the universality of things.

There is a general and particular beauty. By a particular beauty, I mean that by which a thing appears beautiful when considered only with regard to its connection with, and tendency to, some particular things within a limited, and as it were a private sphere. And a general beauty is that by which a thing appears beautiful when viewed most perfectly, comprehensively and universally, with regard to all its tendencies, and its connections with every thing to which it stands related. The former may be without and against the latter. As a few notes in a tune, taken only by themselves and in their relation to one another, may be harmonious, which, when considered with respect to all the notes in the tune, or the entire series of sounds they are connected with, may be very discordant, and disagreeable. That only, therefore, is what I mean by true virtue, which, belonging to the heart of an intelligent being, is beautiful by a general beauty, or beautiful in a comprehensive view, as it is in itself, and as related to every thing with which it stands connected. And therefore, when we are enquiring concerning the nature of true virtue – wherein this true and general beauty of the heart does most essentially consist – this is my answer to the enquiry:

True virtue most essentially consists in *benevolence to being in general*. Or perhaps, to speak more accurately, it is that consent, propensity and union of heart to being in general, which is immediately exercised in a general good will.

The things before observed respecting the nature of true virtue, naturally lead us to such a notion of it. If it has its seat in the heart, and is the general goodness and beauty of the disposition and its exercise, in the most comprehensive view, considered with regard to its universal tendency, and as related to every thing with which it stands connected; what can it consist in, but a consent and good will to being in general? Beauty does not consist in discord and dissent, but in consent and agreement. And if every intelligent being is some way related to being in general, and is a part of the universal system of existence; and so stands in connection with the whole; what can its general and true beauty be, but its union and consent with the great whole?

If any such thing can be supposed as an union of heart to some particular being, or number of beings, disposing it to benevolence to a private circle or system of beings, which are but a small part of the whole; not implying a tendency to an union with the great system, and not at all inconsistent with enmity towards being in general, this I suppose not to be of the nature of true virtue; although it may in some respects be good, and may appear beautiful in a confined and contracted view of things. But of this more afterwards.

It is abundantly plain by the holy scriptures, and generally allowed, not only by Christian divines, but by the more considerable Deists, that virtue most essentially consists in love. And I suppose it is owned by the most considerable writers, to consist in general love of benevolence, or kind affection: though it seems to me the meaning of some in this affair is not sufficiently explained; which perhaps occasions some error or confusion in discourses on this subject.

When I say true virtue consists in love to being in general, I shall not be likely to be understood, that no one act of the mind or exercise of love is of the nature of true virtue, but what has being in general, or the great system of universal existence, for its direct and immediate object: so that no exercise of love, or kind affection to any one particular being, that is but a small part of this whole, has any thing of the nature of true virtue. But that the nature of true virtue consists in a disposition to benevolence towards being in general; though from such a disposition may arise exercises of love to particular beings, as objects are presented and occasions arise. No wonder that he who is of a generally benevolent disposition, should be more disposed than another to have his heart moved with benevolent affection to particular persons, with whom he is acquainted and conversant, and from whom arise the greatest and most frequent occasions for exciting his benevolent temper. But my meaning is, that no affections towards particular persons or beings are of the nature of true virtue, but such as arise from a generally benevolent temper, or from that habit or frame of mind, wherein consists a disposition to love being in general.

And perhaps it is needless for me to give notice to my readers, that when I speak of an intelligent being having a heart united and benevolently disposed to being in general, I thereby mean intelligent being in general. Not inanimate things, or beings that have no perception or will; which are not properly capable objects of benevolence.

Love is commonly distinguished into love of benevolence, and love of complacence. Love of benevolence is that affection or propensity of the heart to any being, which causes it to incline to its well-being, or disposes it to desire and take pleasure in its happiness. And if I mistake not, it is agreeable to the common opinion, that beauty in the object is not always the ground of this propensity; but that there may be a disposition to the welfare of those that are not considered as beautiful, unless mere existence be accounted a beauty. And benevolence or goodness in the divine Being is generally supposed, not only to be prior to the beauty of many of its objects, but to their existence; so as to be the ground both of their existence and their beauty, rather than the foundation of God's benevolence; as it is supposed that it is God's goodness which moved him to give them both being and beauty. So that if all virtue primarily consists in that affection of heart to being, which is exercised in benevolence, or an inclination to its good, then God's virtue is so extended as to include a propensity not only to being actually existing, and actually beautiful, but to possible being, so as to incline him to give a being beauty and happiness.

What is commonly called love of complacence, presupposes beauty. For it is no other than delight in beauty; or complacence in the person or being beloved for his beauty. If virtue be the beauty of an intelligent being, and virtue consists in love, then it is a plain inconsistence, to suppose that virtue primarily consists in any love to its object for its beauty; either in a love of complacence, which is delight in a being for his beauty, or in a love of benevolence, that has the beauty of its object for its foundation. For that would be to suppose, that the beauty of intelligent beings primarily consists in love to beauty; or that their virtue first of all consists in their love to virtue. Which is an inconsistence, and going in a circle. Because it makes virtue, or beauty of mind, the foundation or first motive of that love wherein virtue originally consists, or wherein the very first virtue consists; or, it supposes the first virtue to be the consequence and effect of virtue. Which makes the first virtue both the ground and the consequence, both cause and effect of itself. Doubtless virtue primarily consists in something else besides any effect or consequence of virtue. If virtue consists primarily in love to virtue, then virtue, the thing loved, is the love of virtue: so that virtue must consist in the love of the love of virtue – and so on in infinitum. For there is no end of going back in a circle. We never come to any beginning or foundation; it is without beginning, and hangs on nothing. Therefore, if the essence of virtue, or beauty of mind, lies in love, or a disposition to love, it must primarily consist in something different both from complacence, which is a delight in beauty, and also from any benevolence that has the beauty of its object for its foundation. Because it is absurd to say, that virtue is primarily and first of all the consequence of itself; which makes virtue primarily prior to itself.

Nor can virtue primarily consist in gratitude; or one being's benevolence to another for his benevolence to him. Because this implies the same inconsistence. For it supposes a benevolence prior to gratitude, which is the cause of gratitude. The first benevolence cannot be gratitude. Therefore there is room left for no other conclusion, than that the primary object of virtuous love is being, simply considered; or that true virtue primarily consists, not in love to any particular beings, because of their virtue or beauty, nor in gratitude, because they love us; but in a propensity and union of heart to being simply considered; exciting absolute benevolence, if I may so call it, to being in general. I say true virtue primarily consists in this. For I am far from asserting, that there is no true virtue in any other love than this absolute benevolence. But I would express what appears to me to be the truth on this subject, in the following particulars.

The first object of a virtuous benevolence is being, simply considered; and if being, simply considered, be its object, then being in general is its object; and what it has an ultimate propensity to is the highest good of being in general. And it will seek the good of every individual being unless it be conceived as not consistent with the highest good of being in general. In which case the good of a particular being, or some beings, may be given up for the sake of the highest good of being in general. And particularly, if there be any being statedly and irreclaimably opposite, and an enemy to being in general, then consent and adherence to being in general will induce the truly virtuous heart to forsake that enemy, and to oppose it.

Further, if *being*, simply considered, be the first object of a truly virtuous benevolence, then that object who has most of being, or has the greatest share of existence, other things being equal, so far as such a being is exhibited to our faculties, will have the greatest share of the propensity and benevolent affections of the heart. I say, "other things being equal," especially because there is a secondary object of virtuous benevolence, that I shall take notice of presently, which must be considered as the ground or motive to a purely virtuous benevolence. Pure benevolence in its first exercise is nothing else but being's uniting consent, or propensity to being; and inclining to the general highest good, and to each being, whose welfare is consistent with the highest general good, in proportion to the degree of existence,[1] understand, "other things being equal."

The second object of a virtuous propensity of heart is benevolent being. A secondary ground of pure benevolence is virtuous benevolence itself in its object. When any one under the influence of general benevolence, sees another being possessed of the like general benevolence, this attaches his heart to him, and draws forth greater love to him, than merely his having existence: because so far as the being beloved has love to being in general, so far his own being is, as it were, enlarged; extends to, and in some sort comprehends being in general: and therefore, he that is governed by love to being in general, must of necessity have complacence in him, and the greater degree of benevolence to him, as it were out of gratitude to him for his love to general existence, that his own heart is extended and united to, and so looks on its interest as its own. It is because his heart is thus united to being in general, that he looks on a benevolent propensity to being in general, wherever he sees it, as the beauty of the being in whom it is; an excellency that renders him worthy of esteem, complacence, and the greater good-will.

# Note

1   I say, "in proportion to the degree of existence," because one being may have more existence than another, as he may be greater than another. That which is great has more existence, and is further from nothing, than that which is little. One being may have every thing positive belonging to it, or every thing which goes to its positive existence (in opposition to defect) in an higher degree than another; or a greater capacity and power, greater understanding, every faculty and every positive quality in a higher degree. An archangel must be supposed to have more existence, and to be every way further removed from nonentity, than a worm.

# 15

# Act for Establishing Religious Freedom (1779)

## Thomas Jefferson

## Introduction

In the heyday of Enlightenment rationalism in the late eighteenth century, Thomas Jefferson championed religious freedom by appeal to natural rights philosophy. Against notions of a wrathful, punitive God, Jefferson believed that the Creator endowed mankind with the power of reason, and with the inalienable right to exercise that power in discovering the Creator's design. Jefferson went so far in equating morality with natural reason as to revise the New Testament, deleting all references to miraculous events. How different from Roger Williams, who had championed religious freedom by appeal to Christian revelation! Williams had argued that civil authorities should refrain from interfering with individual conscience because, since the coming of Christ, God worked solely through individuals and no longer directed history through covenants with Israel, or any other nation.

While they defended it from very different religious outlooks, Williams and Jefferson were similar in believing that religious freedom conformed to and strengthened the principles of Christianity and that its absence invited corruption among clergy and complacency among believers. They were also similar in wanting to push the cause of religious liberty further than many of their contemporaries. Few contested the right of states to establish particular churches when the First Amendment to the United States Constitution

Excerpted from Thomas Jefferson, "Act for Establishing Religious Freedom" (1779), reprinted in *James Madison on Religious Liberty*, ed. Robert S. Alley (Buffalo: Prometheus, 1985), 90–1.

prohibiting the federal government from doing so was passed in 1783. In 1786, after much debate, the Commonwealth of Virginia finally passed the "Act for Establishing Religious Freedom" that Jefferson had introduced seven years before. Not until 1833, amidst the enthusiasm for religious voluntarism and evangelical cooperation of the second Great Awakening, did the people of Massachusetts disestablish the Puritan-based Congregational Church.

I. Whereas Almighty God hath created the mind free; that all attempts to influence it by temporal punishments or burthens, or by civil incapacitations, tend only to beget habits of hypocrisy and meanness, and are a departure from the plan of the Holy author of our religion,[1] who being Lord both of body and mind, yet chose not to propagate it by coercions on either, as was in his Almighty power to do; that the impious presumption of legislators and rulers, civil as well as ecclesiastical, who being themselves but fallible and uninspired men, have assumed dominion over the faith of others, setting up their own opinions and modes of thinking as the only true and infallible, and as such endeavouring to impose them on others, hath established and maintained false religions over the greatest part of the world, and through all time; that to compel a man to furnish contributions of money for the propagation of opinions which he disbelieves, is sinful and tyrannical; that even the forcing him to support this or that teacher of his own religious persuasion, is depriving him of the comfortable liberty of giving his contributions to the particular pastor, whose morals he would make his pattern, and whose powers he feels most persuasive to righteousness, and is withdrawing from the ministry those temporary rewards, which proceeding from an approbation of their personal conduct, are an additional incitement to earnest and unremitting labours for the instruction of mankind; that our civil rights have no dependence on our religious opinions, any more than our opinions in physics or geometry; that therefore the proscribing any citizen as unworthy of the public confidence by laying upon him an incapacity of being called to offices of trust and emolument, unless he profess or renounce this or that religious opinion, is depriving him injuriously of those privileges and advantages to which in common with his fellow-citizens he has a natural right; that it tends only to corrupt the principles of that religion it is meant to encourage, by bribing with a monopoly of wor[l]dly honours and emoluments, those who will externally profess and confirm to it; that though indeed these are criminal who do not withstand such temptation, yet neither are those innocent who lay the bait in their way; that to suffer the civil magistrate to intrude his powers into the field of opinion, and to restrain the profession or propagation of principles on supposition of their ill tendency, is a dangerous fallacy, which at once destroys all religious liberty, because he being of course judge of that tendency will make his opinions the rule of judgment; and approve or condemn the sentiments of others only as they shall square with or differ from his own; that it is time enough for the rightful purposes of civil government, for its officers to interfere when principles break out into overt acts against peace and good order; and finally, that truth is great and will prevail if left to herself, that she is the proper and sufficient antagonist to error, and has nothing to fear from the conflict, unless by human interposition disarmed of her natural weapons, free argument and debate, errors ceasing to be dangerous when it is permitted freely to contradict them:

II. *Be it enacted by the General Assembly*, That no man shall be compelled to frequent or support any religious worship, place, or ministry whatsoever, nor shall be enforced restrained, molested, or burthened in his body or goods, nor shall otherwise suffer on account of his religious opinions or belief; but that all men shall be free to profess, and by argument to maintain, their opinion in matters of religion, and that the same shall in no wise diminish, enlarge, or affect their civil capacities.

III.  And though we well know that this assembly elected by the people for the ordinary purposes of legislation only, have no power to restrain the acts of succeeding assemblies, constituted with powers equal to our own, and that therefore to declare this act to be irrevocable would be of no effect in law; yet we are free to declare, and do declare, that the rights hereby asserted are of the natural rights of mankind, and that if any act shall be hereafter passed to repeal the present, or to narrow its operation such act will be an infringement of natural right.

# Note

1   In his autobiography Jefferson states that an effort was made to alter this phrase to read, "a departure from the plan of Jesus Christ, the holy author of our religion." Jefferson contended that in defeating the suggested change the legislators "meant to comprehend, within the mantle of it's protection, the Jew and the Gentile, the Christian and Mahomatan, the Hindoo, and infidel of every denomination."

# 16

# The Code of Handsome Lake
# (ca. 1800)

### Edward Cornplanter

## Introduction

Protestant evangelicals were not the only Americans to experience religious
revivals. At the turn of the nineteenth century, a religious revival led by the
Seneca prophet Handsome Lake swept through a large part of the Iroquois
Confederacy centered in upstate New York. For a century before the American Revolution, the Iroquois had been a powerful political force from the Great
Lakes to the Carolinas, fighting, trading, and negotiating treaties with American,
English, and European people and governments as well as with other Indian
tribes. After the Revolutionary war, which many Iroquois warriors joined on
the British side, the Continental Congress distributed parcels of land once
controlled by the Iroquois as payment to men who had served in the Continental army. Stripped of many of their weapons and treaties as well as much of
their land, the Iroquois people fell into despair, poverty, and disease.

In 1800, Handsome Lake was an old, dissolute warrior who fell into a trance,
and was taken for dead, until his nephew Cornplanter felt some warmth
around the old man's heart and called off preparations for his funeral. When
he revived, Handsome Lake recounted the visit he had taken to the spirit world
and the messages he had received from the Creator. In the spirit world, he had
seen the fork in the road separating those who drank, committed adultery,

Excerpted from Edward Cornplanter, "The Code of Handsome Lake" (recounting Hand-
some Lake's visions of 1800), Sections 94–6, in *The Code of Handsome Lake, the Seneca
Prophet*, ed. Arthur C. Parker (orig. 1913), Book II of *Parker on the Iroquois*, ed. William N.
Fenton (Syracuse: Syracuse University Press, 1968), 67–9.

played cards, and were otherwise destined for the house of the punisher from purer souls destined for a land of clear springs and abundant food. He brought back instructions from the Creator for casting off vices received from whites and for reviving some traditional religious ceremonies, and he presided over the growth of a new religion based on these visions until his death in 1813. Blending ancient ways with new elements enabling people to adapt to Western culture, the religion of Handsome Lake contributed significantly to the survival of Iroquois culture. His Code is still recited today by his followers.

## Section 94

"So they proceeded on their journey and it happened that a vision appeared unto them. They seemed to be advancing toward an approaching man. Soon they met him and passed. Now when they were a distance apart they turned and he was facing them. So they greeted each other. Then said the man, 'Sedwāgo'wanĕ, I must ask you a question. Did you never hear your grandfathers say that once there was a certain man upon the earth across the great waters who was slain by his own people?' That was what he said when he spoke.

"Then answered Sedwāgo'wanĕ, 'It is true. I have heard my grandparents say this.'

"Then answered the man, 'I am he.' (Sega$^{n\prime}$hedŭs, *He who resurrects*). And he turned his palms upward and they were scarred and his feet were likewise and his breast was pierced by a spear wound. It appeared that his hands and his feet were torn by iron nails.

"All this was true. It could be seen and blood was fresh upon him.

"Then said the man, 'They slew me because of their independence and unbelief. So I have gone home to shut the doors of heaven that they may not see me again until the earth passes away. Then will all the people cry to me for succor, and when I come it will be in this wise: my face will be sober and I shall turn it to my people. Now let me ask how your people receive your teachings.'

"He answered, 'It is my opinion that half my people are inclined to believe in me.'

"Then answered he, 'You are more successful than I for some believe in you but none in me. I am inclined to believe that in the end it will also be so with you. Now it is rumored that you are but a talker with spirits (djïs'gä$^n$ dătăha'). Now it is true that I am a spirit and the one of him who was murdered. Now tell your people that they will become lost when they follow the ways of the white man.' "

So that is what he said. Eniaiehuk.

## Section 95

"So they proceeded on their journey and had not gone far when they came to a halt.

"Then the messengers pointed out a certain spot and said, 'Watch attentively,' and beheld a man carrying loads of dirt and depositing them in a certain spot. He carried the earth in a wheelbarrow and his task was a hard one. Then he knew that the name of the man was Sagoyewat′ha, a chief.

"Then asked the messengers, 'What did you see?'

"He answered, 'I beheld a man carrying dirt in a wheelbarrow and that man had a laborious task. His name was Sagoyewat′ha, a chief.'

"Then answered the messengers, 'You have spoken truly. Sagoyewat′ha is the name of the man who carries the dirt. It is true that his work is laborious and this is for a punishment for he was the one who first gave his consent to the sale of Indian reservations. It is said that there is hardship for those who part with their lands for money or trade. So now you have seen the doom of those who repent not. Their eternity will be one of punishment.' "[1]

So they said and he said. Eniaiehuk.

## Section 96

"Now again they took up their journey and had not traveled far when they saw a crowd on both sides of the road. And when they came to where it was they saw that they were at the forks of the road. One road, on the right, was a narrow one and the tracks upon it were mostly those of children and all were pointed in one direction. Few adults had their tracks on this road, the road rough and wide. Now as they watched they saw a woman approaching the forks of the road from behind them. She came to where the road divided and as she halted before the roads a man who stood to the left shouted, 'To this side.' (Now the road of the wicked is owa′ĕtgä$^n$, a rough road.) Then the man on the right said, 'Not so. This woman has done her whole duty. She has truly repented.' Then answered the man on the left, 'You are wrong, for her repentance has been of short duration and so of slight effect. But the man on the right replied, 'Truly in her earth-life she repented and was faithful to her promises. This is all that is required and she will walk upon the narrow road.'

"Now one of the messengers turned to him and said, 'The woman has lived a repented life for three days and has entered into the happy eternity. It was not an easy matter for her to do so of herself, but we, the messengers, have plead before the Creator and he has heard us. Three times we assist every one who believes to continue in the faith of the Gai′wiio′. At this division in the great road we guide the spirits of the earth into Tain′tciadĕ (heaven land). At the forks of the road the spirits of the dead are divided. The narrow road leads to the pleasant lands of the Creator and the wide and rough road leads to the great lodge of the punisher.'"

So they said and he said. Eniaiehuk.

# Note

1  The followers of the Gai′wiio′ to this day mention the name of Red Jacket with contempt. While they acknowledge his mental superiority they have no other admiration for him. He was ever the enemy of Cornplanter and Ganiodaiio with whom he had frequent collision and recognized the sachem-prophet only as an impostor. The teachings of Ganiodaiio have done much to prejudice the Iroquois against Red Jacket.

# 17

# What a Revival of Religion Is (1834)

## Charles Grandison Finney

## Introduction

As a prominent preacher, reformer, and educator during the second Great Awakening of the early nineteenth century, Charles Grandison Finney became famous for "new methods" he introduced into revival meetings. Finney believed that preachers owed it to God, and to the people they served, to employ the most effective means possible of producing a revival, much as a good farmer did the best he could to prepare the soil for a good crop. In support of this approach, Finney maintained that women should not be discouraged from praying aloud during religious meetings because their feelings were easily stimulated and could help soften the harder hearts of men. Finney also invented the "anxious bench," a seat at the front of a religious meeting where a preacher could seat individuals obviously distressed about the state of their souls. Other conversions might follow as congregants watched the preacher lead an anxious person to break down in repentance, and then gratefully accept Christ's forgiveness.

Finney's new methods illustrate a general tendency to pragmatism that runs throughout American religious history. More specifically, they illustrate the enthusiasm for mastering the mechanics of religious life that grew up alongside the new factories, labor-saving devices, entrepreneurship, and marketing strategies associated with industrialization and the emergence of a national

Excerpted from Charles Grandison Finney, "What a Revival of Religion Is" (orig. 1834), in *Lectures on Revivals of Religion* (orig. 1835), ed. William G. McLoughlin (Cambridge, Mass.: Harvard University Press, 1960), 12–15.

economy in the early nineteenth century. As the United States and its territories expanded westward during the nineteenth century, Finney and many of his fellow evangelists were optimistic about the religious destiny of America and the triumph of their own ideas. They pushed Protestant religion and education westward, while some of their cohort headed eastward as missionaries resolved to bring both the gospel and republican government to what they condescendingly perceived as the darkest corners of the heathen world. Because of all these efforts, the second Great Awakening can be seen as a high point of evangelical optimism and enthusiasm for world reform.

# A Revival of Religion Is Not a Miracle

1. A miracle has been generally defined to be, a Divine interference, setting aside or suspending the laws of nature. It is not a miracle, in this sense.[1] All the laws of matter and mind remain in force. They are neither suspended nor set aside in a revival.

2. It is not a miracle according to another definition of the term miracle – *something above the powers of nature*. There is nothing in religion beyond the ordinary powers of nature. It consists entirely in the *right exercise* of the powers of nature. It is just that, and nothing else. When mankind become religious, they are not *enabled* to put forth exertions which they were unable before to put forth. They only exert the powers they had before in a different way, and use them for the glory of God.

3. It is not a miracle, or dependent on a miracle, in any sense. It is a purely philosophical result of the right use of the constituted means – as much so as any other effect produced by the application of means.[2] There may be a miracle among its antecedent causes, or there may not. The apostles employed miracles, simply as a means by which they arrested attention to their message, and established its Divine authority. But the miracle was not the revival. The miracle was one thing; the revival that followed it was quite another thing. The revivals in the apostles' days were connected with miracles, but they were not miracles.

I said that a revival is the result of the *right* use of the appropriate means. The means which God has enjoyed for the production of a revival, doubtless have a natural tendency to produce a revival. Otherwise God would not have enjoined them. But means will not produce a revival, we all know, without the blessing of God. No more will grain, when it is sowed, produce a crop without the blessing of God. It is impossible for us to say that there is not as direct an influence or agency from God, to produce a crop of grain, as there is to produce a revival. What are the laws of nature, according to which, it is supposed, that grain yields a crop? They are nothing but the constituted manner of the operations of God. In the Bible, the word of God is compared to grain, and preaching is compared to sowing seed, and the results to the springing up and growth of the crop. And the result is just as philosophical in the one case, as in the other, and is as naturally connected with the cause.[3]

I wish this idea to be impressed on all your minds, for there has long been an idea prevalent that promoting religion has something very peculiar in it, not to be judged of by the ordinary rules of cause and effect; in short, that there is no connection of the means with the result, and no tendency in the means to produce the effect. No doctrine is more dangerous than this to the prosperity of the church, and nothing more absurd.

Suppose a man were to go and preach this doctrine among farmers, about their sowing grain. Let him tell them that God is a sovereign, and will give them a crop only when it pleases him, and that for them to plow and plant and labor as if they expected to raise a crop is very wrong, and taking the work out of the hands of God, that it interferes with his sovereignty, and is going on in their own strength; and that there is no connection between the means and the result on which they can depend. And now, suppose the farmers should believe such doctrine. Why, they would starve the world to death.

Just such results will follow from the church's being persuaded that promoting religion is somehow so mysteriously a subject of Divine sovereignty, that there is no natural connection between the means and the end. What *are* the results? Why, generation after generation have gone down to hell. No doubt more than five thousand millions have gone down to hell, while the church has been dreaming, and waiting for God to save them without the use of means.[4] It has been the devil's most successful means of destroying souls. The connection is as clear in religion as it is when the farmer sows his grain.

There is one fact under the government of God, worthy of universal notice, and of everlasting remembrance; which is, that the most useful and important things are most easily and certainly obtained by the use of the appropriate means. This is evidently a principle in the Divine administration. Hence, all the *necessaries* of life are obtained with great *certainty* by the use of the simplest means. The luxuries are more difficult to obtain; the means to procure them are more intricate and less certain in their results; while things absolutely hurtful and poisonous, such as alcohol and the like, are often obtained only by torturing nature, and making use of a kind of infernal sorcery to procure the death-dealing abomination. This principle holds true in moral government, and as spiritual blessings are of surpassing importance, we should expect their attainment to be connected with *great certainty* with the use of the appropriate means; and such we find to be the fact; and I fully believe that could facts be known, it would be found that when the appointed means have been *rightly* used, spiritual blessings have been obtained with greater uniformity than temporal ones.[5]

# Notes

1   Typical of the type of revision that Finney made in preparing these lectures for publication in book form is the way in which he broke up into the first two sentences in this paragraph what Joshua Leavitt had written in the *New York Evangelist* as one sentence, namely: "1. It is not a miracle in the sense of a suspension or setting aside of the laws of nature."

2   Anyone who has read Jonathan Edwards's *Faithful Narrative of the Surprising Work of God* or his *Some Thoughts Concerning the Present Revival of Religion in New England* will see at once how different his view of a revival was from that expressed here. Edwards constantly marvels at "this shower of divine blessing," which is "a very extraordinary dispensation of providence; God has in many respects gone out of, and much beyond, his usual and ordinary way." And he applies the words "strange," "remarkable," "wonderful," "uncommon," "amazing" to the revival to indicate its miraculous character: "It is a great and wonderful event, a strange revolution, an unexpected, surprising overturning of things, suddenly brought to pass." In fact, Edwards went out of his way to chastise those who sought to explain in human terms how and why revivals came about: "This is too much for the clay to take upon it with respect to the potter," for "The wind bloweth where it listest" and "We know not the work of God who maketh all." See Jonathan Edwards, *Works*, ed. Sereno E. Dwight (New York, 1829–30), IV, 27, 80, 120–21, and *passim*. (Of course, it should be noted that although Finney denies the miraculous aspect of revivals, he by no means denies that miracles can and do happen.)

3   In the revised edition of 1868 Finney added here, "or more correctly, a revival is as naturally a result of the use of the appropriate means as a crop is of the use of its appropriate means. It is true that religion does not properly belong to the category of cause and effect; but although it is not *caused* by means, yet it has its occasion, and may as naturally and certainly result from its *occasion* as a crop does from its *cause*."

4   In the more rigid expositions of Calvinistic predestination, especially as preached by the New England Congregationalists who followed the theology of Samuel Hopkins, sinners were considered passive in their regeneration. They were told to "wait God's time" and if they were among the predestined elect, God would send the Holy Spirit to infuse grace or impart grace to them when He was ready. If they were not among the elect, then nothing they could do would keep them out of hell. Finney's whole career was devoted to tearing down this generally accepted notion of salvation.

5  This paragraph does not appear in the vision of this lecture that appeared in the *New York Evangelist*, December 6, 1834, p. 194. This "philosophical" justification for teetotalism was often used by later revivalists. The whole paragraph is eloquent proof of Finney's pietistic love of simplicity and his optimistic view of the benevolence of Nature and of Nature's God.

# 18

# The Life and Religious Experience of Jarena Lee (1836)

## Jarena Lee

## Introduction

In important respects, Jarena Lee's account of her religious experience is typical of that of many Protestant evangelicals. Her story begins with her realization of being "a wretched sinner," guilty before God, which weighed her down with remorse and made her long desperately for deliverance. Like many before and after, Lee sought comfort in different places before experiencing a softening of heart and a sense of God's forgiveness and closeness. Her struggles were not over, however, as Satan strengthened his hold. She battled against him until Christ intervened and Lee realized that she must put herself entirely in Christ's hands if Satan were to be overcome.

Having first awakened to her sinfulness under the preaching of a Presbyterian missionary, Lee eventually found deliverance with the Methodists. In this move, her story represents a larger shift in American Protestant culture toward the "methods" of attaining of religious experience and assurance developed by the English preacher John Wesley. With its emphasis on each sinner's ability to choose Christ, openness to new forms of religious expression, and effective system of circuit-riding preachers who kept pace with the settlement of new towns, the Methodist Church was the fastest-growing denomination in nineteenth-century America.

Excerpted from Jarena Lee, *The Life and Religious Experience of Jarena Lee* (1836), in *Sisters of the Spirit: Three Black Women's Autobiographies of the Nineteenth Century*, ed. William L. Andrews (Bloomington: Indiana University Press, 1986), 27–34.

As an African American woman, Lee represents both the democratic character of Protestant evangelicalism and its tendency to define freedom primarily in spiritual and emotional terms. On one hand, evangelical religion in the nineteenth century dignified and empowered blacks and women by emphasizing Christ's affinity with the low and outcast and the value of each individual soul. On the other hand, it stressed that pride was a bad thing and glorified personal suffering and self-sacrifice. As the interplay of these two forces varied from one situation to another, evangelicalism sometimes helped inspire political movements aimed at freedom and civil rights and at other times functioned as a damper against worldly ambition and social change.

> And it shall come to pass . . . that I will pour out my Spirit upon all flesh; and your sons, and your *daughters* shall prophecy.
>
> *Joel ii. 28*

I was born February 11th, 1783, at Cape May, state of New Jersey. At the age of seven years I was parted from my parents, and went to live as a servant maid, with a Mr. Sharp, at the distance of about sixty miles from the place of my birth.

My parents being wholly ignorant of the knowledge of God, had not therefore instructed me in any degree in this great matter. Not long after the commencement of my attendance on this lady, she had bid me do something respecting my work, which in a little while after, she asked me if I had done, when I replied, Yes – but this was not true.

At this awful point, in my early history, the spirit of God moved in power through my conscience, and told me I was a wretched sinner. On this account so great was the impression, and so strong were the feelings of guilt, that I promised in my heart that I would not tell another lie.

But notwithstanding this promise my heart grew harder, after a while, yet the spirit of the Lord never entirely forsook me, but continued mercifully striving with me, until his gracious power converted my soul.

The manner of this great accomplishment was as follows: In the year 1804, it so happened that I went with others to hear a missionary of the Presbyterian order preach. It was an afternoon meeting, but few were there, the place was a school room; but the preacher was solemn, and in his countenance the earnestness of his master's business appeared equally strong, as though he were about to speak to a multitude.

At the reading of the Psalms, a ray of renewed conviction darted into my soul. These were the words, composing the first verse of the Psalms for the service:

Lord, I am vile, conceived in sin,
Born unholy and unclean.
Sprung from man, whose guilty fall
Corrupts the race, and taints us all.

This description of my condition struck me to the heart, and made me to feel in some measure, the weight of my sins, and sinful nature. But not knowing how to run immediately to the Lord for help, I was driven of Satan, in the course of a few days, and tempted to destroy myself.

There was a brook about a quarter of a mile from the house, in which there was a deep hole, where the water whirled about among the rocks; to this place it was suggested, I must go and drown myself.

At the time I had a book in my hand; it was on a Sabbath morning, about ten o'clock; to this place I resorted, where on coming to the water I sat down on the bank, and on my looking into it; it was suggested, that drowning would be an easy death. It seemed as if some one was speaking to me, saying put your head under, it will not distress you. But by some means, of which I can give no account, my thoughts were taken entirely from this purpose, when I went from the place to the house again. It was the unseen arm of God which saved me from self murder.

But notwithstanding this escape from death, my mind was not at rest – but so great was the labour of my spirit and the fearful oppressions of a judgment to come, that I was reduced as one extremely ill. On which account a physician was called to attend me, from which illness I recovered in about three months.

But as yet I had not found him of whom Moses and the prophets did write, being extremely ignorant: there being no one to instruct me in the way of life and salvation as yet. After my recovery, I left the lady, who during my sickness, was exceedingly kind, and went to Philadelphia. From this place I soon went a few miles into the country, where I resided in the family of a Roman Catholic. But my anxiety still continued respecting my poor soul, on which account I used to watch my opportunity to read in the Bible; and this lady observing this, took the Bible from me and hid it, giving me a novel in its stead – which when I perceived, I refused to read.

Soon after this I again went to the city of Philadelphia; and commenced going to the English Church, the pastor of which was an Englishman, by the name of Pilmore, one of the number, who at first preached Methodism in America, in the city of New York.[1]

But while sitting under the ministration of this man, which was about three months, and at the last time, it appeared that there was a wall between me and a communion with that people, which was higher than I could possibly see over, and seemed to make this impression upon my mind, *this is not the people for you*.

But on returning home at noon I inquired of the head cook of the house respecting the rules of the Methodists, as I knew she belonged to that society, who told me what they were; on which account I replied, that I should not be able to abide by such strict rules not even one year; – however, I told her that I would go with her and hear what they had to say.

The man who was to speak in the afternoon of that day, was the Rev. Richard Allen, since bishop of the African Episcopal Methodists in America.[2] During the labors of this man that afternoon, I had come to the conclusion, that this is the people to which my heart unites, and it so happened, that as soon as the service closed he invited such as felt a desire to flee the wrath to come, to unite on trial with them – I embraced the opportunity. Three weeks from that day, my soul was gloriously converted to God, under preaching, at the very outset of the sermon. The text was barely pronounced, which was: "I perceive thy heart is not right in the sight of God" [Acts 8:21], when there appeared to *my* view, in the centre of the heart *one* sin; and this was *malice*, against one particular individual, who had strove deeply to injure me, which I resented. At this discovery I said, *Lord* I forgive *every* creature. That instant, it appeared to me, as if a garment, which had entirely enveloped my whole person, even to my fingers ends, split at the crown of my head, and was stripped away from me, passing like a shadow, from my sight – when the glory of God seemed to cover me in its stead.

That moment, though hundreds were present, I did leap to my feet, and declare that God, for Christ's sake, had pardoned the sins of my soul. Great was the ecstasy of my mind, for I felt that not only the sin of *malice* was pardoned, but all other sins were swept away together. That day was the first when my heart had believed, and my tongue had made confession unto salvation – the first words uttered, a part of that song, which shall fill eternity with its sound, was *glory to God*. For a few moments I had power to exhort sinners, and to tell of the wonders and of the goodness of him who had clothed me with *his* salvation. During this, the minister was silent, until my soul felt its duty had been per-formed, when he declared another witness of the power of Christ to forgive sins on earth, was manifest in my conversion.

From the day on which I first went to the Methodist church, until the hour of my deliverance, I was strangely buffetted by that enemy of all righteousness – the devil.

I was naturally of a lively turn of disposition; and during the space of time from my first awakening until I knew my peace was made with God, I rejoiced in the vanities of this life, and then again sunk back into sorrow.

For four years I had continued in this way, frequently labouring under the awful apprehension, that I could never be happy in this life. This persuasion was greatly strengthened, during the three weeks, which was the last of Satan's power over me, in this peculiar manner: on which account, I had come to the conclusion that I had better be dead than alive. Here I was again tempted to destroy my life by drowning; but suddenly this mode was changed, and while in the dusk of the evening, as I was walking to and fro in the yard of the house, I was beset to hang myself, with a cord suspended from the wall enclosing the secluded spot.

But no sooner was the intention resolved on in my mind, than an awful dread came over me, when I ran into the house; still the tempter pursued me. There was standing a vessel of water – into this I was strongly impressed to plunge my head, so as to extinguish the life which God had given me. Had I have done this, I have been always of the opinion that I should have been unable to have released myself; although the vessel was scarcely large enough to hold a gallon of water. Of me may it not be said, as written by Isaish, (chap. 65, verses 1,2.) "I am sought of them that asked not for me; I am found of them that sought me not." Glory be to God for his redeeming power, which saved me from the violence of my own hands, from the malice of Satan, and from eternal death; for had I have killed myself, a great ransom could not have delivered me; for it is written – "No murderer hath eternal life abiding in him" [1 John 3:15]. How appropriately can I sing –

> "Jesus sought me, when a stranger,
> Wandering from the fold of God;
> He to rescue me from danger,
> Interposed his precious blood."[3]

But notwithstanding the terror which seized upon me, when about to end my life, I had no view of the precipice on the edge of which I was tottering, until it was over, and my eyes were opened. Then the awful gulf of hell seemed to be open beneath me, covered only, as it were, by a spider's web, on which I stood. I seemed to hear the howling of the damned, to see the smoke of the bottomless pit, and to hear the rattling of those chains, which hold the impenitent under clouds of darkness to the judgment of the great day.

I trembled like Belshazzar,[4] and cried out in the horror of my spirit, "God be merciful to me a sinner." That night I formed a resolution to pray; which, when resolved upon, there appeared, sitting in one corner of the room, Satan, in the form of a monstrous dog, and in a rage, as if in pursuit, his tongue protruding from his mouth to a great length, and his eyes looked like two balls of fire; it soon, however, vanished out of my sight. From this state of terror and dismay, I was happily delivered under the preaching of the Gospel as before related.

This view, which I was permitted to have of Satan, in the form of a dog, is evidence, which corroborates in my estimation, the Bible account of a hell of fire, which burneth with brimstone, called in Scripture the bottomless pit; the place where all liars, who repent not, shall have their portion; as also the Sabbath breaker, the adulterer, the fornicator, with the fearful, the abominable, and the unbelieving, this shall be the portion of their cup.

This language is too strong and expressive to be applied to any state of suffering in *time*. Were it to be thus applied, the reality could no where be found in human life; the consequence would be, that *this* scripture would be found a false testimony. But when made to apply to an endless state of perdition, in eternity, beyond the bounds of human life, then this language is found not to exceed our views of a state of eternal damnation.

During the latter part of my state of conviction, I can now apply to my case, as it then was, the beautiful words of the poet:

> "The more I strove against its power,
> I felt its weight and guilt the more;
> 'Till late I hear'd my Saviour say,
> Come hither soul, I am the way."

This I found to be true, to the joy of my disconsolate and despairing heart, in the hour of my conversion to God.

During this state of mind, while sitting near the fire one evening, after I had heard Rev. Richard Allen, as before related, a view of my distressed condition so affected my heart, that I could not refrain from weeping and crying aloud; which caused the lady with whom I then lived, to inquire, with surprise, what ailed me; to which I answered, that I knew not what ailed me. She replied that I ought to pray. I arose from where I was sitting, being in an agony, and weeping convulsively, requested her to pray for me; but at the very moment when she would have done so, some person rapped heavily at the door for admittance; it was but a person of the house, but this occurrence was sufficient to interrupt us in our intentions; and I believe to this day, I should then have found salvation to my soul. This interruption was, doubtless, also the work of Satan.

Although at this time, when my conviction was so great, yet I knew not that Jesus Christ was the Son of God, the second person in the adorable trinity. I knew him not in the pardon of my sins, yet I felt a consciousness that if I died without pardon, that my lot must inevitably be damnation. If I would pray – I knew not how. I could form no connexion of ideas into words; but I knew the Lord's prayer; this I uttered with a loud voice, and with all my might and strength. I was the most ignorant creature in the world; I did not even know that Christ had died for the sins of the world, and to save sinners. Every circumstance, however, was so directed as still to continue and increase the sorrows of my heart, which I now know to have been a godly sorrow which wrought repentance, which is not to be repented of. Even the falling of the dead leaves from the forests, and the dried spires of the mown grass, showed me that I too must die, in like manner. But my case was awfully different from that of the grass of the field, or the wide spread decay of a thousand forests, as I felt within me a living principle, an immortal spirit, which cannot die, and must forever either enjoy the smiles of its Creator, or feel the pangs of ceaseless damnation.

But the Lord led me on; being gracious, he took pity on my ignorance; he heard my wailings, which had entered into the ear of the Lord of Sabaoth. Circumstances so transpired that I soon came to a knowledge of the being and character of the Son of God, of whom I knew nothing.

My strength had left me. I had become feverish and sickly through the violence of my feelings, on which account I left my place of service to spend a week with a coloured physician, who was a member of the Methodist society, and also to spend this week in going to places where prayer and supplication was statedly made for such as me.

Through this means I had learned much, so as to be able in some degree to comprehend the spiritual meaning of the text, which the minister took on the Sabbath morning, as before related, which was, "I perceive thy heart is not right in the sight of God." Acts, chap. 8, verse 21.

This text, as already related, became the power of God unto salvation to me, because I believed. I was baptized according to the direction of our Lord, who said, as he was about to ascend from the mount, to his disciples, "Go ye into all the world and preach my gospel to every creature, he that believeth and is baptized shall be saved" [Mark 16:15–16].

I have now passed through the account of my conviction, and also of my conversion to God; and shall next speak of the blessing of sanctification.

A time after I had received forgiveness flowed sweetly on; day and night my joy was full, no temptation was permitted to molest me. I could say continually with the psalmist, that "God had separated my sins from me, as far as the east is from the west" [Ps. 103:12]. I was ready continually to cry,

> "Come all the world, come sinner thou,
> All things in Christ are ready now."

I continued in this happy state of mind for almost three months, when a certain coloured man, by name William Scott, came to pay me a religious visit. He had been for many years a faithful follower of the Lamb; and he had also taken much time in visiting the sick and distressed of our colour, and understood well the great things belonging to a man of full stature in Christ Jesus.

In the course of our conversation, he inquired if the Lord had justified my soul. I answered, yes. He then asked me if he had sanctified me. I answered, no; and that I did not know what that was. He then undertook to instruct me further in the knowledge of the Lord respecting this blessing.

He told me the progress of the soul from a state of darkness, or of nature, was threefold; or consisted in three degrees, as follows: – First, conviction for sin. Second, justification from sin. Third, the entire sanctification of the soul to God. I thought this description was beautiful, and immediately believed in it. He then inquired if I would promise to pray for this in my secret devotions. I told him, yes. Very soon I began to call upon the Lord to show me all that was in my heart, which was not according to his will. Now there appeared to be a new struggle commencing in my soul, not accompanied with fear, guilt, and bitter distress, as while under my first conviction for sin; but a labouring of the mind to know more of the right way of the Lord. I began now to feel that my heart was not clean in his sight; that there yet remained the roots of bitterness, which if not destroyed, would ere long sprout up from these roots, and overwhelm me in a new growth of the brambles and brushwood of sin.

By the increasing light of the Spirit, I had found there yet remained the root of pride, anger, self-will, with many evils, the result of fallen nature. I now became alarmed at this discovery, and began to fear that I had been deceived in my experience. I was now greatly alarmed, lest I should fall away from what I knew I had enjoyed; and to guard against this I prayed almost incessantly, without acting faith on the power and promises of God to keep me from falling. I had not yet learned how to war against temptation of this kind. Satan well knew that if he could succeed in making me disbelieve my conversion, that he would catch me either on the ground of complete despair, or on the ground of infidelity. For if all I had passed through was to go for nothing, and was but a fiction, the mere ravings of a disordered mind, then I would naturally be led to believe that there is nothing in religion at all.

From this snare I was mercifully preserved, and led to believe that there was yet a greater work than that of pardon to be wrought in me. I retired to a secret place (after having sought this blessing, as well as I could, for nearly three months, from the time brother Scott had instructed me respecting it) for prayer, about four o'clock in the afternoon. I had struggled long and hard, but found not the desire of my heart. When I rose from my knees, there seemed a voice speaking to me, as I yet stood in a leaning posture – "Ask for sanctification." When to my surprise, I recollected that I had not even thought of it in my whole prayer. It would seem Satan had hidden the very object from my mind, for which I had purposely kneeled to pray. But when this voice whispered in my heart, saying, "Pray for sanctification," I again bowed in the same place, at the same time, and said, "Lord *sanctify* my soul for Christ's sake?" That very instant, as if lightning had darted through me, I sprang to my feet, and cried, "The Lord has sanctified my soul!" There was none to hear this but the angels who stood around to witness my joy – and Satan, whose malice raged the more. That Satan was there, I knew; for no sooner had I cried out, "The Lord has sanctified my soul," than there seemed another voice behind me, saying, "No, it is too great a work to be done." But another spirit said, "Bow down for the witness – I received it – *thou art sanctified!*" The first I knew of myself after that, I was standing in the yard with my hands spread out, and looking with my face toward heaven.

I now ran into the house and told them what had happened to me, when, as it were, a new rush of the same ecstasy came upon me, and caused me to feel as if I were in an ocean of light and bliss.

During this, I stood perfectly still, the tears rolling in a flood from my eyes. So great was the joy, that it is past description. There is no language that can describe it, except that which was heard by St. Paul, when he was caught up to the third heaven, and heard words which it was not lawful to utter.[5]

# Notes

1   Joseph Pilmore (1739–1825) accepted John Wesley's call for volunteers to evangelize the American colonies and in 1769 became the first Methodist preacher in Philadelphia. See the sketch of his life in *DANB*, vol. 15, 609–10.

2   Richard Allen (1760–1831), born a slave in Philadelphia, was converted to Christianity and purchased his freedom at the age of seventeen, whereupon he became a wagon driver during the Revolutionary war and began an itinerant preaching career. Discrimination against blacks in the St. George's Methodist Episcopal Church in Philadelphia moved Allen, with the help of Absalom Jones, to organize in protest the Free African Society, on April 12, 1787. Seven years later, the society's first church, the Bethel African Methodist Episcopal Church, was dedicated into service under the preaching leadership of Allen. In 1799 Bishop Francis Asbury ordained Allen a deacon, making him the first black to receive ordination in the Methodist Episcopal

church in America. During the next fifteen years other AME congregations were established in Delaware, Maryland, New York, and neighboring states. On April 9, 1816, Allen and the leaders of these more recent black churches founded the first independent Afro-American denomination in the United States, the African methodist Episcopal church. Allen was consecrated as the first bishop of the AME church on April 11, 1816. See Charles H. Wesley's *Richard Allen: Apostle of Freedom*, 2nd ed. (Washington, DC: Associated Publishers, 1969) and Allen's narrative, *The Life, Experience and Gospel Labors of the Rt. Rev. Richard Allen* (1833).

3  In her narrative, Lee often quotes verses from popular hymns of the day. Her sources include *A Collection of Hymns, for the Use of the Methodist Episcopal Church* (1823) and *The African Methodist Episcopal Church Hymn Book* (1818, rev. 1836).

4  Belshazzar, king of Babylon after Nebuchadnezzar, is the subject of the fifth chapter of the Book of Daniel.

5  Lee alludes to 2 Cor. 12:2–4, although it was not Paul but an unnamed acquaintance of Paul who was "caught up to the third heaven."

# 19

# Nature (1836)

## Ralph Waldo Emerson

## Introduction

No less influential than Jonathan Edwards, Ralph Waldo Emerson is one of America's greatest and most brilliant religious thinkers. Rooted in the liberal side of New England Puritan culture, Emerson translated the Puritan interest in virtue, and the Puritan impatience with religious formalism and hypocrisy, into a new key. Inspired by the German idealists and English Romantics of his day, Emerson wedded their reverence for the divine Spirit manifest in art and nature to a distinctively American respect for common sense, human decency, and democratic principle. Along with other representatives of New England Transcendentalism, Emerson's ideas have contributed much to the fertility and syncretism of American religious history. Their legacy stretches through the broad-minded investigations of religious experience undertaken by the philosopher William James at the turn of the twentieth century to the flowering of American Buddhism a century later, and through the celebration of authentic personhood and defiance of moral convention that rocked American culture in the wake of the Vietnam war to the upsurge in spirituality that contributed to the growth of many religious movements at the turn of the twenty-first century.

Written partly as a means of coping with his grief at the death of his young wife Ellen at the beginning of his public career, "the little book on nature" announced some of the main themes of Emerson's religious thought.

Excerpted from Ralph Waldo Emerson, *Nature* (1836), reprinted in *Selected Writings of Ralph Waldo Emerson*, ed. Brooks Atkinson (New York: Modern Library, 1940), 5–7.

Spirituality required solitude. And solitude, Emerson believed, fostered reverence for nature as the partner of the human spirit and its best source of inspiration. Friendship and compassion for others were also products of solitude and reverence for nature. Only by resisting conformity to conventional tastes and to the ideas of others, he believed, could one find the self-reliance that ushered one into true community with others and to the Spirit coursing through one and all.

# I

To go into solitude, a man needs to retire as much from his chamber as from society. I am not solitary whilst I read and write, though nobody is with me. But if a man would be alone, let him look at the stars. The rays that come from those heavenly worlds will separate between him and what he touches. One might think the atmosphere was made transparent with this design, to give man, in the heavenly bodies, the perpetual presence of the sublime. Seen in the streets of cities, how great they are! If the stars should appear one night in a thousand years, how would men believe and adore; and preserve for many generations the remembrance of the city of God which had been shown! But every night come out these envoys of beauty, and light the universe with their admonishing smile.

The stars awaken a certain reverence, because though always present, they are inaccessible; but all natural objects make a kindred impression, when the mind is open to their influence. Nature never wears a mean appearance. Neither does the wisest man extort her secret, and lose his curiosity by finding out all her perfection. Nature never became a toy to a wise spirit. The flowers, the animals, the mountains, reflected the wisdom of his best hour, as much as they had delighted the simplicity of his childhood.

When we speak of nature in this manner, we have a distinct but most poetical sense in the mind. We mean the integrity of impression made by manifold natural objects. It is this which distinguishes the stick of timber of the wood-cutter from the tree of the poet. The charming landscape which I saw this morning is indubitably made up of some twenty or thirty farms. Miller owns this field, Locke that, and Manning the woodland beyond. But none of them owns the landscape. There is a property in the horizon which no man has but he whose eye can integrate all the parts, that is, the poet. This is the best part of these men's farms, yet to this their warranty-deeds give no title.

To speak truly, few adult persons can see nature. Most persons do not see the sun. At least they have a very superficial seeing. The sun illuminates only the eye of the man, but shines into the eye and the heart of the child. The lover of nature is he whose inward and outward senses are still truly adjusted to each other; who has retained the spirit of infancy even into the era of manhood. His intercourse with heaven and earth becomes part of his daily food. In the presence of nature a wild delight runs through the man, in spite of real sorrows. Nature says – he is my creature, and maugre all his impertinent griefs, he shall be glad with me. Not the sun or the summer alone, but every hour and season yields its tribute of delight; for every hour and change corresponds to and authorizes a different state of the mind, from breathless noon to grimmest midnight. Nature is a setting that fits equally well a comic or a mourning piece. In good health, the air is a cordial of incredible virtue. Crossing a bare common, in snow puddles, at twilight, under a clouded sky, without having in my thoughts any occurrence of special good fortune, I have enjoyed a perfect exhilaration. I am glad to the brink of fear. In the woods, too, a man casts off his years, as the snake his slough, and at what period soever of life is always a child. In the woods is perpetual youth. Within these plantations of God, a decorum and sanctity reign, a perennial festival is dressed, and the guest sees not how he should tire of them in a thousand years. In the woods, we return to reason and faith. There I feel that nothing can befall me in life – no disgrace, no calamity (leaving me my eyes), which nature cannot repair. Standing on the bare ground – my head bathed by the blithe air and uplifted into infinite space – all mean egotism vanishes. I become a transparent eyeball; I am nothing; I see all; the currents of the Universal Being circulate through me; I am part or parcel of God. The name of the nearest friend sounds then foreign and accidental: to be brothers, to be acquaintances, master or servant, is then a trifle and a disturbance. I am the lover of uncontained and immortal beauty. In the wilderness, I find something more dear and connate than in streets or villages. In the tranquil landscape, and especially in the distant line of the horizon, man beholds somewhat as beautiful as his own nature.

The greatest delight which the fields and woods minister is the suggestion of an occult relation between man and the vegetable. I am not alone and unacknowledged. They nod to me, and I to them. The waving of the boughs in the storm is new to me and old. It takes me by surprise, and yet is not unknown. Its effect is like that of a higher thought or a better emotion coming over me, when I deemed I was thinking justly or doing right.

Yet it is certain that the power to produce this delight does not reside in nature, but in man, or in a harmony of both. It is necessary to use these pleasures with great temperance. For nature is not always tricked in holiday attire, but the same scene which yesterday breathed perfume and glittered as for the frolic of the nymphs is overspread with melancholy to-day. Nature always wears the colors of the spirit. To a man laboring under calamity, the heat of his own fire hath sadness in it. Then there is a kind of contempt of the landscape felt by him who has just lost by death a dear friend. The sky is less grand as it shuts down over less worth in the population.

# 20
# Poems (1863–1864)

## Emily Dickinson

## Introduction

While Emerson translated the Puritan concern for virtue into the broader context of modern spirituality, Emily Dickinson brought the Puritan relish for plain speech and honest introspection into modern poetry. Her work has influenced many of America's greatest poets, including Robert Lowell, Robert Frost, Allen Ginsberg, Gary Snyder, and Alice Fulton. Like Emerson, Dickinson looked to nature, and to herself, for inspiration. While never relinquishing attachment to the Bible, she also found revelation in her garden, and within her own heart.

Dickinson lived a quiet life in Amherst, Massachusetts, never married, and rarely wrote about the great events of her day. Like Anne Bradstreet, she found religious meaning in ordinary, domestic life. Her life at home was interrupted by one year at Mount Holyoke Female Seminary, where she successfully withstood pressure to undergo a religious conversion. Calling herself "one of the lingering bad ones" with respect to a religious revival at the school, Dickinson resisted the unrestrained emotionalism of evangelical religion. Like Jonathan Edwards, she was unwilling to equate enthusiasm for religion with grace or moral virtue. But unlike Edwards, she was never convinced of the need to submit to any religious authority outside her own heart. While Edwards certainly would have disapproved of her stubborn

---

Emily Dickinson, "Because I could not stop for Death –," "On a Columnar Self –," "A loss of something ever felt I –," in *The Complete Poems of Emily Dickinson*, ed. Thomas H. Johnson (Boston: Little, Brown, 1960), 350, 384–5, 448–9.

sense of her own rectitude and spiritual authority, and been shocked at the coy attitude she sometimes assumed toward God, her outlook grew out of the emphasis on responsiveness to the beauty of being that he did so much to articulate.

## 712

Because I could not stop for Death –
He kindly stopped for me –
The Carriage held but just Ourselves –
And Immortality.

We slowly drove – He knew no haste
And I had put away
My labor and my leisure too,
For His Civility –

We passed the School, where Children strove
At Recess – in the Ring –
We passed the Fields of Gazing Grain –
We passed the Setting Sun –

Or rather – He passed Us –
The Dews drew quivering and chill –
For only Gossamer, my Gown –
My Tippet – only Tulle –

We paused before a House that seemed
A Swelling of the Ground –
The Roof was scarcely visible –
The Cornice – in the Ground –

Since then – 'tis Centuries – and yet
Feels shorter than the Day
I first surmised the Horses' Heads
Were toward Eternity –
*ca.* 1863                                            1890

## 789

On a Columnar Self –
How ample to rely

In Tumult – or Extremity –
How good the Certainty

That Lever cannot pry –
And Wedge cannot divide
Conviction – That Granitic Base –
Though None be on our Side –

Suffice Us – for a Crowd –
Ourself – and Rectitude –
And that Assembly – not far off
From furthest Spirit – God –
*ca.* 1863                                    1929

## 959

A loss of something ever felt I –
The first that I could recollect
Bereft I was – of what I knew not
Too young that any should suspect

A Mourner walked among the children
I notwithstanding went about
As one bemoaning a Dominion
Itself the only Prince cast out –

Elder, Today, a session wiser
And fainter, too, as Wiseness is –
I find myself still softly searching
For my Delinquent Palaces –

And a Suspicion, like a Finger
Touches my Forehead now and then
That I am looking oppositely
For the site of the Kingdom of Heaven –
*ca.* 1864                                    1945

# 21

# The American Republic:
# Its Constitution, Tendencies,
# and Destiny (1865)

*Orestes Brownson*

## Introduction

Catholics played leading roles in the European settlement of North America, especially in the lands of New France and New Spain, where Many Native Americans were converted to the Roman Church. Catholics settled in Maryland, and figured prominently there, but in England's other American colonies, they were few and Catholic worship was often outlawed. Not until the 1830s, when refugees from Ireland joined new immigrants from Germany and France, did the growth of Catholic population in the United States accelerate. Later in the century, Catholics from Italy and Eastern Europe swelled the populations of New York, Chicago, and other American cities, adding new dimensions to the already complex fabric of American Catholicism. In the twentieth century, the cultural diversity within American Catholicism became even more robust as Latinos became the fastest-growing ethnic population in the United States.

Some of the most influential American Catholics have been converts from Protestantism drawn to the Catholic Church by the beauty and mysticism of its rituals. In the nineteenth century, several New England Transcendentalists appreciated Catholicism in this way, with Orestes Brownson leading the way

Excerpted from Orestes Brownson, *The American Republic: Its Constitution, Tendencies, and Destiny* (New York: P. O'Shea, 1865), 427–8, 439.

with his conversion to the Catholic Church in 1844. For Brownson and others who took his view, Catholicism resonated with the deep individualism celebrated by Emerson and other Transcendentalists while at the same time serving as an antidote for the excessive materialism and superficial individualism they saw in American culture.

Unlike Catholic leaders in Europe who viewed the policies of the modern world, including the separation of church and state, as antithetical to the religious values of the Church, Brownson rejoiced in America's separation of church and state and regarded it as a corrective to the religious passivity associated with membership in an established church. Celebrating both the Catholic Church and the United States as exemplars of divine wisdom, each in its own sphere of activity, he foresaw their historical destinies as being vigorously and fruitfully intertwined.

The United States, constituted in accordance with the real order of things, and founded on principles which have their origin and ground in the principles on which the church herself is founded, can never establish any one of the sects as the religion of the state, for that would violate their political constitution, and array all the other sects, as well as the church herself, against the government. They cannot be called upon to establish the church by law, because she is already in their constitution as far as the state has in itself any relation with religion, and because to establish her in any other sense would be to make her one of the civil institutions of the land, and to bring her under the control of the state, which were equally against her interest and her nature.

The religious mission of the United States is not then to establish the church by external law, or to protect her by legal disabilities, pains, and penalties against the sects, however uncatholic they may be; but to maintain catholic freedom, neither absorbing the state in the church nor the church in the state, but leaving each to move freely, according to its own nature, in the sphere assigned it in the eternal order of things. Their mission separates church and state as external governing bodies, but unites them in the interior principles from which each derives its vitality and force. Their union is in the intrinsic unity of principle, and in the fact that, though moving in different spheres, each obeys one and the same Divine law. With this the Catholic, who knows what Catholicity means, is of course satisfied, for it gives the church all the advantage over the sects of the real over the unreal; and with this the sects have no right to be dissatisfied, for it subjects them to no disadvantage not inherent in sectarianism itself in presence of Catholicity, and without any support from the civil authority.

But the American people need not trouble themselves about their exterior expansion. That will come of itself as fast as desirable. Let them devote their attention to their internal destiny, to the realization of their mission within, and they will gradually see the whole continent coming under their system, forming one grand nation, a really catholic nation, great, glorious, and free.

# 22

# Our Country's Place in History (1869)

## Isaac M. Wise

## Introduction

No religious group has supported the principles of the First Amendment more fervently than American Jews. Their long history of being a religious minority in the old worlds of Europe and the Middle East, and of being hated and persecuted for their religion, made religious liberty extremely precious and desirable. For liberal Jews like Isaac Mayer Wise, the Cincinnati rabbi who epitomized the progressive spirit of Reform Judaism in nineteenth-century America, appreciation for religious liberty was combined with enthusiasm for historical progress, and with belief that Judaism had much to contribute to American life.

As a liberal, progressive Jew, Wise wanted to bring Judaism out of its ghetto existence into full partnership with modern society. He believed that Jews should not restrict themselves from contributing to public life and to important new developments in the arts and sciences by adherence to what he regarded as excessively strict forms of religious observance. As Wise saw it, being an American enabled him to live freely as a Jew, and being a Jew enabled him to understand and contribute to America's providential role in history in a special way. He believed that God acted in history, and continued to act in history, as creator and redeemer of humankind. Rejecting fatalistic notions of

A lecture delivered before the Theological and Religious Library Association of Cincinnati, January 7, 1869. Excerpted from Isaac M. Wise, "Our Country's Place in History" (1869), reprinted in *God's New Israel: Religious Interpretations of American Destiny*, rev. ed., ed. Conrad Cherry (Chapel Hill: University of North Carolina Press, 1998), 224–5, 232–4.

divine providence, he affirmed the importance of free will as part of God's
plan and believed that, through a covenant relationship with God, America
had the potential of becoming the greatest nation on God's earth.

## History and a Place in It

History is Providence realized. It is the experience of the human family,
because it is the compendium of those events which effected the progress
of our race. Individuals and nations, by an undefined impulse, are the
actors who realize the plans of a higher power, to the detriment of all that
is wicked, the development and preservation of all that is good, and
tends to the elevation of man.

A cursory glance upon this physical universe proves the existence of
such an impulse in the vast domain of creation as a force of nature, a
universal law. Primary matter, imagine it as ether, gas, mist or chaos, –
primary matter is potential, imbued with the desire of individuation
(although no such term is known in physics), to form bodies of a
separate existence. So this earth, those stars, and those suns were individualized from primary matter, other celestial bodies are, and will
perpetually be formed by the same law, the same "Word of God." The
great bodies of the universe, in the architecture of heaven, are active and
cooperative individuals. The influence of each contributes directly or
indirectly to the rotation and life of the whole; while the primary or non-
individualized matter is apparently passive, without a role in the grand
drama of the universe.

The same law precisely governs the destiny of man. The human family
is a chaos of persons, each imbued with the desire, to rise above this
chaos to individual immortality. Tribes and nations, composed of persons, are continually stimulated by the same innate desire, to rise above
the level of the chaos to individual existence, to an active and cooperative attitude. Many rise above the chaos, and fulfill their destiny,
to realize the designs of Providence; many more remain particles of the
chaos, or meteors in the celestial plan.

Like the stars in the solar system, the nations who rose to individuality
are clustered around the central and invisible omnipotence, and complete their rotation in obedience to immutable laws. Like the stars, every
people must be a unit in the sum total of history – a unit without which
the whole sum could not exist; an independent unit in its sphere, and an
auxiliary one, attracting and being attracted, bearing and being borne, in
the moral universe of Providence. So and not otherwise, we can imagine
a government administered by the Supreme Wisdom. This theory rests

upon the solid basis of analogy from nature's revelations, and explains the phenomenon of history. In this sense nations have their places in history.[. . .]

The United States occupy the same place in modern history as Greece did in antiquity. Greece, surrounded by water and blessed with numerous harbors, was favored with an extensive commerce and continual intercourse with the world. The same precisely is the case with our country. The oceans are broad enough to protect us against foreign interference in our domestic affairs, which no council of European powers will ever arrange. At the same time our harbors are numerous enough to shelter the navies of the whole world, and to keep us in constant intercourse with all nations. Distances were the great obstacles in our way. But the American mind removed them. The application of steam to navigation and the electro-magnetic force to the telegraph brought us in connection with the world, as closely as Greece ever was, to Egypt, Phoenicia or Italy, and reduced our wide-stretched territories, for all practical purposes, to a compass no larger than that of ancient Greece. Greece was the heiress of an ancient civilization, which was poured into her lap by immigrants from Egypt, Phoenicia, Assyria, Syria and Asia Minor, and the constant intercourse with all those and other nations. Our country is the heiress of the European civilization. All her shipwrecked men and shipwrecked ideas continually pour into our lap with a wealth of thoughts, designs, energies, learning, skill and enterprise which steadily fill our mental coffers, and enlarge our horizon of conceptions. Greece remoulded all those foreign elements into one preeminently Grecial form; so do we continually assimilate and Americanize, absorb and recast all the foreign elements which we receive. So powerful is the affinity of freedom among men that it unites and amalgamates them quicker than any other agency. While the German in Poland, after centuries of domicil, is still a German, the first American-born generation of Germans is American. While the Poles in France remain foreigners, among us they are fastly incorporated. While Czechs in the heart of Germany, after centuries of mutual intercourse, are still Bohemian in feeling, language, customs and ideals; it is extremely easy for us to sustain one language for the whole country. This is one of the most wonderful influences which we know liberty to exercise on man.

Greece did not stop short at her heritage from abroad, but enlarged it, by native genius, to Grecian art, philosophy, science, government and religion; so do we. Our form of government is new. The patent-office at Washington, that great museum of mind, speaks volumes in praise of native genius. The practical sphere, to which necessity has confined and schooled us, testifies sufficiently, that whenever our turn shall come in the idealistic sphere, we will not be found missing in the production of an originally American art, science, philosophy and religion. Greece educated tens thousands of emissaries, to carry her wealth into Asia, Africa and Europe; so do we. We educate millions of free men, to carry our national wealth all over the earth. The very example of our successful revolution set France and all Europe ablaze with hopes of liberty. The millions of letters and journals which we send annually across the ocean, are so many rays of light to oppressed nations, and rouse the millions to think, reflect, wish and hope for freedom, and to appreciate its blessings. Every Negro in our midst is an emissary for the future humanization and civilization of Africa. Those very Chinamen who do now the work of washerwomen in the far West, are our boarding scholars, to become the future teachers of Eastern Asia, which is already near our doors. The very result of our late rebellion encouraged and inspired millions of European hearts with hopes of redemption, and proved that the republic is stronger than any monarchy. This is as important to humanity as our declaration of independence was. Greece, by the conflux of the various families of man, was inhabited by a peculiar people; so is our country. We are originally English, Irish, French, Dutch, German, Polish, Spanish, or Scandinavian; but we are neither. We are Americans. Every child born on this soil is Americanized. Our country has a peculiar people to work out a new and peculiar destiny.

The heiress of the civilized world's blood, experience and wisdom, as Greece was in days of yore; the mistress of the vast domain fortified by heaving oceans, really wealthy as none was before her; the favored high priestess of the goddess of liberty, with the diadem of honor and the breast-plate of justice – though young, gay, fast blundering and wild – occupies already a prominent place in history. Her commerce influences the commerce of the world, as only a few old countries do. But commerce, the source of wealth and the missionary of civilization, is one of the handmaids of progress. Her inventions in the mechanical arts, her strikes and associations of mechanics and laborers, revolutionize the system of labor all over the world, and redeem the laboring man from the oppression of hard labor, the despotism of capital and cunningness. These are powerful contributions to the progress of humanity. Still, industry herself is but another handmaid of progress. Liberty is the cause, progenitor, preserver and protector of all the blessings which we enjoy and impart to others. Liberty is progress itself. The chapter of liberty in the modern record of nations is our country's place in history. All other blessings of the human family grow from the soil of liberty, warmed by the genial rays of this glorious sun, and fructified by the stream of justice. Liberty is our place in history, our national destiny, our ideal, the very soul of our existence. As long as we cling tenaciously to our destiny and long steadily after our ideal, we will maintain our country's place in history. Greece, Rome and all the other empires afford no precedences to our future, for ours is a new world and a new destiny, which is entirely in our hands. Political parties may struggle and strive for the ascendancy. The conservative and the progressive elements of society are its centripetal and centrifugal forces which cause regular rotation, as long as they are governed by the center of gravity, the ideal of liberty. Money may govern the actions of tens of thousands; it is after all the mere foam on the surface which invariably disappears, as often as the ocean exerts its freedom of heaving up its billows. Sects may quarrel over particular dogmas, doctors disagree on the precise nature of the center of the earth. Liberty neutralizes their disputes, and begets new forms of religion and science. Nothing can arrest our progress, nothing drag down our country from her high place in history, except our own wickedness working a wilful desertion of our destiny, the desertion from the ideal of liberty. As long as we cling to this ideal, we will be in honor, glory, wealth and prosperity.

In the family, in school, in the academy, in church, on the public forum, in the press and everywhere else educate champions for the host of freedom; they are our country's guard. Warm, rouse, inspire every heart for liberty; this is our strength, our prosperity, our future, our destiny. Freedom to all nations; freedom to every man, this is our country's place in history; liberty in the name of my God and my country.

# 23

# Pre-Existence of Our Spirits (1872)

## Orson Pratt

## Introduction

Among the variety of new religious movements that originated during the second Great Awakening, none has been more successful than the Church of Jesus Christ of Latter-Day Saints, commonly known as the Mormons. In 1830, the religious visionary Joseph Smith published the Book of Mormon as a translation of hieroglyphic writings he claimed to have found inscribed on golden plates buried in upstate New York. As an extension of biblical revelation, the Book of Mormon chronicled the journey of one of the lost tribes of Israel to North America, their hostile interactions with American Indians, and Christ's visit to America after his resurrection. Smith received many additional revelations, but in trying to establish a "City of Holiness" based on them, he and his growing community of followers were hounded by opponents. After moving from New York to Kirtland, Ohio, then to Independence, Missouri, and then to Nauvoo, Illinois, Smith was arrested, removed to jail in Carthage and lynched without a trial in 1844. His successor, Brigham Young, led the Saints further west, where they established their Zion in territory that, finally in 1896, became the State of Utah.

Much can be said about the distinctly American qualities of the Latter-Day Saints, especially with regard to their desire to advance the Puritan vision of a New Israel. Their emphasis on marriage and family life as the central domain

Excerpted from Orson Pratt, "Pre-Existence of Our Spirits," *Journal of Discourses by President Brigham Young, His Two Counsellors, and the Twelve Apostles*, Vol. XV (Liverpool: Albert Carrington, 1873), 250–3.

of religious life and chief building block of society is also rooted in Puritan thought. In their radical interpretation of Puritan ideas about marriage, Latter-Day Saints believed that married saints had the power to create offspring in heaven who, in their turn, would pass through the earthly state of existence and find relationships of their own. Although both men and women needed to marry in order to produce spiritual offspring, men could become gods through the priesthood. Only women need to marry in order to enter heaven. For Latter-Day Saints as for other conservative descendants of the Puritans, women's dependence on the religious authority of their husbands is a hallmark of family values.

There are many Scriptures in the New Testament that have relation to the previous existence of man, which I do not at this time feel disposed to quote. They can be searched up by the Latter-day Saints, and by all who are curious enough to enquire into these things. There are some other things however, which I feel anxious to bring forth in connection with the pre-existence of man. One thing is our origin more fully. I have already stated that the spirits of the children of men were born unto their parents. Now who are the parents of these children?

There are certain promises made to the Latter-day Saints, one of them being that when we take a wife here in this world, it is our privilege by obedience to the ordinances of heaven, to have that wife married to us for time and for all eternity. This is a promise which God has made by revelation to his Church, hence the Latter-day. Saints believe in the eternity of the marriage covenant. This is one of our fundamental doctrines. We consider that a marriage for time alone is after the old Gentile order, and they have lost all knowledge of the true ordinances and order of heaven. They marry until death separates them. I believe that almost every religious society, in their marriage ceremony, use this phrase, "I pronounce you man and wife until death shall part you!" This sort of a marriage never originated with God; the marriage that origin-ated with him is the same as that of which we had an example in the beginning – the first marriage that was ever celebrated here on the earth. Do you enquire what was the form of that first marriage between Adam and Eve? I will explain it in a few words. They were united as husband and wife by the Lord himself; when they were united they did not know anything about death, for they had not partaken of the fruit of the tree that was forbidden, and they were then immortal beings. Here were two beings united who were as immortal as you will be when you come forth from your graves in the morning of the first resurrection. Under these conditions Adam and Eve were married. I do not believe that the Lord used the ceremony that is now used – I marry you until death shall separate you. By what means did death come into the world? After this marriage by partaking of the forbidden fruit, they brought death on both male and female, or as the Apostle Paul says, By one man sin and death entered into the world, even so shall all be made alive, and every man in his own order.

It seems then, that if there had been no sin death never would have come upon Adam and Eve, and they would have been living to-day, immortal, nearly six thousand years after being placed in the Garden of Eden, and would they not still be husband and wife? Certainly, and so they would continue if millions and millions of ages should pass away, and you could not point out any period in the future, when this relation would cease; no matter how many myriads of ages might pass away, unless they by sin brought death into the world. All will admit, who reflect on the subject, that this marriage was for eternity, and that death interfered with it only for the time being, until the resurrection should bring them forth and re-unite them.

The "Mormons," or Latter-day Saints, believe in this kind of marriage, and the first one ever performed on the earth is a pattern for us. Moreover God has revealed to us the nature of marriage, and that its relationships are to exist after the resurrection, and that it must be attended to in this life in order to secure it for the next life. For instance, if you wish to obtain a great many blessings pertaining to the future world, you have to secure these blessings here. You cannot be baptized in the next state of existence for the remission of sins; that is an ordinance pertaining to the flesh, which you must attend to here. And so with all other ordinances which God has ordained, you have to partake of them here in order to have a claim on the promises hereafter. It is so with regard to marriage; and this agrees with what Jesus has said in relation to their not marrying nor giving in marriage in that world. There will be no such thing there. Why? Because this is the world for all these ordinances to be attended to. Here is the place to secure all the blessings for the next world. We have to show in this probation that we will be obedient in obeying the commandments of heaven so that we may have a claim on every blessing pertaining to the next life. Consequently, we have to secure this marriage for eternity while in this world. When a female in the Latter-day Saint Church marries a person outside the Church it is not a marriage in our estimation, in the scriptural sense of the word, it is only a union until death shall part them. When a person does this we really consider them weak in the faith; indeed it is equivalent in my estimation not only to being weak in the faith, but since these revelations were given on the subject, if people with their eyes wide open will still reject these important things, and marry a person outside the Church, it shows to me very clearly that he or she has no regard for the word of God, nor for their own salvation. They are lacking not only in faith but in the principle of obedience. They have no hope when they marry outside the Church, but when they marry in the Church according to this order, and the persons who officiate in declaring them husband and wife, being commissioned of God and having authority to administer in all the ordinances of his kingdom, that marriage is not only for time, but for all eternity.

Another question. Having been married for eternity, we die and our spirits go into celestial paradise. We come forth in the morning of the first resurrection as immortal males and immortal females. Our wives, married to us for eternity, come forth, and they are ours by virtue of that which God has pronounced upon them through those whom he has appointed, and to whom he has given authority. We have a legal claim upon them at the resurrection. But here comes forth a person that is married outside. She comes up without a husband, he without a wife, or any claim upon any of the blessings. Here is the difference between these two classes of beings. One dwells as an angel, without any power to increase their species, family or dominions, without the power to beget sons and daughters. This class will be angels. Perhaps many of them will be worthy of obtaining a degree of power, glory, and happiness, but not a fullness. Why? Because they have not come up to that position of their Father and their God. He has power to beget and bring forth sons and daughters in the spirit world; and after he has brought forth millions and millions of spirits, he has power to organize worlds, and send these spirits into these worlds to take temporal bodies to prepare them in turn to be redeemed and become Gods, or in other words, the sons of God, growing up like their father, possessing all his attributes, and propagating their species through all eternity. Here then is the difference between these two classes of beings – one having lost what they might have obtained and enjoyed if they had had faith in God and been willing to obey his commandments. But the others are worthy, as the Apostle Paul has said, to obtain a far more exceeding and eternal weight of glory, while the others will be angels or servants, to go and come at the bidding of those who are more exalted.

This is what Paul meant when he said that in the Lord the man is not without the woman, neither is the woman without the man; as much as to say that in order to be in the Lord and to obtain a fullness of his glory and exaltation, you can not be separated; or in other words, to speak according to the common phrase, you can not live old bachelors or old maids and go down to your graves in this condition. That is not the order of heaven, why? Because marriage is essentially necessary to qualify them to propagate their species throughout all eternity, that they in their turn may have worlds created on which these sons and daughters of their own begetting may receive tabernacles of flesh and bones as we have done.

This is the order by which all worlds are peopled by spirits that have been born in the eternal worlds; and these wórlds are organized expressly for them that they may go and have another change, another state of being different from their spiritual state, where they may possess bodies of flesh and bones, which are essentially necessary to the begetting of their own species. Spirits can not bring forth, multiply and increase. They must have bodies.

# 24

# Science and Health with Key to the Scriptures (1875)

## Mary Baker Eddy

## Introduction

In addition to its stress on the need for conversion, evangelical Protestantism in the nineteenth century fostered desire for knowledge about the nature of spiritual reality and its means of operation. Enthusiastic about science as well as religion, more than a few Americans attempted to understand and control the unseen power of the spirit world in scientific ways. Many religious enthusiasts hoped the spirit world would reveal its laws of operation so that practitioners might manage spiritual forces in beneficial ways. Interest in mesmerism, or hypnotic trance, flourished in the nineteenth century, contributing both to the development of psychology and to fascination with Buddhism and Hinduism, religions known for adepts who could enter states of trance at will.

In the context of a larger cultural interest in harmonizing religion and science, the First Church of Christ, Science focused on the healing power of divine love and on recovering the science of healing revealed in the ministry of Jesus. The founder of Christian Science, Mary Baker Eddy, had been an invalid. She recovered her health as a result of reading New Testament accounts of the healing powers of Jesus and then went on to identify key principles, distilled from the New Testament, which would enable practitioners to dispel disease. Disease was nothing more than the materialization of sin, Eddy

Excerpted from Mary Baker Eddy, *Science and Health with Key to the Scriptures* (Boston: First Church of Christ, Science, 1875), xi, 135–6.

believed, and could be eradicated by belief in the power of love, which triumphed over all.

In addition to representing one version of a larger cultural effort to harmonize religion and science, Christian Science is an especially clear example of the desire for recovery from illness or misfortune that so often draws people to religion. In this regard, Christian Science may hark back to the earliest forms of religious expression in shamanism. At the same time, its emphasis on health and well-being might be said to anticipate recent scientific discoveries about the healing effect of prayer and other forms of religious belief.

The physical healing of Christian Science results now, as in Jesus' time, from the operation of divine Principle, before which sin and disease lose their reality in human consciousness and disappear as naturally and as necessarily as darkness gives place to light and sin to reformation. Now, as then, these mighty works are not supernatural, but supremely natural. They are the sign of Immanuel, or "God with us," – a divine influence ever present in human consciousness and repeating itself, coming now as was promised aforetime,

> To preach deliverance to the captives [of sense],
> And recovering of sight to the blind,
> To set at liberty them that are bruised.

[. . .] The same power which heals sin heals also sickness. This is "the beauty of holiness," that when Truth heals the sick, it casts out evils, and when Truth casts out the evil called   Fear and disease, it heals the sick. When Christ cast out the devil of   sickness dumbness, "it came to pass, when the devil was gone out,   identical the dumb spake." There is to-day danger of repeating the offence of the Jews by limiting the Holy One of Israel and asking: "Can God furnish a table in the wilderness?" What cannot God do?

It has been said, and truly, that Christianity must be Science, and Science must be Christianity, else one or the other is false and useless; but neither is unimportant or untrue, and they are alike in demonstration. This proves the   The unity of one to be identical with the other. Christianity as Jesus   Science and taught it was not a creed, nor a system of ceremonies,   Christianity nor a special gift from a ritualistic Jehovah; but it was the demonstration of divine Love casting out error and healing the sick, not merely in the *name* of Christ, or Truth, but in demonstration of Truth, as must be the case in the cycles of divine light.

Jesus established his church and maintained his mission on a spiritual foundation of Christ-healing. He taught his followers that his religion

**The Christ-mission**

had a divine Principle, which would cast out error and heal both the sick and the sinning. He claimed no intelligence, action, nor life separate from God. Despite the persecution this brought upon him, he used his divine power to save men both bodily and spiritually.

# 25

# A Function of the Social
# Settlement (1899)

## Jane Addams

## Introduction

Offering classes ranging from cooking to literacy, and from art appreciation to manual training, settlement houses might be described as an extension of Protestant missionary outreach to immigrants living in the ghettoes of British and American cities. But while missionaries often focused on preaching and obtaining conversions, settlement workers advocated a social gospel that defined the Kingdom of God in terms of better housing, child-labor laws, and concern for the dignity, education, and cultural development of individuals and families. During the late nineteenth and early twentieth centuries, liberals like Jane Addams, who defined religious outreach in terms of education and social reform, increasingly parted ways from conservatives who defined it in terms of saving sinners from hell.

While representing the liberal side of American Protestant benevolence, Addams and her settlement house colleagues moved even further to challenge some of the basic religious assumptions upon which all forms of missionary philanthropy were based. Resisting the idea that society ought to be divided into rich donors and poor recipients of good will, Addams argued that it should rather be a medium for personal development, interpersonal exchange, and collective improvement. In her understanding of the relationship between religion and human life, Addams was an advocate of the

Excerpted from Jane Addams, "A Function of the Social Settlement," *Annals of the American Academy of Political and Social Science* 13 (May 1899): 323–45, reprinted in *Pragmatism: A Reader*, ed. Louis Menand (New York: Vintage, 1997), 273–8.

philosophy of pragmatism, which defined ideas in terms of their effects and measured virtue by its outcomes. On one hand, the pragmatic approach to virtue carried forward the old Puritan idea that grace enabled moral behavior. On the other, it challenged the pretentiousness of all theologies and philosophic systems, including those based in biblical revelation, insofar as they claimed to rise above, or set one apart from, the creative processes of human life and democratic society.

The word "settlement," which we have borrowed from London, is apt to grate a little upon American ears. It is not, after all, so long ago that Americans who settled were those who had adventured into a new country, where they were pioneers in the midst of difficult surroundings. The word still implies migrating from one condition of life to another totally unlike it, and against this implication the resident of an American settlement takes alarm.

We do not like to acknowledge that Americans are divided into "two nations," as her prime minister once admitted of England.[1] We are not willing, openly and professedly, to assume that American citizens are broken up into classes, even if we make that assumption the preface to a plea that the superior class has duties to the inferior. Our democracy is still our most precious possession, and we do well to resent any inroads upon it, even although they may be made in the name of philanthropy.

And yet because of this very democracy, superior privileges carry with them a certain sense of embarrassment, founded on the suspicion that intellectual and moral superiority too often rest upon economic props which are, after all, matters of accident, and that for an increasing number of young people the only possible way to be comfortable in the possession of those privileges, which result from educational advantages, is in an effort to make common that which was special and aristocratic. Added to this altruistic compunction one may easily discover a selfish suspicion that advantages thus held apart slowly crumble in their napkins, and are not worth having.

The American settlement, perhaps, has represented not so much a sense of duty of the privileged toward the unprivileged, of the "haves" to the "have nots," to borrow Canon Barnett's[2] phrase, as a desire to equalize through social effort those results which superior opportunity may have given the possessor.

The settlement, however, certainly represents more than compunctions. Otherwise it would be but "the monastery of the nineteenth century," as it is indeed sometimes called, substituting the anodyne of work for that of contemplation, but still the old attempt to seek individual escape from the common misery through the solace of healing.

If this were the basis of the settlement, there would no longer be need of it when society had become reconstructed to the point of affording equal opportunity for all, and it would still be at the bottom a philanthropy, although expressed in social and democratic terms. There is, however, a sterner and more enduring aspect of the settlement which this paper would attempt to present.

It is frequently stated that the most pressing problem of modern life is that of a reconstruction and a reorganization of the knowledge which we possess; that we are at last struggling to realize in terms of life all that has been discovered and absorbed, to make it over into healthy and direct expression of free living. Dr. John Dewey, of the University of Chicago, has written: "Knowledge is no longer its own justification, the interest in it has at last transferred itself from accumulation and verification to its application to life." And he adds: "When a theory of knowledge forgets that its value rests in solving the problem out of which it has arisen, that of securing a method of action, knowledge begins to cumber the ground. It is a luxury, and becomes a social nuisance and disturber."[3]

We may quote further from Professor James, of Harvard University, who recently said in an address before the Philosophical Union of the University of California: "Beliefs, in short, are really rules of action, and the whole function of thinking is but one step in the production of habits of action," or "the ultimate test for us of what a truth means is indeed the conduct it dictates or inspires."[4]

Having thus the support of two philosophers, let us assume that the dominating interest in knowledge has become its use, the conditions under which, and ways in which it may be most effectively employed in human conduct; and that at last certain people have consciously formed themselves into groups for the express purpose of effective application. These groups which are called settlements have naturally sought the spots where the dearth of this applied knowledge was most obvious, the depressed quarters of great cities. They gravitate to these spots, not with the object of finding clinical material, not to found "sociological laboratories," not, indeed, with the analytical motive at all, but rather in a reaction from that motive, with a desire to use synthetically and directly whatever knowledge they, as a group, may possess, to test its validity and to discover the conditions under which this knowledge may be employed.

That, just as groups of men, for hundreds of years, have organized themselves into colleges, for the purpose of handing on and disseminating knowledge already accumulated, and as other groups have been organized into seminars and universities, for the purpose of research and the extension of the bounds of knowledge, so at last groups have been consciously formed for the purpose of the application of knowledge to life. This third attempt also would claim for itself the enthusiasm and advantage of collective living. It has become to be a group of people who share their methods, and who mean to make experience continuous beyond the individual. It may be urged that this function of application has always been undertaken by individuals and unconscious groups. This is doubtless true, just as much classic learning has always been disseminated outside the colleges, and just as some of the most notable discoveries of pure science have been made outside of the universities. Still both these institutions do in the main accomplish the bulk of the disseminating, and the discovering; and it is upon the same basis that the third group may establish its value.

The ideal and developed settlement would attempt to test the value of human knowledge by action, and realization, quite as the complete and ideal university would concern itself with the discovery of knowledge in all branches. The settlement stands for application as opposed to research; for emotion as opposed to abstraction, for universal interest as opposed to specialization. This certainly claims too much, absurdly too much, for a settlement, in the light of its achievements, but perhaps not in the light of its possibilities.

This, then, will be my definition of the settlement: that it is an attempt to express the meaning of life in terms of life itself, in forms of activity. There is no doubt that the deed often reveals when the idea does not, just as art makes us understand and feel what might be incomprehensible and inexpressible in the form of an argument. And as the artist tests the success of his art when the recipient feels that he knew the thing before, but had not been able to express it, so the settlement, when it attempts to reveal and apply knowledge, deems its results practicable, when it has made knowledge available which before was abstract, when through use, it has made common that knowledge which was partial before, because it could only be apprehended by the intellect.

The chief characteristic of art lies in freeing the individual from a sense of separation and isolation in his emotional experience, and has usually been accomplished through painting, writing and singing; but this does not make it in the least impossible that it is now being tried, self-consciously and most bunglingly we will all admit, in terms of life itself.

A settlement brings to its aid all possible methods to reveal and make common its conception of life. All those arts and devices which express kindly relation from man to man, from charitable effort to the most specialized social intercourse, are constantly tried. There is the historic statement, the literary presentation, the fellowship which comes when great questions are studied with the hope of modifying actual conditions, the putting forward of the essential that the trivial may appear unimportant, as it is, the attempt to select the more typical and enduring forms of social life, and to eliminate, as far as possible, the irrelevant things which crowd into actual living. There are so-called art exhibits, concerts, dramatic representations, every possible device to make operative on the life around it, the conception of life which the settlement group holds. The demonstration is made not by reason, but by life itself. There must, of course, be a certain talent for conduct and unremitting care lest there grow to be a divergence between theory and living, for however embarrassing this divergence may prove in other situations, in a settlement the artist throws away his tools as soon as this thing happens. He is constantly transmitting by means of his human activity, his notion of life to others. He hopes to produce a sense of infection which may ultimately result in identity of interest. [...]

[...] The phrase "applied knowledge" or science has so long been used in connection with polytechnic schools that it may be well to explain that I am using it in a broader sense. These schools have applied science primarily for professional ends. They are not so commercial, but they may easily become quite as specialized in their departments as the chemical laboratories attached to certain large manufacturing concerns. In the early days of Johns Hopkins University, one of the men in the biological department invented a contrivance which produced a very great improvement in the oyster raft at that time in use in the Chesapeake Bay. For months afterward, in all the commencement orations and other occasions when "prominent citizens" were invited to speak, this oyster raft was held up as the great contribution of the University to the commercial interest of the city, and as a justification of the University's existence, much to the mortification of the poor inventor. This [...] is an excellent example of what I do not mean.

The application which I have in mind is one which cannot be measured by its money-making value. I have in mind an application to a given neighborhood of the solace of literature, of the uplift of the imagination, and of the historic consciousness which gives its possessor a sense of connection with the men of the past who have thought and acted, an application of the stern mandates of science, not only to the conditions of sewers and the care of alleys, but to the methods of life and thought; the application of the metaphysic not only to the speculations of the philosopher, but to the events of the passing moment; the application of the moral code to the material life, the transforming of the economic relation into an ethical relation until the sense that religion itself embraces all relations, including the ungodly industrial relation, has become common property.

# Notes

1   [Benjamin Disraeli (1804–81); his novel *Sybil: Or, The Two Nations* was published in 1845.]
2   [Samuel Augustus Barnett (1844–1913), English clergyman and founder of the social settlement movement.]
3   [John Dewey, *The Significance of the Problem of Knowledge* (Chicago: University of Chicago Press, 1897); reprinted in John Dewey, *The Early Works, 1882–1898, Volume 5: 1895–1898: Early Essays*, ed. Jo Ann Boydston (Carbondale: Southern Illinois University Press, 1972), 20–1, slightly condensed and paraphrased.]
4   [William James, "Philosophical Conceptions and Practical Results," the first use of the term "pragmatism" in print. Originally published in the Berkeley *University Chronicle* I (September 1898), 287–310; reprinted in *Pragmatism*, ed. Frederick H. Burkhardt (Cambridge, Mass.: Harvard University Press, 1975), 257–70. James is articulating what he calls "the principle of Peirce, the principle of pragmatism."]

# 26

# The Varieties of Religious Experience (1902)

## William James

## Introduction

No one played a greater role in exploring the pragmatic meaning of religion than the philosopher William James. While Addams and others aimed their pragmatic approach to religion more toward the advancement of democracy and social reform, James was primarily interested in the psychological implications of pragmatism, especially with regard to the power of religious belief and the process of conversion. With a pragmatist's focus on outcome, James argued that religious beliefs could be defined in terms of the effects they produced and that these effects were proof that religion was not just an imaginary phenomenon. Religious belief engaged the whole of a person's life, James believed, and was capable of generating biological and behavioral changes not otherwise possible. People might disagree about how to name the source of religion's power, and develop a vast array of different and even conflicting theologies to explain it, but at the most basic level, James believed, all religions brought people into contact with something real and powerful beyond ordinary consciousness. Belief in this "more," however it was theologically defined, supplied real strength and comfort. Religious conversion was nothing other than an encounter with the "more" that alleviated a person's feelings of isolation, failure, and despair.

Excerpted from William James, *The Varieties of Religious Experience, A Study in Human Nature: Being the Gifford Lectures on Natural Religion Delivered at Edinburgh in 1901–1902* (New York: American Library, 1958), 383–91.

As a best-selling American book on religion, second in all-time US sales only to the Bible, James's *Varieties* marks an important shift in American religious thought. It represented a bold effort to think about religious experience in psychological terms rather than in terms of the doctrinal differences that separate religious groups. As a psychologist of religion, James was especially interested in the transformation of the will associated with the process of conversion and he was profoundly respectful of the power of religious experience in people's lives. But he was more cautious about proclaiming the existence of spiritual forces, and more dubious about the possibility of harnessing those forces, than mesmerists, Christian Scientists, and others who imagined that the metaphysical realities people believed in could be investigated scientifically or defined in scientific terms.

The warring gods and formulas of the various religions do indeed cancel each other, but there is a certain uniform deliverance in which religions all appear to meet. It consists of two parts: –

1. An uneasiness; and
2. Its solution.

1. The uneasiness, reduced to its simplest terms, is a sense that there is *something wrong about us* as we naturally stand.

2. The solution is a sense that *we are saved from the wrongness* by making proper connection with the higher powers.

In those more developed minds which alone we are studying, the wrongness takes a moral character, and the salvation takes a mystical tinge. I think we shall keep well within the limits of what is common to all such minds if we formulate the essence of their religious experience in terms like these: –

The individual, so far as he suffers from his wrongness and criticises it, is to that extent consciously beyond it, and in at least possible touch with something higher, if anything higher exist. Along with the wrong part there is thus a better part of him, even though it may be but a most helpless germ. With which part he should identify his real being is by no means obvious at this stage; but when stage 2 (the stage of solution or salvation) arrives,[1] the man identifies his real being with the germinal higher part of himself; and does so in the following way. *He becomes conscious that this higher part is conterminous and continuous with a M O R E of the same quality, which is operative in the universe outside of him, and which he can keep in working touch with, and in a fashion get on board of and save himself when all his lower being has gone to pieces in the wreck.*

It seems to me that all the phenomena are accurately describable in these very simple general terms.[2] They allow for the divided self and the struggle; they involve the change of personal centre and the surrender of the lower self; they express the appearance of exteriority of the helping power and yet account for our sense of union with it;[3] and they fully justify our feelings of security and joy. There is probably no autobiographic document, among all those which I have quoted, to which the description will not well apply. One need only add such specific details as will adapt it to various theologies and various personal temperaments, and one will then have the various experiences reconstructed in their individual forms.

So far, however, as this analysis goes, the experiences are only psychological phenomena. They possess, it is true, enormous biological worth. Spiritual strength really increases in the subject when he has them, a new life opens for him, and they seem to him a place of conflux where the forces of two universes meet; and yet this may be nothing but his subjective way of feeling things, a mood of his own fancy, in spite of the effects produced. I now turn to my second question: What is the objective 'truth' of their content?[4]

The part of the content concerning which the question of truth most pertinently arises is that 'MORE of the same quality' with which our own higher self appears in the experience to come into harmonious working relation. Is such a 'more' merely our own notion, or does it really exist? If so, in what shape does it exist? Does it act, as well as exist? And in what form should we conceive of that 'union' with it of which religious geniuses are so convinced?

It is in answering these questions that the various theologies perform their theoretic work, and that their divergencies most come to light. They all agree that the 'more' really exists; though some of them hold it to exist in the shape of a personal god or gods, while others are satisfied to conceive it as a stream of ideal tendency embedded in the eternal structure of the world. They all agree, moreover, that it acts as well as exists, and that something really is effected for the better when you throw your life into its hands. It is when they treat of the experience of 'union' with it that their speculative differences appear most clearly. Over this point pantheism and theism, nature and second birth, works and grace and karma, immortality and reincarnation, rationalism and mysticism, carry on inveterate disputes. [...]

The 'more,' as we called it, and the meaning of our 'union' with it, form the nucleus of our inquiry. Into what definite description can these words be translated, and for what definite facts do they stand? It would never do for us to place ourselves offhand at the position of a particular theology, the Christian theology, for example, and proceed immediately to define the 'more' as Jehovah, and the 'union' as his imputation to us of the righteousness of Christ. That would be unfair to other religions, and, from our present standpoint at least, would be an over-belief.

We must begin by using less particularized terms; and, since one of the duties of the science of religions is to keep religion in connection with the rest of science, we shall do well to seck first of all a way of describing the 'more,' which psychologists may also recognize as real. The *subconscious self* is nowadays a well-accredited psychological entity; and I believe that in it we have exactly the mediating term required. Apart from all religious considerations, there is actually and literally more life in our total soul than we are at any time aware of. The exploration of the transmarginal field has hardly yet been seriously undertaken, but what Mr. Myers said in 1892 in his essay on the Subliminal Consciousness[5] is as true as when it was first written: "Each of us is in reality an abiding psychical entity far more extensive than he knows – an individuality which can never express itself completely through any corporeal manifestation. The Self manifests through the organism; but there is always some part of the Self unmanifested; and always, as it seems, some power of organic expression in abeyance or reserve." Much of the content of this larger background against which our conscious being stands out in relief is insignificant. Imperfect memories, silly jingles, inhibitive timidities, 'dissolutive' phenomena of various sorts, as Myers calls them, enter into it for a large part. But in it many of the performances of genius seem also to have their origin; and in our study of conversion, of mystical experiences, and of prayer, we have seen how striking a part invasions from this region play in the religious life.

Let me then propose, as an hypothesis, that whatever it may be on its *farther* side, the 'more' with which in religious experience we feel ourselves connected is on its *hither* side the subconscious continuation of our conscious life. Starting thus with a recognized psychological fact as our basis, we seem to preserve a contact with 'science' which the ordinary theologian lacks. At the same time the theologian's contention that the religious man is moved by an external power is vindicated, for it is one of the peculiarities of invasions from the subconscious region to take on objective appearances, and to suggest to the Subject an external control. In the religious life the control is felt as 'higher'; but since on our hypothesis it is primarily the higher faculties of our own hidden mind which are controlling, the sense of union with the power beyond us is a sense of something, not merely apparently, but literally true.

This doorway into the subject seems to me the best one for a science of religions, for it mediates between a number of different points of view. Yet it is only a doorway, and difficulties present themselves as soon as we step through it, and ask how far our transmarginal consciousness carries us if we follow it on its remoter side. Here the over-beliefs begin: here mysticism and the conversion-rapture and Vedantism and transcendental idealism bring in their monistic interpretations and tell us that the finite self rejoins the absolute self, for it was always one with God and identical with the soul of the world.[6] Here the prophets of all the different religions come with their visions, voices, raptures, and other openings, supposed by each to authenticate his own peculiar faith.

Those of us who are not personally favored with such specific revelations must stand outside of them altogether and, for the present at least, decide that, since they corroborate incompatible theological doctrines, they neutralize one another and leave no fixed result. If we follow any one of them, or if we follow philosophical theory and embrace monistic pantheism on non-mystical grounds, we do so in the exercise of our individual freedom, and build out our religion in the way most congruous with our personal susceptibilities. Among these susceptibilities intellectual ones play a decisive part. Although the religious question is primarily a question of life, of living or not living in the higher union which opens itself to us as a gift, yet the spiritual excitement in which the gift appears a real one will often fail to be aroused in an individual until certain particular intellectual beliefs or ideas which, as we say, come home to him, are touched.[7] These ideas will thus be essential to that individual's religion; – which is as much as to say that over-beliefs in various directions are absolutely indispensable, and that we should treat them with tenderness and tolerance so long as they are not intolerant themselves. As I have elsewhere written, the most interesting and valuable things about a man are usually his over-beliefs.

Disregarding the over-beliefs, and confining ourselves to what is common and generic, we have in *the fact that the conscious person is continuous with a wider self through which saving experiences come*,[8] a positive content of religious experience which, it seems to me, *is literally and objectively true as far as it goes*. If I now proceed to state my own hypothesis about the farther limits of this extension of our personality, I shall be offering my own over-belief – though I know it will appear a sorry under-belief to some of you – for which I can only bespeak the same indulgence which in a converse case I should accord to yours.

The further limits of our being plunge, it seems to me, into an altogether other dimension of existence from the sensible and merely 'understandable' world. Name it the mystical region, or the supernatural region, whichever you choose. So far as our ideal impulses originate in this region (and most of them do originate in it, for we find them possessing us in a way for which we cannot articulately account), we belong to it in a more intimate sense than that in which we belong to the visible world, for we belong in the most intimate sense wherever our ideals belong. Yet the unseen region in question is not merely ideal, for it produces effects in this world. When we commune with it, work is actually done upon our finite personality, for we are turned into new men, and consequences in the way of conduct follow in the natural world upon our regenerative change.[9] But that which produces effects within another reality must be termed a reality itself, so I feel as if we had no philosophic excuse for calling the unseen or mystical world unreal.

God is the natural appellation, for us Christians at least, for the supreme reality, so I will call this higher part of the universe by the name of God.[10] We and God have business with each other; and in opening ourselves to his influence our deepest destiny is fulfilled. The universe, at those parts of it which our personal being constitutes, takes a turn genuinely for the worse or for the better in proportion as each one of us fulfills or evades God's demands. As far as this goes I probably have you with me, for I only translate into schematic language what I may call the instinctive belief of mankind: God is real since he produces real effects.

The real effects in question, so far as I have as yet admitted them, are exerted on the personal centres of energy of the various subjects, but the spontaneous faith of most of the subjects is that they embrace a wider sphere than this. Most religious men believe (or 'know,' if they be mystical) that not only they themselves, but the whole universe of beings to whom the God is present, are secure in his parental hands. There is a sense, a dimension, they are sure, in which we are *all* saved, in spite of the gates of hell and all adverse terrestrial appearances. God's existence is the guarantee of an ideal order that shall be permanently preserved. This world may indeed, as science assures us, some day burn up or freeze; but if it is part of his order, the old ideals are sure to be brought elsewhere to fruition, so that where God is, tragedy is only provisional and partial, and shipwreck and dissolution are not the absolutely final things. Only when this farther step of faith concerning God is taken, and remote objective consequences are predicted, does religion, as it seems to me, get wholly free from the first immediate subjective experience, and bring a *real hypothesis* into play. A good hypothesis in science must have other properties than those of the phenomenon it is immediately invoked to explain, otherwise it is not prolific enough. God, meaning only what enters into the religious man's experience of union, falls short of being an hypothesis of this more useful order. He needs to enter into wider cosmic relations in order to justify the subject's absolute confidence and peace.

That the God with whom, starting from the hither side of our own extra-marginal self, we come at its remoter margin into commerce should be the absolute world-ruler, is of course a very considerable over-belief. Over-belief as it is, though, it is an article of almost every one's religion.

Most of us pretend in some way to prop it upon our philosophy, but the philosophy itself is really propped upon this faith. What is this but to say that Religion, in her fullest exercise of function, is not a mere illumination of facts already elsewhere given, not a mere passion, like love, which views things in a rosier light. It is indeed that, as we have seen abundantly. But it is something more, namely, a postulator of new *facts* as well. The world interpreted religiously is not the materialistic world over again, with an altered expression; it must have, over and above the altered expression, *a natural constitution* different at some point from that which a materialistic world would have. It must be such that different events can be expected in it, different conduct must be required.

This thoroughly 'pragmatic' view of religion has usually been taken as a matter of course by common men. They have interpolated divine miracles into the field of nature, they have built a heaven out beyond the grave. It is only transcendentalist metaphysicians who think that, without adding any concrete details to Nature, or subtracting any, but by simply calling it the expression of absolute spirit, you make it more divine just as it stands. I believe the pragmatic way of taking religion to be the deeper way. It gives it body as well as soul, it makes it claim, as everything real must claim, some characteristic realm of fact as its very own. What the more characteristically divine facts are, apart from the actual inflow of energy in the faith-state and the prayer-state, I know not. But the over-belief on which I am ready to make my personal venture is that they exist. The whole drift of my education goes to persuade me that the world of our present consciousness is only one out of many worlds of consciousness that exist, and that those other worlds must contain experiences which have a meaning for our life also; and that although in the main their experiences and those of this world keep discrete, yet the two become continuous at certain points, and higher energies filter in. By being faithful in my poor measure to this over-belief, I seem to myself to keep more sane and true. I *can*, of course, put myself into the sectarian scientist's attitude, and imagine vividly that the world of sensations and of scientific laws and objects may be all. But whenever I do this, I hear that inward monitor of which W. K. Clifford once wrote, whispering the word 'bosh!' Humbug is humbug, even though it bear the scientific name, and the total expression of human experience, as I view it objectively, invincibly urges me beyond the narrow 'scientific' bounds. Assuredly, the real world is of a different temperament, – more intricately built than physical science allows. So my objective and my subjective conscience both hold me to the over-belief which I express. Who knows whether the faithfulness of individuals here below to their own poor over-beliefs may not actually help God in turn to be more effectively faithful to his own greater tasks?

# Notes

1   Remember that for some men it arrives suddenly, for others gradually, whilst others again practically enjoy it all their life.

2   The practical difficulties are: 1, to 'realize the reality' of one's higher part; 2, to identify one's self with it exclusively; and 3, to identify it with all the rest of ideal being.

3   "When mystical activity is at its height, we find consciousness possessed by the sense of a being at once *excessive* and *identical* with the self: great enough to be God; interior enough to be *me*. The 'objectivity' of it ought in that case to be called *excessivity*, rather, or exceedingness." Récéjac: Essai sur les fondements de la conscience mystique, 1897, p. 46.

4   The word 'truth' is here taken to mean something additional to bare value for life, although the natural propensity of man is to believe that whatever has great value for life is thereby certified as true.

5   Proceedings of the Society for Psychical Research, vol. vii; p. 305. For a full statement of Mr. Myers's views, I may refer to his posthumous work, 'Human Personality in the Light of Recent Research,' which is already announced by Messrs. Longmans, Green & Co. as being in press. Mr. Myers for the first time proposed as a general psychological problem the exploration of the subliminal region of consciousness throughout its whole extent, and made the first methodical steps in its topography by treating as a natural series a mass of subliminal facts hitherto considered only as curious isolated facts, and subjecting them to a systematized nomenclature. How important this exploration will prove, future work upon the path which Myers has opened can alone show. Compare my paper: 'Frederic Myers's Services to Psychology,' in the said Proceedings, part xlii., May, 1901.

6   One more expression of this belief, to increase the reader's familiarity with the notion of it: –

"If this room is full of darkness for thousands of years, and you come in and begin to weep and wail, 'Oh, the darkness,' will the darkness vanish? Bring the light in, strike a match, and light comes in a moment. So what good will it do you to think all your lives, 'Oh, I have done evil, I have made many mistakes'? It requires no ghost to tell us that. Bring in the light, and the evil goes in a moment. Strengthen the real nature, build up yourselves, the effulgent, the resplendent, the ever pure, call that up in every one whom you see. I wish that every one of us had come to such a state that even when we see the vilest of human beings we can see the God within, and instead of condemning, say, 'Rise, thou effulgent One, rise thou who art always pure, rise thou birthless and deathless, rise almighty, and manifest your nature.' ... This is the highest prayer that the Advaita teaches. This is the one prayer: remembering our nature." ... "Why does man go out to look for a God? ... It is your own heart beating, and you did not know, you were mistaking it for something external. He, nearest of the near, my own self, the reality of my own life, my body and my soul. – I am Thee and Thou art Me. That is your own nature. Assert it, manifest it. Not to become pure, you are pure already. You are not to be perfect, you are that already. Every good thought which you think or act upon is simply tearing the veil, as it were, and the purity, the Infinity, the God behind, manifests itself – the eternal Subject of everything, the eternal Witness in this universe, your own Self. Knowledge is, as it were, a lower step, a degradation. We are It already; how to know It?" Swami Viveka-nanda: Addresses, No. XII., Practical Vedanta, part iv., pp. 172, 174, London, 1897; and Lectures, The Real and the Apparent Man, p. 24, abridged.

7    For instance, here is a case where a person exposed from her birth to Christian ideas had to wait till they came to her clad in spiritistic formulas before the saving experience set in: –

"For myself I can say that spiritualism has saved me. It was revealed to me at a critical moment of my life, and without it I don't know what I should have done. It has taught me to detach myself from worldly things and to place my hope in things to come. Through it I have learned to see in all men, even in those most criminal, even in those from whom I have most suffered, undeveloped brothers to whom I owed assistance, love, and forgiveness. I have learned that I must lose my temper over nothing, despise no one, and pray for all. Most of all I have learned to pray! And although I have still much to learn in this domain, prayer ever brings me more strength, consola-tion, and comfort. I feel more than ever that I have only made a few steps on the long road of progress; but I look at its length without dismay, for I have confidence that the day will come when all my efforts shall be rewarded. So Spiritualism has a great place in my life, indeed it holds the first place there." Flournoy Collection.

8    "The influence of the Holy Spirit, exquisitely call the Comforter, is a matter of actual *experience*, as solid a reality as that of electro-magnetism." W. C. Brownell, Scribner's Magazine, vol. xxx., p. 112.

9    That the transaction of opening ourselves, otherwise called prayer, is a perfectly definite one for certain persons, appears abundantly in the preced-ing lectures. I append another concrete example to reinforce the impression on the reader's mind: –

"Man can learn to transcend these limitations [of finite thought] and draw power and wisdom at will.... The divine presence is known through experience. The turning to a higher plane is a distinct act of consciousness. It is not a vague, twilight or semi-conscious experience. It is not an ecstasy; it is not a trance. It is not super-consciousness in the Vedantic sense. It is not due to self-hypnotization. It is a perfectly calm, sane, sound, rational, common-sense shifting of consciousness from the phenomena of sense-perception to the phenomena of seership, from the thought of self to a distinctively higher realm.... For example, if the lower self be nervous, anxious, tense, one can in a few moments compel it to be calm. This is not done by a word simply. Again I say, it is not hypnotism. It is by the exercise of power. One feels the spirit of peace as definitely as heat is perceived on a hot summer day. The power can be as surely used as the

sun's rays can be focused and made to do work, to set fire to wood." The
Higher Law, vol. iv., pp. 4, 6, Boston, August, 1901.

10   Transcendentalists are fond of the term 'Over-soul,' but as a rule they use it
in an intellectualist sense, as meaning only a medium of communion. 'God'
is a causal agent as well as a medium of communion, and that is the aspect
which I wish to emphasize.

# 27

# The Scofield Reference Bible (1909)

## Introduction

In reaction against the kind of broad-minded, inclusive interpretations of religion advanced by William James, Jane Addams, and other liberal thinkers, conservative Protestants claimed that true religion was defined solely and exclusively by the doctrines and revelations of the Bible. From this perspective, there was no common ground between Christianity and other religions, as James believed. And from this perspective, the notion that Christianity could be redefined in terms of a democratic impulse, or an investment in the liberal arts, as Addams believed, was a sell-out to secular culture. Conservative Protestants emphasized the uniqueness of Christian revelation and took a much darker view of the moral tendency of modern society, stressing the wickedness of humanity and the catastrophic power of divine judgment.

The study Bible edited by Cyrus I. Scofield was an important resource for conservative Protestants who wished to define Christianity in terms of what they regarded as fundamental Christian doctrines, such as the virgin birth of Jesus, the resurrection of the dead, and the inerrancy of scripture. In extensive notes surrounding the actual text of the Bible, Scofield cross-referenced New Testament passages and Old Testament prophesies. As well as presenting these cross-references as proof of the Bible's inerrancy, Scofield interpreted them as evidence of a dispensational scheme of history that would culminate in a terrible day of judgment for humanity. In its emphasis on the

Daniel 9:20–4 and Revelation 12:7–17 and 13:1, excerpted from the *Scofield Reference Bible* (New York: Oxford University Press, 1909), 914–15, 1341.

special importance of apocalyptic texts, the Scofield Bible challenged the tendency of liberal Christians (and liberal Jews as well) to emphasize the ongoing, creative partnership between God and humanity and celebrate history as the progressive unfolding of divine will.

## Daniel 9

*The seventy weeks of years*

20 And whiles I *was* speaking, and praying, and confessing my sin and the sin of my people Israel, and presenting my supplication before the LORD my God for the holy mountain of my God;

21 Yea, whiles I *was* speaking in prayer, even the man *b*Gabriel, whom I had seen in the vision at the beginning, being caused to fly swiftly, touched me about the time of the evening oblation.

22 And he informed *me*, and talked with me, and said, O Daniel, I am now come forth to give thee skill and understanding.

23 At the beginning of thy supplications the commandment came forth, and I am come to shew *thee*; for thou *art* greatly beloved: therefore understand the matter, and consider the vision.

24 Seventy ¹weeks are determined upon *c*thy people and upon thy holy city, to finish the transgression, and to make an end of sins, and to make reconciliation for iniquity, and to bring in everlasting righteousness, and to seal up the vision and prophecy, and to anoint the most Holy.

## Notes

*b* Dan.8.16.

*c* Cf. Hos.1.9. The Jews, rejected, are "thy people," i.e. Daniel's, not Jehovah's though yet to be restored.

1 These are "weeks" or, more accurately, sevens of years; seventy weeks of seven years each. Within these "weeks" the national chastisement must be ended and the nation re-established in everlasting righteousness (v. 24). The seventy weeks are divided into seven = 49 years; sixty-two = 434 years; one = 7 years (vs. 25–27). In the seven weeks = 49 years, Jerusalem was to be rebuilt in "troublous times." This was fulfilled, as Ezra and Nehemiah record. Sixty-two weeks = 434 years, thereafter Messiah was to come (v. 25). This was fulfilled in the birth and manifestation of Christ. Verse 26 is obviously an indeterminate period. The date of the crucifixion is not fixed. It is only said to be "after" the threescore and two weeks. It is the first event

in verse 26. The second event is the destruction of the city, fulfilled A.D. 70. Then, "unto the end," a period not fixed, but which has already lasted nearly 2000 years. To Daniel was revealed only that wars and desolations should continue (cf. Mt. 24. 6–14). The N.T. reveals, that which was hidden from the O.T. prophets (Mt. 13. 11–17; Eph. 3. 1–10), that during this period should be accomplished the mysteries of the kingdom of Heaven (Mt. 13. 1–50), and the outcalling of the Church (Mt. 16. 18; Rom. 11. 25). When the Church-age will end, and the seventieth week begin, is nowhere revealed. Its duration can be but seven years. To make it more violates the principle of interpretation already confirmed by fulfillment. Verse 27 deals with the last week. The "he" of verse 27 is the "prince that shall come" of verse 26, whose people (Rome) destroyed the temple, A.D. 70. He is the same with the "little horn" of chapter 7. He will covenant with the Jews to restore their temple sacrifices for one week (seven years), but in the middle of that time he will break the covenant and fulfil Dan. 12. 11; 2 Thes. 2. 3, 4. Between the sixty-ninth week, after which Messiah was cut off, and the seventieth week, within which the "little horn" of Dan. 7. will run his awful course, intervenes this entire Church-age. Verse 27 deals with the last three and a half years of the seven, which are identical with the "great tribulation" (Mt. 24. 15–28); "time of trouble" (Dan. 12.1); "hour of temptation" (Rev. 3. 10). (See "Tribulation," Psa. 2.5; Rev. 7. 14.)

## Revelation 12–13

### The archangel

7 And there was ${}^{l}$war in heaven: ${}^{m}$Michael and his ${}^{n}$angels ${}^{o}$fought against the dragon; and the dragon fought and his angels,

8 And prevailed not; neither was their place found any more in heaven.

9 And the great ${}^{p}$dragon was cast out, ${}^{q}$that old serpent, called the ${}^{r}$Devil, and ${}^{s}$Satan, which ${}^{t}$deceiveth the whole ${}^{u}$world: he was cast out into the earth, and his ${}^{v}$angels were cast out with him.

10 And I heard a loud voice saying in heaven, Now is come ${}^{w}$salvation, and ${}^{x}$strength, and the ${}^{1}$kingdom of our God, and the ${}^{y}$power of his Christ: for the accuser of our brethren is cast down, which accused them before our God day and night.

11 And they overcame him ${}^{z}$by the ${}^{a}$blood of the Lamb, and ${}^{z}$by the word of their testimony; and they loved not their lives unto the death.

12 Therefore rejoice, *ye* heavens, and ye that dwell in them. Woe to the inhabiters of the earth and of the seal for the devil is come down unto you, having great ${}^{b}$wrath, because he knoweth that he hath ${}^{c}$but a short time.

*Satan and Israel in the tribulation*

13 And when the dragon saw that he was cast unto the earth, he *<sup>d</sup>*persecuted the woman which brought forth the man *child*.

14 And to the woman were given two *<sup>e</sup>*wings of a great eagle, that she might fly into the wilderness, into her *<sup>f</sup>*place, where she is nourished for a time, and times, and half a time, from the face of the serpent.

15 And the serpent *<sup>g</sup>*cast out of his mouth water as a flood after the woman, that he might cause her to be carried away of the flood.

16 And the earth helped the woman, and the earth opened her mouth, and *<sup>h</sup>*swallowed up the flood which the dragon cast out of his mouth.

*The Jewish remnant*

17 And the dragon was wroth with the woman, and went to make war with the *<sup>i</sup>*remnant of her seed, which keep the *<sup>j</sup>*commandments of God, and have the testimony of *<sup>k</sup>*Jesus Christ.

CHAPTER 13

*The Beast out of the sea*

And I stood upon the sand of the sea, and saw a *<sup>l</sup>*beast *<sup>2</sup>*rise up out of the sea, having seven heads and ten horns, and upon his horns ten *<sup>m</sup>*crowns, and upon his heads the *<sup>n</sup>*name of blasphemy.

# Notes

*l*  *Contra*; Lk.19.38.
*m*  Cf. Jude 9; cf. Dan.10.21.
*n*  Heb.1.4, *note*.
*o*  *went to war with.*
*p*  *Satan.* vs.3,4, 7–17; Rev.20.2,7, 10. (Gen.3.1; Rev.20.10.)
*q*  *the ancient serpent.* Gen.3.1; Isa.14.12–19.
*r*  Cf. 1 Pet.5.8.
*s*  Cf. 1 Cor.5.5.
*t*  Cf. 2 Cor.4.4.
*u*  *oikoumene = inhabited earth.* (Lk.2.1.)
*v*  Heb.1.4, *note*.
*w*  *the salvation.* Rom.1.16, *note*.
*x*  *the power.*
*y*  *authority.*
*z*  *because of.*
*a*  Heb.2.14.
*b*  v.17; cf.1 Pet.5.8.
*c*  *Contra*, John 9.4; cf.Lk.9.42.
*d*  Cf. Mt.24.9.

*e*   Cf.Ex.19.4; cf.Isa.40.31.

*f*   v.6; cf.Hos.2.14, 15.

*g*   Cf. Isa.8.7,8; cf.Jer.46.8; cf.Isa.17.12,13.

*h*   Cf.2 Chr.20.23,24.

*i*   *Remnant.* Rev. 14.1–5. (Isa.1.9; Rom.11.5.)

*j*   *Law (of Moses).* Rev.14.12. (Ex. 19.1; Gal.3.1–29.)

*k*   *Jesus.*

*l*   *The Beast.* vs.1–8; Rev.19.19,20. (Dan.7.8; Rev. 19.20.)

*m*   *diadems.*

*n*   *names.*


1   The Dispensation of the Kingdom (2 Sam. 7.16, *refs.*) begins with the return of Christ to the earth, runs through the "thousand years" of His earth-rule, and ends when He has delivered up the kingdom to the Father (1 Cor. 15. 24, *note*).

2   Daniel's fourth beast (Dan. 7. 26, *note*). The "ten horns" are explained in Dan. 7. 24, Rev. 17. 12, to be ten kings, and the whole vision is of the last form of Gentile world-power, a confederated ten-kingdom empire covering the sphere of authority of ancient Rome. Rev. 13. 1–3 refers to the ten-kingdom *empire*; vs. 4–10 to the *emperor*, who is emphatically *"the* Beast" (Rev. 19. 20, *note*).

# 28

# Christianity and Liberalism (1923)

## J. Gresham Machen

## Introduction

One of the most articulate defenders of Reform Protestant orthodoxy in the twentieth century, J. Gresham Machen defined the battlelines against liberalism for years to come. In voicing the concerns of many conservative Protestants, Machen focused on what he saw as the decline of spiritual inspiration, moral values, and family life. He regarded efforts to translate Christianity to conform to the materialistic standards of modern society completely wrongheaded and severely criticized Marxist and Freudian theories that attempted to define the meaning of life in terms of economic forces or sexual drive. He appreciated the extent to which scientific discoveries over the last century enabled people to master the material forces of the world more than ever before. But grandiose theories that attempted to reduce everything to natural forces only claimed to be scientific. He believed that science was more restrained, disciplined, focused, and humble.

Machen criticized liberal theologians for what he saw as their willingness to compromise what he believed were the essential doctrines of Christian faith. True Christianity centered on devotion to a transcendent reality, he believed, not on manipulating the material world to make society run better or enhance one's own well-being. From Machen's perspective, God inspired believers with higher truth and courage, and condemned the arrogance of materialistic thinking and the profane, flat world it yielded.

Excerpted from J. Gresham Machen, *Christianity and Liberalism* (Philadelphia: Presbyterian Guardian, 1923), 2–3, 7–8, 14–15, 154.

In fact, Machen did not really do justice to Christian liberalism. But as the decades unfolded, his criticism of liberal thought became increasingly popular. In response to two World Wars and the development of weapons of mass destruction, many people were drawn to interpretations of Christianity that stressed the conflict between biblical values and those of modern society. Even among religious liberals, previous ideas about historical progress seemed naive and renewed interest in the transcendence and mystery of God more appealing.

In the sphere of religion, in particular, the present time is a time of conflict; the great redemptive religion which has always been known as Christianity is battling against a totally diverse type of religious belief, which is only the more destructive of the Christian faith because it makes use of traditional Christian terminology. This modern non-redemptive religion is called "modernism" or "liberalism." Both names are unsatisfactory; the latter, in particular, is question-begging. The movement designated as "liberalism" is regarded as "liberal" only by its friends; to its opponents it seems to involve a narrow ignoring of many relevant facts. And indeed the movement is so various in its manifestations that one may almost despair of finding any common name which will apply to all its forms. But manifold as are the forms in which the movement appears, the root of the movement is one; the many varieties of modern liberal religion are rooted in naturalism – that is, in the denial of any entrance of the creative power of God (as distinguished from the ordinary course of nature) in connection with the origin of Christianity. The word "naturalism" is here used in a sense somewhat different from its philosophical meaning. In this non-philosophical sense it describes with fair accuracy the real root of what is called, by what may turn out to be a degradation of an originally noble word, "liberal" religion.

The rise of this modern naturalistic liberalism has not come by chance, but has been occasioned by important changes which have recently taken place in the conditions of life. The past one hundred years have witnessed the beginning of a new era in human history, which may conceivably be regretted, but certainly cannot be ignored, by the most obstinate conservatism. The change is not something that lies beneath the surface and might be visible only to the discerning eye; on the contrary it forces itself upon the attention of the plain man at a hundred points. Modern inventions and the industrialism that has been built upon them have given us in many respects a new world to live in; we can no more remove ourselves from that world than we can escape from the atmosphere that we breathe.

But such changes in the material conditions of life do not stand alone; they have been produced by mighty changes in the human mind, as in their turn they themselves give rise to further spiritual changes. The industrial world of to-day has been produced not by blind forces of nature but by the conscious activity of the human spirit; it has been produced by the achievements of science. The outstanding feature of recent history is an enormous widening of human knowledge, which has gone hand in hand with such perfecting of the instrument of investigation that scarcely any limits can be assigned to future progress in the material realm.

The application of modern scientific methods is almost as broad as the universe in which we live. Though the most palpable achievements are in the sphere of physics and chemistry, the sphere of human life cannot be isolated from the rest, and with the other sciences there has appeared, for example, a modern science of history, which, with psychology and sociology and the like, claims, even if it does not deserve, full equality with its sister sciences. No department of knowledge can maintain its isolation from the modern lust of scientific conquest; treaties of inviolability, though hallowed by all the sanctions of age-long tradition, are being flung ruthlessly to the winds. [. . .]

Two lines of criticism, then, are possible with respect to the liberal attempt at reconciling science and Christianity. Modern liberalism may be criticized (1) on the ground that it is un-Christian and (2) on the ground that it is unscientific. We shall concern ourselves here chiefly with the former line of criticism; we shall be interested in showing that despite the liberal use of traditional phraseology modern liberalism not only is a different religion from Christianity but belongs in a totally different class of religions. But in showing that the liberal attempt at rescuing Christianity is false we are not showing that there is no way of rescuing Christianity at all; on the contrary, it may appear incidentally, even in the present little book, that it is not the Christianity of the New Testament which is in conflict with science, but the supposed Christianity of the modern liberal Church, and that the real city of God, and that city alone, has defences which are capable of warding off the assaults of modern unbelief. However, our immediate concern is with the other side of the problem; our principal concern just now is to show that the liberal attempt at reconciling Christianity with modern science has really relinquished everything distinctive of Christianity, so that what remains is in essentials only that same indefinite type of religious aspiration which was in the world before Christianity came upon the scene. In trying to remove from Christianity everything that could possibly be objected to in the name of science, in trying to bribe off the enemy by those concessions which the enemy most desires, the apologist has really abandoned what he started out to defend. Here as in many other departments of life it appears that the things that are sometimes thought to be hardest to defend are also the things that are most worth defending.

In maintaining that liberalism in the modern Church represents a return to an un-Christian and sub-Christian form of the religious life, we are particularly anxious not to be misunderstood. "Un-Christian" in such a connection is sometimes taken as a term of opprobrium. We do not mean it at all as such. Socrates was not a Christian, neither was Goethe; yet we share to the full the respect with which their names are regarded. They tower immeasurably above the common run of men; if he that is least in the Kingdom of Heaven is greater than they, he is certainly greater not by any inherent superiority, but by virtue of an undeserved privilege which ought to make him humble rather than contemptuous.

Such considerations, however, should not be allowed to obscure the vital importance of the question at issue. If a condition could be conceived in which all the preaching of the Church should be controlled by the liberalism which in many quarters has already become preponderant, then, we believe, Christianity would at last have perished from the earth and the gospel would have sounded forth for the last time. If so, it follows that the inquiry with which we are now concerned is immeasurably the most important of all those with which the Church has to deal. Vastly more important than all questions with regard to methods of preaching is the root question as to what it is that shall be preached. [. . .]

The truth is that the materialistic paternalism of the present day, if allowed to go on unchecked, will rapidly make of America one huge "Main Street," where spiritual adventure will be discouraged and democracy will be regarded as consisting in the reduction of all mankind to the proportions of the narrowest and least gifted of the citizens. God grant that there may come a reaction, and that the great principles of Anglo-Saxon liberty may be rediscovered before it is too late! But whatever solution be found for the educational and social problems of our own country, a lamentable condition must be detected in the world at large. It cannot be denied that great men are few or non-existent, and that there has been a general contracting of the area of personal life. Material betterment has gone hand in hand with spiritual decline.

Such a condition of the world ought to cause the choice between modernism and traditionalism, liberalism and conservatism, to be approached without any of the prejudice which is too often displayed. In view of the lamentable defects of modern life, a type of religion certainly should not be commended simply because it is modern or condemned simply because it is old. On the contrary, the condition of mankind is such that one may well ask what it is that made the men of past generations so great and the men of the present generation so small. In the midst of all the material achievements of modern life, one may well ask the question whether in gaining the whole world we have not lost our own soul. Are we forever condemned to live the sordid life of utilitarianism? Or is there some lost secret which if rediscovered will restore to mankind something of the glories of the past?

Such a secret the writer of this little book would discover in the Christian religion. [...] According to Christian belief, man exists for the sake of God; according to the liberal Church, in practice if not in theory, God exists for the sake of man.

But the social element in Christianity is found not only in communion between man and God, but also in communion between man and man. Such communion appears even in institutions which are not specifically Christian.

The most important of such institutions, according to Christian teaching, is the family. And that institution is being pushed more and more into the background. It is being pushed into the background by undue encroachments of the community and of the state. Modern life is tending more and more toward the contraction of the sphere of parental control and parental influence. The choice of schools is being placed under the power of the state; the "community" is seizing hold of recreation and of social activities. It may be a question how far these community activities are responsible for the modern breakdown of the home; very possibly they are only trying to fill a void which even apart from them had already appeared. But the result at any rate is plain – the lives of children are no longer surrounded by the loving atmosphere of the Christian home, but by the utilitarianism of the state. A revival of the Christian religion would unquestionably bring a reversal of the process; the family, as over against all other social institutions, would come to its rights again.

# 29

# From Union Square to Rome (1939)

## Dorothy Day

## Introduction

One of the best-known Catholic activists of the twentieth century, Dorothy Day was dedicated to the poor and to sharing their suffering. As a young woman, she embraced Marxist philosophy and its analysis of capitalism and the oppression of workers. But she converted to Catholicism because she found there a spiritual identification with the poor that Marxism lacked. Catholic ideas about the sacredness of life also provided a framework for understanding the intense feelings she experienced giving birth to her daughter Tamar a few years after an abortion she deeply regretted. Inspired by the philosophy of Catholic personalism developed in France, Day believed that human beings experienced personhood most fully in union with Christ. This union could be attained through the sacraments of the Church, she found, and then developed further through identification with the poor. As an indefatigable organizer and writer, Day helped to found and support Catholic Worker houses across the United States that offered shelter, food, and friendship to the poor. She also protested government actions that caused suffering and violence, published a newspaper for radical Catholics and their friends, and attracted many followers and admirers.

Drawing from the idealization of poverty developed in Catholic monasticism, Day believed that Christians could purify themselves by participating in the lives of the poor, where the kind of suffering that Christ experienced was

Excerpted from Dorothy Day, *From Union Square to Rome* (Silver Spring, Md.: Preservation of the Faith Press, 1938), 10–13, 17.

manifest. In addition to drawing from this ancient, mystical approach to suffering, Day anticipated the social activism that emerged among Catholics after the second Vatican Council, which affirmed the pastoral responsibility of all Catholics, as members of the body of Christ, to reach out to people in need. For American Catholics dedicated both to the religious teachings of the Church and to the development of lay activism on behalf of the poor, Dorothy Day is an inspiring model and strong candidate for beatitude and sainthood.

But always the glimpses of God came most when I was alone. Objectors cannot say that it was fear of loneliness and solitude and pain that made me turn to Him. It was in those few years when I was alone and most happy that I found Him. I found Him at last through joy and thanksgiving, not through sorrow.

Yet how can I say that either? Better let it be said that I found Him through His poor, and in a moment of joy I turned to Him. I have said, sometimes flippantly, that the mass of bourgeois smug Christians who denied Christ in His poor made me turn to Communism, and that it was the Communists and working with them that made me turn to God.

Communism, says our Holy Father, can be likened to a heresy, and a heresy is a distortion of the truth. Many Christians have lost sight, to a great extent, of the communal aspect of Christianity, so the collective ideal is the result. They have failed to learn a philosophy of labor, have failed to see Christ in the worker. So in Russia, the worker, instead of Christ, has been exalted. They have the dictatorship of the proletariat maintained by one man, also a dictator. The proletariat as a class has come to be considered the Messiah, the deliverer.

A mystic may be called a man in love with God. Not one who loves God, but who is *in love with God*. And this mystical love, which is an exalted emotion, leads one to love the things of Christ. His footsteps are sacred. The steps of His passion and death are retraced down through the ages. Almost every time you step into a Church you see people making the Stations of the Cross. They meditate on the mysteries of His life, death, and resurrection, and by this they are retracing with love those early scenes and identifying themselves with the actors in those scenes.

When we suffer, we are told we suffer with Christ. We are "completing the sufferings of Christ." We suffer His loneliness and fear in the garden when His friends slept. We are bowed down with Him under the weight of not only our own sins but the sins of each other, of the whole world. We are those who are sinned against and those who are sinning. We are identified with Him, one with Him. We are members of His Mystical Body.

Often there is a mystical element in the love of a radical worker for his brother, for his fellow worker. It extends to the scene of his sufferings, and those spots where he has suffered and died are hallowed. The names of places like Everett, Ludlow, Bisbee, South Chicago, Imperial Valley, Elaine, Arkansas, and all those other places where workers have suffered and died for their cause have become sacred to the worker. You know this feeling as does every other radical in the country. Through ignorance, perhaps, you do not acknowledge Christ's name, yet, I believe you are trying to love Christ in His poor, in His persecuted ones. Whenever men have laid down their lives for their fellows, they are doing it in a measure for Him. This I still firmly believe, even though you and others may not realize it.

"Inasmuch as ye have done it unto one of the least of these brethren, you have done it unto me." Feeling this as strongly as I did, is it any wonder that I was led finally to the feet of Christ?

I do not mean at all that I went around in a state of exaltation or that any radical does. Love is a matter of the will. You know yourself how during a long strike the spirit falters, how hard it is for the leaders to keep up the morale of the men and to keep the fire of hope burning within them. They have a hard time sustaining this hope themselves. Saint Teresa says that there are three attributes of the soul: memory, understanding, and will. These very leaders by their understanding of the struggle, how victory is gained very often through defeat, how every little gain benefits the workers all over the country, through their memory of past struggles, are enabled to strengthen their wills to go on. It is only by exerting these faculties of the soul that one is enabled to love one's fellow. And this strength comes from God. There can be no brotherhood without the Fatherhood of God.

Take a factory where fifty per cent of the workers themselves [are] content, [and] do not care about their fellows. It is hard to inspire them with the idea of solidarity. Take those workers who despise their fellow-worker, the Negro, the Hungarian, the Italian, the Irish, where race hatreds and nationalist feelings persist. It is hard to overcome their stubborn resistance with patience and with love. That is why there is coercion, the beating of scabs and strikebreakers, the threats and the hatreds that grow up. That is why in labor struggles, unless there is a wise and patient leader, there is disunity, a rending of the Mystical Body.

Even the most unbelieving of labor leaders have understood the expediency of patience when I have talked to them. They realize that the use of force has lost more strikes than it has won them. They realize that when there is no violence in a strike, the employer through his armed guards and strikebreakers may try to introduce this violence. It has happened again and again in labor history.

What is hard to make the labor leader understand is that we must love even the employer, unjust though he may be, that we must try to overcome his resistance by non-violent resistance, by withdrawing labor, *i.e.*, by strikes and by boycott. These are non-violent means and most effective. We must try to educate him, to convert him. We must forgive him seventy times seven just as we forgive our fellow-worker and keep trying to bring him to a sense of solidarity. [. . .]

A conversion is a lonely experience. We do not know what is going on in the depths of the heart and soul of another. We scarcely know ourselves.

# 30

# The Future of the American Jew (1948)

## Mordecai M. Kaplan

## Introduction

The death of six million Jews – one-third of all living Jews – by Nazi Germany in the 1930s and 1940s created a religious crisis for many survivors as well as a mandate for political activism. While some Jews saw the Holocaust as God's judgment against Jews for their sinfulness, many others wondered what kind of God could allow such devastation. Some argued that to continue to believe in a God who could do such a thing was unimaginable and that atheism was the only moral option. Others believed that, in giving humanity free will, God deliberately limited his own power in the world. Only by restraining himself in this way would people become truly capable of both good and evil, and thus truly human.

In his response to the Holocaust, Rabbi Mordecai Kaplan challenged all these views. He believed that God was life itself and that supernatural conceptions of God that made him independent of human life, and human striving, were misguided. The purpose of religion, and of Judaism in particular, was not to explain God but to enable human beings to love and serve life and, in essence, to become more human. As the chief victims of the Nazi regime, Jews understood as well as any group the human need for religious freedom

Excerpted from Mordecai M. Kaplan, *The Future of the American Jew*, orig. 1948 (New York: Reconstructionist Press, 1967), 283–5. Reproduced with permission from the Reconstructionist Press. More information about the Reconstructionist movement may be obtained by visiting www.jrf.org.

and self-government. As a religious people who traced their inner devotion to freedom back to the Exodus of Hebrew slaves from Egypt, Jews had a special reverence for freedom as a moral and spiritual treasure, Kaplan believed, that could enable them to contribute significantly to the development of democracy in the United States and around the world.

In founding the Reconstructionist movement, Kaplan wanted to preserve the ancient traditions of Judaism but also to revise them in ways that addressed the challenges and opportunities of modern life in the most spirited way possible. In subsequent efforts to revitalize Jewish tradition, Kaplan's followers carried forward his sense that religious creativity was essential to Jewish authenticity. Reconstructionist Jews often took the lead in affirming the equality of women and homosexuals as a means of renewing the vitality of Jewish practice and liturgy.

# Inner Freedom

American Jews have a more crucial stake than any other group in the struggle of democracy against the new barbarism with which mankind is threatened. So long as the rest of the world is in danger of political serfdom and economic slavery, the Jewish people is in danger of annihilation. Its only hope is in the triumph of democracy. *Destiny has placed us Jews on the firing line in defense of freedom.*

The triumph of democracy is the triumph of social order based upon freedom. Any attempt to keep alive in the Jewish people the hope of survival and redemption, associated with the triumph of democracy, must seek to make us aware of the meaning of freedom. We must understand what constitutes freedom, and what we must do to attain it.

Democracy is freedom conceived as a condition of society, or as a quality of social relationships. It is freedom embodied in political forms or institutions – in universal suffrage, parliamentarism, the bill of rights. Those forms are based on two principles. The first of these is the principle of the "government of the people, by the people," which implies that all adult persons are entitled to participate in the government under which they live. The second is the principle of government "for the people," the subordination of the state to the welfare of the people, on the assumption that the state exists for the people, not the people for the state.

But if democracy is to hold its own in the struggle against antidemocratic forces, political freedom must be sustained by an inner freedom, a freedom of the spirit. *Freedom must be conceived not only as a condition of society, but also as a state of mind.* We Jews may not have played a considerable role in the shaping of the political instruments of democracy; but from the time that our fathers identified God as the Power that brought us forth from the "house of bondage," freedom became part of our religious tradition with which we sought to inform our personal habits. The understanding of the close relationship between freedom as a state of mind and freedom as a condition of society is what Jews are in a position to contribute to the struggle for democracy. Such a contribution would be more effective in securing the eventual triumph of democracy than any, however important, that we are now making toward the progress of science or the development of industry. For, in democracy's struggle for survival, the decision will rest upon the extent to which those who fight under its banner will possess inner freedom.

What is this inner freedom, the state of mind or quality of character that is indispensable to the triumph of democracy? *It is the unyielding refusal to recognize the legitimacy of brute force, or to bow before its authority.* This inner freedom determines a person's entire attitude toward the world, toward his fellowman, toward his group, toward his momentary wishes and impulses. It makes his whole life one long protest against all the brute forces that would interpose obstacles to the achievement of his worthiest aims.

These brute forces operate through various media. They operate through the violent phenomena of nature, through storms, floods, earthquakes, famine, pestilence, and cosmic upheavals. They operate no less through human tyrannies, like those of despots, great or small, or like those of organized multitudes, whether mobs or nations, whether savage or highly civilized. Brute force, to defy which is a mark of inner freedom, is as varied in its forms of expression as in the media it employs. It may take the form of blind destructiveness or of planned devastation, of sheer physical strength or of diabolic cunning, of outright violence or of fomented treachery, of undisguised banditry or of smooth-tongued diplomacy.

But whatever medium brute force employs, and in whatever form it expresses itself, to the man who has inner freedom, it is ever an abomination. If he must live with it, he will never leave off resisting it, taming it, seeking to master it. That is how freedom as a state of mind, or quality of character, asserts itself. To resist brute force, to tame it and master it takes all that a man has in him. His entire personality is involved – heart, mind and will. But the initial sign of inner freedom is always "the unreconciled heart."

# 31

# "Foreword," The Sacred Pipe (1953)

## Black Elk

## Introduction

The Oglala Sioux holy man Black Elk exemplifies the persistent vitality of Native traditions in American religious history. Amidst the hardship and demoralization of his people on one hand and the opposition to Native rituals expressed by American missionaries and government agents on the other, Black Elk led the way in the revitalization of the Sun Dance and other defining rituals of Plains Indian culture. As perhaps the greatest theologian of Native American spirituality, Black Elk redefined the rituals of Plains Indian culture as essential both to the survival of Native identity and to the well-being of the earth and all its people.

Black Elk also exemplifies the syncretism that has often characterized American religious history and contributed to the larger vitality of American religious life. As a Roman Catholic catechist as well as an Oglala holy man, Black Elk understood both traditions and believed, as many Natives have, that Christianity and Native religious traditions complement and ultimately improve one another. Among Oglala people today, those most devoted to the practice of traditional Oglala religion are often Christians as well as followers of Black Elk.

Black Elk's belief in the underlying resonance between Christian and Native traditions helps explain his appeal to Americans without Native ancestry as

Excerpted from Black Elk, "Foreword" (recorded winter of 1947–8), in *The Sacred Pipe: Black Elk's Account of the Seven Rites of the Oglala Sioux*, ed. Joseph Epes Brown (Norman: University of Oklahoma Press, 1953), xix–xx.

well as to Natives themselves. Many young Americans turned to Black Elk in the 1960s and 1970s for the nature spirituality they perceived lacking in Christianity and Judaism. Partly as a result of Black Elk's indirect influence, both liberal and conservative branches of these traditions developed ecological themes. Thus Black Elk contributed significantly to the widespread greening of American religious life.

In the great vision which came to me in my youth, when I had known only nine winters, there was something which has seemed to me to be of greater and greater importance as the moons have passed by. It is about our sacred pipe and its importance to our people.

We have been told by the white men, or at least by those who are Christian, that God sent to men His son, who would restore order and peace upon the earth; and we have been told that Jesus the Christ was crucified, but that he shall come again at the Last Judgment, the end of this world or cycle. This I understand and know that it is true, but the white men should know that for the red people too, it was the will of *Wakan-Tanka*, the Great Spirit, that an animal turn itself into a two-legged person in order to bring the most holy pipe to His people; and we too were taught that this White Buffalo Cow Woman who brought our sacred pipe will appear again at the end of this "world," a coming which we Indians know is now not very far off.

Most people call it a "peace pipe," yet now there is no peace on earth or even between neighbors, and I have been told that it has been a long time since there has been peace in the world. There is much talk of peace among the Christians, yet this is just talk. Perhaps it may be, and this is my prayer that, through our sacred pipe, and through this book in which I shall explain what our pipe really is, peace may come to those peoples who can understand, an understanding which must be of the heart and not of the head alone. Then they will realize that we Indians know the One true God, and that we pray to Him continually.

I have wished to make this book through no other desire than to help my people in understanding the greatness and truth of our own tradition, and also to help in bringing peace upon the earth, not only among men, but within men and between the whole of creation.

We should understand well that all things are the works of the Great Spirit. We should know that He is within all things: the trees, the grasses, the rivers, the mountains, and all the four-legged animals, and the winged peoples; and even more important, we should understand that He is also above all these things and peoples. When we do understand all this deeply in our hearts, then we will fear, and love, and know the Great Spirit, and then we will be and act and live as He intends.

# 32

# "Sunflower Sutra" (1955) and "Kaddish" (1958)

## Allen Ginsberg

## Introduction

No one represents the creative syncretism of American religious life better than Allen Ginsberg. The son of Jewish immigrants from Russia, Ginsberg grew up in New York and New Jersey among people struggling to define their religious and political identities in the context of urban American culture. As a young poet, he found inspiration in the writings of the New England Transcendentalists, especially Walt Whitman's rapturous *Leaves of Grass*. His friendship with the Catholic mystic and lover of Buddhism Jack Kerouac led him to become a serious student of Buddhism. As perhaps the best-known poet of the Beat generation that jangled many people's nerves in the 1950s, Ginsberg lashed out like the Hebrew prophet Jeremiah against the moral complacency and spiritual emptiness of American culture. In his efforts to bring Buddhism to America and revitalize American Transcendentalism in the process, he sought to awaken Americans to the ecstatic juices of life as well as to the horrors of death and suffering.

"Sunflower Sutra" reflects the Buddhist idea that life and death are inseparable. Seeing the beauty of a sunflower in its dead and dusty manifestation beside the railroad tracks is like seeing the Buddha in a corpse, or like finding

Allen Ginsberg, "Sunflower Sutra," in *Howl and Other Poems* (San Francisco: City Lights, 1956), 28–30; and "Kaddish" Part I (excerpt), in *Kaddish and Related Poems* (1959–60), reprinted in Allen Ginsberg, *Collected Poems 1947–1980* (New York: Harper & Row, 1984), 209–12. Copyright © 1959 by Allen Ginsberg. Copyright renewed. Reprinted by permission of Harper Collins Publishers, Inc.

enlightenment, as the Buddha did, simply by sitting down under a tree and becoming completely attuned to the mind-stream of reality. "Kaddish," Ginsberg's poem about his mother, reflects his indebtedness to Buddhist philosophy and New England Transcendentalism as well as to Jewish thought and practice. The title of the poem refers to the Jewish prayer for the dead, traditionally recited for a parent once a day for eleven months and then on each anniversary of death.

## Sunflower Sutra

I walked on the banks of the tincan banana dock and sat down under the huge
    shade of a Southern Pacific locomotive to look at the sunset over the box
    house hills and cry.
Jack Kerouac sat beside me on a busted rusty iron pole, companion, we thought
    the same thoughts of the soul, bleak and blue and sad-eyed, surrounded
    by the gnarled steel roots of trees of machinery.
The oily water on the river mirrored the red sky, sun sank on top of final Frisco
    peaks, no fish in that stream, no hermit in those mounts, just ourselves
    rheumy-eyed and hung-over like old bums on the river-bank, tired and
    wily.
Look at the Sunflower, he said, there was a dead gray shadow against the sky, big
    as a man, sitting dry on top of a pile of ancient sawdust –
– I rushed up enchanted – it was my first sunflower, memories of Blake – my
    visions – Harlem
and Hells of the Eastern rivers, bridges clanking Joes Greasy Sandwiches, dead
    baby carriages, black treadless tires forgotten and unretreaded, the poem
    of the riverbank, condoms & pots, steel knives, nothing stainless, only the
    dank muck and the razor-sharp artifacts passing into the past –
and the gray Sunflower poised against the sunset, crackly bleak and dusty with
    the smut and smog and smoke of olden locomotives in its eye –
corolla of bleary spikes pushed down and broken like a battered crown, seeds
    fallen out of its face, soon-to-be-toothless mouth of sunny air, sunrays
    obliterated on its hairy head like a dried wire spiderweb,
leaves stuck out like arms out of the stem, gestures from the sawdust root, broke
    pieces of plaster fallen out of the black twigs, a dead fly in its ear,
Unholy battered old thing you were, my sunflower O my soul, I loved you then!
The grime was no man's grime but death and human locomotives,
all that dress of dust, that veil of darkened railroad skin, that smog of cheek, that
    eyelid of black mis'ry, that sooty hand or phallus or protuberance of
    artificial worse-than-dirt – industrial – modern – all that civilization
    spotting your crazy golden crown –
and those blear thoughts of death and dusty loveless eyes and ends and withered
    roots below, in the home-pile of sand and sawdust, rubber dollar bills,
    skin of machinery, the guts and innards of the weeping coughing car, the

empty lonely tincans with their rusty tongues alack, what more could I
  name, the smoked ashes of some cock cigar, the cunts of wheelbarrows
  and the milky breasts of cars, wornout asses out of chairs & sphincters of
  dynamos – all these
entangled in your mummied roots – and you there standing before me in the
  sunset, all your glory in your form!
A perfect beauty of a sunflower! a perfect excellent lovely sunflower existence! a
  sweet natural eye to the new hip moon, woke up alive and excited
  grasping in the sunset shadow sunrise golden monthly breeze!
How many flies buzzed round you innocent of your grime, while you cursed the
  heavens of the railroad and your flower soul?
Poor dead flower? when did you forget you were a flower? when did you look at
  your skin and decide you were an impotent dirty old locomotive? the
  ghost of a locomotive? the specter and shade of a once powerful mad
  American locomotive?
You were never no locomotive, Sunflower, you were a sunflower!
And you Locomotive, you are a locomotive, forget me not!
So I grabbed up the skeleton thick sunflower and stuck it at my side like a
  scepter,
and deliver my sermon to my soul, and Jack's soul too, and anyone who'll listen,
– We're not our skin of grime, we're not our dread bleak dusty imageless
  locomotive, we're all golden sunflowers inside, blessed by our own seed
  & hairy naked accomplishment-bodies growing into mad black formal
  sunflowers in the sunset, spied on by our eyes under the shadow of the
  mad locomotive riverbank sunset Frisco hilly tincan evening sitdown
  vision.

*Berkeley, 1955*

# Kaddish

*For Naomi Ginsberg, 1894–1956*

I
Strange now to think of you, gone without corsets & eyes, while I walk on the
  sunny pavement of Greenwich Village.
downtown Manhattan, clear winter noon, and I've been up all night, talking,
  talking, reading the Kaddish aloud, listening to Ray Charles blues shout
  blind on the phonograph
the rhythm the rhythm – and your memory in my head three years after –
  And read Adonais' last triumphant stanzas aloud – wept, realizing
  how we suffer –
And how Death is that remedy all singers dream of, sing, remember, prophesy as
  in the Hebrew Anthem, or the Buddhist Book of Answers – and my own
  imagination of a withered leaf – at dawn –

Dreaming back thru life, Your time – and mine accelerating toward Apocalypse,
the final moment – the flower burning in the Day – and what comes after,
looking back on the mind itself that saw an American city
a flash away, and the great dream of Me or China, or you and a phantom Russia,
   or a crumpled bed that never existed –
like a poem in the dark – escaped back to Oblivion –
No more to say, and nothing to weep for but the Beings in the Dream, trapped in
   its disappearance,
sighing, screaming with it, buying and selling pieces of phantom, worshipping
   each other,
worshipping the God included in it all – longing or inevitability? – while it lasts, a
   Vision – anything more?
It leaps about me, as I go out and walk the street, look back over my shoulder,
   Seventh Avenue, the battlements of window office buildings shouldering
   each other high, under a cloud, tall as the sky an instant – and the sky
   above – an old blue place.
or down the Avenue to the south, to – as I walk toward the Lower East Side –
   where you walked 50 years ago, little girl – from Russia, eating the first
   poisonous tomatoes of America – frightened on the dock –
then struggling in the crowds of Orchard Street toward what? – toward Newark –
toward candy store, first home-made sodas of the century, hand-churned ice
   cream in backroom on musty brownfloor boards –
Toward education marriage nervous breakdown, operation, teaching school, and
   learning to be mad, in a dream – what is this life?
Toward the Key in the window – and the great Key lays its head of light on top of
   Manhattan, and over the floor, and lays down on the sidewalk – in a single
   vast beam, moving, as I walk down First toward
the Yiddish Theater – and the place of poverty
you knew, and I know, but without caring now – Strange to have moved thru
   Paterson, and the West, and Europe and here again,
with the cries of Spaniards now in the doorstoops doors and dark boys on the
   street, fire escapes old as you
– Tho you're not old now, that's left here with me –
Myself, anyhow, maybe as old as the universe – and I guess that dies with us –
   enough to cancel all that comes – What came is gone forever every time –
That's good! That leaves it open for no regret – no fear radiators, lacklove,
   torture even toothache in the end –
Though while it comes it is a lion that eats the soul – and the lamb, the soul, in
   us, alas, offering itself in sacrifice to change's fierce hunger – hair and
   teeth – and the roar of bonepain, skull bare, break rib, rot-skin,
   braintricked Implacability.
Ai! ai! we do worse! We are in a fix! And you're out, Death let you out, Death had
   the Mercy, you're done with your century, done with God, done with the
   path thru it – Done with yourself at last – Pure – Back to the Babe dark
   before your Father, before us all – before the world –
There, rest. No more suffering for you. I know where you've gone, it's good.

No more flowers in the summer fields of New York, no joy now, no more fear of
    Louis,
and no more of his sweetness and glasses, his high school decades, debts, loves,
    frightened telephone calls, conception beds, relatives, hands –
No more of sister Elanor, – she gone before you – we kept it secret – you killed
    her – or she killed herself to bear with you – an arthritic heart – But
    Death's killed you both – No matter –
Nor your memory of your mother, 1915 tears in silent movies weeks and weeks –
    forgetting, agrieve watching Marie Dressler address humanity, Chaplin
    dance in youth,
or Boris Godunov, Chaliapin's at the Met, halling his voice of a weeping Czar –
    by standing room with Elanor & Max – watching also the Capitalists take
    seats in Orchestra, white furs, diamonds,
with the YPSL's hitch-hiking thru Pennsylvania, in black baggy gym skirts pants,
    photograph of 4 girls holding each other round the waste, and laughing
    eye, too coy, virginal solitude of 1920
all girls grown old, or dead, now, and that long hair in the grave – lucky to have
    husbands later –
You made it – I came too – Eugene my brother before (still grieving now and will
    gream on to his last stiff hand, as he goes thru his cancer – or kill – later
    perhaps – soon he will think –)
And it's the last moment I remember, which I see them all, thru myself, now –
    tho not you
I didn't foresee what you felt – what more hideous gape of bad mouth came first
    – to you – and were you prepared?
To go where? In that Dark – that – in that God? a radiance? A Lord in the Void?
    Like an eye in the black cloud in a dream? Adonoi at last, with you?
Beyond my remembrance! Incapable to guess! Not merely the yellow skull in the
    grave, or a box of worm dust, and a stained ribbon – Deathshead with
    Halo? can you believe it?
Is it only the sun that shines once for the mind, only the flash of existence, than
    none ever was?
Nothing beyond what we have – what you had – that so pitiful – yet Triumph,
to have been here, and changed, like a tree, broken, or flower – fed to the ground
    – but mad, with its petals, colored, thinking Great Universe, shaken, cut
    in the head, leaf stript, hid in an egg crate hospital, cloth wrapped, sore –
    freaked in the moon brain, Naughtless.
No flower like that flower, which knew itself in the garden, and fought the knife –
    lost
Cut down by an idiot Snowman's icy – even in the Spring – strange ghost thought
    – some Death – Sharp icicle in his hand – crowned with old
    roses – a dog for his eyes – cock of a sweatshop – heart of electric irons.
All the accumulations of life, that wear us out – clocks, bodies, consciousness,
    shoes, breasts – begotten sons – your Communism – "Paranoia" into
    hospitals.

You once kicked Elanor in the leg, she died of heart failure later. You of stroke.
Asleep? within a year, the two of you, sisters in death. Is Elanor happy?

Max grieves alive in an office on Lower Broadway, lone large mustache over
midnight Accountings, not sure. His life passes – as he sees – and what
does he doubt now? Still dream of making money, or that might have
made money, hired nurse, had children, found even your Immortality,
Naomi?

I'll see him soon. Now I've got to cut through – to talk to you – as I didn't when
you had a mouth.

Forever. And we're bound for that, Forever – like Emily Dickinson's horses –
headed to the End.

# 33

# Nonviolence and Racial Justice (1957)

## Martin Luther King, Jr.

## Introduction

As a Baptist preacher, social activist, and sophisticated theologian, Martin Luther King, Jr. had a profound impact on American culture and its many religious institutions. Drawing especially on the Exodus story of God's freeing the Hebrews from Egyptian slavery, he reawakened the Puritan vision of America as the Promised Land. Combining faith in history's underlying tendency toward justice with belief in God's judgment against oppression and complacency, he challenged Americans across the religious landscape to catch hold of this vision. The Civil Rights movement he led altered the racial dynamics of American society. It also planted seeds of religious opposition to the war in Vietnam and stimulated the growth of feminist theology.

At one level, King carried forward the social gospel of Jane Addams and other liberal Protestants who saw democracy as the incarnation of Christian principle. At the same time, he drew from some of the criticisms leveled against religious liberalism to emphasize the transcendence of God and modern society's need for the infusion of spiritual forces. No less important, King drew from the intense religious feeling associated with the American revivalist tradition and its commitment to experiences of conversion and

Excerpted from Martin Luther King, Jr., "Nonviolence and Racial Justice," *The Christian Century* (6 February, 1957): 165–7, reprinted in *Sources of Christian Theology in America*, ed. Mark G. Toulouse and James O. Duke (Nashville: Abingdon Press, 1999), 481–5.

sanctification, especially as this tradition was embodied in African American life. As a theologian, King was a personalist who believed that God acted first and foremost through the lives of individuals and that the meaning of Christianity had everything to do with the development of personhood. Although he was neither as politically radical nor as theologically conservative as Dorothy Day, his social activism was similar to hers in its focus on the personal connection between God and each believer, and on the organic connection between each believer and society.

It is commonly observed that the crisis in race relations dominates the arena of American life. This crisis has been precipitated by two factors: the determined resistance of reactionary elements in the south to the Supreme Court's momentous decision outlawing segregation in the public schools, and the radical change in the Negro's evaluation of himself. While southern legislative halls ring with open defiance through "interposition" and "nullification," while a modern version of the Ku Klux Klan has arisen in the form of "respectable" white citizens' councils, a revolutionary change has taken place in the Negro's conception of his own nature and destiny. Once he thought of himself as an inferior and patiently accepted injustice and exploitation. Those days are gone.

The first Negroes landed on the shores of this nation in 1619, one year ahead of the Pilgrim Fathers. They were brought here from Africa and, unlike the Pilgrims, they were brought against their will, as slaves. Throughout the era of slavery the Negro was treated in inhuman fashion. He was considered a thing to be used, not a person to be respected. He was merely a depersonalized cog in a vast plantation machine. The famous Dred Scott decision of 1857 well illustrates his status during slavery. In this decision the Supreme Court of the United States said, in substance, that the Negro is not a citizen of the United States; he is merely property subject to the dictates of his owner.

After his emancipation in 1863, the Negro still confronted oppression and inequality. It is true that for a time, while the army of occupation remained in the south and Reconstruction ruled, he had a brief period of eminence and political power. But he was quickly overwhelmed by the white majority. Then in 1896, through the Plessy v. Ferguson decision, a new kind of slavery came into being. In this decision the Supreme Court of the nation established the doctrine of "separate but equal" as the law of the land. Very soon it was discovered that the concrete result of this doctrine was strict enforcement of the "separate," without the slightest intention to abide by the "equal." So the Plessy doctrine ended up plunging the Negro into the abyss of exploitation where he experienced the bleakness of nagging injustice.

## A Peace That Was No Peace

Living under these conditions, many Negroes lost faith in themselves. They came to feel that perhaps they were less than human. So long as the Negro maintained this subservient attitude and accepted the "place" assigned him, a sort of racial peace existed. But it was an uneasy peace in which the Negro was forced patiently to submit to insult, injustice and exploitation. It was a negative peace. True peace is not merely the absence of some negative force – tension, confusion or war; it is the presence of some positive force – justice, good will and brotherhood.

Then circumstances made it necessary for the Negro to travel more. From the rural plantation he migrated to the urban industrial community. His economic life began gradually to rise, his crippling illiteracy gradually to decline. A myriad of factors came together to cause the Negro to take a new look at himself. Individually and as a group, he began to re-evaluate himself. And so he came to feel that he was somebody. His religion revealed to him that God loves all his children and that the important thing about a man is "not his specificity but his fundamentum," not the texture of his hair or the color of his skin but the quality of his soul.

This new self-respect and sense of dignity on the part of the Negro undermined the south's negative peace, since the white man refused to accept the change. The tension we are witnessing in race relations today can be explained in part by this revolutionary change in the Negro's evaluation of himself and his determination to struggle and sacrifice until the walls of segregation have been finally crushed by the battering rams of justice.

## Quest for Freedom Everywhere

The determination of Negro Americans to win freedom from every form of oppression springs from the same profound longing for freedom that motivates oppressed peoples all over the world. The rhythmic beat of deep discontent in Africa and Asia is at bottom a quest for freedom and human dignity on the part of people who have long been victims of colonialism. The struggle for freedom on the part of oppressed people in general and of the American Negro in particular has developed slowly and is not going to end suddenly. Privileged groups rarely give up their privileges without strong resistance. But when oppressed people rise up against oppression there is no stopping point short of full freedom. Realism compels us to admit that the struggle will continue until freedom is a reality for all the oppressed peoples of the world.

Hence the basic question which confronts the world's oppressed is: How is the struggle against the forces of injustice to be waged? There are two possible answers. One is resort to the all too prevalent method of physical violence and corroding hatred. The danger of this method is its futility. Violence solves no social problems; it merely creates new and more complicated ones. Through the vistas of time a voice still cries to every potential Peter, "Put up your sword!" The shores of history are white with the bleached bones of nations and communities that failed to follow this command. If the American Negro and other victims of oppression succumb to the temptation of using violence in the struggle for justice, unborn generations will live in a desolate night of bitterness, and their chief legacy will be an endless reign of chaos.

## Alternative to Violence

The alternative to violence is nonviolent resistance. This method was made famous in our generation by Mohandas K. Gandhi, who used it to free India from the domination of the British empire. Five points can be made concerning nonviolence as a method in bringing about better racial conditions.

First, this is not a method for cowards; it *does* resist. The nonviolent resister is just as strongly opposed to the evil against which he protests as is the person who uses violence. His method is passive or nonaggressive in the sense that he is not physically aggressive toward his opponent. But his mind and emotions are always active, constantly seeking to persuade the opponent that he is mistaken. This method is passive physically but strongly active spiritually; it is nonaggressive physically but dynamically aggressive spiritually.

A second point is that nonviolent resistance does not seek to defeat or humiliate the opponent, but to win his friendship and understanding. The nonviolent resister must often express his protest through noncooperation or boycotts, but he realizes that noncooperation and boycotts are not ends themselves; they are merely means to awaken a sense of moral shame in the opponent. The end is redemption and reconciliation. The aftermath of nonviolence is the creation of the beloved community, while the aftermath of violence is tragic bitterness.

A third characteristic of this method is that the attack is directed against forces of evil rather than against persons who are caught in those forces. It is evil we are seeking to defeat, not the persons victimized by evil. Those of us who struggle against racial injustice must come to see that the basic tension is not between races. As I like to say to the people in Montgomery, Alabama: "The tension in this city is not between white people and Negro people. The tension is at bottom between justice and injustice, between the forces of light and the forces of darkness. And if there is a victory it will be a victory not merely for 50,000 Negroes, but a victory for justice and the forces of light. We are out to defeat injustice and not white persons who may happen to be unjust."

A fourth point that must be brought out concerning nonviolent resistance is that it avoids not only external physical violence but also internal violence of spirit. At the center of nonviolence stands the principle of love. In struggling for human dignity the oppressed people of the world must not allow themselves to become bitter or indulge in hate campaigns. To retaliate with hate and bitterness would do nothing but intensify the hate in the world. Along the way of life, someone must have sense enough and morality enough to cut off the chain of hate. This can be done only by projecting the ethics of love to the center of our lives.

## The Meaning of "Love"

In speaking of love at this point, we are not referring to some sentimental emotion. It would be nonsense to urge men to love their oppressors in an affectionate sense. "Love" in this connection means understanding good will. There are three words for love in the Greek New Testament. First, there is *eros*. In Platonic philosophy *eros* meant the yearning of the soul for the realm of the divine. It has come now to mean a sort of aesthetic or romantic love. Second, there is *philia*. It meant intimate affectionateness between friends. *Philia* denotes a sort of reciprocal love: the person loves because he is loved. When we speak of loving those who oppose us we refer to neither *eros* nor *philia*; we speak of a love which is expressed in the Greek word *agape*. *Agape* means nothing sentimental or basically affectionate; it means understanding, redeeming good will for all men, an overflowing love which seeks nothing in return. It is the love of God working in the lives of men. When we love on the *agape* level we love men not because we like them, not because their attitudes and ways appeal to us, but because God loves them. Here we rise to the position of loving the person who does the evil deed while hating the deed he does.

Finally, the method of nonviolence is based on the conviction that the universe is on the side of justice. It is this deep faith in the future that causes the nonviolent resister to accept suffering without retaliation. He knows that in his struggle for justice he has cosmic companionship. This belief that God is on the side of truth and justice comes down to us from the long tradition of our Christian faith. There is something at the very center of our faith which reminds us that Good Friday may reign for a day, but ultimately it must give way to the triumphant beat of the Easter drums. Evil may so shape events that Caesar will occupy a palace and Christ a cross, but one day that same Christ will rise up and split history into A.D. and B.C., so that even the life of Caesar must be dated by his name. So in Montgomery we can walk and never get weary, because we know that there will be a great camp meeting in the promised land of freedom and justice.

This, in brief, is the method of nonviolent resistance. It is a method that challenges all people struggling for justice and freedom. God grant that we wage the struggle with dignity and discipline. May all who suffer oppression in this world reject the self-defeating method of retaliatory violence and choose the method that seeks to redeem. Through using this method wisely and courageously we will emerge from the bleak and desolate midnight of man's inhumanity to man into the bright daybreak of freedom and justice.

# 34

# God's Judgment of White America (1963)

## Malcolm X

## Introduction

More radical both politically and theologically than Martin Luther King, Malcolm X condemned Christianity as the religion of white people who invoked the name of God to cover their oppression of others. Islam was the true religion of God, Malcolm believed, rooted in the religious history described in the Hebrew Bible, but fulfilled in God's revelations to the Prophet Muhammad and uncorrupted by the distortions introduced by Jews and Christians. Interestingly, Malcolm's anticipation of God's wrath coming down on America's head reflects the persistence of a deeply entrenched, biblical vision of America. Despite its rejection of Christianity, his denunciation of the moral corruption of American society has much in common with the "jeremiads" preached in the spirit of the Old Testament prophet Jeremiah by many Puritan ministers and their successors.

On a path that a number of American blacks followed, Malcolm X gravitated from the Nation of Islam, a sectarian religious group founded in the United States by W. D. Farad and Elijah Muhammad, toward Sunni Islam, the main branch of Islam to which the majority of the world's Muslims belong. The Nation of Islam, led by Elijah Muhammad and his successor Louis Farrakhan, condemned the white race as the evil invention of a mad scientist and called blacks to strengthen and defend themselves. Malcolm aligned himself

Excerpted from Malcolm X, "God's Judgment of White America" (December 1, 1963), reprinted in *Malcolm X: The Man and His Times*, ed. John Henrik Clarke (Trenton: Africa World Press, 1990; orig. 1969), 282–7.

with the beliefs of this separatist group until a pilgrimage to Mecca in 1964 changed his mind. Profoundly moved by the universality of Islamic teaching and practice, and by the colorblindness of Muslim society he experienced in Mecca, Malcolm promoted an inclusive understanding of Islam until his assassination in 1965. His shift in understanding Islam foreshadowed the movement of a significant minority of American blacks toward Sunni Islam and their increasing involvement with Muslims from other ethnic backgrounds.

White America is doomed! Death and devastating destruction hang at this very moment in the skies over America. But why must her divine execution take place? Is it too late for her to avoid this catastrophe?

All the prophets of the past listed America as number one among the guilty nations that would be too proud and blind to repent and atone when God's last messenger is raised in her midst to warn her. America's last chance, her last warning, is coming from the lips of the Honorable Elijah Muhammad today. Accept him and be saved; reject him and be damned!

It is written that white America will reject him; it is also written that white America will be damned and doomed – and the prophets who make these prophecies are never wrong in their divine predictions.

White America refuses to study, reflect, and learn a lesson from history; ancient Egypt didn't have to be destroyed. It was her corrupt government, the crooked politicians, who caused her destruction. Pharaoh hired Hebrew magicians to try and fool their own people into thinking they would soon be integrated into the mainstream of that country's life. Pharaoh didn't want the Hebrews to listen to Moses' message of separation. Even in that day separation was God's solution to the "slaves' problems." By opposing Moses, the magicians were actually choosing sides against the God of their own people.

In like manner, modern Negro magicians are hired by the American Government to oppose the Honorable Elijah Muhammad today. They pose as Negro "leaders." They have been hired by this white Government (white so-called liberals) to make our people here think that integration into this doomed white society will soon solve our problem.

The only permanent solution to America's race problem is the complete separation of these 22 million ex-slaves from our white slave master, and the return of these ex-slaves to our own land, where we can then live in peace and security among our own people.

The American Government is trying to trick her 22 million ex-slaves with false promises that she never intends to keep. The crooked politicians in the government are working with the Negro civil rights leaders, but not to solve the race problem. The greedy politicians who run this Government give lip service to the civil rights struggle, only to further their own selfish interests, and their main interest as politicians is to stay in power.

In this deceitful American game of power politics, the Negroes (i.e., the race problem, the integration and civil rights issues) are nothing but tools, used by one group of whites called liberals against another group of whites called conservatives, either to get into power, or to remain in power.

The white liberal differs from the white conservative only in one way: The liberal is more deceitful than the conservative. The liberal is more hypocritical than the conservative.

Both want power, but the white liberal is the one who has perfected the art of posing as the Negro's friend and benefactor; and by winning the friendship, allegiance, and support of the Negro, the white liberal is able to use the Negro as a pawn or tool in this political football game that is constantly raging between the white liberals and white conservatives.

Politically, the American Negro is nothing but a football, and the white liberals control this mentally dead ball through tricks of tokenism: false promises of integration and civil rights. In this profitable game of deceiving and exploiting the political potential of the American Negro, those white liberals have the willing cooperation of the Negro civil rights leaders. These "leaders" sell out our people for just a few crumbs of token gains. These "leaders" are satisfied with token victories and token progress because they themselves are nothing but token leaders.

According to a New York *Tribune* editorial (dated February 5, 1960), out of 11 million qualified Negro voters, only 2,700,000 actually took time to vote. This means that, roughly speaking, only 3 million out of 11 million Negroes who are qualified to vote actually take an active part, and the remaining 8 million remain voluntarily inactive, and yet this small (3 million) minority of Negro voters holds the decisive edge in determining who will be the next President.

If who will be the next President is influenced by only 3 million Negro voters, it is easy to understand why the presidential candidates of both political parties put on such a false show with the Civil Rights Bill and with false promises of integration. They must impress the 3 million voting Negroes who are the actual "integration seekers."

If such a fuss is made over these 3 million integration seekers, what would presidential candidates have to do to appease the 8 million non-voting Negroes, if they ever decide to become politically active?

The 8 million non-voting Negroes are in the majority; they are the downtrodden black masses. The black masses have refused to vote, or to take part in politics, because they reject the Uncle Tom approach of the Negro leadership that have been handpicked for them by the white man.

These Uncle Tom leaders do not speak for the Negro majority; they do not speak for the black masses. They speak for the black bourgeoisie, the brainwashed, white-minded, middle- class minority, who are ashamed of black, and don't want to be identified with the black masses, and are therefore seeking to lose their black identity by mixing, inter-marrying, and integrating with the white man.

The race problem can never be solved by listening to this white-minded minority. The white man should try to learn what the black masses want, and the only way to learn what the black masses want is by listening to the man who speaks for the black masses of America. The one man here in America who speaks for the downtrodden, dissatisfied black masses is this same man so many of our people are flocking to see and hear. This same Mr. Muhammad who is labeled by the white man as a black supremacist, and as a racist.

If the 3 million white-minded Negroes are casting their ballots for integration and intermarriage, what do the non-voting black masses want? Find out what the black masses want, and then perhaps America's race problem can be solved.

The white liberals hate the Honorable Elijah Muhammad, because they know their present position in the power structure stems from their ability to deceive and to exploit the Negro, politically as well as economically.

They know that the Honorable Elijah Muhammad's divine message will make our people (1) wake up, (2) clean up, and (3) stand up. They know that once the Honorable Elijah Muhammad is able to resurrect the Negro from this mental grave of ignorance by teaching him the truth about himself and his real enemy, the Negro learns to think for himself, he will no longer allow the white liberal to use him as a helpless football in the white man's crooked game of "power politics."

The white liberals control the Negro and the Negro vote by control-ling the Negro civil rights leaders. As long as they control the Negro civil rights leaders, they can also control and contain the Negro's struggle, and they can control the Negro's so-called "revolt."

The Negro revolution is controlled by foxy white liberals, by the Government itself. But the Black Revolution is controlled only by God.

The Black Revolution is the struggle of the non-whites of this earth against their white oppressors. The Black Revolution has swept white supremacy out of Africa, out of Asia, and is getting ready to sweep it out of Latin America. Revolutions are based upon land. Revolutionaries are the landless against the landlord. Revolutions are never peaceful, never loving, never non-violent, nor are they ever compromising. Revolutions are destructive and bloody. Revolutionaries don't compromise with the enemy; they don't even negotiate. Like the flood in Noah's day, revolution drowns all opposition... or like the fires in Lot's day, the Black Revolution burns everything that gets in its path.

History must repeat itself! Because of America's evil deeds against these 22 million Negroes, like Egypt and Babylon before her, America herself now stands before the bar of justice. White America is now facing her day of judgment, and she can't escape because today God Himself is the judge. God Himself is now the administrator of justice, and God Himself is to be her divine executor!

Is it possible for America to escape this divine disaster? If America can't atone for the crimes she has committed against the 22 million Negroes, if she can't undo the evils she has brutally, mercilessly heaped upon our people these past four hundred years, then America has signed her own doom, and our people would be foolish to accept her deceitful offers of integration into her doomed society at this late date!

How can America atone for her crimes? The Honorable Elijah Muhammad teaches us that a desegregated theater or lunch counter won't solve our problems. An integrated cup of coffee isn't sufficient pay for four hundred years of slave labor, and a better job in the white man's factory or position in his business is, at best, only a temporary solution. The only lasting or permanent solution is complete separation on some land that we can call our own.

The Honorable Elijah Muhammad teaches us that the race problem can easily be solved, just by sending these 22 million ex-slaves back to our own homeland where we can live in peace and harmony with our own kind. But this Government should provide the transportation, plus everything else we need to get started again in our own country. This Government should provide everything we need in machinery, materials, and finance; enough to last us from twenty to twenty-five years, until we can become an independent people in our own country.

If this white Government is afraid to let her 22 million ex-slaves go back to our country and to our own people, then America must set aside some separate territory here in the Western Hemisphere, where the two races can live apart from each other, since we certainly don't get along peacefully while we are here together.

The size of the territory can be judged according to our own population. If our people number one seventh of America's total population, then give us one seventh of this land. We don't want any land in the desert, but where there is rain and much mineral wealth.

We want fertile, productive land on which we can farm and provide our own people with sufficient food, clothing, and shelter. This Government must supply us with the machinery and other tools needed to dig into the earth. Give us everything we need for them from twenty to twenty-five years, until we can produce and supply our own needs.

If we are a part of America, then part of what she is worth belongs to us. We will take our share and depart, then this white country can have peace. What is her net worth? Give us our share in gold and silver and let us depart and go back to our homeland in peace.

We want no integration with this wicked race that enslaved us. We want complete separation from this race of devils. But we should not be expected to leave America and go back to our own homeland empty-handed. After four hundred years of slave labor, we have some *back pay* coming, a bill owed to us that must be collected.

If the Government of white America truly repents of its sins against our people, and atones by giving us our true share, only then can America save herself!

But if America waits for Almighty God Himself to step in and force her into a just settlement, God will take this entire continent away from her; and she will cease to exist as a nation. Her own Christian scriptures warn her that when God comes He can give the "entire Kingdom to whomsoever He will," which only means that the God of justice on Judgment Day can give this entire continent to whomsoever He wills!

White America, wake up and take heed, before it is too late!

# 35

# "Preface,"
# The Protestant Establishment
# (1964)

## E. Digby Baltzell

## Introduction

Since the seventeenth century at least, Americans have struggled with the problems of tribalism. The natural desire to strengthen group identity and protect lineage inevitably led to conflict with other groups and discrimination against them. In Puritan New England, basic human tendencies to promote one's tribe vied with the idealistic belief that spiritual election was not a matter of birth, and that God chose whom he willed. First-generation New England Puritans hoped that God would elect all their descendants, and baptized their children in that hope. But conflict broke out when baptized children who had not managed to go through the full process of church membership presented their own offspring for baptism. Did these grandchildren deserve special consideration? What about "outsiders"? On what grounds might they present children for baptism?

During the eighteenth century, emphasis on the need for "new birth" helped to democratize American religious life by making religious experience, not family lineage, the main criterion of religious status. The belligerent declaration of 1776 that "all men are created equal" did even more for democracy. But the urge to tribalism reasserted itself with new force. Beginning in the nineteenth century, as the size and diversity of the American

Excerpted from E. Digby Baltzell, "Preface," in *The Protestant Establishment: Aristocracy & Caste in America* (New Haven: Yale University Press, 1964), vii–xv.

population expanded, and as industrialization created a national economy based increasingly on divisions of labor and wealth, a de facto establishment of wealthy Anglo-Saxon Protestants controlled an increasingly disproportionate amount of land, commerce, government, and education. Many in this group believed that this inequitable situation reflected God's will. Others, like Digby Baltzell, did their best to unhook the connection between social entitlement and Anglo-Saxon ethnicity and to expose the tribalism of American society as a failure of both democratic process and religious idealism.

On a fine May morning in 1910, representatives of some seventy nations, including nine kings, five heirs apparent, forty other imperial highnesses, seven queens and Theodore Roosevelt of the United States, the greatest assemblage of rank and royalty the world had ever seen, rode through the streets of London in the funeral cortege of Edward VII, who has often been called the "Uncle of Europe." Theodore Roosevelt, without titled rank and dressed in civilian clothes, was hardly pleased to be walking at the very end of the long procession of titled dignitaries dressed in their resplendent uniforms. But his friend and one of the dead king's nephews, Wilhelm II of Imperial Germany, mounted on a white charger and dressed in the scarlet uniform of a British field marshal, was proud to be riding at the right hand of the new king. He was also pleased to be among his relatives in a city where, for the present at least, he was quite popular. Big Ben tolled nine in the morning as the royal procession, followed by all the formal pomp of England, left the palace grounds. But on Clio's clock it was nearer sunset, for the sun of white Western world empire was symbolically setting in a dying blaze of splendor never to rise again.

Within a decade, millions of men would have laid down their lives to stem the tide of the Kaiser's armies. And the series of wars and revolutions which began on the fields of Flanders and ended with our dropping of the Bomb on Hiroshima marked the end of the Pax Britannica and the transfer of Western leadership to the United States. Whereas generations of British gentlemen had proudly, and sometimes smugly, assumed it their natural right and duty to rule the world, there is something uncharacteristic in America's assuming such leadership. But, then, we Americans have been trained to succeed rather than to lead, and all too many of us would gladly forgo the need for greatness which has been so suddenly thrust upon us.

As far as our relations with the rest of the world are concerned, we are faced with infinitely more complex problems than were our British predecessors. In the first place, we live in a crowded world community where global war and genocide are ever present, but unthinkable, possibilities. At the same time, the authority of the white race, largely built up by the Anglo-Saxon gentlemen of England between the ages of Francis Drake and Benjamin Disraeli, is now being called into question around the world. The optimistic and imperialistic ideology of the white man's burden, materially based in the Anglo-American lead in the Industrial Revolution, has now turned into a nightmare, frighteningly fed by the demon dreams of the racists in our midst. Although the decline of established authority in the modern world community is most obviously reflected in the polarization of power between the defenders of democratic capitalism on the one hand and of totalitarian communism on the other, there is, I think, a latent but far greater danger that moral authority may degenerate into complete chaos and violence if ever the world should become divided into two opposing racial camps. In other words, the central question in the second half of this century may well be whether the white Western world, led by America, will be able to retain its traditional freedoms in an overpopulated world and, at the same time, succeed in sharing the fruits of an industrial-scientific civilization with the rising races which make up the rest of manking. In this process, white Western man must, above all, learn to share the leadership of some sort of new world community with his nonwhite peers, many of them now educated in the West, before a stable world establishment with moral authority can be re-created.

It is, in this connection, indeed appropriate that the United Nations, a struggling, still impotent, but ever hopeful attempt at creating some kind of world authority, should be located in New York City. For New York is racially and ethnically the most heterogeneous city in the world. Throughout history, of course, the elite of all nations and races have walked the streets of the great cosmopolitan centers; yet New York is historically unique in that its population is a heterogeneous one, as it were, from top to bottom. Even today its citizenry, almost half of whom are foreign-born or the children of the foreign-born, includes more Negroes than most cities in Africa, a greater concentration of Jews than at any other time or place in their long history, more Puerto Ricans than any other city outside of San Juan, more persons of Italian descent than most cities in Italy, and more sons of Ireland than Dublin. Finally, at the top of the pyramid of wealth and social prestige in the city, there is a White–Anglo-Saxon–Protestant establishment which, as this book will show, has been gradually losing its power and authority in the course of the twentieth century. New York, in short, mirrors in microcosm the problems of the world.

All over the world the people, if not always their leaders, look to America for leadership. But America's continuing authority in the world depends on our ability to solve the problem of authority here at home. The stability of authority in any community depends to a very great extent on the maintenance of a continuity of cultural traditions. There have always been, I suppose, two kinds of people, those who have been proud of their heritage and have wanted to share it with others, and those who have been jealous of their heritage and have tried to monopolize it for themselves. A crisis in moral authority has developed in modern America largely because of the White–Anglo-Saxon–Protestant establishment's unwillingness, or inability, to share and improve its upper-class traditions by continuously absorbing talented and distinguished members of minority groups into its privileged ranks. [...]

[...] It is my central thesis that in order for an upper class to maintain a continuity of power and authority, especially in an opportunitarian and mobile society such as ours, its membership must, in the long run, be representative of the composition of society as a whole. Thus Theodore Roosevelt's generation, which came to maturity at the close of the optimistic nineteenth century (which had its Indian summer in the Edwardian era), was authoritatively dominated by an old-stock upper class whose members were the business, cultural and intellectual leaders of a nation which was, at the higher levels of society at least, still overwhelmingly white, Anglo-Saxon and Protestant in origins and convictions.

Since Roosevelt's day, America has become, at all levels of society, the most ethnically and racially heterogeneous nation on earth. In response to this new heterogeneity, a dialectical struggle developed within the ranks of the White–Anglo-Saxon–Protestant establishment. On the one hand, the vast majority of old-stock patricians, following the caste ideals of the Old Regime in France, concentrated on success and the protection of their privileges at the expense of power and leadership; and the Republican Party, which had protected its interests since the Civil War, gradually lost authority in the land after 1929. On the other hand, a small but growing minority of old-stock aristocrats, following the Whig tradition in England, were willing to share their privileges with distinguished members of minority groups in order to maintain their traditional power and authority within the ranks of some sort of new and heterogeneous establishment; they first became Progressives under Theodore Roosevelt, eventually supported Woodrow Wilson, and finally joined, and often led, the Democratic Party during the Great Depression; and many of their sons were inspired by the aristocratic style of the New Frontier.

Following Tocqueville's classic analysis of the decline of authority in France, I have tried to show that an authoritative leadership structure will evolve in this country only when and if a new and representative upper class and establishment are created, whose members will then be able to *discriminate* on the basis of the distinguished accomplishments of individuals rather than *classifying* men categorically on the basis of their ethnic or racial origins.

Essentially this book, both in its method and in its theoretical point of view, is a continuation of another which I completed several years ago. The earlier book was a detailed analysis of how a national and associational upper class replaced the local and communal gentry in America between the close of the Civil War and 1940.[...]I deliberately concluded my analysis of upper-class institutions with the year 1940, when a rather secure establishment of Anglo-Saxon—Protestant gentlemen still ran the city. Looking to the future, however, the book ended on the following note:

> One more question remains to be raised if it cannot be answered: What is the future function of a predominantly Anglo-Saxon and Protestant upper class in an ethnically and religiously heterogeneous democracy? In many ways, this is the most important question of all. As Joseph Patrick Kennedy, Boston millionaire and American Ambassador to the Court of St. James under Roosevelt, once put it: "How long does our family have to be here before we are called Americans rather than Irish-Americans?" As has been shown throughout this volume, the American upper class has been from the beginning open to new men of talent and power and their families. By the middle of the twentieth century, however, upper-class status appears to be limited primarily to families of colonial and northern European stock and Protestant affiliations. Glancing back to the turn of the century, when a flood tide of immigrants came to these shores from southern and eastern Europe, to say nothing of the Irish Catholics who came earlier, one wonders if this American democracy has not produced somewhat of a caste situation at the upper-class level. Or are the talented and powerful descendants of these newer immigrants going to be assimilated into some future upper class way of life and social organization?[1]

[...] It still takes some time, even in an age which has just watched its first real murder on television, to translate a raw manuscript into the printed page of a book. Soon after I had completed the final, tedious revisions on this manuscript and sent it off to my publishers for what I thought was to be the last time, John Fitzgerald Kennedy was tragically killed. Death, I suppose, transforms admiration into reverence. Yet in this final revision of the text, I have resisted any temptations to alter its original tone and have limited myself to revising the tenses of verbs when they referred to the late President and the New Frontier which he so gallantly led.

As I sat, in a state of shock and sorrow, watching the President's funeral last Monday, my mind kept going back to the funeral of Edward

VII, when a sorrowful yet confident royal establishment, still assuming it ruled the world, followed the dead king's favorite charger, Kildare, through the streets of London. I thought of how far the world had traveled since that gay and formal age. At the same time, I could not help feeling that Theodore Roosevelt would have been far prouder to have taken part in the procession which was now walking from the White House to St. Matthew's Cathedral, with all the majesty of democratic dignity, behind the nervous black charger, whose absent rider symbolized so well the leadership and hopes of a new world which was so desperately trying to be born in his generation. For surely faith and hope rank higher than confidence in the hierarchy of human virtues. Thus Theodore Roosevelt was a dreamer of dreams who dared to hope that America would, in the long run, conquer the values of caste and someday send a distinguished Catholic, and eventually a Jew, to the White House. Among other things, this funeral dramatized the fact that part of his hopes have now been realized. I have written this book with the hope that when the American establishment finally rejects the caste ideas of the country-club set in favor of the ideals once dramatized at Camelot, which inspired Woodrow Wilson, the two Roosevelts, and the late John Fitzgerald Kennedy, this whole dream will surely come to be.

Thanksgiving Day, 1963

# Note

1    E. Digby Baltzell, *Philadelphia Gentlemen, The Making of a National Upper Class* (Glencoe, Ill.: The Free Press, 1958), 395–6. See also paperback reprint, *An American Business Aristocracy* (New York: Collier Books, 1962).

# 36

# Religious Freedom (1966)

## John Courtney Murray

## Introduction

As the chief author of *Dignitatis Humanae Personae*, the declaration on religious freedom ratified at the second Vatican Council in 1965, the Jesuit scholar John Courtney Murray led the Roman Catholic Church toward an understanding of the relationship between church and state that resonated with a good deal of American religious thought. By 1965, five years after the election of John F. Kennedy as President of the United States, many American Catholics, as well as Protestants and Jews, were already committed to religious freedom and the separation of church and state. But until Vatican II, official teaching affirmed that, as the one true church of God, the Catholic Church should offer spiritual guidance to the state and that the state owed the Church its loyalty and support.

While they agreed that the Catholic Church was the one true church, many American Catholics were committed to a democratic form of government that guaranteed each individual's freedom to worship as they pleased. To be sure, this support for religious freedom resulted partly from the fact that Catholics were members of a religious minority who knew that if the United States did have an established church it would not be theirs. But for many American Catholics, investment in religious freedom was not simply a matter of accepting the lesser of two evils. As Orestes Brownson argued a century

Excerpted from John Courtney Murray, "Religious Freedom," preface to *Dignitatis Humanae Personae*, in *The Documents of Vatican II*, ed. Walter M. Abbott (Piscataway: New Century, 1966), 672–4.

before Vatican II, religious freedom was a positive contribution to faith because it encouraged active commitment to the Church and discouraged unthinking, passive obedience.

As a successor to the ideas of Brownson and other Americanist Catholics, Murray understood that religious freedom lay at the crux of a host of reforms. The Church could open wide its doors to the modern world only by letting go of nostalgia for medieval relations between church and state. Ecumenical dialogue was possible only when Catholics respected other claims to truth. And lay people would step fully into their roles as participants of the body of Christ and ministers to the world only when the priestly hierarchy of the Church affirmed the dignity and freedom of all humanity.

On November 19, 1963, the first schema (draft text) on religious freedom was presented to the conciliar Fathers by the Secretariat for Promoting Christian Unity. In the course of two years, five corrected versions of the text appeared in print, each being the work of many revisions within the secretariat. Three public debates were held in the Aula, during which some one hundred and twenty speeches were made. Some six hundred written interventions were sent to the secretariat, many of them signed by groups of bishops. Moreover, critiques of the successive schemas were made, either orally or in writing, by a considerable number of bishops and theologians who were consulted by the secretariat. Also consulted were a number of the observers at the Council. Before the final vote was taken, more than two thousand *modi* (suggested corrections) were considered (many of them, of course, were identical).

Thus, the greatest argument on religious freedom in all history happily broke forth in the Church. The debate was full and free and vigorous, if at times confused and emotional.

The first text had appeared as Chapter V of the Decree on Ecumenism. The second text had appeared as a Declaration, but in an appendix to the Decree on Ecumenism. With the third text the Declaration assumed independent status. From the outset, its intention was pastoral, as was the general intention of the Council in all its utterances. This, however, does not mean that the Declaration contains simply practical advice. Its content is properly doctrinal. In particular, three doctrinal tenets are declared: the ethical doctrine of religious freedom as a human right (personal and collective); a political doctrine with regard to the functions and limits of government in matters religious; and the theological doctrine of the freedom of the Church as the fundamental principle in what concerns the relations between the Church and the socio-political order.

It can hardly be maintained that the Declaration is a milestone in human history – moral, political, or intellectual. The principle of religious freedom has long been recognized in constitutional law, to the point where even Marxist-Leninist political ideology is obliged to pay lip-service to it. In all honesty it must be admitted that the Church is late in acknowledging the validity of the principle.

In any event, the document is a significant event in the history of the Church. It was, of course, the most controversial document of the whole Council, largely because it raised with sharp emphasis the issue that lay continually below the surface of all the conciliar debates – the issue of the development of doctrine. The notion of development, not the notion of religious freedom, was the real sticking-point for many of those who opposed the Declaration even to the end. The course of the development between the *Syllabus of Errors* (1864) and *Dignitatis Humanae Personae*[1] (1965) still remains to be explained by theologians. But the Council formally sanctioned the validity of the development itself; and this was a doctrinal event of high importance for theological thought in many other areas.

Moreover, taken in conjunction with the Pastoral Constitution on the Church in the Modern World, the Declaration opens a new era in the relations between the People of God and the People Temporal. A long-standing ambiguity has finally been cleared up. The Church does not deal with the secular order in terms of a double standard – freedom for the Church when Catholics are a minority, privilege for the Church and intolerance for others when Catholics are a majority. The Declaration has opened the way toward new confidence in ecumenical relationships, and a new straightforwardness in relationships between the Church and the world.

Finally, though the Declaration deals only with the minor issue of religious freedom in the technical secular sense, it does affirm a principle of wider import – that the dignity of man consists in his responsible use of freedom. Some of the conciliar Fathers – not least those opposed to the Declaration – perceived that a certain indivisibility attaches to the notion of freedom. The word and the thing have wrought wonders in the modern world; they have also wrought havoc. The conciliar affirmation of the principle of freedom was narrowly limited – in the text. But the text itself was flung into a pool whose shores are wide as the universal Church. The ripples will run far.

Inevitably, a second great argument will be set afoot – now on the theological meaning of Christian freedom. The children of God, who receive this freedom as a gift from their Father through Christ in the Holy Spirit, assert it within the Church as well as within the world, always for the sake of the world and the Church. The issues are many – the dignity of the Christian, the foundations of Christian freedom, its object or content, its limits and their criterion, the measure of its responsible use, its relation to the legitimate reaches of authority and to the saving counsels of prudence, the perils that lurk in it, and the forms of corruption to which it is prone. All these issues must be considered in a spirit of sober and informed reflection.

The issue of religious freedom was in itself minor. But Pope Paul VI was looking deep and far when he called the Declaration on Religious Freedom "one of the major texts of the Council."

## Note

1  These are the opening words, in Latin, of the Declaration on Religious Freedom. The opening words of conciliar documents may be cited as titles (usually with each word capitalized, according to the practice for papal encyclicals), but the more common title is the one that heads the document.

# 37

# Beyond God the Father (1973)

## Mary Daly

## Introduction

No one has taken the Catholic mandate for religious reform further than the maverick philosopher Mary Daly. As an unofficial observer at the second Vatican Council, overlooking the splendor of St. Peter's basilica filled with cardinals in crimson gowns, Daly experienced a sort of negative epiphany as she watched a single line of black-clad nuns shuffle unevenly toward the altar to receive communion. These pious women were grateful for the opportunity to celebrate their faith in this extraordinary setting. But they struck Daly in a most irreverent way – to her, they looked like ants at a picnic, lined up for crumbs, and poison crumbs at that. Like so much else in the Church, she believed, this ritual constructed women's inferiority.

In the years that followed, Daly went even further in her criticism of Christianity. She gave up being a reformer who urged Christians to affirm women's equality to condemn Christianity as nothing more than an elaborate system for elevating the authority of men at the expense of women's dignity and well-being. The most authentic form of religious life, Daly came to believe, centered on women's identification with, and celebration of, the elemental beauty, power, and being of the natural world. For much of human history, Daly believes, men had succeeded in their attempts to sever religion from the dynamic forces of nature, and to usurp women's spiritual authority and power.

Excerpted from Mary Daly, *Beyond God the Father: Toward a Philosophy of Women's Liberation* (Boston: Beacon Press, 1973), 69–71, 73–5.

Most feminist theologians have not gone as far as Daly in rejecting Christianity as hopelessly misogynist. But even feminists who have not rejected Christianity or Judaism for Goddess theology or neo-pagan Wiccan practices are often indebted to her insights. Daly has led the way in analyzing how religion constructed gender roles, and in analyzing how beliefs about nature functioned to define gender roles and their legitimation by religion. Through these insights into how religion worked to construct gender, Daly has influenced a number of different branches of religious thought worldwide.

## Beyond Christolatry: A World Without Models

> Take the snake, the fruit-tree and the woman from the tableau, and we have no fall, nor frowning Judge, no Inferno, no everlasting punishment – hence no need of a Savior. Thus the bottom falls out of the whole Christian theology. Here is the reason why in all the Biblical researches and higher criticisms, the scholars never touch the position of women.
> **Elizabeth Cady Stanton**

> Historical Christianity has fallen into the error that corrupts all attempts to communicate religion.... It has dwelt, it dwells, with noxious exaggeration about the *person* of Jesus.
> **Ralph Waldo Emerson**

The distortion in Christian ideology resulting from and confirming sexual hierarchy is manifested not only in the doctrines of God and of the Fall but also in doctrines concerning Jesus. A great deal of Christian doctrine has been docetic, that is, it has not seriously accepted the fact that Jesus was a limited human being. A logical consequence of the liberation of women will be a loss of plausibility of Christological formulas which reflect and encourage idolatry in relation to the person of Jesus.

As the idolatry and the dehumanizing effects of reifying and therefore limiting "God" become more manifest in women's expanded consciousness, it will become less plausible to think of Jesus as the "Second Person of the Trinity" who "assumed" a human nature in a unique "hypostatic union." Indeed, it is logical that the prevalent emphasis upon the total uniqueness and supereminence of Jesus will become less meaningful. To say this is not at all to deny the charismatic and revelatory power of the personality of Jesus (or of other persons). The point is, rather, to attempt a realistic assessment of traditional ways of looking at and using his image.

It is still not unusual for Christian priests and ministers, when confronted with the issue of women's liberation, to assert that God "became incarnate" uniquely as a male and then to draw arguments for male supremacy from this. Indeed the Christological tradition itself tends to justify such conclusions. The underlying – and often explicit – assumption in the minds of theologians down through the centuries has been that the divinity could not have deigned to "become incarnate" in the "inferior" sex, and the "fact" that "he" did not do so of course confirms male superiority. The erosion of consent to male dominance on the part of women is undermining such assumptions of the tradition. [. . .]

I am proposing that Christian idolatry concerning the person of Jesus is not likely to be overcome except through the revolution that is going on in women's consciousness. It will, I think, become increasingly evident that exclusively masculine symbols for the ideal of "incarnation" or for the ideal of the human search for fulfillment will not do. As a uniquely masculine image and language for divinity loses credibility, so also the idea of a single divine incarnation in a human being of the male sex may give way in the religious consciousness to an increased awareness of the power of Being in all persons.

Seeds of this awareness are already present in the traditional doctrine that all human beings are made to the image of God and in a less than adequate way in the doctrine of grace. Now it should become possible to work out with increasing realism the implications in both of these doctrines that human beings are called to self-actualization and to the creation of a community that fosters the becoming of women and men. This means that no adequate models can be taken from the past.

It may be that we will witness a remythologizing of religion. Symbolism for incarnation of the divine in human beings may continue to be needed in the future, but it is highly unlikely that women or men will continue to find plausible that symbolism which is epitomized in the image of the Virgin kneeling in adoration before her own son. Perhaps this will be replaced by the emergence of imagery that is not hierarchical. The point is not to deny that a revelatory event took place in the encounter with the person Jesus. Rather, it is to affirm that the creative presence of the Verb can be revealed at every historical moment, in every person and culture. [. . .]

## Jesus Was a Feminist, But So What?

In an admirable and scholarly article Leonard Swidler has marshaled historical evidence to show convincingly that Jesus was a feminist.[1] The response that appears to be forthcoming from many women goes something like this: "Fine. Wonderful. But even if he wasn't, *I am*." Professor Swidler's work has the advantages of striving for historical accuracy and of maintaining continuity with tradition. At the same time, there are inherent difficulties in this approach. First, his assumption that one can extract "religious truth" from "time-conditioned categories" seems to mean that we can shuck off the debris of a long history of oppressiveness and get to the pristine purity of the original revelation. This is problematic in that it tends to be backward-looking, assuming at least implicitly that past history (that is, some peak moments of the past) has some sort of prior claim over present experience, as if recourse to the past were necessary to legitimate experience now. A second difficulty with the "Jesus was a feminist" approach to feminism is interrelated with the first: Implicit in this approach is the notion that there *are* adequate models that can be extracted from the past. The traditional idea of *imitatio Christi* is the not-so-hidden agenda of this method. [. . .]

Aside from the impossibility of looking to the *past* for adequate guidance, I propose that there are inherent difficulties in looking to Jesus, or to anyone else, as a model. The very concept of model, as commonly understood, is one of those conceptual products that either should be rejected as not applicable to persons or else made into a new word by being lifted out of its old context. The same term may be retained, materially speaking, but what we are about is breaking models in the old sense of the term. It seems to have been part of the patriarchal mind-set to imitate slavishly a master or father-figure with an almost blind devotion and then to reject this figure in order to be oneself. It is perhaps significant that the Latin term *modulus* means a small measure: it is necessary to shrink the self in order to imitate a model in this sense. This imitation-rejection syndrome is not what is going on with women now. Those who have come far enough in consciousness to break through the destructive conditioning imposed through "models" offered to the female in our culture are learning to be critical of all ready-made models. This is not to say that strong and free women do not have an influence, but this is transmitted rather as an infectious freedom. Those who are really living on the boundary tend to spark in others the courage to affirm their own unique being. [. . .] If reading the Gospels – or anything else – sparks this kind of freedom in some persons today, this is hardly to be disparaged. But then Jesus or any other liberated person who has this effect functions as a model precisely in the sense of being a model-breaker, pointing beyond his or her own limitations to the potential for further liberation.

# 38

# Ceremony (1977)

## Leslie Marmon Silko

## Introduction

Along with other gifted novelists and short-story writers, Leslie Silko helped make Native American spirituality part of the larger American conversation about religious life. Utilizing Western forms of literature such as the novel and short story, Silko and other Native writers have enabled many Americans to better understand Native worldviews. In lifting up and elaborating upon aspects of these worldviews that they believe other Americans ought to understand, these creative artists have also contributed to the vitality, authority, and historical development of their own Native traditions.

In her novel *Ceremony*, Silko broke new ground in depicting Native American stories and rituals as antidotes for the ailments of modern society. As the story unfolds, ordinary events take on cosmic significance as the protagonist Tayo undergoes a healing process and finds his way through many difficulties. His personal journey deepens as he discerns the underlying structure of events revealed in Navajo and Laguna mythology. As Tayo becomes increasingly aware, his handling of dangerous events and feelings has enormous implication, not only for his own survival but also for that of the world.

As a religious writer, Silko approaches Native American stories as guides to the well-being of individuals, communities, and the earth. In this respect, she takes the religious beliefs of Native Americans very seriously indeed. But at the same time, she treats Native stories – and by implication all religious

Excerpted from Leslie Marmon Silko, *Ceremony* (New York: New American Library, 1977), 1–3.

stories and ceremonies – as works of imagination. To persist through time, Silko believes, and to do their work of holding the world and its people together, sacred stories need to be continually relived, reimagined, and represented in new ways.

> Ts'its'tsi'nako, Thought-Woman,
>   is sitting in her room
> and whatever she thinks about
>     appears.
>
> She thought of her sisters.
>   Nau'ts'ity'i and I'tcts'ity'i,
> and together they created the Universe
>   this world
>   and the four worlds below.
>
> Thought-Woman, the spider,
>   named things and
>   as she named them
>     they appeared.
>
> She is sitting in her room
> thinking of a story now
>
> I'm telling you the story,
> she is thinking.

# Ceremony

> I will tell you something about stories,
>   [he said]
> They aren't just entertainment.
>   Don't be fooled.
> They are all we have, you see,
>   all we have to fight off
>     illness and death.
>
> You don't have anything
> if you don't have the stories.
>
> Their evil is mighty
> but it can't stand up to our stories.
> So they try to destroy the stories

let the stories be confused or forgotten.
They would like that
They would be happy
Because we would be defenseless then.

He rubbed his belly.
I keep them here
  [he said]
Here, put your hand on it
  See, it is moving.
  There is life here
  for the people.

And in the belly of this story
the rituals and the ceremony
are still growing.

*What She Said:*
The only cure
I know
is a good ceremony,
that's what she said.

# 39

# "American Indian Religious Freedom," Public Law 95–341 (1978)

## Introduction

When North America was first colonized, many Euro-Americans thought that Native peoples had nothing that could be dignified by the name religion. Even settlers sensitive to the humanity of Native peoples, like Roger Williams, often believed that Native worship was inspired by Satan. Throughout much of American history, Indians were constantly pressured by Euro-Americans to abandon their traditional beliefs and practices and accept Christianity. At the same time, however, some Euro-Americans accepted Native beliefs and practices, usually in bits and pieces, but occasionally by joining Indian tribes and becoming Indians themselves. In the nineteenth century, New England Transcendentalists and other Americans influenced by romanticism began to appreciate Native religions as wholesome alternatives to the corruptions of civilization. And at the end of the century, anthropologists began to view Native religions as precious cultural resources on the verge of extinction that ought to be documented before it was too late.

"American Indian Religious Freedom," Public Law 95–341, August 11, 1978, reprinted in *Native American Traditions: Sources and Interpretations*, 1st ed., ed. Sam D. Gill (Belmont, Calif.: Wadsworth, 1983), 15–16. Copyright © 1983. Reprinted with permission of Wadsworth, an imprint of the Wadsworth Group, a division of Thomson Learning, fax 800 730 2215.

Meanwhile, Native people were revising their religious traditions to account for colonization, assimilate Christianity, and survive in the modern world. Instead of dying out, Native religions often played a vital role in the persistence and reinvention of Native American identity. As part of this complicated historical process, spokespersons for Native identity argued that religious rituals practiced by Native peoples were worthy of national protection. As an affirmation of this position, the American Indian Religious Freedom law of 1978 aimed to protect Native religious sites and objects from destruction or exploitation and to restrict developers, archeologists, and tourists with respect to sacred places, bones, and artifacts. The law also aimed to protect Native religious activities that might otherwise be deemed unlawful, such as taking eagle feathers, hunting whales, or ingesting peyote. While not unchallenged or entirely effective, the law is nevertheless a landmark both in Native American religious history and in the history of American interpretations of religious freedom.

Whereas the freedom of religion for all people is an inherent right, fundamental to the democratic structure of the United States and is guaranteed by the First Amendment of the United States Constitution;

Whereas the United States has traditionally rejected the concept of a government denying individuals the right to practice their religion and as a result, has benefited from a rich variety of religious heritages in this country;

Whereas the religious practices of the American Indian (as well as Native Alaskan and Hawaiian) are an integral part of their culture, tradition and heritage, such practices forming the basis of Indian identity and value systems;

Whereas the traditional American Indian religions, as an integral part of Indian life, are indispensable and irreplaceable;

Whereas the lack of a clear, comprehensive, and consistent Federal policy has often resulted in the abridgment of religious freedom for traditional American Indians;

Whereas such religious infringements result from the lack of knowledge or the insensitive and inflexible enforcement of Federal policies and regulations premised on a variety of laws;

Whereas such laws were designed for such worthwhile purposes as conservation and preservation of natural species and resources but were never intended to relate to Indian religious practices and, therefore, were passed without consideration of their effect on traditional American Indian religions;

Whereas such laws and policies often deny American Indian access to sacred sites required in their religions, including cemeteries;

Whereas such laws at times prohibit the use and possession of sacred objects necessary to the exercise of religious rites and ceremonies;

Whereas traditional American Indian ceremonies have been intruded upon, interfered with, and in a few instances banned: Now, therefore, be it

*Resolved by the Senate and House of Representatives of the United States of America in Congress assembled,* That henceforth it shall be the policy of the United States to protect and preserve for American Indians their inherent right of freedom to believe, express, and exercise the traditional religions of the American Indian, Eskimo, Aleut, and Native Hawaiians, including but not limited to access to sites, use and possession of sacred objects, and the freedom to worship through ceremonials and traditional rites.

# 40

# Sexism and God-Talk (1983)

## Rosemary Radford Ruether

## Introduction

If Mary Daly led the charge against Christianity as an inherently misogynist religion, Rosemary Radford Ruether took the lead in reconstructing Christianity in feminist terms. She was among the first to proclaim Jesus as a feminist and to interpret the gospel accordingly. Amidst a cadre of revolutionary theologians who argued for a gospel of social justice and liberation, Ruether was the first to insist that justice and liberation be measured in terms of women's suffering and freedom of expression. Believing that Christianity should be a force against oppression, she argued that since women were the most common victims of oppression, concern for their suffering, and commitment to their well-being, inclusion, and empowerment should be at the heart of Christian life. In drawing out the implications of this theology, Ruether focused on the need to revise language about God, arguing that describing God in authoritarian male terms made women feel submissive and inferior while more inclusive language, such as naming God mother, encouraged women's empowerment.

Ruether hailed American women of the past who were inspired by the liberating force of Christianity to oppose slavery and oppression. She also celebrated heroic women in other religions. And she built on Mary Daly's discovery that language about nature, women, and God was interconnected. Arguing that sensitivity to women's lives implied concern for the earth,

Excerpted from Rosemary Radford Ruether, *Sexism and God-Talk: Toward a Feminist Theology* (Boston: Beacon Press, 1983), 85, 264–6.

Ruether maintained that, wherever it was found, true religion was ecological as well as feminist.

## Toward an Ecological-Feminist Theology of Nature

An ecological-feminist theology of nature must rethink the whole Western theological tradition of the hierarchical chain of being and chain of command. This theology must question the hierarchy of human over nonhuman nature as a relationship of ontological and moral value. It must challenge the right of the human to treat the nonhuman as private property and material wealth to be exploited. It must unmask the structures of social domination, male over female, owner over worker that mediate this domination of nonhuman nature. Finally, it must question the model of hierarchy that starts with nonmaterial spirit (God) as the source of the chain of being and continues down to nonspiritual "matter" as the bottom of the chain of being and the most inferior, valueless, and dominated point in the chain of command. [...]

## The Big Lie

Those who rule pay their professors to proliferate lies, to generate a mental universe that turns everything upside down. The Big Lie makes those who toil appear to be idle, while those who speak into dictaphones appear to be the hard workers. It makes women appear the offspring of males, and males the primary creators of babies. It makes matter the final devolution of the mind, and mind the original source of all being. It regards the body as an alien tomb of the soul, and the soul as growing stronger the more it weakens the body. It abstracts the human from the earth and God from the cosmos, and says that that which is abstracted is the original, and the first, and can exist alone and independent.

The Big Lie tells us that we are strangers and sojourners on this planet, that our flesh, our blood, our instincts for survival are our enemies. Originally we lived as disincarnate orbs of light in the heavenly heights. We have fallen to this earth and into this clay through accident or sin. We must spend our lives suppressing our hungers and thirsts and shunning our fellow beings, so that we can dematerialize and fly away again to our stars.

It is said that mothers particularly are the enemy, responsible for our mortal flesh. To become eternal and everlasting we must flee the body, the woman, and the world. She is the icon of the corruptible nature, seduced by the serpent in the beginning. Through her, death entered the world. Even now she collaborates with devils to hold men in fast fetters to the ground. A million women twisted on the rack, smoldered in burning fagots to pay homage to this Lie.

It is said that enlightened man must drive the devils and witches from the world, restore order, put himself in charge, reduce nature to his control. With numbers and formulas he can search out her innermost secrets, learn all the laws of her ways, become her lord and master. The cosmos is reduced to elements, molecules, atoms, positive and negative charges, infinitely manipulatable, having no nature of her own, given to him to do with what he will. He will mount upon her with wings, fly away to the moon, blow her up in the flash of atomic energy, live forever in a space capsule, entombed in plastic, dining on chemicals.

## The Collapse of the House of Cards: The Disclosure of Divine Wisdom

The facade starts to crumble. We discover buried histories. "We Shall Overcome." "Sisterhood Is Powerful." "Viva la Huelga." "Bury My Heart at Wounded Knee." We begin to understand the hidden costs. "Hello, carbon dioxide; the air, the air is everywhere." Carcinogens in our health food, strontium 90 in mother's milk. Atomic fallout in our swimming pool. Threats to generations yet unborn. We are held hostage by the colonized, blackmailed by the poor rich in raw materials. The Petroleum Age starts to run out of gas.

Through the fissures of the system we glimpse the forgotten world of our homeland. We learn to walk again; to watch sunsets; to examine leaves; to plant seeds in soil. Turn off the TV; talk to each other to ease the frenetic pace; get in touch with our circulatory system, with the rhythms of our menstrual cycle that link us to the pull of the moon and tides of the sea.

The scales begin to fall from our eyes, and all around us we see miracles. Babies grow in wombs without help from computers. The sun rises every day. Con Ed sends no bill for sunshine. The harmony is still there, persisting, supporting, forgiving, preserving us in spite of ourselves. Divine Grace keeps faith with us when we have broken faith with her. Through the years of alien madness, she did not abandon us; she kept the planets turning, the seasons recurring, even struggled to put the upside down right side up, to cleanse the channels of the garbage, to blow the smog out to sea.

To return Home: to learn the harmony, the peace, the justice of body, bodies in right relation to each other. The whence we have come and whither we go, not from alien skies but here, in the community of earth. Holy One, Thy Kingdom come, Thy will done on earth. All shall sit under their own vines and fig trees and none shall be afraid. The lion will lay down with the lamb and the little child will lead them. A new thing is revealed; the woman will encompass the warrior. Thou shalt not hurt, thou shalt not kill in all my holy mountain.

The Shalom of the Holy; the disclosure of the gracious *Shekinah*; Divine Wisdom; the empowering Matrix; She, in whom we live and move and have our being – She comes; She is here.

# 41

# The Voice of Sarah (1990)

## Tamar Frankiel

## Introduction

As representative of a growing number of Americans committed to Orthodox Judaism, Tamar Frankiel adheres strictly to the rules of Jewish law, or
halakhah, governing everything from Sabbath restrictions to food and sex. In
Orthodox Judaism, gender roles are clearly defined, with men responsible for
religious study and leadership, while women's lives are defined primarily in
terms of fertility, child nurture, and family life. Despite limitations on women's
religious leadership, and restrictions on sex based on women's menstrual
cycles, Frankiel found her identity as a woman deepened, and more satisfying
and pleasurable, because of the religious meaning imparted through these
observances. As she discovered through her conversion to Orthodoxy, the
whole purpose of halakhah was to become more aware of God in all aspects
of life.

This kind of spirituality is not feminist in the way Rosemary Ruether or
Mary Daly use the term. In fact, Orthodox Jews and other religious conservatives have often opposed feminism and celebrated their own traditions as
alternatives to feminism's blurring of gender roles and perceived tendency to
secularism. At the same time, however, conservative religious women have
appropriated a number of feminist strategies, including deliberate revision of
negative stereotypes about women, self-conscious networking, commitment

Excerpted from Tamar Frankiel, *The Voice of Sarah: Feminine Spirituality and Traditional
Judaism* (New York: Harper Collins, 1990), 79–83. Copyright © 1990 by Tamar Frankiel.
Reprinted by permission of HarperCollins Publishers, Inc.

to men's participation in the responsibilities of family life, and concerted effort to promote new forms and interpretations of spirituality that celebrate women and enhance their status.

> Niddah.
> Can you come close?
> Can I touch you?
> Will you be mine?
> Must I be yours?
> What is this dance we play
> me and you, I and thou,
> far away and close, passing in the night –
> how can I know you like this?
> how can you know me?
> how can I know me?
> Together and apart
> we become something new
> a new possibility in creation.

Many regard the rituals of *taharat hamishpocheh*, "family purity," as obsolete today. Yet we find more and more young women taking them on. What leads women to choose a practice that involves sexual abstinence part of the time? More generally, what are we to make of a system that gives women no choice about the expression of their sexuality? The halacha stipulates that for our entire menstrual period plus seven more days each month we must practice abstinence from sexual relations. So, of course, must our husbands, who also have no choice. (They have a less direct relation to the system, since it is the woman's biology that dictates the times of separation and union.)

Should we be coerced by our biology at all, though? Although we are women and our breasts give milk, although because we resonate to symbols of food and nourishment, we do not necessarily become chief cook and table setter in the household. Why then, because of our periods, must we follow a sexual schedule? Is this some scheme to make sure we have more babies?

It is tempting to turn to the interesting studies that have been conducted in the past several years on the differences women experience in their feelings, inclinations, and abilities at different times in their menstrual cycle. For example, some have argued that there are rhythms in most women's lives that are represented by the poles of ovulation and menstruation. The time of menstruation is characterized by withdrawal and inwardness, often accompanied by vivid dreams; the pole of ovulation is marked by outgoingness and greater openness to socializing. Recent Canadian research in women's cognitive ability indicates that women operate more skillfully in different areas according to their low or high estrogen levels, verbal and fine motor skills being at their peak when estrogen is high (ovulation), spatial skills when it is low (menstruation). Claims have been made (and disputed) that the chemistry of our bodies is such that it is actually healthier to avoid sex during and immediately after menstruation.

But none of the extant studies is definitive; and none can really tell us how we should act when menstruating or ovulating, only what variations and consequences we can expect when we undertake certain kinds of activity. We are not like animals whose sexual activity is restricted to certain times: we can do almost anything from sex to mathematics at any time we please, and most of us suffer no ill effects.

Still, we may find that we are more in harmony with our own nature if we follow the rhythms in our bodies. These bodily changes, however, are subtle. Beyond physical symptoms and a heightened emotionality or irritability at certain times, many of us are not very much aware of how our personal moon phase, so to speak, affects what we are doing and how we are relating. Even if we are aware, we are taught to hide or belittle the differences. Tribal and ancient cultures set up a variety of rituals of seclusion for women, but in the modern West culture has killed our sensitivity to nature.

As a result, we have arrived at the point where we can be expected to perform on a nine-to-five, fifty-week-a-year job, or cook and keep house equally well every week for our families, or accomplish our multitudinous tasks with equal efficiency every day. We might be forgiven for some oversights during "that time of the month," but these are considered weaknesses rather than signs that we might do better directing our energy in another path. These attitudes reveal that despite our intentions to be positive, open, and honest about our physiology our culture is still intolerant of menstruation. We no longer view the menstruating woman as actually dangerous, one who pollutes all she touches and who must be segregated. But we have no positive vision of this time. Our culture has offered instead the sexless, or at least hormoneless, woman: she who never falters or shows extremes no matter what her body is doing.

Jewish tradition suggests a different path, neither the tribal way of radical seclusion nor modern culture's path of ignoring feminine rhythms. The Torah defines precisely what is at issue. Variable moods, inclinations, or abilities are only the superficial symptoms of something much deeper. Even the obvious physical purposes of ovulation and menstruation – repeatedly preparing the body for pregnancy – are really on the surface. The entire process is something else: a scale drawing, so to speak, of the creativity of the universe.

The pivotal point of that creativity is the union of male and female. As we saw earlier, this is manifest ritually in the movement of Shabbat and the cycle of the year. The female rhythms lay the foundation, the male brings forth the spark. On the human level, her rhythms are decisive: there is a time for union and a time for separation. While the descriptions of the time of niddah are usually translated "impurity" or "uncleanness," they do not connote magical danger or pollution, let alone dirt. The time is viewed negatively only from the point of view that now creative union cannot properly take place. No other pollution is involved, no other relationships are forbidden. The only things not permitted at this time are entering into sexual relations, and gestures between husband and wife that might lead to such relations.

There are many implications of following these rhythms. The separation for nearly two weeks alters the relationship between husband and wife. Many of us know, from the times we suffer discomfort from our periods, that we want warmth and caring without sexual demands. If we are not suffering, we do not notice this need so sharply. But many observant women report that their relationships are enriched by the cycle precisely because of the shift to another style of relationship between husband and wife. "It's not just on the physical level," many say. Caring takes place in a different way. As when a woman feels too ill to cook, her continual loving-through-nourishment shifts into another gear, so when she becomes more inward or needy, her husband must transform his sexual loving into another form.

For us apart from our partners there are other benefits. At the time of niddah a woman does not come near her husband. This is our solitude, our darkness, our hiddenness – an opportunity to go inward, that can lead to a spiritual focus. When we take additional time out for spiritual pursuits during the days of niddah, it can sometimes relieve emotional distress – the anxiety, deflated energy, or depression that many of us experience at this time. Some women find it a fortuitous time for dreams or visualizations that give us insight or comfort.

The time of niddah is also a time of preparation. After finding our place of solitude, we move into the other rhythm, preparing to join again with our husbands. Jewish mysticism tells us that when husband and wife unite at permitted times, and especially on Shabbat or at the end of her period of niddah when it is a mitzvah to do so, their union reflects the union of masculine and feminine in the divine. This is a special kind of holy act: two people in their physical being and their natural energies reflect the culmination of the divine creative process, making a unity from what had been a duality. The two who had been separated, like Adam and Chava, now come together as God and the world.

This is the essential reason why Jews do not practice celibacy. Marriage is important – so important that the blessing on a newborn infant is that he or she will be raised to "Torah, *chupah* [marriage], and good deeds." More than in any other tradition, marriage is of the essence of Jewish work in the world. Only in the union between man and woman can we touch with our own natures the process that the whole world is about: to come together, to overcome our separation, to be at one. At-one-ness in Judaism comes in an act of pleasure and creativity, as though God made the world just for this.

In these rituals we can also hear the echo, in our own practice, of the holiness discussed in chapter 2: sexuality is to be guarded, preserved for the right times, as a powerful source of creativity. In marriage we develop the discipline that makes this possible. Romantic love is egotistical, seeking one round after another of pleasurable feelings, but with no further aim. Even extended "relationships" that go beyond mere romance are founded primarily on the desires of the partners for companionship and security – essentially self-centered aims. As Jewish women, as sexual beings, we aim at holiness, so our partnership is different, beginning with the sexual dimension. It is essential to set apart the time and place. We count the days, prepare ourselves for the monthly renewal that comes with immersion in a mikvah. Together with our husbands, we develop the discipline of abstinence and careful attention to the nature of our contact and speech.

Then our monthly immersion is truly an experience of renewal. Water, especially the gathering of waters in a pool, is part of a nearly universal feminine symbolism.[1] "Mikvah" means the gathering of waters, and immersion is always in either a natural body such as a pond or sea or an indoor pool specially constructed so as to be connected to naturally gathered waters, like a pool of fresh rainwater. The waters of a mikvah are, as Rabbi Aryeh Kaplan pointed out, connected to the waters of Eden,[2] the original rivers that flowed from the garden. They make for us each month a rebirth of spiritual virginity.

The rhythm of this "woman's mitzvah" highlights a different dimension of her experience of herself in relationship – not this time through nourishing and nurturing, but through the dynamic of withdrawal and joining, separation and union. We move from inwardness to transformation and renewal, then to the willingness to give ourselves to another in a coming together that mirrors the union of the world with its source. Individuality and independence are balanced at a deep level with interdependence and mutual surrender. The rites and practices make for a demanding path in some ways, while in other respects nothing could seem more natural. The practices of *taharat hamishpocheh* ensure that the structure of intimacy in a family is founded on the woman's inner rhythms, an anchor to the inner psychic life of the family and the people, a ground of holiness in our relationships.

# Notes

1   In Judaism we may note that Rikvah, Rachel, and Zipporah were all connected with wells. Eliezer met Rikvah at a well and brought her home to Isaac; Jacob and Moses each met their future wives at wells.
2   Rabbi Aryeh Kaplan, *The Waters of Eden: An Exploration of the Concept of Mikvah Renewal and Rebirth*, 2nd ed. (New York: National Conference of Synagogue Youth, 1982).

# 42

# Thoughts Without a Thinker (1995)

## Mark Epstein

## Introduction

Since the 1960s, Buddhism's impact on American culture has increased dramatically, partly as a result of changes in immigrant quotas enabling more Asian Americans to enter the United States, and partly as a result of Buddhism's attractiveness to Americans from Jewish and Christian backgrounds. During the late twentieth century, new centers for Buddhist study and practice sprang up across the country and Buddhist teachers drew large and dedicated followings. As Buddhism became an increasingly vital part of the American religious landscape, Americans also stimulated important new developments within Buddhism. Americans devised new forms of Buddhist social action, encouraged more democratic attitudes toward women, and experimented with new forms of meditation for ordinary people. As Mark Epstein and a number of other mental health practitioners discovered, the field of psychotherapy proved especially hospitable to Buddhist influence. Buddhist meditation techniques enabled people to achieve better perspective on their lives and find relief from stress. And the Buddhist concept of *anatman*, or no self, proved to be an effective aid in treating the self-absorption from which many Americans suffered.

Excerpted from Mark Epstein, *Thoughts Without a Thinker: Psychotherapy from a Buddhist Perspective* (New York: Basic Books, 1995), 47–8. Copyright © 1995 by Mark Epstein, MD. Reprinted by permission of Basic Books, a member of Perseus Books Group Ltd.

Buddhist ideas often seeped into American culture in unorganized and sometimes unorthodox ways. As they made their way into art, literature, music, sports, advertising, and psychotherapy, Buddhist philosophy affected the attitudes of many Americans who never participated in officially recognized Buddhist communities. In their application to different areas of life – ranging from improving a golf game to overcoming drug addiction and from lessons in cooking to lessons in business management – Buddhist ideas have entered the mainstream of American culture.

# The Image of Self

The original Greek myth of Narcissus derives its power from just this core uncertainty about the reality of the self. Enamored of his own image, unable to tear himself away from his reflection in a pond, Narcissus died of languor. The power of his image was such that Narcissus gave himself over to it. He was captivated by the completeness of the image, which alleviated his sense of unreality and gave him something (apparently) solid to hang on to. Not only was the reflection illusory, of course, but Narcissus perished by virtue of his attachment to this image of perfection.

Consider again the Buddhist perspective on this captivating image of self, as articulated by the Buddha in that first teaching:

All worry about the self is vain; the ego is like a mirage, and all the tribulations that touch it will pass away. They will vanish like a nightmare when the sleeper awakes.

He who has awakened is freed from fear; he has become Buddha; he knows the vanity of all his cares, his ambitions, and also of his pains.

It easily happens that a man, when taking a bath, steps upon a wet rope and imagines that it is a snake. Horror will overcome him, and he will shake from fear, anticipating in his mind all the agonies caused by the serpent's venomous bite. What a relief does this man experience when he sees that the rope is no snake. The cause of his fright lies in his error, his ignorance, his illusion. If the true nature of the rope is recognised, his tranquillity of mind will come back to him; he will feel relieved; he will be joyful and happy.

This is the state of mind of one who has recognised that there is no self, that the cause of all his troubles, cares, and vanities is a mirage, a shadow, a dream.[1]

Far from the narcissistic pursuit that many psychoanalysts and religious scholars have labeled it, Buddhist meditation is rather an attempt to break through and expose narcissism in its every haunt. The Buddha sees us all as Narcissus, gazing at and captivated by our own reflections, languishing in our attempted self-sufficiency, desperately struggling against all that would remind us of our own fleeting and relative natures. His message is a wake-up call. He seeks to rouse us from our Narcissus-like reverie, to redirect our attention from a preoccupation with shoring up an inevitably flawed sense of self to knowledge of what he calls "the Noble Truth."

Birth, old age, sickness, and death are distasteful not just because they are painful but also because they are humiliating. They violate our self-regard and are blows to our narcissism. In one of his first writings about this, Freud recognized that the inability to tolerate unpleasant truths about oneself was essential to narcissism. The Buddha's teachings make this observation the cornerstone of his psychology. We are all subject to this tendency, taught the Buddha. We do not want to admit our lack of substance to ourselves and, instead, strive to project an image of completeness, or self-sufficiency. The paradox is that, to the extent that we succumb to this urge, we are estranged from ourselves and are *not real.* Our narcissism requires that we keep the truth about our selves at bay.

# Note

1   Lucien Stryck, *World of the Buddha* (New York: Grove Weidenfeld, 1968), 52–3.

## 43

# Active Faith (1996)

### Ralph Reed

## Introduction

As one of the leading spokesmen for the Christian Coalition, Ralph Reed has been in the vanguard of recent efforts to utilize national politics as a means of bringing American culture more in line with conservative Christian values. As suggested by the subtitle of *Active Faith: How Christian Are Changing the Soul of American Politics*, Reed reserves the term "Christian" for conservative evangelicals who oppose abortion, gay rights, and the idea that government has an inherent responsibility for the poor. Like J. Gresham Machen several generations before, Reed would define Christianity and liberalism as two completely different points of view.

 Conservative evangelicals became more politically visible at the end of the twentieth century partly in reaction to the alleged deterioration of family values in the United States, and partly as a result of effective use of the media by conservative leaders. No less important, their activism expresses faith in the power of religious experience to transform individual lives, and through those lives, to strengthen the social fabric of American culture. In some respects, this activism resembles the energetic spirit of social reform generated in earlier periods of religious revival. In addition, new forms of interaction among black and white evangelicals that emerged in the context of this activism resemble the interracial character of earlier revivals. In other respects, however, political activism among conservative evangelicals reflects

Excerpted from Ralph Reed, *Active Faith: How Christians Are Changing the Soul of American Politics* (New York: Free Press, 1996), 276–81.

something new. As an effort to reclaim priority for conservative Protestant values, it is part of a new and increasingly pluralistic religious landscape where enthusiasm for religious experience is no longer a predominantly Protestant phenomenon. Thus in a somewhat ironic way, the success of conservative evangelicals in claiming a place at the table of American public policy discussions reflects the strength of liberal democracy and the vibrancy of the pluralistic culture that conservative evangelicals have sometimes decried. As they join the process of political debate among competing interest groups, religious conservatives committed to implementing their ideas for reforming American society find themselves revising their ideas in order to appeal to other groups, and making amends with people they have disdained in the past.

When I hear some conservatives proposing that we eliminate government welfare programs altogether, I fear they do not understand the full consequences of their proposal. Charitable giving in the United States in 1995 totaled approximately $124 billion, but only a fraction of that finds its way to the poor. A truly Christian approach would be to gradually phase out many government welfare programs over a period of years, with an adequate transition period for private and faith-based charities to pick up the slack. Even after that transition, there should always be local government assistance for the truly disabled and for abandoned children. Otherwise, lives that are already hanging precariously by a thread could fall by the wayside, and the already crime-ridden, tension-filled urban centers could likely explode. This is not a defense of the existing welfare system or of federal entitlements, but it is a warning not to go too far too fast.

A second area that must move higher among the priorities of the religious conservative movement is the issue of race relations. As people of faith have sought to re-enter the political arena, they have been hamstrung by the painful legacy of Jim Crow, a history which remains shackled to their culture like a ball and chain. The past complicity of the white evangelical community in the mistreatment of blacks under the regime of segregation cannot be denied. White evangelicals stood in the front lines defending segregation and invoking Scripture to justify its cruelty. I believe that our moral authority on issues such as abortion and religious freedom will never carry sufficient weight to change the nation's culture until we thoroughly remove the stain of past racism from our own culture. Dan T. Carter argues in his recent biography of George C. Wallace that today's religious conservative message is an outgrowth of Wallace's anti-government, traditional values message stripped of its now disreputable racial appeal. That charge is overdrawn. Yes, there are some white racists on the right. But they do not speak for our movement, any more than Louis Farrakhan speaks for liberal

African-Americans. Where were many of today's conservative leaders when Wallace was standing in the schoolhouse door? Pat Robertson was integrating white churches in Virginia at the height of massive resistance, Newt Gingrich supported Rockefeller against Nixon in 1968 solely because of the race issue, and William F. Buckley's *National Review* argued that a vote for Wallace was the least defensible ballot that could be cast that year. In more recent times, Pat Robertson has condemned David Duke on his nationally televised news program. This hardly qualifies as a veiled appeal to race.

But the pro-family movement must do more. The Promisekeepers, a movement to encourage men to be better husbands and fathers, have made racial reconciliation a major priority. In February, 1996, the Christian Coalition joined other pro-family groups in urging Congress to hold hearings on the recent rash of bombings directed against black churches in the South. I later wrote a letter to Attorney General Janet Reno urging that the FBI put the investigation and prosecution of the arsonists and vandals of black churches at the top of its list of pending cases. The dominant media predictably ignored these appeals to racial justice, but the evolution of our movement from a lily-white phenomenon to a multi-racial community is occurring slowly but surely. Most religious conservative groups have also been slow to take a formal position on reforming affirmative action, primarily because they fear that it could inflame racial tensions and divide the American people. But what is needed today is a major effort to build bridges with the African-American community based on our many shared values. That effort must be preceded by a genuine, public repentance for past racism. Only when our community is thoroughly cleansed of that taint can we move forward and heal the body politic. [...]

[...] There will be times when we find ourselves too engaged in the political and will need to pull back. There will be other times when we have to be even more politically forceful than we have been. But in our times of questioning, we still have a history to look back on. It is a history that teaches us the importance of being politically sophisticated – of knowing that there are times to fight harder, times to speak loudly, times to say nothing. It is a history that teaches us the importance of remembering where we are going – to a place where families are valued, children are educated, and hope and opportunity abound. We are proud to stand on the shoulders of those who have come before us – and we wish to ensure that our movement will be viewed in the years to come not as a flash in the pan, but as a long-term participant in American public life. History has shown that people of faith can follow two paths in politics. Either we can become inflamed with zeal, and make much sound and fury before our fervor and influence ultimately dissipate; or we can assume the role of a responsible player within the democratic polity, so that the voices of Christians will always be heard in public discourse. The latter vision requires religious conservatives to understand our movement's purpose, and to comprehend the role of each individual within the movement and the larger society.

As it happens, I draw much of my own inspiration from the example of Martin Luther King, Jr. He faced this difficult dilemma of balancing a movement's passionate faith with the requirements of political sophistication. His response varied, but one of the things he did say in no uncertain terms was that his must be a movement defined by love. To ensure that everyone was clear about what this meant, each and every volunteer in his SCLC [Southern Christian Leadership Conference] signed a pledge card mandating that they would:

1. *Meditate* daily on the teachings and life of Jesus.
2. *Remember* always that the . . . movement  . . . seeks justice and reconciliation, not victory.
3. *Walk* and *talk* in the manner of love, for God is love.
4. *Pray* daily to be used by God in order that all men might be free.
5. *Sacrifice* personal wishes in order that all men might be free.
6. *Observe* with both friend and foe the ordinary rules of courtesy.
7. *Seek* to perform regular service for others and for the world.
8. *Refrain* from the violence of fist, tongue, or heart.

With this solemn promise in place, King and his army were able to move out in love, transforming the country and bringing to fruition the dreams of tens of millions of Americans – a transformation whose spirit has outlived both King and the movement he led. I am not comparing our movement to King's. We can never know the indignity, suffering, violence, and death that the civil rights pioneers experienced. But we can seek to make this creed our own, and hope to wield a fraction of the influence that they had on the hearts of their fellow citizens.

A century from now, when some student leafs through the yellowed pages of books talking about the religious conservative movement led by the Christian Coalition – as I did looking back on the populists and the Progressives while writing this book – it is my hope that he or she will be amazed. Not because of our political power, our grassroots strength, or our ability to turn out a huge vote on Election Day, though I am proud of all those things, but because our movement of common people had an uncommon commitment to caring for those in need, loving those who attacked us, and displaying the love, dignity, and decency that are the hallmarks of an active faith.

# Index